HIEROCLES THE STOIC: *ELEMENTS OF ETHICS*, FRAGMENTS, AND EXCERPTS

Society of Biblical Literature

Writings from the Greco-Roman World

Number 28

Hierocles the Stoic:
Elements of Ethics,
Fragments, and Excerpts

Volume Editor: David Konstan

HIERROCLES THE STOIC: *ELEMENTS OF ETHICS*, FRAGMENTS, AND EXCERPTS

By

Ilaria Ramelli

Translated by

David Konstan

Society of Biblical Literature
Atlanta

HIEROCLES THE STOIC: *ELEMENTS OF ETHICS*, FRAGMENTS, AND EXCERPTS

Library of Congress Cataloging-in-Publication Data

Ramelli, Ilaria, 1973–
Hierocles the Stoic : Elements of ethics, fragments and excerpts / by Ilaria Ramelli ; translated by David Konstan.
p. cm. — (Society of Biblical Literature writings from the Greco-Roman world ; v. 28)
Includes bibliographical references and index.
ISBN-13: 978-1-58983-418-7 (paper binding : alk. paper)
1. Hierocles, the Stoic, 2nd cent.—Translations into English. 2. Ethics—Early works to 1800. 3. Stoics—Early works to 1800. I. Konstan, David. II. Hierocles, the Stoic, 2nd cent. Elements of ethics. English. III. Hierocles, the Stoic, 2nd cent. On appropriate acts. English. IV. Title. V. Title: Elements of ethics.
B577.H42E57 2009a
188—dc22 2009029913

17 16 15 14 13 12 11 10 09 5 4 3 2 1
Printed in the United States of America on acid-free, recycled paper conforming to ANSI/NISO Z39.48-1992 (R1997) and ISO 9706:1994 standards for paper permanence.

Contents

Translator's Preface

The present work is a translation of Ilaria Ramelli's text, translation, introduction, and commentary on the complete surviving works of Hierocles. In preparing the translation, I have rendered afresh, directly from the original texts, all Greek and Latin sources, whether of Hierocles himself or of any other writer cited in the introduction, commentary, and notes. I had to hand Ramelli's own versions, and she went over mine with her customary care and thoroughness. Any differences of interpretation or nuance were fully discussed (this is true as well of my rendering of Ramelli's Italian). While full responsibility for the present edition rests with Ramelli, I must accept the blame for any infelicities in style; more particularly, my own habit in translation tends to the literal, and I am aware of often having spoiled the charm of Ramelli's more elegant Italian versions. In addition to translating, in my role as volume editor I worked together with Ramelli on matters of format, citation of secondary literature, and the like, to bring the book into conformity with the style of the series, Writings from the Greco-Roman World.

It remains to say only that working closely with Ilaria Ramelli has been a pleasure and a privilege. My esteem for her as a scholar is matched by my profound affection for her as a friend. The present translation of her book is my tribute to her in both these roles.

David Konstan

Author's Preface

All that I wish and really need to say is to thank my colleagues and friends very much. First of all, my warmest gratitude goes to David Konstan both for his excellent translation and for the joy of working together and sharing thoughts in friendship. This was really a splendid gift. I heartily thank John Fitzgerald, who generously served as the general editor for this volume and encouraged this work since the beginning, when he and the editorial board took an interest in my essay, translation, and commentary on Hierocles. His careful reading and his suggestions, as well as our discussion of moral progress in Stoicism, proved immensely helpful. Warm thanks also to Bob Buller, whose editorial assistance has been exemplary and invaluable; to the editors of Hierocles' *Elements of Ethics*, Guido Bastianini and Anthony Long; and to Olschki Editore, the publisher of *CPF*, which kindly gave permission to make use of the edition of the *Elements*. I am grateful in particular to Anthony Long for reading portions of this work. I also express special gratitude to Will Deming, who put his translation and notes of some of the excerpts from Stobaeus at my disposal and for his helpful suggestions. Finally, I wish to thank all the colleagues and friends who have constantly gladdened me in my research.

Ilaria Ramelli

Abbreviations

Primary Sources

Abst.	Porphyry, *De abstinentia* (*On Abstinence*)
Acad. pr.	Cicero, *Academica priora* (*Prior Academics*)
Aet.	Philo, *De aeternitate mundi* (*On the Eternity of the World*)
An.	Alexander of Aphrodisias, *De anima* (*On the Soul*)
Anth.	Stobaeus, *Anthologium* (*Anthology*)
Apol.	Plato, *Apologia* (*Apology of Socrates*)
Autol.	Theophilus, *Ad Autolycum* (*To Autolycus*)
Cels.	Origen, *Contra Celsum* (*Against Celsus*)
Comm. not.	Plutarch, *De communibus notitiis contra Stoicos* (*On Common Notions*)
Comm. Tim.	Calcidius, *Commentarius in Platonis Timaeum* (*Commentary on Plato's* Timaeus)
Corp. Herm.	*Corpus Hermeticum*
De an.	Aristotle, *De anima* (*On the Soul*)
Deipn.	Athenaeus, *Deipnosophistae* (*Sophists at a Banquet*)
Diss.	*Dissertationes* (*Discourses*)
Ep.	Seneca, *Epistulae morales* (*Moral Epistles*)
Etym.	Isodore, *Etymologiae* (*Etymologies*)
Fab.	Aesop, *Fabulae* (*Fables*)
Fin.	Cicero, *De finibus* (*On Moral Ends*)
Foet. form.	Galen, *De foetuum formatione libellus* (*On the Formation of the Fetus*)
Frat.	Plutarch, *De fraterno amore* (*On Fraternal Love*)
Gorg.	Plato, *Gorgias*
Haer.	*Adversus haereses* (*Against Heresies*)
Hier.	Horapollo, *Hieroglyphica* (*Hieroglyphics*)
Hipp.	Euripides, *Hippolytus*
Hist. an.	Aristotle, *Historia animalium* (*History of Animals = Investigation into Animals*)

Hist. Rom.	Dio Cassius, *Historiae Romanae* (*Roman History*)
Il.	Homer, *Iliad*
Leg.	Cicero, *De legibus* (*On the Laws*); Plato, *Leges* (*Laws*)
Marc.	Porphyry, *Ad Marcellam* (*Letter to Marcella*)
Math.	Sextus Empiricus, *Adversus Mathematicos* (*Against Scholars*)
Mem.	Xenophon, *Memorabilia*
Metam.	Apuleius, *Metamorphoses* (*The Golden Ass*)
Metaph.	Aristotle, *Metaphysica* (*Metaphysics*)
Mixt.	Alexander of Aphrodisias, *De mixtione* (*On Mixture*)
Mor.	Plutarch, *Moralia*
Nat.	Pliny the Elder, *Naturalis historia* (*Natural History* = *Investigation into Nature*)
Nat. an.	Aelian, *De natura animalium* (*Nature of Animals*)
Nat. hom.	Nemesius of Emesa, *De natura hominis* (*On the Nature of Man*)
Noct. Att.	Aulus Gellius, *Noctes Atticae* (*Attic Nights*)
Od.	Homer, *Odyssea* (*Odyssey*)
Oec.	Xenophon, *Oeconomicus* (*Household Management*)
Off.	Cicero, *De officiis* (*On Duty*)
Or.	Dio Chrysostom, *Orationes* (*Orations*)
Paed.	Clement of Alexandria, *Paedagogus* (*Christ the Educator*)
Phaed.	Plato, *Phaedo*
Piet.	Philodemus, *De pietate* (*On Piety*)
Plac. philos.	[Plutarch], *Placita philosophorum* (*Opinions of the Philosophers*)
Poet.	Aristotle, *Poetica* (*Poetics*)
Prog.	*Progymnasmata* (*Preliminary Exercises*)
Prov.	Chrysippus, *De providentia* (*On Providence*)
Pyr.	Sextus Empiricus, *Pyrrhoniae hypotyposes* (*Outline of Pyrrhonism*)
Resp.	Plato, *Respublica* (*Republic*)
Rhet.	Aristotle, *Rhetorica* (*Rhetoric*)
Rust.	Varro, *De re rustica* (*Agriculture*)
Sat.	Persius, *Satirae* (*Satires*)
Sent.	*Sententiae* (*Sentences*)
Soll. an.	Plutarch, *De sollertia animalium* (*On the Cleverness of Animals*)
Stoic.	Philodemus, *De Stoicis* (*On the Stoics*)
Stoic. rep.	Plutarch, *De Stoicorum repugnantiis* (*On the Contradictions of the Stoics*)

Strom.	Clement of Alexandria, *Stromata* (*Miscellanies*)
Theol.	Cornutus, *Theologiae Graecae compendium* (*Compendium of Greek Theology*)
Ther.	Nicander, *Theriaca*
Tim.	Plato, *Timaeus*
Tusc.	Cicero, *Tusculanae disputationes* (*Tusculan Disputations*)
Vit. phil.	Diogenes Laertius, *Vitae philosophorum* (*Lives of the Philosophers*)

Secondary Sources

AClass	*Acta Classica*
AGPh	*Archiv für Geschichte der Philosophie*
AJP	*American Journal of Philology*
AncPhil	*Ancient Philosophy*
ANRW	*Aufstieg und Niedergang der römischen Welt: Geschichte und Kultur Roms im Spiegel der neueren Forschung*. Part 2, *Principat*. Edited by Hildegard Temporini and Wolfgang Haase. Berlin: de Gruyter, 1972–.
AU	*Altsprachliche Unterricht*
Bib	*Biblica*
BJRL	*Bulletin of the John Rylands University Library of Manchester*
BSGRT	Bibliotheca scriptorum Graecorum et Romanorum Teubneriana
CCTC	Cambridge Classical Texts and Commentaries
CErc	*Cronache ercolanesi*
CIL	*Corpus inscriptionum latinarum*
CISA	Contributi dell'Istituto di storia antica dell'Università Cattolica del S. Cuore di Milano
CP	*Classical Philology*
CPF	*Corpus dei papiri filosofici greci e latini: Testi e lessico nei papiri di cultura greca e latina*. Florence: Olschki.
CPhPJ	*Cahiers de philosophie politique et juridique*
CQ	*Classical Quarterly*
ÉPRO	Études préliminaires aux religions orientales dans l'Empire romain
GR	*Greece and Rome*
GRBS	*Greek, Roman, and Byzantine Studies*
Int	*Interpretation*

JBL	*Journal of Biblical Literature*
JHI	*Journal for the History of Ideas*
JHS	*Journal of Hellenic Studies*
JPh	*The Journal of Philosophy*
JSNTSup	Journal for the Study of the New Testament Supplement Series
HSCP	*Harvard Studies in Classical Philology*
LEC	Library of Early Christianity
MH	*Museum Helveticum*
NovT	*Novum Testamentum*
NovTSup	Supplements to Novum Testamentum
NTS	*New Testament Studies*
OSAP	*Oxford Studies in Ancient Philosophy*
PCPhS	*Proceedings of the Cambridge Philological Society*
PhAnt	Philosophia antiqua
PhilosAnt	*Philosophie antique*
PhJ	*Philosophisches Jahrbuch*
PP	*La parola del passato*
PW	*Paulys Real-Encyklopädie der classischen Altertumswissenschaft.* New edition by Georg Wissowa and Wilhelm Kroll. 50 vols. in 84 parts. Stuttgart: Metzler and Druckenmüller, 1894–1980.
QS	*Quaderni di storia*
RAC	*Reallexikon für Antike und Christentum: Sachwörterbuch zur Auseinandersetzung des Christentums mit der antiken Welt.* Edited by Theodor Kluser et al. Stuttgart: Hiersemann, 1950–.
REA	*Revue des études anciennes*
REAug	*Revue des études augustiniennes*
RFIC	*Rivista di filologia e di istruzione classica*
RFN	*Rivista di Filosofia Neoscolastica*
RhM	*Rheinisches Museum*
RHT	*Revue d'histoire des textes*
RIL	*Rendiconti dell'Istituto lombardo, Classe di lettere, scienze morali e storiche*
RIPh	*Revue internationale de philosophie*
RPFE	*Revue philosophique de la France et de l'étranger*
SAPERE	Scripta antiquitatis posterioris ad ethicam religionemque pertinentia
SBLRBS	Society of Biblical Literature Resources for Biblical Study

SBLTT	Society of Biblical Literature Texts and Translations
SBLWGRW	Society of Biblical Literature Writings from the Greco-Roman World
SCHNT	Studia ad corpus Hellenisticum Novi Testamenti
SIFC	*Studi Italiani di Filologia Classica*
SMSR	*Studi e Materiali di Storia delle Religioni*
STAC	Studien und Texte zu Antike und Christentum/Studies and Texts in Antiquity and Christianity
STCPF	Studi e testi per il Corpus dei papiri filosofici greci e latini
StudPhil	*Studia Philosophica*
StudPhilAnn	*Studia Philonica Annual*
SVF	*Stoicorum veterum fragmenta*. Edited by Hans Friedrich August von Arnim. 4 vols. Leipzig: Teubner, 1903–24. Volumes 1 and 2 are cited by volume and text number; volume 3 by volume, text, and page number.
TAPA	*Transactions of the American Philological Association*
TrGF	*Tragicorum Graecorum fragmenta*. Edited by Bruno Snell et al. 5 vols. in 6. Göttingen: Vandenhoeck & Ruprecht, 1971–2004.
TSAJ	Texts and Studies in Ancient Judaism/Texte und Studien zum antiken Judentum
WUNT	Wissenschaftliche Untersuchungen zum Neuen Testament
YCS	*Yale Classical Studies*
ZNW	*Zeitschrift für die neutestamentliche Wissenschaft*
ZPE	*Zeitschrift für Papyrologie und Epigraphik*

Short References

Bastianini and Long = Guido Bastianini and Anthony A. Long, "Ierocle: Elementi di Etica." Pages 296–362 in vol. 1.1.2 of *Corpus dei papiri filosofici greci e latini: Testi e lessico nei papiri di cultura greca e latina*. Florence: Olschki, 1992. Although the publisher of *CPF* uses asterisks to label the individual books that constitute a volume (e.g., 1*; 1**; 1***), I follow the lead of Anthony Long (*Phoenix* 51 [1997]: 90) and other sources and cite Bastianini and Long by listing the part, volume, book, and page(s). Thus, *CPF* 1.1.2:283 refers to *CPF* part 1, volume 1, book 2, page 283.

Brunschwig, "The Cradle Argument" = Jacques Brunschwig, "The Cradle Argument in Epicureanism and Stoicism." Pages 113–45 in *The Norms*

of Nature: Studies in Hellenistic Ethics. Edited by Malcolm Schofield and Gisela Striker. Cambridge: Cambridge University Press, 1986.

Engberg-Pedersen, *The Stoic Theory of Οἰκείωσις* = Troels Engberg-Pedersen, *The Stoic Theory of Οἰκείωσις: Moral Development and Social Interaction in Early Stoic Philosophy*. Studies in Hellenistic Civilization 2. Aarhus: Aarhus University Press, 1990.

Inwood, "Hierocles" = Brad Inwood, "Hierocles: Theory and Argument in the 2nd Century A.D." *OSAP* 2 (1984): 151–84.

Isnardi, "Ierocle" = Margherita Isnardi Parente, "Ierocle stoico: Oikeiôsis e doveri sociali." *ANRW* 36.3:2201–26.

Meineke = August Meineke, *Iōannou Stobaiou Anthologion*. 4 vols. Leipzig: Teubner: 1855–57.

Praechter, *Hierokles* = Karl Praechter, *Hierokles der Stoiker*. Leipzig: Dieterich, 1901. Repr. as pages 311–474 in idem, *Kleine Schriften*. Edited by Heinrich Dörrie. Hildesheim: Olms, 1973.

Radice, *Oikeiôsis* = Roberto Radice, *Oikeiôsis: Ricerche sul fondamento del pensiero stoico e sulla sua genesi*. Introduction by Giovanni Reale. Temi metafisici e problemi del pensiero antico: Studi e testi 77. Milan: Vita e Pensiero, 2000.

Ramelli, *Allegoria* = Ilaria Ramelli, *L'età classica*. Vol. 1 of *Allegoria*. Milan: Vita e Pensiero, 2004.

Ramelli, *Cornuto* = Ilaria Ramelli, *Anneo Cornuto: Compendio di teologia greca*. With essays, edition, translation, and commentary. Milan: Bompiani, 2003.

Ramelli, *Musonio Rufo* = Ilaria Ramelli, *Musonio Rufo: Diatribe, frammenti, testimonianze*. With introductory essay, Greek text, translation, notes, apparatuses, and bibliography. Milan: Bompiani, 2001.

Ramelli, *Stoici romani minori* = Ilaria Ramelli, *Stoici romani minori*. With critical essays, texts, translations, commentaries, and bibliographies of Manilius, Musonius, Cornutus, Chaeremon, Persius, Lucan, Juvenal, and an appendix on Mara Bar Serapion. Milan: Bompiani, 2008.

Reale, *Diogene Laerzio* = Giovanni Reale, *Diogene Laerzio: Vite e dottrine dei più celebri filosofi*. In collaboration with Ilaria Ramelli and Giuseppe Girgenti, with introductory essay, edition, commentary, and bibliography by Ilaria Ramelli, translation by Giovanni Reale, and indexes by Giuseppe Girgenti. Milan: Bompiani, 2005.

Reydams-Schils, *Roman Stoics* = Gretchen Reydams-Schils, *The Roman Stoics: Self, Responsibility, and Affection*. Chicago: University of Chicago Press, 2005.

von Arnim, *Ethische Elementarlehre* = Hans Friedrich August von Arnim, ed., in collaboration with Wilhelm Schubart, *Ethische Elementarlehre (Papyrus 9780): Nebst den bei Stobaios erhaltenen ethischen Exzerpten aus Hierokles*. Berliner Klassikertexte 4. Berlin: Weidmann, 1906.

Wachsmuth and Hense = Curt Wachsmuth and Otto Hense, eds., *Ioannis Stobaei anthologium*. 5 vols. in 4. Berlin: Weidmann, 1884–1923.

Introductory Essay: Hierocles between the Old Stoic Tradition and Middle and Neo-Stoic Innovations

1. Identity, Modern Studies, and Historical Context

Hierocles was a Stoic philosopher in the first half of the second century A.D.—a Neo-Stoic, accordingly—and was often confused, prior to the nineteenth century, with the Alexandrian Neoplatonic philosopher of the same name who lived in the fifth century A.D. and was the author of a commentary on the *Carmen aureum* (*Golden Verses*) of Pythagoras and a treatise *De providentia* (*On Providence*). Our author, however, belongs rather to the world of Neo-Stoicism or Roman Stoicism, which is closely related to Ancient and Middle Stoicism but also has various characteristics that are specific to it.[1]

1. The treatise of Hierocles of Alexandria, which at first was confused with that of Hierocles the Stoic, has survived in extracts by Photius, *Bibliotheca*, codd. 214 and 251; as for commentary, there is the edition by Friedrich Wilhelm Köhler, *Hieroclis in aureum Pythagoreorum carmen commentarius* (BSGRT; Leipzig: Tuebner, 1974); see also idem, *Kommentar zum Pythagoreischen goldenen Gedicht* (Griechische und lateinische Schriftsteller; Stuttgart: Teubner, 1983). On Hierocles of Alexandria, see especially Theo Kobusch, *Studien zur Philosophie des Hierokles von Alexandria* (Munich: Berchmans, 1976); Ilsetraut Hadot, *Le problème du néoplatonisme alexandrin: Hiéroclès et Simplicius* (Paris: Études augustiniennes, 1978); Noël Aujoulat, *Le néo-platonisme alexandrin: Hiéroclès d'Alexandrie* (PhAnt 45; Leiden: Brill, 1986); Leendert G. Westerink, "Hierokles II (Neuplatoniker)," *RAC* 15:109–17; Ilsetraut Hadot, "Le démiurge comme principe dérivé dans le système ontologique d'Hiéroclès," *Revue des Études Grecques* 103 (1990): 241–62; Noël Aujoulat, "Hiéroclès d'Alexandrie d'après Damaskios et la Souda," *Pallas* 44 (1996): 65–77; Hermann S. Schibli, *Hierocles of Alexandria* (Oxford: Oxford University Press, 2002).

Several works on Roman Stoicism have appeared recently, among which I note especially Giovanni Reale, *Scetticismo, Eclettismo, Neoaristotelismo e Neostoicismo* (vol. 6 of *Storia della filosofia greca e romana*; Milan: Bompiani, 2004), 247–410, which offers a general characterization of Neo-Stoicism (247–57) and treats Seneca, Musonius, Epictetus,

and Marcus Aurelius individually; in addition, Marcia L. Colish, *The Stoic Tradition from Antiquity to the Early Middle Ages* (2 vols.; Studies in the History of Christian Thought 34–35; Leiden: Brill, 1985; corr. repr., 1995); Brad Inwood, "Seneca in His Philosophical Milieu," *HSCP* 97 (1995): 63–76; Ramelli, *Musonio Rufo*, in particular the introductory essay (ch. 1); idem, "La concezione di Giove negli stoici romani di età neroniana," *Rendiconti dell'Istituto lombardo accademia di scienze e lettere* 131 (1997): 292–320; idem, "Stoicismo e Cristianesimo in area siriaca nella seconda metà del I secolo d.C.," *Sileno* 25 (1999): 197–212; idem, "La tematica *de matrimonio* nello Stoicismo romano: alcune osservazioni," *'Ilu* 5 (2000): 145–62; idem, "'*Tristitia*': Indagine storica, filosofica e semantica su un'accusa antistoica e anticristiana del I secolo," *Invigilata Lucernis* 23 (2001): 187–206; George R. Boys-Stones, *Post-Hellenistic Philosophy: A Study of Its Development from the Stoics to Origen* (Oxford: Oxford University Press, 2001), with my review in *Aevum* 78 (2004): 196–200; Mark P. O. Morford, *The Roman Philosophers: From the Time of Cato the Censor to the Death of Marcus Aurelius* (London: Routledge, 2002), 161–239; Ilaria Ramelli, "Anneo Cornuto e gli Stoici Romani," *Gerión* 21 (2003): 283–303; idem, "Aspetti degli sviluppi del rapporto fra Stoicismo e Cristianesimo in età imperiale," *Stylos* 12 (2003): 103–35; idem, *Anneo Cornuto: Compendio di teologia greca* (Milan: Bompiani, 2003), particularly the introductory essay; idem, *L'età classica* (vol. 1 of *Allegoria*; Milan: Vita e Pensiero, 2004), particularly chs. 6–7; David N. Sedley, ed., *The Cambridge Companion to Greek and Roman Philosophy* (Cambridge: Cambridge University Press, 2003), especially ch. 6: Jacques Brunschwig and David N. Sedley, "Hellenistic Philosophy," 151–83, who emphasize the substantial continuity between the Old Stoa and Roman Stoicism; ch. 7: Anthony A. Long, "Roman Philosophy," 184–210, with discussion of the Neo-Stoics Seneca, Musonius, Cornutus, Epictetus, and Marcus Aurelius; ch. 8: Martha C. Nussbaum, "Philosophy and Literature," 211–41, for Seneca and Lucan; and ch. 11: Glenn W. Most, "Philosophy and Religion," 300–22, for the effort of the Roman Stoics to preserve the traditional, inherited theology by means of allegory; Brad Inwood, ed., *The Cambridge Companion to the Stoics* (Cambridge: Cambridge University Press, 2003), with my review in *RFN* 97 (2005): 152–58; in *The Cambridge Companion to the Stoics*, see in particular Christopher Gill, "The School in the Roman Imperial Period," 33–58, who underlines (40ff.) the importance of ethics in Neo-Stoicism and, within ethics in turn, judges that the practical side is given preference to the speculative; Gretchen Reydams-Schils, *The Roman Stoics: Self, Responsibility, and Affection* (Chicago: University of Chicago Press, 2005), with my review in *RFN* 8 (2006): 605–10, above all on the question of how to define which philosophers may be included under the heading "Roman Stoicism" (she only treats Hierocles, Musonius, Seneca, Epictetus, and Marcus Aurelius, in addition to Cicero as a source). See also my *Stoici romani minori* (Milan: Bompiani, 2008), with further documentation on recent studies, especially in the introductory essay to Musonius. Clearly, I do not mean to provide here individual bibliographies on the several Neo-Stoic philosophers, which would be very extensive, from the more important figures (Seneca, Epictetus, Marcus Aurelius) to the minor ones (e.g., Musonius, Cornutus, Persius, Chaeremon, Thrasea, Pseudo-Seneca, Hierocles), to which we might add poets of a stoicizing tendency or who manifest a strong Stoic influence, such as Manilius, Lucan, or Juvenal, and even, in lesser degree, Silius Italicus, or a Syriac Stoic such as Mara Bar Serapion, who lived toward the end of the first century, on whom see my "Stoicismo e Cristianesimo"; idem, "La lettera di Mara Bar Serapion," *Stylos* 13 (2004): 77–104; and above all idem, "Gesù tra i sapienti greci perseguitati ingiustamente in un antico documento filosofico pagano di lingua siriaca," *RFN* 97 (2005):

It was a study by Praechter that signaled the rediscovery of the Stoic Hierocles and the distinction between him and the homonymous Platonist.[2] Shortly afterwards, the discovery of a papyrus containing a treatise by the Stoic Hierocles confirmed Praechter's hypotheses, which were subsequently further buttressed by Hans von Arnim, who edited the papyrus and was the author of an important monograph on Hierocles the Stoic, in addition to his fundamental and well-known collection of the *Stoicorum veterum fragmenta*. Von Arnim demonstrated definitively, on the basis of stylistic and structural parallels already in part identified by Praechter, that the Hierocles of the Stobaean extracts was the same Stoic writer whose work was preserved on papyrus and who was without question distinct from the much later Neoplatonist.[3] There were other important contributions by Moricca and Pohlenz as well.[4] Nevertheless, broadly speaking the silence that surrounded Hierocles, interrupted just once in 1933 by an article by Philippson,[5] lasted until the 1970s, when it was finally broken, thanks to an article by Pembroke on *oikeiôsis* and studies

---

545–70; and idem, "Mar Bar Serapion," in *Stoici romani minori*, 2555–98. In agreement with me on the dating of the letter of Mara Bar Serapion and the strong presence of Stoic elements in it are, most recently, Ephrem-Isa Yousif, *La floraison des philosophes syriaques* (Paris: L'Harmattan, 2003), 27–28; and David Rensberger, "Reconsidering the Letter of Mara Bar Serapion," in *Aramaic Studies in Judaism and Early Christianity* (ed. Paul V. M. Flesher and Eric M. Meyers; Duke Judaic Studies Monograph Series 3; Winona Lake, Ind.: Eisenbrauns, forthcoming); Annette Merz and Teun L. Tieleman, "The Letter of Mara Bar Sarapion: Some Comments on Its Philosophical and Historical Context," in *Empsychoi Logoi—Religious Innovations in Antiquity: Studies in Honour of Pieter Willem van der Horst* (ed. Alberdina Houtman, Albert de Jong, and Magda Misset-van de Weg; Ancient Judaism and Early Christianity 73; Leiden: Brill, 2008); I am very grateful to Teun Tieleman and Annette Merz for letting me read their study prior to publication.

2. Karl Praechter, *Hierokles der Stoiker* (Leipzig: Dieterich, 1901), repr. in idem, *Kleine Schriften* (ed. Heinrich Dörrie; Hildesheim: Olms, 1973), 311–474.

3. Hans Friedrich August von Arnim, ed., in collaboration with Wilhelm Schubart, *Ethische Elementarlehre (Papyrus 9780): Nebst den bei Stobaios erhaltenen ethischen Exzerpten aus Hierokles* (Berliner Klassikertexte 4; Berlin: Weidmann, 1906), esp. viii–xi: "The Stoic Hierocles who wrote on ethics in Stobaeus and the author of our *Elements of Ethics* are one and the same person" (my trans.). As for von Arnim's *SVF*, the texts are wholly reproduced, with Italian translation, in Roberto Radice, *Stoici antichi: Tutti i frammenti secondo la raccolta di H. von Arnim* (Milan: Rusconi, 1998, frequently reprinted).

4. U. Moricca, "Un trattato di etica stoica poco conosciuto," *Bilychnis* 34 (1930): 77–100; Max Pohlenz, *Die Stoa* (Göttingen: Vandenhoeck & Ruprecht, 1949), Italian translation by Ottone De Gregorio and Beniamino Proto, *La Stoa: Storia di un movimento spirituale* (2 vols.; Florence: La nova Italia, 1967), 2:25ff.

5. Robert Philippson, "Hierokles der Stoiker," *RhM* 82 (1933): 97–114.

of different aspects of Stoic ethics and psychology by Kerferd, Long, Sandbach, Forschner, Inwood, and Brunschwig, as well as an important article by van der Horst in the *Corpus Hellenisticum Novi Testamenti.*[6] Recently, Badalamenti and Delle Donne have investigated Hierocles in articles, Isnardi Parente in an encyclopedia entry, and Radice in a monograph on Stoic *oikeiôsis*, as have other scholars interested in this philosophical issue, for example, Engberg-Pedersen and, more sketchily, Morford in a general work on Roman philosophy, Erler in an article, and Reydams-Schils in a volume on the Roman Stoics.[7] This brief overview indicates the increas-

---

6. S. G. Pembroke, "Oikeiôsis," in *Problems in Stoicism* (ed. Anthony A. Long; London: Athlone, 1971), 114–49; George B. Kerferd, "The Search for Personal Identity in Stoic Thought," *BJRL* 55 (1972): 177–96; Anthony A. Long, *Hellenistic Philosophy: Stoics, Epicureans, Sceptics* (London: Duckworth, 1974), 116 and 186; idem, "Soul and Body in Stoicism," *Phronesis* 27 (1982): 34–57, esp. 46–47; Pieter W. van der Horst, "Hierocles the Stoic and the New Testament: A Contribution to the Corpus Hellenisticum," *NovT* 17 (1975): 156–60; Francis H. Sandbach, *The Stoics* (London: Chatto & Windus, 1975) 149, 170–72; Maximilian Forschner, *Die stoische Ethik: Über den Zusammenhang von Natur-, Sprach- und Moralphilosophie im altstoischen System* (Stuttgart: Klett-Cotta, 1981), esp. 145–46, 148, 158; Inwood, "Hierocles: Theory and Argument in the 2nd Century A.D." *OSAP* 2 (1984): 151–84; see also idem, *Ethics and Human Action in Early Stoicism* (Oxford: Clarendon, 1985), esp. 188–89, 191–94, 219, 262 n. 5, 310–11 n. 27, 320 n. 8 on Hierocles; Jacques Brunschwig, "The Cradle Argument in Epicureanism and Stoicism," in *The Norms of Nature: Studies in Hellenistic Ethics* (ed. Malcolm Schofield and Gisela Striker; Cambridge: Cambridge University Press, 1986), 113–45, esp. 138–44.

7. Guido Badalamenti, "Ierocle stoico e il concetto di *synaisthesis*," *Annali del Dipartimento di Filosofia dell'Università di Firenze* 3 (1987): 53–97; Vittorio Delle Donne, "Per una nuova edizione dei Principi di etica di Ierocle Stoico (*P. Berol. 9780*)," *Annali dell'Istituto Italiano per gli Studi Storici* 10 (1987–88): 113–44; Margherita Isnardi Parente, "Ierocle stoico: Oikeiôsis e doveri sociali," *ANRW* 36.3:2201–26; Troels Engberg-Pedersen, *The Stoic Theory of Οἰκείωσις: Moral Development and Social Interaction in Early Stoic Philosophy* (Studies in Hellenistic Civilization 2; Aarhus: Aarhus University Press, 1990), esp. 240–41 on Hierocles; Vittorio Delle Donne, "Sulla nuova edizione della Ἠθικὴ στοιχείωσις di Ierocle stoico," *SIFC* 13 (1995): 29–99 (with critical and exegetical notes that have been taken into consideration here); Roberto Radice, *Oikeiôsis: Ricerche sul fondamento del pensiero stoico e sulla sua genesi* (intro. by Giovanni Reale; Temi metafisici e problemi del pensiero antico: Studi e testi 77; Milan: Vita e Pensiero, 2000), 189–95; Mark Morford, *The Roman Philosophers*, 10–11; Julia Annas, "My Station and Its Duties: Ideals and the Social Embeddedness of Virtue," *Proceedings of the Aristotelian Society* 102 (2002): 109–23; Michael Erler, "Stoic *Oikeiosis* and Xenophon's Socrates," in *The Philosophy of Zeno* (ed. Theodore Scaltsas and Andrew S. Mason; Larnaka, Cyprus: Municipality of Larnaca, 2002), 239–58, who argues that for their theory of *oikeiôsis* the Stoics were inspired by Socrates' thought as described in Xenophon's *Memorabilia*; Gretchen Reydams-Schils, *The Roman Stoics*, 3–4 and *passim* in chs. 4–5.

ing interest in this writer in recent years, which has been capped off by a new edition by Guido Bastianini and Anthony A. Long of his major work preserved on papyrus ("Ierocle: Elementi di Etica," in *Corpus dei papiri filosofici greci e latini* [Florence: Olschki, 1992], 1.1.2:268–362).

This edition, in turn, has stimulated further critical studies of Hierocles' thought, although, strange to say, up to now there was still no complete English translation of all of Hierocles' writings that have come down to us. Indeed, the present translation of his *Elements of Ethics* is the first English translation ever (some portions were translated by Anthony A. Long and David N. Sedley, *The Hellenistic Philosophers* [2 vols.; Cambridge: Cambridge University Press, 1987], §§53B, 57C–D). As for his work *On Appropriate Acts*, there have of course been several previous English translations of the Stobaean excerpts that contain fragments of it. Among the first was that of Thomas Taylor, *Political Fragments of Archytas, Charondas, Zaleucus, and Other Ancient Pythagoreans Preserved by Stobaeus, and Also, Ethical Fragments of Hierocles, the Celebrated Commentator on the Golden Pythagorean Verses, Preserved by the Same Author* (Chiswick: Whittingham, 1822), 75–115; Taylor naturally believed that this was the work of Hierocles the Platonist. A translation also appeared in the first edition of Kenneth Sylvan Guthrie, *Pythagoras: Source Book and Library* (2 vols.; Yonkers: Platonist, 1920). It is reprinted in Kenneth Sylvan Guthrie, comp. and trans., *The Pythagorean Sourcebook and Library* (ed. David R. Fiedler; 2nd ed.; Grand Rapids: Phanes, 1987), 275–86, where it is still wrongly ascribed to Hierocles the Neoplatonist. The most important English translation of the excerpts that has appeared so far is that of Abraham J. Malherbe, *Moral Exhortation: A Greco-Roman Sourcebook* (LEC 4; Philadelphia: Westminster, 1986), 85–104.

Both Praechter and von Arnim based their argument for the dating of Hierocles on a passage in Aulus Gellius (*Noct. att.* 9.5.8), which attributes to Gellius's own teacher, the Platonist Calvenus Taurus, a description of Hierocles as a "virtuous and serious man" (*vir sanctus et gravis*);[8] both scholars maintained that these words prove that Taurus personally attended the lectures of Hierocles, who is frequently cited by Taurus for his criticism of Epicurean hedonism. The only scholar who challenged

8. Praechter, *Hierokles*, 106; von Arnim, *Ethische Elementarlehre*; von Arnim repeats his description of Hierocles as a "Stoic of the time of Hadrian" (s.v. "Hierokles," PW 8.2:1479).

this identification was A. Bonhoeffer,[9] and although it is accepted by Margherita Isnardi Parente, she herself evinces some doubts about the date: she notes that this same Taurus, in another passage, describes Panaetius in similar terms as "serious and learned"—and surely Taurus never met Panaetius in person.[10] Similarly, Zeller's description of Hierocles as one of Gellius's own teachers does not seem adequately documented.[11] Furthermore, the identification of our Stoic with Hierocles of Hyllarima, in Caria, is bound to remain a mere hypothesis unless further evidence is uncovered; this Hierocles is mentioned by Stephanus of Byzantium as a boxer who later devoted himself to philosophy—not necessarily Stoic philosophy.[12] But it appears, nevertheless, "quite probable that we are dealing with the same Hierocles mentioned by Stobaeus" (Isnardi Parente), who is also, perhaps, the very Hierocles cited as the author of nine papyrus rolls in Papyri Varsovienses 5, a catalogue of books among which there appear some authored by two Stoic philosophers who may fall between the Old and Middle Stoa, namely, Diogenes of Babylon and either Antipater of Tarsus or Zeno of Tarsus.[13]

The parallels in style and content that can be observed, however, between that part of Hierocles' work that has reached us through the indirect tradition via the Stobaean extracts, and the *Discourses* of the Neronian-age Stoic Musonius Rufus (edited by his disciple Lucius and also known chiefly thanks to Stobaeus) and the orations of his pupil Dio Chrysostom, composed between the time of Vespasian and of Trajan (that is, between the end of the first and the beginning of the second century A.D.), do seem to have considerable value as evidence.[14] These similarities,

---

9. "Hierokles," *Deutsche Literaturzeitung* 2 (1907): 86–89, esp. 87.

10. Aulus Gellius, *Noct. Att.* 12.5.10: *Panaetii gravis et docti*; see Isnardi, "Ierocle," 2201.

11. Eduard Zeller, *Die Philosophie der Griechen* (4th ed.; 3 vols. in 6; Leipzig: Reisland, 1922, repr. 1963), 3.1:715: "sein Schüler Gellius" ("his disciple Gellius"); refutation in Isnardi, "Ierocle," 2202.

12. For the Stephanus text, see August Meineke, *Stephani Byzantii ethnicorum quae supersunt* (Berlin: Reimer, 1849), 647. See also Praechter, *Hierokles*, 107; Bastianini and Long, *CPF* 1.1.2:283.

13. Bastianini and Long, *CPF* 1.1.2:284. For Papyri Varsovienses 5, see *CPF* 1.1.1:103.

14. I have translated the diatribes of Musonius in *Musonio Rufo*. The redaction of these diatribes by Lucius, a disciple of Musonius, puts in question the phrase "Musonius Rufus's prose" (my trans.) used by Isnardi, "Ierocle," 2202. See Ilaria Ramelli, "Musonio Rufo," in *Enciclopedia Filosofica* (ed. Virgilio Melchiorre; 2nd ed.; Milan: Bompiani, 2006),

8:7696–97. For important studies on parallels between Musonius and Hierocles, see Tim Whitmarsh, *Greek Literature and the Roman Empire* (Oxford: Oxford University Press, 2001), 141–55; Ilaria Ramelli, "La tematica *di matrimonio*," 145–62; David M. Engel, "The Gender Egalitarianism of Musonius Rufus," *AncPhil* 20 (2000): 377–91; Barbara Levick, "Women, Power, and Philosophy at Rome and Beyond," in *Philosophy and Power in the Graeco-Roman World* (ed. Gillian Clark and Tessa Rajak; Oxford: Oxford University Press, 2002), 134–55; Martha Nussbaum, "The Incomplete Feminism of Musonius Rufus, Platonist, Stoic, and Roman," in *The Sleep of Reason: Erotic Experience and Sexual Ethics in Ancient Greece and Rome* (ed. Martha Nussbaum and Juha Sihvola; Chicago: University of Chicago Press, 2002), 283–326; Georg Wöhrle, "Wenn Frauen Platons Staat lesen, oder: Epiktet und Musonius konstruieren Geschlechtenrollen," *Würzburger Jahrbücher für die Altertumswissenschaft* 26 (2002): 135–43; Kathy L. Gaca, *The Making of Fornication: Eros, Ethics, and Political Reform in Greek Philosophy and Early Christianity* (Berkeley and Los Angeles: University of California Press, 2003), 60, 82–86, 90–93, 113–15; Valéry Laurand, "Souci de soi et mariage chez Musonius Rufus: Perspectives politiques de la κρᾶσις stoïcienne," in *Foucault et la philosophie antique* (ed. Frédéric Gros and Carlos Lévy; Paris: Editions Kimé, 2003), 85–116; Reydams-Schils, *Roman Stoics*, chs. 4–5; Ilaria Ramelli, "Transformations of the Household and Marriage Theory between Neo-Stoicism, Middle-Platonism, and Early Christianity," *RFN* 100 (2008): 369–96. For further references, see the commentary.

On Dio Chrysostom, Paolo Desideri, *Dione di Prusa* (Messina: D'Anna, 1978) is still important, as is Giovanni Salmeri, *La politica e il potere: Saggio su Dione di Prusa* (Catania: Facoltà di Lettere e Filosofia, Università di Catania, 1982); see also John Moles, "Dio und Trajan," in *Philosophie und Lebenswelt in der Antike* (ed. Karen Piepenbrink; Darmstadt: Wissenschaftliche Buchgesellschaft, 2003), 165–85. On various philosophical and rhetorical points of comparison with Hierocles, see Berthold Häsler, *Favorin über die Verbannung* (Berlin: Postberg, 1935), with still useful observations on Musonius, Dio, and Roman Stoicism; Gerard Mussies, *Dio Chrysostom and the New Testament* (SCHNT 2; Leiden: Brill, 1972); Peter A. Brunt, "Aspects of the Social Thought of Dio Chrysostom and of the Stoics," *PCPhS* 19 (1973): 9–34; I. M. Nachov, "Le cynisme de Dion Chrysostome" [in Russian], *Voprosy Klassiceskoj Filologii* 6 (1976): 46–104; Domenico Ferrante, *La Semantica di logos in Dione Crisostomo alla luce del contrasto tra retorica e filosofia* (Naples: Loffredo, 1981); Edmund Berry, "Dio Chrysostom the Moral Philosopher," *GR* NS 30 (1983) 70–80; Alain Michel, "Rhétorique et philosophie au second siècle ap. J.-C.," *ANRW* 34.1:5–74; Claudio Moreschini, "Aspetti della cultura filosofica negli ambienti della Seconda Sofistica," *ANRW* 36.7:5101–33; Simon Swain, ed., *Dio Chrysostom: Politics, Letters, and Philosophy* (Oxford: Oxford University Press, 2000), in particular Michael B. Trapp, "Plato in Dio," 213–39; Aldo Brancacci, "Dio, Socrates, and Cynicism," 240–60; and Frederick E. Brenk, "Dio on the Simple and Self-Sufficient Life," 261–78; Hans-Josef Klauck, ed., *Dion von Prusa: Olympikos und Peri tês prôtês tou theou ennoias* (Darmstadt: Wissenschaftliche Buchgesellschaft, 2000); J. Samuel Houser, "Eros and Aphrodisia in Dio Chrysostom," in Nussbaum and Sihvola, *The Sleep of Reason*, 327–53; Heinz-Günther Nesselrath, Balbina Bäbler, Maximilian Forschner, and Albert De Jong, eds., *Dion von Prusa: Menschliche Gemeinschaft und göttliche Ordnung: Die Borysthenes-Rede* (Darmstadt: Wissenschaftliche Buchgesellschaft, 2003). Fragments of some philosophical works by Dio have now been published in Maria Tanja Luzzatto, "Dio Prusaensis," *CPF* 1.1.2:34–85. The bibliography on Dio, including translations, commentaries, and critical studies, is becoming ever more extensive, and

which I highlight in the commentary to the Stobaean extracts (where I seek to add some to the number of those already identified), were noted by Praechter,[15] who used them to demonstrate the difference between the Stoic and the Neoplatonic Hierocles. Isnardi has exploited them, in turn, to propose as a chronological framework for our author "some time after Posidonius and in all likelihood around the beginning of the imperial period," with the additional arguments that Hierocles is not mentioned in the Herculanean "Index of Stoics," which includes the Middle Stoics, and that one can point also to parallels with Seneca (as we shall see more clearly in the commentary, where they will be supplemented by parallels with Musonius as well) and to their common dependency on Posidonius.[16] An important *terminus ante quem* is provided by the dating of the papyrus that contains the principal work by the Stoic Hierocles: von Arnim attributed the handwriting of the papyrus broadly to the first century A.D., Pearson and Stephens to the end of the second, Schubart to the end of the second or the beginning of the third, Seider to the mid-second century, while Bastianini and Long, whose edition I follow, suggest the second half of the second century A.D.[17] Hierocles is without a doubt prior to that period and so may be safely dated prior to 150 A.D.; Bastianini and Long hold that "Hierocles was active, in all likelihood, around the middle of the second century A.D."[18]

---

only a sample is provided here. There is now being prepared, in Milan, a volume by several hands, edited by Eugenio Amato, *Dione Crisostomo: Tutti i discorsi*, with rich documentation in the introductory essay. For Dio's reflections on the origin of philosophy, see Ilaria Ramelli, "Le origini della filosofia: greche o barbare? L'enigmatico mito del Boristenitico di Dione," *RFN* 99 (2007): 185–214. On Dio as a philosopher, see my *Stoici romani minori*, 689–943.

15. Praechter, *Hierokles*, 90–95.

16. Augusto Traversa, ed., *Index Stoicorum Herculanensis* (Genoa: Istituto di filologia classica, 1952); Isnardi, "Ierocle," 2202.

17. See "Hierocles: Elementa moralia," in Bastianini and Long, *CPF* 1.1.2:268, 272.

18. Bastianini and Long, *CPF* 1.1.2:281–82. For the historical context of Hierocles the Stoic, the following few notices may suffices: Julian Bennet, *Trajan: Optimus Princeps* (London: Routledge, 1997); Anthony R. Birley, *Hadrian: The Restless Emperor* (London: Routledge, 1997); Miriam Griffin, "Nerva to Hadrian," in *The High Empire, A.D. 70–192* (vol. 11 of *The Cambridge Ancient History*; ed. Alan K. Bowman, John B. Bury, and Averil Cameron; 2nd ed.; Cambridge: Cambridge University Press, 2000), 84–131; Philip A. Stadter and Luc Van der Stockt, eds., *Sage and Emperor: Plutarch, Greek Intellectuals and Roman Power in the Time of Trajan (98–117 A.D.)* (Leuven: Leuven University Press, 2002); Elizabeth Speller, *Following Hadrian: A Second-Century Journey through the Roman Empire* (Oxford: Oxford University Press, 2003).

2. Works and Topics

Hierocles concerned himself above all with ethics, in conformity with that side of philosophy favored by Roman Stoicism. He was the author of *The Elements of Ethics* (Ἠθικὴ στοιχείωσις), partially preserved, as I have mentioned, on papyrus (Papyrus Berolinensis 9780) and probably deriving from Hermoupolis in Egypt. Today we have an excellent edition of this work in the *Corpus dei papiri filosofici greci e latini*, which I adopt for the present translation (incorporating subsequent emendations by the editors). The *Elements* joins a fair number of extracts in Stobaeus that had been falsely ascribed to Hierocles of Alexandria and that derive, it would seem, from a work *On Appropriate Acts* (Περὶ τῶν καθηκόντων); we do not know whether the Stobaean extracts *On Marriage* (Περὶ γάμου) and *Household Management* (Οἰκονομικός) formed part of *On Appropriate Acts* as chapters or thematic sections or whether they were rather brief independent treatises.[19]

The *Suda*, s.v. ἐμποδών, also attests the title Φιλοσοφούμενα, which Isnardi, on the basis of the excerpt preserved by the *Suda*, characterizes as, in all likelihood, a "doxographical and anecdotal mélange, containing maxims and aphorisms."[20] It is worth remarking that the discourses or diatribes of Maximus of Tyre (end of the second century A.D.) in their chief manuscript, Parisinus graecus 1962, are called διαλέξεις in the title but in the subscription are labeled Μαξίμου Τυρίου φιλοσοφούμενα, "the philosophical discourses of Maximus of Tyre." Moreover, Φιλοσοφούμενα is also the first title of Hippolytus's *Refutation of All Heresies*, handed down under the name of Origen and found in a single manuscript from Mount Athos (now Parisinus suppl. gr. 464): the titles given by these manuscripts are Φιλοσοφούμενα ἢ κατὰ πασῶν αἱρέσεων ἔλεγχος, "Philosophical Dis-

19. The papyrus and extracts may be found in von Arnim, *Ethische Elementarlehre*. The portion preserved on papyrus is now published, edited by Bastianini and Long, with an Italian transation, in *CPF* 1.1.2:268ff. and 418ff.; for a description of the papyrus, see 270ff.: the *recto* of the papyrus contained a part of Didymus's commentary on the *Philippics* of Demosthenes; on the *verso*, a different hand transcribed the *Elements* of Hierocles.

20. Isnardi, "Ierocle," 2209. On Maximus's title, see Michael B. Trapp, *Maximus of Tyre: The Philosophical Orations* (Oxford: Oxford University Press, 1997), xiii. The full title in this manuscript reads: Μαξίμου Τυρίου Πλατωνικοῦ φιλοσόφου τῶν ἐν Ῥώμῃ διαλέξεων τῆς πρώτης ἐπιδημίας, α', "The first of the discussions of the Platonic philosopher Maximus of Tyre, delivered in Rome during his first visit."

courses or Refutation of All Heresies." This might suggest a polemical aim also for Hierocles' work.

Indeed, in the above-mentioned passage of Gellius (*Noct. att.* 9.5.8), Taurus is cited as mentioning an anti-Epicurean remark by Hierocles, which might imply the existence of a polemical work against Epicureanism, as Isnardi hesitantly suggests;[21] this idea may find some support in a few anti-Epicurean innuendoes in the *Elements of Ethics*, which are noted in the commentary.

Apart from lost or dubious works, it is important to establish the mutual relations between the only two texts by Hierocles that we possess, although in fragmentary condition: the *Elements of Ethics* and the treatise *On Appropriate Acts*. Von Arnim presented arguments that cannot be ignored, with a view to proving that these were probably two parts of a single work, or perhaps different works but very closely related in content:[22] he maintained, as Praechter had already seen,[23] that the Stobaean extracts were part of a tract *On Appropriate Acts* and that it was as an introduction to that treatise that Hierocles composed the *Elements of Ethics*. Its original length was probably twenty to twenty-one columns, although today only eleven are preserved in fragmentary condition.[24] Nevertheless, the discussion of the *oikeiôsis* of animals toward themselves, which occupies the entire surviving text of the *Elements*, makes it impossible to suppose that the entirety of Stoic ethics was treated in an equally thorough way in but a single roll. Yet, because no book number appears alongside the title in the papyrus, we must conclude that the *Elements of Ethics* was wholly contained in one roll, of which the surviving part, according to von Arnim, represents almost two-thirds of the entire papyrus. Von Arnim himself, indeed, anticipated the alternative hypothesis that the papyrus text was a specialized work and that it might have been free-standing.[25] From this angle, then, von Arnim's thesis is open

21. Isnardi, "Ierocle," 2203.

22. Von Arnim, *Ethische Elementarlehre*, xi–xiii; on page xi he writes: "The *Elements of Ethics* in the papyrus constitutes a surviving portion of the same work of Hierocles from which the Stobaean excerpts also derive," and on p. xiv: "As a result of the discussion conducted so far, I regard it as highly probable that the *Elements of Ethics* in the papyrus constituted the introductory chapter of the work that was excerpted by Stobaeus" (my trans.).

23. *Hierokles*, 7–12.

24. See Bastianini and Long, *CPF* 1.1.2:268ff.

25. Von Arnim, *Ethische Elementarlehre*, xiii: "But the title indicates no book number

to question. Besides, von Arnim too hastily rejected—as Max Pohlenz observed[26]—the above-mentioned note in the *Suda* concerning the Φιλοσοφούμενα, the title that Stobaeus might have used for his extracts from Hierocles. Von Arnim, in fact, having wondered whether the first book of the Φιλοσοφούμενα might be identified with the *Elements of Ethics* and the second with the treatise *On Appropriate Acts*, from the Stobaean excerpts, discarded the idea and maintained that the work cited by the *Suda*, the title of which was not suitable for a systematic manual such as the *Elements* but rather for a collection of individual philosophical topics, was distinct from both the *Elements of Ethics* and from the source of the excerpts in Stobaeus.[27]

Praechter argued in passing for the distinction between the *Elements* and the Stobaean extracts, chiefly on the basis of style, and promised to return to the matter in more detail;[28] in fact, however, he never treated the topic again. Philippson accepted the close connection between the two texts—the *Elements* and the Stobaean extracts—and in the end decided that they were certainly parts of the same work; he maintained, however, that the introductory treatise, namely, the *Elements*, originally extended to two rolls and not just one, and he believed that the whole work bore the title Φιλοσοφούμενα.[29] He went so far as to suppose, though not on very secure grounds, that Hierocles had planned to write additional books on logic and physics.

Today it is generally accepted by scholars, such as by Isnardi and by Bastianini and Long,[30] that the two suviving works of Hierocles, the *Ele-*

---

next to Στοιχείωσις ἠθική. Thus, we could conclude that this work did not exceed the limit of one scroll.... The surviving part includes about two thirds of the original scroll"; xiv: "The fundamental doctrine, even apart from the larger context, had a value of its own.... Our manuscript is not a book but a private copy" (my trans.).

26. In his review of von Arnim's edition, in *Göttingische Gelehrte Anzeigen* 11 (1906): 914–20, esp. 916.

27. Von Arnim, *Ethische Elementarlehre*, xiv–xv, esp. xv: "Above all, the title Φιλοσοφούμενα does not suit a systematic textbook, such as we find in the Στοιχείωσις and in Stobaeus, but rather an independent discussion of individual philosophical questions. Therefore, I believe that the Φιλοσοφούμενα cited by *Suidas* are different from this partially preserved work" (my trans.).

28. *Hierokles*, 589 n. 1.

29. Philippson, "Hierokles der Stoiker," 97–114.

30. Isnardi, "Ierocle," 2203; Bastianini and Long, *CPF* 1.1.2:286: "For the purpose of understanding Hierocles as it is preserved in the papyrus, the excerpts from Hierocles in Stobaeus may be, in principle, left aside" (my trans.). On Stoic logic at the time

ments of Ethics and the Stobaean excerpts on "duties" (καθήκοντα), are distinct. The *Elements* appear to be intended for the Stoic school: they have a systematic character and employ a fairly specialized language; the work *On Appropriate Acts*, on the contrary, is more literary and addressed to a larger public, especially since it includes precepts on marriage and household management.

3. The *Elements of Ethics* and the Doctrine of *Oikeiôsis*

I examine the individual arguments of the *Elements of Ethics* in detail in the commentary, where I provide an outline of each section as occasion arises. Here I am concerned to highlight the general lines of the treatise[31] and certain specific aspects of the topic that is central the work, namely, *oikeiôsis*, "appropriation" or "familiarization."

In the first place, then, it is useful to provide a general overview of the contents of what survives of this treatise by Hierocles.

I.1–30: The best starting point for the elements of ethics is the "first thing that is one's own" or "is familiar," the πρῶτον οἰκεῖον of an animal. To determine what this is, one must first of all consider what the beginning of an animal's life is (here Hierocles avails himself of an argument *ab origine* that was employed by the Stoics in other contexts as well):[32] it is birth, when nature (φύσις),

---

of Hierocles, see Jonathan Barnes, *Logic and the Imperial Stoa* (PhAnt 75; Leiden: Brill, 1997); a classic work on Stoic logic, but with little diachronic perspective, is Michael Frede, *Die stoische Logik* (Göttingen: Vandenhoeck & Ruprecht, 1974); see also Brad Inwood, "Kanones kai syllogistiki sti stoiki Ithiki," *Deukalion* 15 (1997): 107–43; Livia Marrone, "La logica degli epicurei e degli stoici," *CErc* 30 (2000): 111–18.

31. There is an excellent account of the contents of the papyrus in von Arnim's introduction to his *Ethische Elementarlehre*, as well as in Isnardi, "Ierocle," 2203–8 and in Bastianini and Long, *CPF* 1.1.2:286–92, which I follow in the schematic description of the material below.

32. For example, the method of referring to origins as a privileged site in which to discover the truth is evident, especially in Middle and Neo-Stoicism, in allegorical treatises: as Annaeus Cornutus puts it with particular clarity, a few decades before Hierocles, in his *Theol.* 35, the ancients, who were the creators of myths and traditions, were philosophers who had attained the truth and expressed it by way of symbols and riddles. See my *Allegoria*, chs. 6 and 9, and my commentary on ch. 35 of Cornutus in Ramelli, *Cornuto*. For the argument *ab origine* developed here, and in general for the use of this type of reasoning with reference to the behavior or traits of children, see Brunschwig, "The Cradle Argument."

in which plants too have a share, is transformed into soul (ψυχή), which is specific to animals.

I.30–37: Characteristic of animals are sensation or perception (αἴσθησις) and impulse (ὁρμή). It is the first of these that will be primarily discussed, since it is essential to understanding the "first thing that is one's own" (or "familiar") of an animal.

I.37–50: The offspring of every animal, immediately upon birth, has perception of itself. There follows the proof of this claim in I.51–VI.24.

1. Animals perceive themselves, as is demonstrated by the fact that:
   — they perceive their individual parts (I.51–II.3);
   — they perceive their individual means of defense (II.3–18);
   — they perceive their own weaknesses and strengths (II.18–III.19);
   — they perceive the threat posed by the abilities of other animals (III.19–52);
2. Animals perceive themselves continuously (III.54–56), as is shown by the fact that:
   — their body and soul interact continuously (III.56–IV.53);
   — animals perceive themselves even in sleep (IV.53–V.38).
3. Animals perceive themselves from the time when they are mere pups, immediately after birth, as is shown by the fact that:
   — the continuous perception of self implies self-perception from the very beginning of life (V.38–43);
   — no moment is more plausible as the beginning of self-perception than the beginning of life itself (V.43–52);
   — the perception of external things, which begins with birth, implies self-perception (V.52–VI.10);
   — self-perception precedes the perception of anything else (VI.10–24).

VI.49–53; VII.48–50: An animal, right from birth, becomes its own or familiar to itself (οἰκειοῦται ἑαυτῷ) and to its own constitution (σύστασις). Proof of this is the fact that: (1) an animal

seems pleased at the representation (φαντασία) that it has of itself (VI.24–49); and (2) animals always seek self-preservation (VI.53–VII.48).

VII.50–VIII.27: The representation (φαντασία) is sharpened as the animal develops.

<30 lines are illegible>

IX.1–10: Adult animals have four types of *oikeiôsis*, and among these is their affection for their offspring, which is equal to that for themselves.

<two columns are lacunose>

XI.14–19: Man is a social animal.

I examine the course of Hierocles' argument analytically and in detail in the commentary. Here it is best to focus on the doctrine that occupies the surviving portion of the *Elements*, that of *oikeiôsis*.[33]

33. The philosophical doctrine of *oikeiôsis* has been studied from many angles over the past half century; see especially Charles O. Brink, "*Oikeiôsis* and *oikeiotês*: Theophrastus and Zeno on Nature in Moral Theory," *Phronesis* 1–2 (1955–57): 123–45; Brad Inwood, "Comments on Professor Görgemanns' Paper: The Two Forms of Oikeiôsis in Arius and the Stoa," in *On Stoic and Peripatetic Ethics: The Work of Arius Didymus* (ed. William W. Fortenbaugh; New Brunswick, N.J.: Transaction, 1983), 190–201; Anthony A. Long, "Arius Didymus and the Exposition of Stoic Ethics," in Fortenbaugh, *On Stoic and Peripatetic Ethics*, 41–65; Gisela Striker, "The Role of οἰκείωσις in Stoic Ethics," *OSAP* 1 (1983): 145–67; Inwood, "Hierocles"; Troels Engberg-Pedersen, "Discovering the Good: Οἰκείωσις and καθήκοντα in Stoic Ethics," in Schofield and Striker, *The Norms of Nature*, 145–83; Isnardi, "Ierocle," 2201–26; Gerhard Schönrich, "*Oikeiôsis*: Zur Aktualität eines stoischen Grundbegriffs," *PhJ* 96 (1989): 34–51; Engberg-Pedersen, *The Stoic Theory of Οἰκείωσις*; Mary Whitlock Blundell, "Parental Nature and Stoic οἰκείωσις," *AncPhil* 10 (1990): 221–42; Giuseppina Magnaldi, *L'οἰκείωσις peripatetica in Ario Didimo e nel De finibus di Cicerone* (Firenze: Casa Editrice Le Lettere, 1991); Brad Inwood, "L'οἰκείωσις sociale chez Épictète," in *Polyhistor: Studies in the History and Historiography of Ancient Philosophy* (ed. Keimpe A. Algra, Pieter W. van der Horst, and David T. Runia; PhAnt 72; Leiden: Brill, 1996), 243–64; Radice, *Oikeiôsis*; Chang-Uh Lee, *Οἰκείωσις: Stoische Ethik in naturphilosophischer Perspektive* (Freiburg: München Alber, 2002); Gretchen Reydams-Schils, "Human Bonding and οἰκείωσις in Roman Stoicism," *OSAP* 2 (2002): 221–51; Robert Bees, *Die Oikeiosislehre der Stoa I: Rekonstruktion ihres Inhaltes* (Würzburg: Königshausen & Neumann, 2004), 16–45 (on Seneca's *Ep.* 121), 46–51 (on *oikeiôsis* in Posidonius), 52–68 (on Seneca and Posidonius), 121–47 (on Cicero, *Nat. d.* 2), 148ff. (on the cosmic dimension of *oikeiosis*), 186–98 (on associative *oikeiôsis*), 259–60 (on *oikeiôsis* and the ethical end); Barbara

The doctrine of *oikeiôsis*, which has a long history in earlier Stoicism as well as in other philosophical schools and even beyond the confines of philosophy,[34] is clearly significant in the construction of Hierocles' treatise: he treats as basic to ethical theory the discussion of "the first thing that is one's own and familiar" (my compound expression for the πρῶτον οἰκεῖον), that is, that which each being senses as primarily its own. Hierocles' discussion takes as its point of departure the very beginning of life in each animal, which, prior to being born, is composed of *pneuma*; the latter only becomes soul (ψυχή) at birth, and is characterized by the properties of sensation (or perception) and impulse. Thanks to sensation, an animal, which while still in gestation is similar to a budding plant and has no more than "nature" (φύσις), can perceive that which is "primarily its own and familiar to itself."

The perception of an animal is directed both toward external things and, simultaneously, toward itself, as Hierocles maintains in a polemic against unnamed opponents, whom I attempt to identify in the commentary. Animals, as Hierocles amply illustrates, are conscious of parts of their own bodies and of the uses to which they can be put; they perceive their own capacities and the weaknesses of others and thus can protect themselves against attack. An animal, moreover, not only perceives itself but does so continuously, and to prove this point Hierocles specifies the nature of the relationship between soul and body—both of which are, according to orthodox Stoicism, material entities—as total mixture (κρᾶσις δι' ὅλου)[35] and as συμπάθεια, that is, a sharing of reactions (πάθη) in such a way that those of the body affect the soul and vice versa. Now, self-perception is not only continuous but, as Hierocles demonstrates with various arguments, also primary, in the sense that even a newborn animal, from

Guckes, *Zur Ethik der älteren Stoa* (Göttingen: Vandenhoeck & Ruprecht, 2004); Mary-Anne Zagdoun, "Problèmes concernant l'*oikeiôsis* stoïcienne," in *Les Stoïciens* (ed. Gilbert Romeyer-Dherbey and Jean-Baptiste Gourinat; Paris: Presses universitaires de France, 2005), 319–34; Tad Brennan, *The Stoic Life: Emotions, Duties, and Fate* (Oxford: Clarendon, 2005), 154–69.

34. In particular, Radice, *Oikeiôsis*, maintains that this doctrine developed originally in a medical and scientific—above all biological—context (see esp. 263–312) and that it subsequently entered into philosophical discourse, where it was elaborated above all by the Stoics, but not only by them. For *oikeiôsis* among the Peripatetics and Epicureans, see 121–51 and 161–82, respectively.

35. For the treatment of the relationship between soul and body in Stoicism, both of which are material entities united in a complete mixture, see the commentary to *Elements of Ethics*, n. 26. The problem is analyzed by Long, "Soul and Body in Stoicism," 34–57.

the first instant of independent life, begins to perceive itself and to do so even before perceiving external things.

Since this primary self-perception is bound up with a tendency to self-preservation and self-love, it follows that an animal, even when tiny and at the very beginning of its life, has the property of οἰκείωσις, insofar as it becomes "its own and familiar to itself" and to its own constitution (σύστασις). Nevertheless, the representation or appearance (φαντασία) of *oikeiôsis*[36] is not initially clear, due to the excessive density and scant exercise or use of the soul. Hierocles alludes here to a controversy between Chrysippus and Cleanthes that is difficult to define, on account of the fragmentary state of the text—as is the case for the entire final section of the papyrus.

At this point Hierocles mentions the various types of *oikeiôsis*, namely, that toward oneself, that toward others (the so-called sociable *oikeiôsis*), and that toward external things. Thus, in accord with the aspect of relations toward others that is specific to sociable *oikeiôsis*, Hierocles affirms the social nature of human beings (συναγελαστικόν), a topic that will be important also in his treatise *On Appropriate Acts*, where this social nature is subdivided into several classes of interpersonal relations.

Hierocles draws the doctrine of *oikeiôsis* from the earliest phase of Stoicism, where it is attested explicitly and uncontroversially in the first book of Chrysippus's work Περὶ τελῶν or *On Ends*. For Chrysippus, as Diogenes Laertius confirms, the first instinct of a living being is that of self-preservation, insofar as nature makes it "its own" in relation to itself from birth: thus, the πρῶτον οἰκεῖον for each individual is its specific σύστασις or constitution and the συνείδησις (consciousness) or συναίσθησις (perception) that it has of it.[37] Plutarch further reports that Chrysippus repeated this

36. Isnardi, "Ierocle," 2205, maintains that it is *oikeiôsis* and nothing else that is under discussion here. On possible interpretations of the passage in question, which is lacunose, see the commentary.

37. Diogenes Laertius, *Vit. phil*. 7.85 (*SVF* 3.178:43), records the view of the Stoics, on the basis of the first book of Chrysippus's *On Ends*: an animal has, as its first impulse, that of preserving itself, because nature from the beginning causes it to appropriate and make itself familiar (οἰκειόω) to itself. The first element that is its own and most familiar to every living creature is its own constitution and the consciousness (συνείδησις) it has of this, which causes it to reject whatever is harmful to it and to approach whatever is proper and familiar to it. In the passage in Diogenes, the term συνείδησις appears in the text printed by von Arnim and subsequently in the new Teubner critical edition (1999) by Miroslav Marcovich (translated by Giovanni Reale, with an essay and commentary by me,

theory in every one of his writings on physics and ethics (*SVF* 3.179:43), and he labels it precisely the theory of οἰκείωσις (*SVF* 2.724).[38]

Zeno, nevertheless, seems already to have highlighted this doctrine, even if there seems to be no testimony in Greek to his use of the technical term. Cicero, however, in his *Prior Academics* (*Acad. pr.* 131 = *SVF* 1.181) employs the term *conciliatio* in reference to Zeno and says that he "posited as the highest good living honestly, which derives from 'reconciliation' with nature"; we also know that Cicero in other contexts renders the Greek οἰκείωσις precisely by *conciliatio*. Radice has recently shown, with additional arguments that to my mind are convincing, the likelihood that this doctrine was already present in Zeno, adducing above all *SVF* 1.197 and 198.[39]

---

in *Diogene Laerzio: Vite e dottrine dei più celebri filosofi* [Milan: Bompiani, 2005], 808–9, with relevant notes in the commentary).

Max Pohlenz, *Grundfragen der stoischen Philosophie* (Göttingen: Vandenhoeck & Ruprecht, 1940), whose proposal has been hesitantly endorsed by Isnardi, "Ierocle," 2209 n. 26, suggested reading συναίσθησις instead, since the self-consciousness implied by the term συνείδησις seemed to him to be ill-adapted to animals, to which indeed the passage refers: Pohlenz adduced other examples of συναίσθησις and συναισθάνεσθαι used in reference to the doctrine of *oikeiôsis* in various texts, including non-Stoic ones, such as Arius Didymus as cited in Stobaeus, *Anth.* 2.7.3c (2:47,13 Wachsmuth and Hense), or the anonymous author of the commentary on the *Theaetetus* V.36. To be sure, several examples of this usage may be found also in Hierocles; see Badalamenti, "Ierocle stoico," 53–97.

For the doctrine of *oikeiôsis* in Arius Didymus, see Magnaldi, *L'οἰκείωσις peripatetica*; Radice, *Oikeiôsis*, 121–47; in Hierocles, see Radice, *Oikeiôsis*, 189–95; Inwood, "Comments on Professor Görgemanns' Paper," 195–96, 200 nn. 6 and 13; Striker, "The Role of οἰκείωσις," 145 n. 3 and 153; Isnardi, "Ierocle," 2209–14. In the commentary I analyze the Chrysippean passage in greater detail.

38. *SVF* 3.179:43, from Plutarch, *Stoic rep.* 12.1038B: "Why, then, does Chrysippus torture us by writing in every book on physics and, by Zeus, on ethics: 'immediately, from the time we are born, we make ourselves, our limbs, and our own offspring familiar to ourselves'?"; *SVF* 2.724, from Plutarch, *Stoic rep.* 12, 1038B: "In the first book of *On Justice*, Chrysippus writes: 'Even wild animals, they say, in a way commensurate with their needs, make their offspring their own and familiar to themselves, except for fish, for their newborn feed themselves.' For appropriation seems to be the perception and apprehension of what is one's own."

39. *SVF* 1.197, from Porphyry, *Abst.* 3.19 οἰκειώσεως πάσης καὶ ἀλλοτριώσεως ἀρχὴ τὸ αἰσθάνεσθαι· τὴν δὲ οἰκείωσιν ἀρχὴν τίθενται δικαιοσύνης οἱ ἀπὸ Ζήνωνος: "perception is the principle [or origin] of every 'making one's own' and of every alienation; the followers of Zeno make appropriation the principle of justice"; this, clearly, refers to sociable, deontological, or rational *oikeiôsis*. See *SVF* 1.98, from Cicero, *Fin.* 4.16.45: *Mihi autem aequius videbatur Zenonem cum Polemone disceptantem, a quo quae essent principia natu-*

Isnardi, moreover, exploits the text of Hierocles himself to confirm that *oikeiôsis* is Zenonian: where Hierocles, in VIII.9–11, reports a divergence of opinion between Cleanthes and Chrysippus in respect to

---

rae acceperat, a communibus initiis progredientem videre, ubi primum insisteret, et unde causa controversiae nasceretur, non stantem cum iis, qui ne dicerent quidem sua summa bona esse a natura profecta, uti isdem argumentis, quibus illi uterentur, isdemque sententiis: "To me, it seemed that Zeno, proceeding on the basis of common points of departure, when he argued against Polemo, from whom he had learned what the principles of nature are [that is, what the Greeks call πρῶτα κατὰ φύσιν, on which the doctrine of *oikeiôsis* is founded], saw better where he first took his stand and whence the reason for the controversy arose, without standing with those who did not even claim that their highest goods had their origin in nature, although he used the same arguments that they used, and the same expressions."

For the presence of the doctrine of *oikeiôsis* in Zeno, see above all Radice, *Oikeiôsis*, 248–62, whose arguments seem to me to be well taken. Franz Dirlmeier, *Die Oikeiôsis-Lehre Theophrasts* (Philologus Supplementband 30.1; Leipzig: Dieterich, 1937), 48–49, holds that in *SVF* 1.197 the term οἰκείωσις is already employed in a technical sense and maintains that *SVF* 1.198 says simply that Zeno proceeded from the same principles as Polemo. Radice, however, corrects the first of Dirlmeier's assertions on the basis of the anonymous commentator on the *Theaetetus*, who attributes sociable *oikeiôsis* to the followers of Zeno (οἱ ἀπὸ Ζήνωνος in the fragment cited above), and objects also to the second, taking the term *principia naturae* in *SVF* 1.198 in the strict philosophical sense, since it expresses a concept closely connected, in other passages as well, with the doctrine of *oikeiôsis*, at least in its initial, preservative phase. Besides, on the basis of *SVF* 1.356 Radice shows (disagreeing here with Anna Maria Ioppolo, *Aristone di Chio e lo Stoicismo antico* [Naples: Bibliopolis, 1980], 149ff.) that Aristo, the disciple of Zeno, had a theory of *oikeiôsis*. It thus seems probable, if the premises, at least, of the doctrine of *oikeiôsis* were present in Polemo and if the doctrine itself was present in Aristo, that Zeno too maintained it, since he was the disciple of the former and the teacher of the latter. In addition, as one may conclude from *SVF* 1.230–31, Zeno had already pushed the theory of duties strongly, which makes one suspect that he also had a complex theory of *oikeiôsis*, not just the preservative sort but also the sociable, as *SVF* 1.197 suggests as well, for it points to *oikeiôsis* as the basis of justice. In sum, according to Radice (255), the multiplication of *oikeiôseis*, of which John M. Rist, "Zeno and Stoic Consistency," *Phronesis* 22 (1977): 161–74, esp. 172; and Kerferd, "Search for Personal Identity," 177–96, esp. 191, speak, should not be dated after Chrysippus but is in all likelihood already present in Zeno. Indeed, Radice concludes his inquiry by affirming: "the picture that emerges from an analysis of the texts confirms the thesis that the first Stoic already had a theory of *oikeiôsis* in a philosophically developed form" (262). "Reconciliation" is also expressed by the terms καταλλαγή and καταλλάσσω and their congeners, on which see John T. Fitzgerald, "Paul and Paradigm Shifts: Reconciliation and Its Linkage Group," in *Paul beyond the Judaism/Hellenism Divide* (ed. Troels Engberg-Pedersen; Louisville: Westminster John Knox, 2001), 241–62, with extensive bibliography on 260–62.

indefinite representation,[40] she supposes that this difference must be in reference to "the representation that a rational living being has of its relation to itself" and regards this as "a firm piece of evidence that Cleanthes and Chrysippus had already offered distinct intepretations of οἰκειοῦσθαι αὑτοῖς [becoming one's own and familiar to oneself], to all appearances without substantial disagreement but differing in the way that the process of a gradual coming to consciousness of the phenomenon was represented; and this undoubtedly means that the theory of οἰκειοῦσθαι ἑαυτοῖς had already taken shape previously." Thus, it was already present in Zeno.

Thus, Isnardi, like Radice, rejects the supposition that the theory of *oikeiôsis* cannot be attributed to Zeno, although Nicholas P. White has maintained, on the contrary, that it could not, and Ioppolo is in agreement with this. Ioppolo indeed goes further in denying that even the theory of πρῶτα κατὰ φύσιν, or "first things [or goods] according to nature," is Zenonian, in her interpretation of Cicero, *Fin.* 4.16.45, which she claims is heavily dependent on Antiochus of Ascalon.[41] Zeno seems rather, she holds, to have adopted from Polemo the theory of "first goods according to nature," those *prima commoda naturae* attributed to him by Cicero in *Acad. pr.* 131 and 138 (= frags. 125–126 Gigante), which he then combined with his own theory of indifferents, which are in turn divisible into those that are "preferable" and those that "are to be rejected" (προηγμένα, ἀποπροηγμένα). The "first goods in accord with nature" are preferable but are not subject to choice, inasmuch as one does not choose whether one wishes to live or perceive. However, Cicero, in *Fin.* 4.16.45 (*SVF* 1.198), reports that Zeno "spoke with Polemo, from whom he *acceperat* what the first principles of nature were." The context indicates that *acceperat* is better taken here as "agreeing" or "sharing the opinion," rather than

40. Isnardi, "Ierocle," 2210; see the commentary below for problems of interpretation connected with this mutilated passage.

41. See Pohlenz, *Grundfragen der stoischen Philosophie*, 20ff.; Kurt von Fritz, "Polemon," PW 21.2:2524–29; Nicholas P. White, "The Basis of Stoic Ethics," *HSCP* 83 (1979): 143–78; Ioppolo, *Aristone di Chio*; Isnardi, "Ierocle," 2210–13: "that Cicero adopts the argument of Antiochus of Ascalon, a passionate follower of Polemo, against the 'faithless' Zeno in this connection, is not a good reason to deny *in toto* Zeno's dependency on Polemo's theses, the very Polemo of whom it is known for sure that Zeno attended his school"; "there does not seem to me to be much weight to the claim that 'if Zeno had maintained the doctrine of *oikeiôsis*, Aristo would have had to make his own point of view clear in this regard, openly declaring his disagreement' [Ioppolo, *Aristone di Chio*, 156], since we know very little of the works of Aristo." See Radice, *Oikeiôsis*, esp. 101–20 for *oikeiôsis* in Cicero's *De finibus* and in Polemo; 251–55 for the refutation of Ioppolo's arguments.

as "learning," and that the *principia naturae* are equivalent to the πρῶτα κατὰ φύσιν. Zeno's originality will have consisted, then, in including these latter among the preferred indifferents and in treating them as a particular case of nonelective preferables, as well as in combining the two theories of "first goods according to nature" and universal relationship: he formulated the theory of relationship, appropriation, and familiarity (οἰκείωσις) with ourselves as the "first goods according to nature" par excellence and as "the first thing that is our own and familiar (πρῶτον οἰκεῖον).[42] In the subsequent tradition, the "first goods according to nature" and *oikeiôsis*—a doctrine that went beyond the boundaries of the school to such an extent that the anonymous commentator on the *Theaetetus* calls it πολυθρύλητος, "very commonly used" or "well known" (VII.20), and that will turn up later in Antiochus of Ascalon and in Cicero, as well as in Arius Didymus and in Seneca[43]—will be indissolubly linked. It is this latter doctrine that serves as the most suitable point of departure in the *Elements of Ethics*,

---

42. Isnardi, "Ierocle," 2212–14.

43. Esp. Cicero, *Fin.* 5.13.37; Arius Didymus in Stobaeus, *Anth.* 2.7.13–26 (2:116,19–152,25 Wachsmuth and Hense); Seneca, *Ep.* 95; 121. On Arius Didymus, the doxographer at the time of Augustus with Peripatetic and Stoic leanings, see above, n. 37; Fortenbaugh, *On Stoic and Peripatetic Ethics*; David E. Hahm, "The Ethical Doxography of Arius Didymus," *ANRW* 36.4:2935–3055, 3234–43; Tryggve Göransson, *Albinus, Alcinous, Arius Didymus* (Göteborg: Acta Universitatis Gothoburgensis, 1995); Jan N. Bremmer, "Aetius, Arius Didymus and the Transmission of Doxography," *Mnemosyne* 51 (1998): 154–60; Arthur J. Pomeroy, trans., *Arius Didymus, Epitome of Stoic Ethics* (SBLTT 44; Atlanta: Society of Biblical Literature, 1999); Jaap Mansfeld, "Chrysippus' Definition of Cause in Arius Didymus," *Elenchos* 22 (2001): 99–109.

On Antiochus of Ascalon, an important figure in the Academy and a turning point between the skeptical Academy and Middle Platonism, see John Glucker, *Antiochus and the Late Academy* (Göttingen: Vandenhoeck & Ruprecht, 1978); Eva Di Stefano, "Antioco di Ascalona tra Platonismo scettico e Medioplatonismo," in *Momenti e problemi di storia del platonismo* (ed. Samuel Scolnicov; Symbolon 1; Catania: Univerità di Catania, 1984), 37–52; Harold Tarrant, "Peripatetic and Stoic Epistemology in Antiochus and Boethus," *Apeiron* 20 (1987): 17–37; Jonathan Barnes, "Antiochus of Ascalon," in *Essays on Philosophy and Roman Society* (vol. 1 of *Philosophia Togata*; ed. Jonathan Barnes and Miriam T. Griffin; Oxford: Clarendon, 1989), 51–96; Michelangelo Giusta, "Antioco di Ascalona e Carneade nel libro V del *De finibus bonorum et malorum* di Cicerone," *Elenchos* 11 (1990): 29–49; Ludwig Fladerer, *Antiochos von Askalon* (Graz: Berger & Söhne, 1996); Enzo Puglia, "Le biografie di Filone e di Antioco nella Storia dell'Academia di Filodemo," *ZPE* 130 (2000): 17–28; François Prost, "L'éthique d'Antiochus d'Ascalon," *Philologus* 145 (2001): 244–68; Jeffrey W. Tatum, "Plutarch on Antiochus of Ascalon," *Hermes* 129 (2001): 139–42.

according to Hierocles, and so he highlights in this work precisely the idea of *oikeiôsis*.

As Radice notes, the principle or ἀρχή of Hierocles' *Elements of Ethics* is not strictly speaking ethical but biological, or rather ethological, in that his observations take as their starting point animal behavior. This seems to agree with Radice's other claim that the theory of *oikeiôsis* arose in an extraphilosophical, and more precisely medical and biological, context.[44] For Hierocles, "an animal, immediately after birth, has perception [αἰσθάνεται] of itself" (I.38–39). Sensation (αἴσθησις) is given by nature both for the perception of external things and for self-perception (I.44ff.). For animals perceive right from the beginning both their own parts and their use: "winged creatures, on the one hand, are aware of the readiness and aptness of their wings for flying, and, on the other hand, every land animal is aware both that it has its own members and of their use" (I.52). The proof of this is that, "when we wish to see something, we direct our eyes toward the visible object, and not our ears" (I.58). This perception of our own parts and their use provides us, for example, with a knowledge of our own weak and strong points: thus, bulls know which parts of their own bodies can be used as weapons (II.18ff. and 3ff.). Analogously, animals perceive the strength of others, and all of them fear humans, since they are aware of humans' superiority (III.20ff. and 46ff.). In humanity in particular, this knowledge is present from the very beginning, since it derives from the tight bond between soul and body (III.56ff.) that is characteristic of human beings.

Hierocles illustrates as follows the simultaneous presence of the perception of external objects and self-perception: together with the perception of white, we perceive ourselves as "whitened" (or, better, we catch ourselves in the act of perceiving white); together with the perception of sweet, we perceive ourselves as "sweetened"; and with the perception of heat, we perceive ourselves as warmed, and so forth. Thus, together with what is perceived, we pick up ourselves as perceivers: "since an animal invariably perceives something as soon as it is born, and perception of itself is naturally joined to the perception of something else, it is clear that

44. Radice, *Oikeiôsis*, 189; see 263–312 for the origin of the doctrine of *oikeiôsis* in medical circles (on which see above, n. 34). Radice looks especially at biology in Hellenistic medicine, at the concept of assimilation in the *Corpus Hippocraticum*, and at the theory of nutrition and assimilation in Aristotle, Theophrastus, Praxagoras, and their disciples, and also in Galen. The theory of appropriation or *oikeiôsis* will, it is argued, have arisen out of these biological ideas concerning assimilation.

animals must perceive themselves right from the beginning."[45] Perception of oneself depends, then, on the perception of external entities; therefore, among other things, small babies are afraid of the dark, since, when they are deprived of visual perception of external objects, they also lose the perception of themselves and fear coming to an end.

Besides, along with the perceiver and the perceived, every pereception implies also the perception of perceiving; in other words, perception includes perception of itself. Hierocles explains this by way of the following syllogism:

> Major premise: every basic [or primary: *arkhikê*] faculty begins with itself;
>
> Minor premise: perception (αἴσθησις) is a basic faculty;
>
> Conclusion: thus, before perceiving anything else, perception must involve perception of itself (VI.20ff.).

On this basis, with one additional step, we get *oikeiôsis*, since every living creature, for its own subsistence, not only is able but also desires to keep itself alive.[46] This is why Hierocles (VI.51–52) concludes that "an animal, when it has received the first perception [αἴσθησις] of itself, immediately becomes its own and familiar to itself [ᾠκειώθη πρὸς ἑαυτῷ] and to its constitution [σύστασις]." One must, then, make a move from self-awareness to self-preservation, with the intermediary step of sensing as one's own and familiar (that is, as οἰκεῖον) both oneself and one's own individual identity, and thus holding oneself and one's individuality dear.

To the perceiver, the perceived, and the perception of perceiving there is thus added self-love, which is characteristic of every creature by nature (VII.4): it is this last that makes survival possible. Self-preservation is the result of *oikeiôsis*.[47] Bastianini and Long rightly observe that for Hierocles,

45. The phenomena of exteroception and proprioception have been studied by Charles S. Sherrington, *The Integrative Action of the Nervous System* (New York: Scribner, 1906), 336–49; and Kerferd, "Search for Personal Identity," 177–94, esp. 179, where he emphasizes the innerwardness of *oikeiôsis* and its self-referentiality, and 186–96, where the doctrine of *oikeiôsis* is said to have Stoic origins and is concerned with the development, whether internal or external, of a person who first succeeds in recognizing himself and then relates to others, to the extent of rendering them part of himself. See Oliver W. Sacks, *The Man Who Mistook His Wife for a Hat* (London: Duckworth, 1985), 43–52.

46. See Radice, *Oikeiôsis*, 191.

47. See Schönrich, "*Oikeiôsis*," 34–51, esp. 41.

who bases his ethical treatise on self-perception, "what an animal values depends on the way it perceives itself."[48] For even newborns, whether human beings or the pups of animals, have a "self" right away, a point of view from which they view and evaluate everything with which they enter into contact. The ethical principle for Hierocles is thus "the basic perception and valorization of oneself that all animals experience."

In relation to this doubling of external and internal, Hierocles in IX.4–5 offers an observation that is most important for an understanding of his entire theory of *oikeiôsis*: he states that "*oikeiôsis* is called by many names," since it is divided into interior and exterior. The interior *oikeiôsis*, in turn, is split into that which looks to the self (εὐνοητική) and the *oikeiôsis* that looks to one's own constitution (ἐκλεκτική), whereas the exterior is divided into *oikeiôsis* that looks to external good (αἱρετική, "choiceworthy") and that which regards other people (στερκτική, "affectionate"). Given this subdivision, Bastianini and Long observe that precisely the multiplicity of objects of *oikeiôsis* opens up the possibility of a conflict among these objects.[49]

The problem that Radice has brought to light seems especially noteworthy in this regard.[50] On the basis of Hierocles' analysis it turns out that we must wish to live, since we love ourselves, must know ourselves and our constitution, and know as well external objects and evaluate whether they are useful or harmful for our lives, as Hierocles himself says (III.19–54). But this last bit would seem to be affirmed only on an empirical basis rather than demonstrated rationally, as a philosophical argument requires. For even though perception, according to the Stoics, admits of rational assent, this does not mean that the perceived object is analyzed rationally, since such assent judges whether perception in fact represents external objects but does not analyze such objects for their properties and does not evaluate whether they are harmful for us or pleasurable and the like.[51] Hierocles treats the process of perception (αἴσθησις), even in the

48. *CPF* 1.1.2:390; so too Radice, *Oikeiôsis*, 192. Regarding the importance of the self and self-perception in ancient philosophy, see Richard Sorabji, "Soul and Self in Ancient Philosophy," in *From Soul to Self* (ed. M. James C. Crabbe; London: Routledge, 1999), 8–32.

49. *CPF* 1.1.2:449.

50. Radice, *Oikeiôsis*, 193.

51. *SVF* 2.993, under Chrysippus, from Plutarch, *Stoic. rep.* 47, 1056E: "Apart from these points, if representations do not occur in accord with fate, how could fate be the cause of assents? If it is because he has it that representations lead to assent, and assents are

case of exterior objects, as always accompanied by interiorization, thanks to which a sense of satisfaction or danger can be associated with one or another sensation. He does not, however, indicate what determines this connection, unless perhaps he has recourse to a principle by which nature acts in a supporting role, as it were, and works in a person's behalf;[52] but if so, it is a thesis that Hierocles does not make explicit.

If, however, we leave aside this matter, which would seem to be a knot still to be untied, Hierocles' contribution to the understanding of *oikeiôsis* can be evaluated positively, in that he makes clear the complexity of pereception and the deep connection between its inner and outer aspects. *Oikeiôsis* is an appropriation of oneself that is consequent upon the perception and love of oneself and that is immediately projected outward as well, in the activity of an animal. This element of projection outward is not absent in formulations of the doctrine outside of Hierocles, for example in Cicero and in the Old Stoa.[53] If this extroversion did not occur, indeed, with an immediate choice between useful and harmful objects, then *oikeiôsis*, reduced to *amor sui* and *sensus sui*, would not influence the behavior of animals. Yet it does influence their behavior, so much so, indeed, that it can even have, for the Stoics, ethical implications, and fundamental ones at that.[54]

Hierocles' treatise is important also because, in investigating self-perception (that is, perception of one's own continuous individuality) and the perception of one's own constitution, in accord with one's stage of development, Hierocles makes it clear that one's constitution or σύστασις is a consequence of the structure that connects the parts of the body, whereas

said to occur in accord with fate, how does fate not contradict itself, since it frequently, and in highly important matters, produces contrasting representations and draws the mind in opposite directions? But they say that people err when they choose one or the other instead of suspending judgment; thus, if they choose unclear representations, they stumble into mere semblances; if false ones, they are deceived; and if generally noncomprehensive ones, then they merely have opinion. But since there are three possibilities, it must be the case either that every representation is the product of fate, or that every reception of an impression and assent is infallible, or that not even fate itself is faultless. For I do not know how fate can be blameless if it produces such representations, since it is blameworthy not to oppose and withstand them but instead to follow and yield to them."

52. See Radice, *Oikeiôsis*, 194 n. 47 and 189–90; Rist, "Zeno and Stoic Consistency," 161–74, esp. 167.

53. Cicero, *Fin.* 3.1.4–2.5; *SVF* 3.181:43–44 and 183:44.

54. For an analysis of ethical *oikeiôsis*, see Radice, *Oikeiôsis*, 196–233.

consciousness or συνείδησις is our awareness of their existence and use, as Seneca too notes.[55]

Above all, the doctrine of *oikeiôsis* as presented by Hierocles in the *Elements of Ethics* is important because, at the end, where he treats the several kinds of *oikeiôsis*, he touches on the problem of interpersonal relations, a topic he analyzes also in his other work, *On Appropriate Acts*; in this way, Hierocles' treatment is related to the passage by Porphyry in which *oikeiôsis* is said to be the source of justice, according to the Stoics: "the followers of Zeno treat *oikeiôsis* as the principle of justice."[56] This is a theory that the anonymous Academic (a Middle Platonist) who wrote the commentary on Plato's *Theaetetus* opposed (V.24ff.).[57] This writer is thoroughly familiar

55. *Ep.* 121.5. See, on this letter, Brunschwig, "The Cradle Argument," esp. 135ff.; Radice, *Oikeiôsis*, 195–96; and the commentary on the *Elements of Ethics* below, ad loc.

56. Porphyry, *Abst.* 3.19 (*SVF* 1.197): τήν τε οἰκείωσιν ἀρχὴν τίθενται δικαιοσύνης οἱ ἀπὸ Ζήνωνος. See above, n. 39. See also Malcolm Schofield, "Two Stoic Approaches to Justice," *Justice and Generosity: Studies in Hellenistic Social and Political Philosophy, Proceedings of the Sixth Symposium Hellenisticum* (ed. André Laks and Malcolm Schofield; Cambridge: Cambridge University Press, 1995), 191–212.

57. Hermann Diels and Wilhelm Schubart, eds., *Anonymer Kommentar zu Platons Theaetet (Papyrus 9782): Nebst drei Bruchstücken philosophischen Inhalts (Pap. n. 8; p. 9766. 9569)* (Berliner Klassikertexte 2; Berlin: Weidmann, 1905), 5–6; today there is a new edition by Guido Bastianini and David N. Sedley in *CPF* 3:227–562. See Jaap Mansfeld, "Notes on Some Passages in Plato's *Theaetetus* and in the Anonymous Commentary," in *Zetesis: Album amicorum aangeboden aan E. de Strycker* (Antwerp: Nederlandsche boekh, 1973), 108–14; Giuseppe Invernizzi, "Un commento medioplatonico al *Teeteto* e il suo significato filosofico," *RFN* 68 (1976): 215–33; James A. Doull, "A Commentary on Plato's *Theaetetus*," *Dionysius* 1 (1977): 5–47; Claudio Mazzarelli, "Bibliografia medioplatonica, I: Gaio, Albino e Anonimo commentatore del *Teeteto*," *RFN* 72 (1980): 108–44; Harold Tarrant, "The Date of Anonymous *In Theaetetum*," *CQ* 33 (1983): 161–87, who proposes a date toward the end of the first century B.C.—and no later than the second century A.D., which is the date of the papyrus on which it is preserved—and a connection with Eudorus of Alexandria; Harold Tarrant, *Scepticism or Platonism? The Philosophy of the Fourth Academy* (Cambridge: Cambridge University Press, 1985), 66–88; David N. Sedley, "Three Platonist Interpretations of the *Theaetetus*," in *Form and Argument in Late Plato* (ed. Christopher Gill and Mary Margaret McCabe; Oxford: Oxford University Press, 1996), 79–103; Salvatore Lilla, *Introduzione al Medio-platonismo* (Rome: Istituto patristico Augustinianum, 1992) 9, 178; Jan Opsomer, *In Search of the Truth: Academic Tendencies in Middle Platonism* (Brussels: Paleis der Academiën, 1998), 36–48. The commentator thought it impious to justify ethics merely on the basis of *oikeiôsis* or human nature and not of God. Whereas Tarrant and Sedley date the commentary on the *Theaetetus* to the late first or the beginning of the second century A.D., Opsomer places it squarely in the second century, reverting to the position initially proposed on the basis of the dating of the papyrus. See also the commentary below on the *Elements of Ethics*, n. 51.

with the idea of *oikeiôsis*, which is introduced by Socrates and by certain sophists in Plato's dialogues (VII.20–25), but he does not accept it as the basis of justice, since elementary *oikeiôsis*, which regards the self and is essentially self-preserving in nature, is incomparably more intense that the sociable kind, that is, the kind of *oikeiôsis* that is not toward oneself but toward the others. Indeed, the idea of an equivalence between these types of *oikeiôsis* would be "contrary to what is evident [ἐνάργεια] and to the self-perception [συναίσθησις] of a person" (V.34–35: the vocabulary is the same as that of Hierocles; in the commentary it is shown that the classification of kinds of *oikeiôsis* is also similar in both writers).

In truth, the theory of "duties," which is connected with that of *oikeiôsis* directed toward one's neighbor, seems to be characteristic of a certain "softening" of the rigorous, Old Stoic line, which begins to be visible in Middle Stoicism, with its easing of the principle of ἀπάθεια, with which the implications of the doctrine of *oikeiôsis* seemed to be incompatible. As is well known, Panaetius is regarded as the most important exponent of this Middle Stoic mitigation of Old Stoic ethics. Of course, the idea of duties or καθήκοντα, as distinct from κατορθώματα, was already present in early Stoicism and is indeed attested to by Zeno, as indicated above; nevertheless, it was chiefly Panaetius who deepened the conception of καθήκοντα and connected it with a reevaluation of indifferents (ἀδιάφορα), which is one of the most important features of the softening of the Old Stoic approach to ethics.[58]

58. See Giovanni Reale, *Cinismo, epicureismo e stoicismo* (vol. 5 of *Storia della filosofia greca e romana*; Milan: Bompiani, 2004), 481–514, for Middle Stoicism, and esp. 492–94, arguing that Panaetius reconsidered the nature of ἀδιάφορα and deepened the existing concept of καθήκοντα, which was the title of his fundamental work, now lost. For Panaetius, see the collections of fragments edited by Modestus van Straaten, *Panaetii Rhodii Fragmenta* (3rd ed.; PhAnt 5; Leiden: Brill, 1962); Francesca Alesse, *Panezio di Rodi, Testimonianze* (Naples: Bibliopolis, 1997); with introduction and commentary, Emmanuele Vimercati, *Panezio: Testimonianze e frammenti* (Milan: Bompiani, 2002). Some studies specifically on Panaetius's ethics, which underscore what is new in comparison with the Old Stoa, are: Alberto Grilli, *Il problema della vita contemplativa nel mondo greco-romano* (Milan: Fratelli Bocca, 1953), 108–24 and 137–64; idem, "Studi paneziani," *SIFC* 29 (1957): 31–97; John M. Rist, *Stoic Philosophy* (Cambridge: Cambridge University Press, 1980), 173–200; Hans Armin Gärtner, *Cicero und Panaitios: Beobachtungen zu Ciceros Schrift* De officiis (Heidelberg: Winter, 1974); Annekatrin Puhle, *Persona: Zur Ethik des Panaitios* (Frankfurt: Lang, 1987); Paolo Garro, "La concezione dei πάθη da Zenone e Crisippo a Panezio," *SMSR* 13 (1989): 183–95; Irene Frings, "Struktur und Quellen des Prooemiums zum I. Buch Ciceros *De officiis*," *Prometheus* 19 (1993): 169–82; Francesca Alesse, *Panezio di Rodi e la tradizione*

Moreschini, moreover, has suggested that the Academic Antiochus of Ascalon, who was strongly influenced by Stoic thought, was the one who recognized the incompatibility between *oikeiôsis* and *apatheia*;[59] indeed, Antiochus tempered the doctrine of *apatheia* and the paradoxes associated with Stoic ethics (Cicero, *Acad. pr.* 43.133ff.) and at the same time affirmed that virtue, which continues to be the *summum bonum* as in all Stoicism (Cicero, *Fin.* 5.9.26), is sufficient for happiness, but not for "perfect happiness," which requires also material goods, as the Peripatetics held (Cicero, *Acad. pr.* 43.134ff.; *Fin.* 5.9.24; 5.24.72).[60] Hierocles himself seems

---

stoica (Naples: Bibliopolis, 1994); François Prost, "La psychologie de Panétius," *Revue des Études Latines* 79 (2001): 37–53; most recently, Teun L. Tieleman, "Panaetius' Place in the History of Stoicism, with Special Reference to His Moral Psychology," in *Pyrrhonists, Patricians, Platonizers: Hellenistic Philosophy in the Period 155–86 BC. Tenth Symposium Hellenisticum* (ed. Anna Maria Ioppolo and David N. Sedley; Naples: Bibliopolis, 2007), 107–42. For the theory of καθήκοντα in Panaetius: Andrew R. Dyck, "The Plan of Panaetius' *Peri tou Kahêkontos*," *AJP* 100 (1979): 408–16; Eckard Lefèvre, *Panaitios' und Ciceros Pflichtenlehre* (Stuttgart: Steiner, 2001).

59. Claudio Moreschini, *Apuleio e il platonismo* (Firenze: Olschki, 1978), 141. See Reale, *Scetticismo, Eclettismo, Neoaristotelismo*, 87–92, who on 88 defines Antiochus as "a Stoic with only a partly Platonic camouflage." For the doctrines, particularly the ethical ones, of Antiochus, see above n. 43 and Woldemar Görler, "Älterer Pyrrhonismus—Jüngere Akademie: Antiochos von Askalon," in *Grundriss der Geschichte der Philosophie* (ed. Friedrich Ueberweg and Hellmut Flashar; Basel: Schwabe, 1994), 4.2:717–989, esp. 938–80; Prost, "L'éthique d'Antiochus," 244–68.

60. See Diogenes Laertius, *Vit. phil.* 7.127–128 (= *SVF* 1.187 and 3.49:13): "Besides, according to the Stoics, virtue by itself is sufficient for happiness [αὐτάρκη εἶναι πρὸς εὐδαιμονίαν], as Zeno, Chrysippus in the first book of his *On Virtues*, and Hecato in book 2 of his *On Goods* affirm. This is their reasoning: if greatness of soul [μεγαλοψυχία] is sufficient by itself [αὐτάρκης ἐστίν] to render us superior to all else, and if it is a part of virtue, then virtue too is sufficient by itself for happiness [αὐτάρκης ἐστὶ καὶ ἡ ἀρετὴ πρὸς εὐδαιμονίαν], disdaining all that seems to entail perturbation. Panaetius and Posidonius maintain, however, that virtue is not sufficient by itself [οὐκ αὐτάρκη], but that health, resources, and strength are also needed." See Reale, *Diogene Laerzio*, 844–45, with my nn. 274–75; on eudaimonism in Hellenistic philosophy, see Julia Annas, *The Morality of Happiness* (Cambridge: Cambridge University Press, 1993), Italian translation under the title *La morale della felicità in Aristotele e nei filosofi dell'età ellenistica*, with preface by Giovanni Reale (Temi metafisici e problemi del pensiero antico: Studi e testi 64; Milan: Vita e Pensiero, 1998). See also Hecato frag. 3 (Heinz Gomoll, ed., *Der stoische Philosoph Hekaton, seine Begriffswelt und Nachwirkung unter Beigabe seiner Fragmente* [Bonn: Cohen, 1933]); Panaetius frag. 110 (van Straaten, *Panaetii Rhodii Fragmenta*); Posidonius frag. 173 (Ludwig Edelstein and I. G. Kidd, eds., *Fragments 150–293* [vol. 2.2 of *Posidonius*; Cambridge: Cambridge University Press, 1988]) and 425c (Willy Theiler, ed., *Poseidonios: Die Fragmente* [Berlin: de Gruyter, 1982]). One may compare Diogenes Laer-

to participate in this tendency to mitigate the severe ideal of *apatheia* in such a way as to render it compatible with a sociable (i.e., deontological and rational) *oikeiôsis*, that is, the kind of *oikeiôsis* that is not directed toward oneself but toward the others and entails duties or appropriate actions toward them. More particularly, Isnardi has suggested that Hierocles may lie behind a passage in Aulus Gellius's *Noctes atticae* (12.5.7ff.), in which Gellius's teacher, Taurus, affirms that the *principia naturae* are self-love and concern for ourselves and our safety, "which the ancients called πρῶτα κατὰ φύσιν," and he praises Panaetius for having recognized that

---

tius, *Vit. phil.* 7.103 (= frag. 171, Edelstein and Kidd, *Fragments 150–293*; 245a, Theiler, *Poseidonios*): for the old Stoics, "wealth is not a good, and neither is health. Posidonius, however, asserts that these too enter into the list of goods" (see Reale, *Diogene Laerzio*, 822–23 with my n. 213).

But a philosopher who straddles the Old and Middle Stoa, Antipater of Tarsus, a disciple of Chrysippus and of Diogenes of Babylon, already seems to have distanced himself from strictly orthodox Stoicism in conceding a certain importance to external goods, that is, those that were traditionally considered indifferents in Stoicism and not true goods. See Seneca, *Ep.* 92.5 (*SVF* 3.53:13): "Some, however, are of the opinion that the highest good [*summum bonum*] may be increased, since it would not be complete if matters subject to fortune were against it. Antipater too, who is among the great authorities of this school, affirms that something, even if it is very little, must be granted to external things [*aliquid se tribuere dicit externis*]." On Antipater, see the commentary on the treatise *On Appropriate Acts* below, n. 17, where I note the close connection with the Neo-Stoic ideas on marriage. See also §5b of the introductory essay (below), with notes, on the doctrine of the τέλος in Antipater, which seems indeed to herald some departure from Old Stoicism. In fact, not only from a chronological point of view, but also in respect to content and deviations from orthodox doctrine, Antipater seems to belong no longer to the Old but rather to the Middle Stoa. Francesca Alesse, "Socrate dans la littérature de l'ancien et du moyen stoïcisme," *PhilosAnt* 1 (2001): 119–35, analyzes references to Socrates and his fundamental ideas in Zeno, Cleanthes, and Antipater and considers the last of these to be already an undoubted exponent of Middle Stoicism, even though his fragments are included in *SVF*. Various fragments in von Arnim's edition are devoted to his polemic against the Academic probabilism of Carneades, well analyzed by Myles F. Burnyeat, "Antipater and Self-Refutation: Elusive Arguments in Cicero's *Academica*," in *Assent and Argument: Studies in Cicero's Academic Books: Proceedings of the 7th Symposium Hellenisticum (Utrecht, August 21–25, 1995)* (ed. Brad Inwood and Jaap Mansfeld; PhAnt 76; Leiden: Brill, 1997), 277–310: probabilism strengthened the Academic position and became the official doctrine of the Academy, thanks also to this debate with Antipater, who was by now a Middle Stoic. The context is that of the dispute between Academics and Stoics analyzed in detail by Anna Maria Ioppolo, *Opinione e scienza: Il dibattito tra stoici e accademici nel III e nel II secolo a.C.* (Naples: Bibliopolis, 1986). For Antipater, see also Ramelli, *Allegoria*, ch. 2.6.1–2 on Antipater's theology, his use of etymology and allegoresis, and an analysis of *SVF* 3.63:16, drawn from his *On Marriage*, together with the citations of poetry in this work.

one cannot accept the theory of *oikeiôsis* with all its implications and at the same time maintain the doctrine of *apatheia* in all its rigor (frag. 111 van Straaten, *Panaetii Rhodii Fragmenta*).[61] Whether this passage actually derives from Hierocles, as is possible, or not, it seems clear, at all events, that Hierocles adopted the same line as Panaetius in acknowledging that the interpersonal consequences of the theory of sociable, deontological, and rational *oikeiôsis*, that is, the kind of *oikeiôsis* that is directed toward others, require an attenuation of the doctrine of *apatheia*.

4. Hierocles' Treatise *On Appropriate Acts*

Since Cicero translated the Greek term καθῆκον, which he found in Panaetius, as *officium*, we render the title of Hierocles' treatise Περὶ τῶν καθηκόντων as *On Appropriate Acts*.[62]

The presence of the concept and the term καθῆκον already in Zeno is attested to by Diogenes Laertius (*Vit. phil.* 7.108 [*SVF* 1.230]), who also testifies to the etymology that Zeno himself provided, in accord with a practice dear to Stoics:[63]

> now, duty [καθῆκον] was first so called by Zeno, with a name drawn from "going in accord with others" [κατά τινας ἥκειν]. It is an act that is appropriate [or proper, one's own: οἰκεῖον] to constitutions in accord with nature [κατὰ φύσιν]. Of acts done in accord with impulse, indeed, some are duties, but others are contrary to duty, <and still others are neither duties nor contrary to duty>. Duties, then, are those that reason chooses

61. Isnardi, "Ierocle," 2214.

62. See Gerhard Nebel, "Der Begriff ΚΑΘΗΚΟΝ in der alten Stoa," *Hermes* 70 (1935): 439–60, who translates the Greek term as "das Sich-Gehörende"; Damianos Tsekourakis, *Studies in the Terminology of Early Stoic Ethics* (Wiesbaden: Steiner, 1974) 36, 44, and *passim*; Ioppolo, *Aristone di Chio*, 98ff.; Isnardi, "Ierocle," 2206 and 2215–16; Gill, "The School in the Roman Imperial Period," 33–58, esp. 41; Long and Sedley, *The Hellenistic Philosophers*, §§58–59, esp. 1:358–59, who translate καθήκοντα as "proper functions," as does David N. Sedley, "The Stoic-Platonist Debate on *kathêkonta*," in *Topics in Stoic Philosophy* (ed. Katerina Ierodiakonou; Oxford: Clarendon, 1999), 128–52, esp. 130–33. For further discussion and documentation on *kathêkonta*, see the commentary on the Stobaean extracts from *On Appropriate Acts*, n. 21.

63. For the importance of etymology in Stoic philosophy see, e.g., my "Saggio introduttivo" and "Saggio integrativo," in Ramelli, *Cornuto*, chs. 2 and 9. For the fragment in the passage of Diogenes Laertius, see the translation by Reale in *Diogene Laerzio*, 827, and my notes 221, 222, and 223.

> to enact, for example honoring one's parents, siblings, and country and surrounding oneself with friends.

Just these duties toward parents, siblings, country, and friends, which were valorized, as we have seen, by Panaetius in the passage on ethical theory, are those treated as well by Hierocles in his work *On Appropriate Acts*.

The theory of duties is still more closely associated not only with what is "in accord with nature" but also with the "first goods according to nature" and *oikeiôsis* in a testimony provided by Cicero, *Fin.* 3.7.23,[64] in which duties (*officia*) are said to derive from the *principia naturae* and from the *conciliatio*, that is, *oikeiôsis*, of a person in respect to whatever is according to nature (Cicero, *Fin.* 3.6.20; see *SVF* 3.188:45, which, again in reference to duties, nicely traces the complex picture and development of Stoic *oikeiôsis*).[65] Analogously, *SVF* 3.492:135 defines "the duties …

64. *SVF* 3.186:45: *Cum autem omnia officia a principiis naturae proficiscantur, ab iisdem necesse est proficisci ipsam sapientiam. Sed quemadmodum saepe fit, ut is qui commendatus sit alicui pluris eum faciat cui commendatus sit quam illum a quo sit, sic minime mirum est primo nos sapientiae commendari ab initiis naturae, post autem ipsam sapientiam nobis cariorem fieri quam illa sint, a quibus ad hanc venerimus*: "Since all duties derive from principles of nature, it is necessary that wisdom itself derive from the same principles. But, just as it often happens that a person who has been recommended to someone values more highly the one to whom he has been recommended than he does the person by whom he was recommended, so too it is no wonder that we are first recommended to wisdom by the principles of nature, but afterwards wisdom itself becomes more dear to us than those very principles by which we arrived at wisdom."

65. *SVF* 3.188:45, from Cicero, *Fin.* 3.6.20, included among the fragments of Chrysippus: "Once, therefore, those principles have been established, namely, that those things that are in accord with nature should be acquired for their own sake, whereas contrary things in turn should be avoided, the first duty [*primum officium*]—for this is how I translate καθῆκον—is that one preserve oneself in the state of nature, next that one maintain those things that are in accord with nature and reject those that are contrary. Once choice and avoidance [*selectione et item reiectione*] have been determined, there follows choice together with duty [*cum officio selectio*], then choice that is permanent [*perpetua*], and finally that which is constant and in agreement with nature, in which for the first time there begins to inhere and to be understood what it is that can be called truly good [*vere bonum*]. For first is a human being's appropriation [*conciliatio*] in respect to those things that are in accord with nature. At the same time as one has acquired intelligence or rather thought, which the Stoics call ἔννοια, and has seen the order or, so to speak, the harmony of the things that are to be done, he values that much more than all those things that he loved previously, and so by his knowledge and reason he concludes that he should decide that precisely in that harmony is located that highest good [*summum bonum*] for a human being, which is to be praised and sought for itself [*per se laudandum et expetendum*]. And

which, for a human being, derive from the first *conciliatio* toward nature." Thus, *oikeiôsis* toward oneself and toward one's neighbor, along with the duties that it entails, pertains for the Stoics to everyone, whether the wise or the foolish (the σοφοί or the φαῦλοι, in the traditional Stoic classification), just on account of its basic and general character: it is a "duty common to the wise person and the fool," as Cicero reports (*Fin.* 3.18.59; *SVF* 3.498:135–36).

Despite stylistic differences, and high likelihood that the two surviving works of Hierocles are distinct, there is a clear thematic continuity between the *Elements of Ethics* and the treatise *On Appropriate Acts*, which is no surprise, given what has been said concerning the deep connection between the topic of duties and that of *oikeiôsis*. Isnardi, however, emphasizes rather the way in which the argument in the first of Hierocles' treatises seems to break off exactly at the point at which the second begins.[66] Indeed, in the extracts from Stobaeus collected by von Arnim, which are also translated in this volume, a series of duties is listed and discussed under the heading "how one must behave toward…" (πῶς χρηστέον, *quomodo sit utendum*),[67] arranged according to people or entities with whom we relate or toward whom behave in a certain way, beginning with the most important: the gods, one's country, parents, siblings, spouse. This last, which involves domestic comportment, is treated under the above-mentioned rubrics *On Marriage* and *Household Management* (unless these were independent works), and it is possible, as I attempt to show in the commentary on *On Appropriate Acts*, to draw a series of useful comparisons with similar tracts by other Roman Stoics, above all Musonius Rufus, for both these themes, and with earlier writers too, such as Antipater of Tarsus, midway between the Old and Middle Stoa, for the first of these topics, and with the *Oeconomicus* of Xenophon for the second. Among the kinds of behavior analyzed by Hierocles there is also that which

---

when the highest good is located in that which the Stoics call ὁμολογία and when the Good is located in that to which all things referred…."

66. Isnardi, "Ierocle," 2206. For a brief analysis of the extracts from Stobaeus, not taken into consideration by Bastianini and Long or by Radice, who concern themselves only with the *Elements of Ethics*, see Isnardi, "Ierocle," 2206–8.

67. The Latin translation is that of Seneca, *Ep.* 95.45–67 = Posidonius frag. 452 in Theiler, *Poseidonios* (partially = frag. 176 in Edelstein and Kidd, *Fragments 150–293*); commentary in Theiler, *Poseidonios*, 394ff., which incidentally cites a work by Marcus Brutus Περὶ τοῦ καθήκοντος or *On Appropriate Acts*. On the χρῆσθαι theme in Stoicism, see Thomas Bénatouïl, *Faire usage: La pratique du stoïcisme* (Paris: Vrin, 2006).

one should maintain in respect to oneself (*apud* Stobaeus, *Anth.* 4.27.23 (4:672,12 Wachsmuth and Hense), this instance clearly linked with the theory of *oikeiôsis* discussed in the *Elements of Ethics.*

The first extract looks to duties toward the gods, who in the scale of relations come first since they are the most important moral subjects with whom each person can be related via the activity of *oikeiôsis.* In his exposition in this section, Hierocles offers first of all a typically Stoic definition of virtue as based on ἀμεταπτωσία and βεβαιότης, "immutability and stability," which harkens back directly to Zeno (*SVF* 1.202), who defined virtue as "stable and immutable" (βέβαιος καὶ ἀμετάπτωτος); this quality is possessed in the highest degree by the gods, who, in the Stoic view, constitute the primary paradigm for human ethics.[68] Divinity neither wishes nor does anything but good, as Hierocles affirms, citing by the way a passage from Plato's *Respublica* (1.335D) and doubtless drawing inspiration from Platonic thinking; if the gods dispense any evil to humans, it is exclusively a matter of just punishments.[69] Hierocles subsequently observes that humans bring down upon themselves the evils that are freely chosen by them (αὐθαίρετα), and he contrasts, as Plato had done, the free choice of human beings with the self-excusing fashion of attributing responsibility for our misfortunes to God, though this too is in line with Stoic reflections on human free will.[70] For in accord with traditional Stoic views, Hierocles affirms that vice alone is the cause of evils, just as only virtue is the cause of goods; thus, everything that is neither virtue nor vice can only be either in accord with or contrary to nature:[71] there follow examples of this latter class, with the

68. See the commentary below on *On Appropriate Acts*, n. 2, with further documentation.

69. See the documentation in the commentary to *On Appropriate Acts*, nn. 4–6.

70. Evidence is provided in the commentary below on *On Appropriate Acts*, nn. 7–9.

71. There is a problem here, however, that arises in connection with terminology but extends to the much larger question concerning Hierocles' adherence to the traditional Stoic theory, according to which all things are divided into goods, evils, and indifferents or ἀδιάφορα, which are neither goods nor evils and which in turn are subdivided into preferables and things to be rejected, as Diogenes Laertius (*Vit. phil.* 7.101–107) attests (see Reale, *Diogene Laerzio*, 822–27 with my nn. 211–20); see esp. §§101–102: "They say that, of the things that are, some are goods [ἀγαθά], some are evils [κακά], and some are neither [οὐδέτερα]. Goods are the virtues…, evils are their opposites…, and neither goods nor evils are all those things that neither benefit nor harm, for example, life, health, pleasure, beauty, strength, wealth…. For these things are not goods, but rather indifferents [ἀδιάφορα], in the class of preferables [προηγμένα]." Hierocles, however, in the passage under consideration does not say that things that are neither goods nor evils are ἀδιάφορα but calls them

rather μέσα, that is, intermediates between good and evil or virtue and vice, although the old Stoics maintained that there was no middle between virtue and vice. For the notion of ἀγαθόν in Stoicism, see Michael Frede, "On the Stoic Conception of the Good," in Ierodiakonou, *Topics in Stoic Philosophy*, 71–94. Diogenes Laertius again testifies to this view (*Vit. phil.* 7.127 = *SVF* 3.536:143): "They believe that there is nothing between virtue and vice [μεταξὺ ἀρετῆς καὶ κακίας], whereas the Peripatetics say that between virtue and vice there is moral progress [προκοπή]. For the Stoics say that a piece of wood must be either straight or crooked, and so too a person must be either just or unjust, and not more just or more unjust; and similarly for the other virtues." But Hierocles does not mean moral progress as the middle between virtue and vice, on the importance of which in Middle and Neo-Stoicism, see Geert Roskam, *On the Path to Virtue: The Stoic Doctrine of Moral Progress and Its Reception in (Middle-)Platonism* (Ancient and Medieval Philosophy 33; Leuven: Leuven University Press, 2005), 33–144; John T. Fitzgerald, "The Passions and Moral Progress: An Introduction," in *Passions and Moral Progress in Greco-Roman Thought* (ed. John T. Fitzgerald; London: Routledge, 2008), esp. 15–16; rather, as is evident from the context, the μέσα between virtue and vice of which he speaks, and which can be in accord with or contrary to nature, are none other than the indifferents, whether preferables or to be rejected. He offers as examples illness, poverty, and so forth, which, together with their contraries, form part of the traditional set of indifferents mentioned by the Stoics. This is why, in the passage of Hierocles under consideration, I employ the term "indifferents" in my translation. Hierocles' purpose is to show that God is the cause of all goods and only of goods, but it is for us to choose them and, among the indifferents, those that are in accord with nature. Indeed, it seems to me that there is a confirmation of this interpretation in a passage in Epictetus's *Dissertationes* (2.19.13 = *SVF* 3.39:218, under Diogenes of Babylon), where the indifferents are explicitly defined as μεταξύ between goods and evils, or virtues and vices: "Of the things that are, some are goods, some are evils, and some are indifferents [ἀδιάφορα]. The virtues [ἀρεταί] and whatever participates in them are goods; the vices [κακίαι] and whatever participates in the vices are evils; and what is between these [τὰ μεταξὺ τούτων] are indifferents: wealth, health, life, death, pleasure, and toil. —Whence do you know this? —Hellanicus says so in his *Egyptiaca*. —For what is the difference between saying this and what Diogenes says in his *Ethics*, or Chrysippus, or Cleanthes?" Analogous is *SVF* 3.118:28, under Chrysippus, from Stobaeus, *Anth.* 2.7.7 (2:79,4–7 Wachsmuth and Hense): "The Stoics call 'indifferents' [ἀδιάφορα] things that are intermediate between goods and evils [τὰ μεταξὺ τῶν ἀγαθῶν καὶ τῶν κακῶν], … that is, what is neither good nor evil [τὸ μήτε ἀγαθὸν μήτε κακόν]." This doctrine, then, was precisely Stoic orthodoxy. Clearly, it is a different formulation from that in Diogenes Laertius: when he says that for the orthodox Stoics there is nothing μεταξύ virtue and vice, he means to say that there is nothing that is partly virtue and partly vice, as one might understand to be the case with moral progress; however, when the indifferents are defined as μεταξύ goods and evils, that is, once again, between virtue and vice, what is meant is that these, in themselves, are neither goods nor evils, as is clear from frag. 118 of Chrysippus.

In this connection it is worth mentioning that it is the Stoics who paid special attention to the notion of moral progress, as is rightly maintained by Fitzgerald in "The Passions and Moral Progress," 1–25. At the same time, it would seem that, among the Stoics, those who made the most of the notion of moral progress were the Middle Stoics and the Roman Stoics, whereas the Old Stoics, in contrast to the Peripatetics, according to Diogenes Laertius (*Vit. phil.* 7.227 = *SVF* 3.536:143), did not admit of it; this is the prevailing view among

scholars. For the debated question of moral progress in the Old Stoa, see Roskam, *On the Path to Virtue*, 15–33, who denies that the Old Stoa allowed for moral progress; Otto Luschnat, "Das Problem des ethischen Fortschritts in der alten Stoa," *Philologus* 102 (1958): 178–214. On the other hand, *SVF* 1.234, cited in n. 98 below, suggests that for Zeno there did exist moral progress and that he conceived of it as of progress toward the predominance of the rational faculty in a person's life, actions, and choices. This tension seems to reappear also in later authors, such as Musonius (see my "Ierocle Neostoico in Stobeo: I *Kathêkonta* e l'evoluzione dell'etica stoica," in *Deciding Culture: Stobaeus' Collection of Excerpts of Ancient Greek Authors* [ed. Gretchen Reydams-Schils; Turnhout: Brepols, 2009]). The tension within the sources may be at least partially explained if we take into consideration the whole of Chrysippus's fragments concerning προκοπή. First of all, he considers nature to manifest a continual progress, understood as a strengthening and perfecting of the *logos*: *ipsam per se naturam longius progredi, quae etiam nullo docente … confirmat ipsa per se rationem et perficit*: "Nature on its own progresses further, and although nobody teaches her … she strengthens and brings to perfection reason [i.e., the *logos*] by herself" (*SVF* 3.220:52). The source is reliable, Cicero, *Leg.* 1.9.27, and *progredi* clearly denotes progress. The problem is whether this is physical or moral progress, given that both seem to be progress toward the *logos*; one may even suppose that, from the Stoic holistic and monistic point of view, they constitute one and the same progress. In *SVF* 3.219:52, deriving from another reliable source, Seneca (*Ep.* 49.11), a similar idea seems to be expressed: *dociles natura nos edidit et rationem dedit imperfectam, sed quae perfici posset*: "Nature generated us susceptible of education and gave us a reason that was imperfect but capable of becoming perfect." Here, too, progress is seen as the natural perfecting of the *logos*. Another fragment confirms that this natural progress of reason was regarded as related to progress in virtue: "the Stoics maintained that since the beginning, by nature [ἐκ φύσεως], there exists the noteworthy progress toward the virtues [πρὸς τὰς ἀρετὰς τὴν ἀξιόλογον προκοπήν], which the Peripatetics, too, called natural virtue [φυσικὴν ἀρετήν]" (*SVF* 3.217:51). This fragment was ascribed by von Arnim to Chrysippus, although the source, Simplicius in his commentary on Aristotle's *Categoriae*, speaks of "the Stoics" in general. The last three fragments seem to indicate the natural perfecting of the *logos* and, with this, a natural progress toward virtue. This kind of progress, linked to the development of the *logos*, seems to be referred to in the fragment of Zeno mentioned above (*SVF* 1.234; cited in n. 98). Natural progress is important, but perfection in virtue depends, not only on nature, but also on education. For, "even those who have a poor natural disposition to virtue, if they receive an adequate education [παιδεία], reach moral perfection, and, on the contrary, those who have an excellent natural disposition become evil on account of carelessness [ἀμελείᾳ γεγόνασι κακοί]" (*SVF* 3.225:52, from Clement of Alexandria). It is clear that education and training are linked to moral progress, which is confirmed, to my mind, by a letter of Zeno quoted by Diogenes Laertius (*Vit. phil.* 7.8) on the basis of a first-century B.C. Stoic source, Apollonius of Tyre. Zeno is replying to Antigonus Gonatas, who asked him to come to Macedonia to instruct him (παιδεύω) in virtue and thus enable him to achieve perfect happiness (τελείας εὐδαιμονίας). Zeno praises the true παιδεία, the philosophical education, that leads to happiness, evidently through moral progress. The ingredients of this process are adequate exercise (μετρία ἄσκησις) and a master who is energetic in his teaching. The goal of moral progress will be "the complete acquisition of virtue" (τελεία ἀνάληψις τῆς ἀρετῆς) and thus the attainment of perfect happiness. According to David Hahm, "Zeno before and after Stoicism" (in Scaltsas and Mason, *The Philosophy of*

Zeno, 29–56, esp. 39), this letter of Zeno's reflects Chrysippus's teaching on education and moral progress toward perfect virtue and happiness. We find several fragments—all ascribed to Chrysippus in von Arnim's collection—in which it is said that moral progress toward virtue does exist, and virtues themselves are susceptible of increment (*SVF* 3.226:52, from Chrysippus's *On Zeus*), but at the same time it is asserted that those who are still involved in passions and are only approaching virtue but have not yet reached it are as miserable as those who have made no progress at all. *SVF* 3.535:143 comes from a hostile source (Plutarch), who moreover speaks not specifically of Chrysippus but of "the Stoics" and thus must be taken *cum grano salis*, but its sense is clear: the Stoics admit of προκοπή—although Plutarch remarks that this concept of theirs remains an αἴνιγμα to him—"but those who have not yet liberated themselves from absolutely all passions and illnesses are as miserable [κακοδαιμονοῦντας] as those who have not yet got rid of the worst of them." The very same idea is expressed in *SVF* 3.530:142, which comes from a trustworthy source (Cicero, *Fin.* 3.14.48), who records the similes that the Stoics employed to make their view clear: *Ut enim qui demersi sunt in aqua nihilo magis respirare possunt, si non longe absunt a summo ut iam iamque possint emergere, quam si etiamtum essent in profundo, nec catulus ille qui iam appropinquat ut videat plus cernit quam is qui modo est natus, item qui processit aliquantum ad virtutis habitum nihilominus in miseria est quam ille qui nihil processit*: "Just as those who are immersed in water, if they are not far removed from the surface, so that they can emerge in time, cannot breathe more than if they were still in the depths, and a puppy that is on the verge of seeing can see no more than a newborn pup, so the person who has made some progress toward the state of virtue is no less in misery than the one who has made no progress at all.". The very same examples of persons immersed in water and of blind newborn puppies are reported by Plutarch in *SVF* 3.539:143, and exactly the same idea is repeated in *SVF* 3.532:142, also from Cicero (*Fin.* 4.9.21): those who are approaching virtue but have not yet reached it are as *miseri* as those who are very remote from it. Thus, the Old Stoics did admit of progress toward virtue but maintained that happiness, which attaches only to virtue itself, is not achieved until one has reached complete virtue (thus, in *SVF* 3.534:142 it is rightly stated that the Stoics, i.e., the Old Stoics, "grant virtue only to perfect philosophy, whereas the Peripatetics and others grant this honor also to those who are imperfect"; see also 3.510:137–38). This does not mean that the Old Stoics did not ascribe importance to moral progress. That they spoke of the persons progressing (προκόπτοντες) and distinguished them from both the totally vicious or ignorant (ἀπαίδευτοι) and the perfectly virtuous or educated (πεπαιδευμένοι) is also attested by Proclus in *SVF* 3.543:145: the vicious blame others for their own misery; those who are making progress blame only themselves for their errors; the virtuous accuse neither others nor themselves, because they do not err and are not miserable.

To my mind, the above helps to explain how it is that Diogenes Laertius can report that for the Stoic there was no intermediate state between virtue and vice because an action is either virtuous or vicious, while at the same time a fragment of Zeno attests that the founder of the Stoa did admit of the possibility of progress.

It is on the basis of the above-mentioned testimonites concerning Chrysippus's interest in moral progress that A. M. Colombo, "Un nuovo frammento di Crisippo," *PP* 9 (1954): 376–81, argued that a testimony to the Stoic concept of moral progress contained in P.Mil.Vogl. Inv. 1241 (a papyrus belonging to the State University of Milan, probably dating to the second century A.D.) may be a fragment of Chrysippus. This argument is based on the presence in the papyrus of a comparison between the fool (ἄφρων) and the

qualification, not strictly in line with Stoic orthodoxy, as we shall see, that what is contrary to nature occurs only in the terrestrial world as opposed to the heavens, which are composed of the most pure substance.[72]

The second extract from Hierocles' *On Appropriate Acts* concerns due behavior toward one's country, which is conceived of as the "system" to which an individual belongs: in importance, this comes immediately after the gods. Hierocles focuses on a proof of the significance of part and whole, a topic that was surely discussed in the Old Stoa:[73] Chrysippus himself wrote a treatise in several books entitled *On Parts* (*De Partibus* = Περὶ μερῶν), as Plutarch attests (*Comm. not.* 1082),[74] and Sextus Empiricus (*Math.* 11.23)[75] seems to testify to an ongoing debate on the subject in Sto-

blind person, which is attested for Chrysippus in *SVF* 3.530:142 and 532:142, as mentioned above, and of an allusion to the doctrine of the προκοπή. If this identification is right, and if the fragments of Chrysippus cited above are reliable, as I think they are, the doctrine of moral progress may be considered to have been maintained already in the Old Stoa. The only doubtful point is whether these fragments may be assigned to Chrysippus as opposed to other Old Stoics. Fernanda Decleva Caizzi and Maria Serena Funghi, "Un testo sul concetto stoico di progresso morale (PMilVogliano Inv. 1241)," in *Aristoxenica, Menandrea, fragmenta philosophica* (ed. Aldo Brancacci et al.; Florence: Olschki, 1988), 85–124, who provide a complete edition, with an Italian translation and commentary, of the papyrus fragment, are not convinced that it should be ascribed to Chrysippus. See also Marcello Gigante, "Dossografia stoica," in *Varia papyrologica* (ed. Fernanda Decleva Caizzi et al.; STCPF 5; Florence: Olchki, 1991), 123–26; Fernanda Decleva Caizzi, "The Porch and the Garden: Early Hellenistic Images of the Philosophical Life," in *Images and Ideologies: Self-Definition in the Hellenistic World* (ed. Anthony Bulloch et al.; Berkeley and Los Angeles: University of California Press, 1994), 303–29; Roskam, *On the Path to Virtue*, 25–27, also offers a translation and some textual emendations and supplements.

72. See the commentary below on *On Appropriate Acts*, nn. 10 (on the orthodox Stoic claim that vice is the only cause of evils and virtue as the only cause of goods) and 11 (for the specific remark by Hierocles on the negative nature of matter and on the distinction between the heavenly and sublunary worlds, a distinction that does not seem to be typically Stoic, even if the pure substance of the celestial regions has an analogue in the Stoic ether, that fiery, extremely subtle element that is conceived of as fire and as *pneuma* in its most pure form, as the hegemonic function of the cosmos, and as the primary manifestation of the divine that is immanent in it).

73. See the commentary below on *On Appropriate Acts*, n. 14, with bibliography.

74. This title is missing in the long list of Chrysippus's works preserved at the end of book 7 of Diogenes Laertius, but this list, although it is the fullest, is notoriously incomplete, since book 7 is truncated at a certain point: see my introductory essay, "Diogene Laerzio storico del pensiero antico tra biografia e dossografia, 'successioni di filosofi' e scuole filosofiche," in Reale, *Diogene Laerzio*, xxxiii–cxxxvi, esp. xliii–xlv, ciii–cx.

75. See *SVF* 2.80, under Chrysippus's logical fragments = Sextus Empiricus, *Math.* 9.352: "Given such dilemmas at this stage, the dogmatic thinkers typically say that an

icism. Hierocles shows how absurd it is to worry about the safety of only a single part, since, if the whole should perish, that part too would perish, and yet he also affirms that "the whole is nothing without its parts," in this respect differing from Aristotle, who, basing himself on the priority of the act (*Metaph.* 8.1045a9ff.), decidedly devalued the parts in respect to the whole. Some of the characterizations of country that Hierocles offers here are based on traditional rhetoric: "a second divinity," "one's first parent"; national customs constitute an "unwritten law" (ἄγραφος νόμος) that must be revered, a concept especially relevant to the Stoics, who considered the νομοθέται, alongside mythographers, as philosophers capable of expressing the truth, the latter in myths, the former in the institutions, cults, and customs of each city.[76]

Hierocles next treats duties to parents and kin, in passages that are tinged with rhetoric and figurative expressions. Parents are not only the best craftsmen, inasmuch as they are creators, but indeed household gods, whom we ought to serve as priests: Hierocles then dwells on a description of the various gestures of gratitude that we can perform toward them. The discourse on kin is based broadly on a particularly successful and rightly famous illustration: around our own minds, conceived of as the center, there run a series of ever wider concentric circles, beginning with that representing our own body, then the circles representing our parents, siblings, spouse and children, and on to more remote relatives, and then to members of the same deme and tribe, to fellow citizens, to those who

---

external, perceptible object is neither a whole nor a part but that it is we who predicate both whole and part of it. For the whole [τὸ ὅλον] is a relation [πρός τι], in that the whole is conceived in relation to the parts [τὰ μέρη], but the parts too are a relation in turn, since the parts are conceived in relation to the whole. But relations are located in our co-memory [συμμνημόνευσις], and our co-memory is within us. Therefore, both the whole and the part are within us. The external, perceptible object is neither a whole nor a part, but a thing of which we predicate our own co-memory." See also *SVF* 3.75:18, under the ethical fragments of Chrysippus = Sextus Empiricus, *Math.* 11.24: "Parts, say the followers of the Stoics, are not the same things as wholes, nor are they something of another kind, just as a hand is not the same thing as a whole person (for a hand is not a whole person), but neither is it other than the whole (for a whole person is conceived of with a hand). Therefore, since virtue is a part of a good man and a friend, but parts are neither the same as wholes nor other than wholes, the good man and friend is said not to be other than benefit. Thus, every good is contained in the definition [sc. 'the good coincides with benefit or with what is not other than benefit'], whether it is benefit straight out or not other than benefit."

76. Isnardi, "Ierocle," 2207.

belong to the same people or *ethnos*, until we arrive at the widest circle, which is that of the entire human race. The width of the circles and their distance from the center constitutes the standard by which to measure the intensity of our ties, and therefore of our duties, toward people.[77] The commentary illustrates in more detail the question of the need indicated by Hierocles to perform a kind of "contraction of the circles," that is, to reduce as much as possible the distance from each circle to the next one out and thus to create the closest possible *oikeiôsis*, even going so far as to employ the onomastic strategem of designating others by names appropriate to a degree of relationship one step closer to us than that which characterizes them in reality.[78] A similar purpose seems to motivate as well the assimilation of our feelings toward various categories of others to those due to one's father and mother, thereby basing those feelings principally on respect and love.[79] We shall have occasion to note how Hierocles warns of the objective impossibility of maintaining toward the whole human race, or even just large groups of people, the same goodwill that we manifest toward those most dear to us. He recommends, accordingly, preserving goodwill toward those who are most near and dear to us, and more broadly a sense of our affinity toward all human beings,[80] which in Stoicism is grounded also in a consciousness of the divine paternity common to all.[81]

The two extracts on marriage and household management are also closely related to the two fundamantal themes in Hierocles' ethics, that of duties and that concerning *oikeiôsis*, which are themselves tightly connected, as we have seen, given that duties are what characterize the *oikeiôsis* that is directed toward one's neighbor. As for the treatment of marriage, this is a topic that was developed several times by Stoics, which is the only philosophical school that considered marriage in a truly positive light and deemed it wholly suitable for the *sapiens*; the term καθῆκον occurs in this tract several times, above all in reference to the "choice of

77. See Kerferd, "Search for Personal Identity," 177–96, esp. 193–96; Bastianini and Long, *CPF* 1.1.2:290–91; Reydams-Schils, *The Roman Stoics*, 3–4.

78. See the commentary below on the Stobaean extracts from *On Appropriate Acts*, n. 42.

79. See the commentary on the Stobaean extracts from *On Appropriate Acts*, n. 43.

80. See the commentary below on the Stobaean extracts from *On Appropriate Acts*, nn. 39–41.

81. See the references below in the commentary on the Stobaean extracts from *On Appropriate Acts*, nn. 12 and 43.

duties" that are considered to be in harmony with one's own nature.[82] In addition, in the tract on marriage there is a clear link with the doctrine of *oikeiôsis*, when Hierocles explains how every creature must live in accord with nature: if plants do not possess a soul, as is stated in regard to the period of gestation in the *Elements of Ethics*, animals, on the contrary, form representations that lead them naturally to what is "their own and familiar" (τὰ οἰκεῖα) to them. Human beings, in addition, have *logos*, which determines the act of choosing (ἐκλογή). Hierocles dwells at length on an illustration of the advantages of married life in terms that, as is indicated in the commentary, closely recall those of Antipater of Tarsus,[83] but also those of other, later Stoics such as Musonius Rufus, with whom he shares a positive evaluation of the capacities of women and a view of the matrimonial bond as having as its goal not just procreation but also, and above all, a life of shared harmony and the joint pursuit of virtue, just as in the case of friendship between philosophers. Spouses do not have just each other's bodies in common, but also their souls, in a bond of ὁμόνοια and φιλία.[84]

So too, the discussion of household management, at least insofar as we can judge from the extracts that have reached us, is connected directly with Hierocles' ideas *de matrimonio*, to the extent that it is a matter of shared activities between husband and wife. Here again there are numerous motifs in common with Musonius Rufus, such as the possibility a mutual sharing of tasks, which is of considerable importance for solidifying still further the communion between a married couple and their commitment to virtue.[85] Points of contact with other texts, although less close, include echoes of Socrates in Xenophon's *Oeconomicus*, which shed light also on the importance and nature of the Socratic heritage in Hierocles and the Neo-Stoics,[86] and of Dio Chrysostom, for the agricultural ideal that he shares with Musonius and Hierocles, and which in Musonius

82. For full documentation both of parallel texts and bibliography, see the commentary below on the Stobaean extracts from *On Appropriate Acts*, nn. 17–29.

83. See the commentary below on the Stobaean extracts from *On Appropriate Acts*, esp. nn. 17 and 29.

84. See the commentary below on the Stobaean extracts from *On Appropriate Acts*, nn. 19 and 23, with full documentation.

85. See the commentary below on the Stobaean extracts from *On Appropriate Acts*, nn. 44 and 47, where I present the relevant evidence.

86. Details and bibliography in the commentary below on the Stobaean extracts from *On Appropriate Acts*, n. 31.

in particular assumes so powerful an ethical significance as to render it the activity best suited to the philosopher.[87]

In sum, the treatise *On Appropriate Acts*, like that on the doctrine of *oikeiôsis*, locates Hierocles wholly and in an exemplary fashion in the world of the Stoic debate over ethics. It is worth attempting, at this point, to establish whether there exist, and if so to identify, themes that the Neo-Stoic Hierocles, who has so much in common with other Neo-Stoics, adopted from the Old and Middle Stoa.

5. Some Aspects of the Old and Middle Stoa in Hierocles

5.1. In the *Elements of Ethics*

There is a marked presence of doctrines drawn from the Old Stoa in Hierocles, as we have had occasion to mention several times and as was long ago emphasized by von Arnim:[88] such references are discussed in detail in the commentary on the *Elements of Ethics*, where they are continual, especially with respect to Chrysippus. In the extracts from Stobaeus, too, there are several indications of strong affinity with orthodox Stoicism. Nevertheless, the work *On Appropriate Acts*, as I have had occasion to observe, assumes a certain distance from the Old Stoa, in part by adopting a somewhat milder or attenuated position in regard to ethics inspired by Middle Stoicism but driven above all by the requirements of the doctrine of other-directed *oikeiôsis*, which seemed incompatible with the more rigorous *apatheia* required of the sage. Indeed, *Elements of Ethics* bears the same title as a treatise by the Middle Stoic Eudromus (as indicated in the commentary).[89]

In this latter work, in any case, it is notable that Hierocles maintains a certain "orthodox" commitment to a significant dimension of Old Stoic ethical theory, even though he stands apart from it in many respects. I may illustrate this briefly here, putting together the major points of the

---

87. See the references provided in the commentary below on the Stobaean extracts from *On Appropriate Acts*, n. 46.

88. *Ethische Elementarlehre*, xviiff. Von Armin devotes a lengthy discussion to the question "whether the new text offers anything new in respect to the Old Stoic doctrine, and what" (xvii). His conclusion is: "In the new text I have indicated the most important points relating to the knowledge of the Old Stoic doctrine, as regards content.... it is all, in fact, in perfect accord with Chrysippean orthodoxy" (xxxv–xxxvi, my trans.).

89. For details, see the commentary below on the *Elements of Ethics*, n. 1.

argument first advanced by von Arnim and then elaborated upon above all by Inwood, Isnardi, and Bastianini and Long, an argument that in my view is still valid.[90] Broadly, then, the doctrine of *oikeiôsis*, involving the thesis that animals, immediately from birth, become "their own and familiar" to themselves—that is, primary and individual *oikeiôsis*, of the sort that looks inward—does belong to Stoic orthodoxy, as does the decision to make *oikeiôsis* the point of departure for ethical theory as a whole, as we have seen above (§3), where we discussed traces of the idea of *oikeiôsis* that date back in all likelihood to Zeno and without any doubt at all to Chrysippus. What is specifically characteristic of Hierocles himself are (1) his initial discussion of the life and condition of animals in the state of gestation, for which no parallels in other Stoic treatments of *oikeiôsis* have come down to us; (2) the rich detail with which he illustrates animal behavior (this is further examined in the commentary, along with close parallels in Seneca, *Ep.* 121);[91] and (3) the large amount of space that he devotes to demonstrating that self-perception is the basis of *oikeiôsis*.

We may consider here several specific points in which Hierocles clearly depends on Old Stoic doctrines. First of all, Hierocles applies to the earliest or primary self-perception of an animal the substantive συναίσθησις, which, together with συνείδησις, seems to have been a technical term in the Stoa and used in connection with the doctrine of *oikeiôsis*.[92] In addition, the attribution of soul to animals in a state of gestation, which are treated like little plants, along with the theory of the intimate connection between soul and body—the total mixture of the two, together with the corporeal nature of the soul, as though it were something fluid and diffuse[93]—though absent in our sources for Old Stoicism, nevertheless seem to be directly inspired by Old Stoic doctrines (in particular, there is a close correspondence with fragments *SVF* 2.471–473 of Chrysippus). So too συμπάθεια, that is, the "sharing of affects" between soul and body, affirmed by Hierocles, is already present in Cleanthes, for whom the soul "shares

90. Inwood, "Hierocles"; Isnardi, "Ierocle," 2216–19; Bastianini and Long, *CPF* 1.1.2:289–92.

91. See the commentary below on the *Elements of Ethics*, nn. 9, 11, 12, 21, 41, 44, 46.

92. See the commentary below on the *Elements of Ethics*, nn. 12 and 44.

93. See the commentary below on the *Elements of Ethics*, nn. 24 and 26–28, with full documentation. On little ones in gestation considered like tiny plants by the Stoics, see Jean-Baptiste Gourinat, "L'embryon végétatif et la formation de l'âme selon les stoïciens," in *L'embryon dans l'Antiquité et au Moyen-Âge* (ed. Luc Brisson and Marie-Helène Congourdeau; Paris: Vrin, 2008), 59–77.

affects with the body" (συμπάσχει τῷ σώματι, *SVF* 1.518), and then again in Chrysippus (*SVF* 2.473), so that it need not be ascribed specifically to Posidonius.[94] Similarly, the idea that body is what "offers resistance" is common to Hierocles and the Old Stoa. In addition, as we shall note in more detail, the description of the physical genesis of the soul through the "cooling down," at the moment of birth, of what until then was basically a plant, also goes back to the Old Stoa: the theory is attested for early Stoicism by Plutarch (*SVF* 2.806) and by Aetius (*SVF* 2.756).[95]

For Hierocles, the soul exists in a relation of equality with the body, even though its functions are superior, and this seems to be a decidedly archaizing feature in comparison with the more common tendency of Stoicism under the Roman Empire, from Seneca to Epictetus and Marcus Aurelius, to devalue the body with respect to the rational soul. The extended examples of animal behavior in the *Elements* and the parallels between animals and human beings, which have the same kind of *oikeiôsis*, have Old Stoic credentials, for example in Cleanthes, with his interest in the *sollertia animalium*, which he uses to support his thesis of nature as creative and providential, as in *SVF* 1.515a–b:

> Cleanthes, although he did not allow that animals have a share in reason [λόγος], admitted that he had witnessed the following scene. Some ants were approaching another anthill as they carried a dead ant; the other ants climbed out of their hill, as though to meet them, and then descended into it again. This happened two or three times. Finally, those that emerged from their hill brought a larva as ransom for the corpse; the others accepted it and, having returned the corpse, they departed [from Plutarch, *Soll. an.* 967E]. They say that this story obliged Cleanthes of Assos to yield and to take note of the proposition that animals possess the elements of reason [λογισμοῦ], which he had so energetically and sincerely denied before. (from Aelian, *Nat. an.* 6.50)[96]

94. As Karl Reinhardt maintained, "Poseidonios von Apameia," PW 22.1:653ff.; rightly criticized by Isnardi, "Ierocle," 2217.

95. Analysis in the commentary below on the *Elements of Ethics*, n. 6.

96. Chrysippus, however, followed by Posidonius, emphasized the legal disparity between human beings and animals arising from the fact that *logos* is present only in the former: "Furthermore, they [the Stoics] believe that for us there is no justice toward other animals because of their dissimilarity, according to what Chrysippus affirms in the first book of his *On Justice* and Posidonius in the first book of *On Duty*" (*SVF* 3.367:89, from Diogenes Laertius, *Vit. phil.* 7.129). This claim of Chrysippus's is repeated in *SVF* 3.371:90 (from Cicero, *Fin.* 3.20.67): "And just as they believe that, with human beings, there are

Again, the continuous function of self-perception or (συν)αἴσθησις, defended and demonstrated by Hierocles in the *Elements*,[97] seems to echo an Old Stoic idea, more precisely one of Zeno, who employed this premise as a basis for his proof that there is progress toward virtue. According to Zeno, on the basis of our psychological reactions during sleep and dreams we can become aware—συναισθάνεσθαι—of our advance toward virtue (*SVF* 1.234).[98]

If up to this point I have attempted to survey, very generally, some significant points of convergence between Hierocles' views in the *Elements of Ethics* and those of the Old Stoa, it is also possible to indicate a few particulars in both vocabulary and thought in which he distances himself from Chrysippean orthodoxy and that of the Old Stoa generally.[99] Here too the details are reserved for the commentary; for the present, I wish to note just one important feature. Hierocles seems to part company with Chrysippus's well-known thesis concerning the location of the hegemonic function in the heart (attested, e.g., in *SVF* 2.879 and still present in Marcus Aurelius, *To Himself* 3.19), when he affirms that the soul exercises its directive function from "the highest regions of the body," which in all likelihood are to be identified with the head, not the heart.[100] In the development of Stoicism, it would seem to have been Cleanthes[101] who abandoned the cardiocentric position, and several Old Stoics followed him in this, according to the testimony in *SVF* 2.836, in which the doxographer Aetius speaks of "Stoics" who equated the position of the sun in the universe with that of the hegemonic function in the head: "the

bonds of justice toward other human beings, so they believe that for a human being there is no justice with animals. For Chryippus is absolutely clear that other animals are born for the sake of human beings and the gods.... Thus human beings can use animals for their own benefit without offense."

97. See the commentary below on the *Elements of Ethics*, nn. 22ff.

98. "Note also what Zeno's view was like; he believed that each person can be aware [συναισθάνεσθαι] of his own progress on the basis of his dreams, if he sees that he takes pleasure in nothing shameful and that he does not approve or do anything terrible or strange, but rather, as in the clear depths of a calm sea, without waves, the imaginative and the emotive parts of his soul shine forth, bathed in reason [λόγος]." See n. 71 for the problems that this fragment entails in respect to the assumption that the Old Stoics did not admit of moral progress.

99. See the discussion in Isnardi, "Ierocle," 2220–21.

100. For the question of the location of the hegemonic function in Old Stoicism, see the commentary below on the *Elements of Ethics*, nn. 28 and 31.

101. This is the hypothesis of Isnardi, "Ierocle," 2220.

hegemonic function, like the sun in the cosmos, is located in our head, which is spherical in shape [ἐν τῇ ἡμετέρᾳ σφαιροειδεῖ κεφαλῇ]." A still clearer testimony, I think, is Philodemus, *Piet.* 16 (*SVF* 2.910): "Some Stoics maintain that the hegemonic function is located in the head [ἐν τῇ κεφαλῇ]; for this is intelligence [φρόνησις], and that is why they call it Metis.[102] Chrysippus, however, places the hegemonic function in the chest [στῆθος] and asserts that Athena, who is intelligence [φρόνησις], was born precisely from there." Philodemus also cites the work *On Athena* by Diogenes of Babylon, a disciple of Chrysippus, who attacked the critics of his teacher's cardiocentric doctrine.[103] Hierocles, then, in proposing that the hegemonic function is located in the head, does not seem to have distanced himself strictly speaking from the Old Stoa but simply from the line that Chrysippus adopted.

Furthermore, according to Isnardi, there is a particular aspect of Hierocles' gnoseology that seems to depart from the older Stoic theories.[104] Hierocles presents consciousness as an assimilation to objects, since there is no perception of an external thing without self-perception of ourselves as modified in the act of perceiving the object; thus, when we have an αἴσθησις of white, we have one as well of ourselves as whitened, and when we have a perception of sweet, we have one also of ourselves as sweetened, and so forth.[105] This idea does not seem to be attested for the Old Stoa; we know only that Chrysippus, in opposing Zeno's own theory of "imprinting" (τύπωσις), conceived of the process of perception in terms of "alteration" or ἑτεροίωσις (*SVF* 2.56). This point is discussed further in the commentary, since Isnardi's interpretation does not seem to be entirely uncontroversial; besides, the fragmentary condition of the Old Stoic evidence does not allow for full confidence in the *argumentum ex silentio*, which is problematic in the best of circumstances.

Nevertheless, the *Elements of Ethics* seems to depend to a considerable degree on Old Stoicism, and this on the part of a writer who, as Inwood

---

102. The mother of Athena, identified by the Stoic allegorists with φρόνησις itself: see the materials collected in Ramelli, *Cornuto*, introductory essay and commentary on ch. 19; idem, *Allegoria*, ch. 2.

103. The same fragment is cited, indeed, in *SVF* 3.33:217, precisely under Diogenes. For Diogenes' work *On Athena* and the role of Stoic theology and allegoresis in it, see Ramelli, *Allegoria*, ch. 2.5.1–2.

104. Isnardi, "Ierocle," 2222.

105. See the points noted in the commentary below on the *Elements of Ethics*, n. 41.

has cogently argued,[106] was no mediocre thinker and was fully aware of the reasons behind the claims he made. Hierocles appears, indeed, anything but a mere popularizer of earlier doctrines; rather, he is fully up to defending Stoic theories and his own contributions in open philosophical debate. Although he has not the vitality and subtlety of Chrysippus as a speculative thinker (any more than any other late Stoic did), he had a coherent overall position, displaying both a continuity with the Old Stoa and a consistency in his own thought, even if he was not always able to offer an incontrovertible defense of his theses.

If the continuity of Hierocles' views with those of the Old Stoa seems clear, albeit marked by an evolution in thinking and incorporating some Middle Stoic accretions, it is less easy to give a complete and precise answer to Inwood's perfectly fair invitation to locate Hierocles within the philosophical scene of his own time, in part because of the difficulty of situating him chronologically, even though it is likely that he wrote later than Seneca and prior to the middle of the second century A.D. The commentary will indicate how Hierocles, at the beginning of his treatise, seeks to refute two groups of adversaries on matters relating to self-perception:[107] according to Bastianini and Long,[108] the ample space granted to this polemic favors the supposition that he is here dealing with contemporary opponents of a non-Stoic stripe. In fact, in Hierocles' time, *oikeiôsis* had long been absorbed as a basic ethical concept even among Peripatetic and Academic philosophers,[109] and it is not implausible to suppose that Hierocles dedicated so much attention to self-perception because this concept, present in Stoicism from its very origin, had to be defended against thinkers who did not take proper account of it in their treatment of *oikeiôsis*. In addition, as I have noted, the significance that Hierocles accords to the doctrine of perception in *oikeiosis* is perhaps due to the fact that he himself supplied the connection,[110] missing in the ethical theory of the Old Stoa, between primary *oikeiôsis*—that of the individual toward oneself—and the social kind that is related to justice, that is, the so-called sociable, deontological, or rational *oikeiôsis*. For, while Cicero

106. Inwood, "Hierocles," 151–84.

107. See the commentary below on the *Elements of Ethics*, nn. 11–12.

108. *CPF* 1.1.2:289–90.

109. For full documentation on the question, see Radice, *Oikeiôsis*, esp. chs. 4–5, 9.

110. Criticized by Inwood, "Hierocles," 151–84; idem, "Comments on Professor Görgemanns' Paper," 190–201, esp. 195, though it is revived by Engberg-Pedersen, *The Stoic Theory of Οἰκείωσις*, esp. 122–26.

in *Fin.* 3.19.62 introduces social *oikeiôsis*, as Inwood calls it, he does not really connect it with the primary kind that he treats at 3.16ff., whereas Hierocles discusses social *oikeiôsis* in column IX, immediately after his treatment of the primary kind and of the development in the representation of oneself and one's environment in column VIII. The connection must be as follows: the individual, as he (or she) matures, comes to perceive not only himself as "his own and familiar" to himself, but also others who are within his sphere, such as his children. Thus, by perceiving and loving himself, he at the same time perceives and loves his own children as well.[111]

Although one cannot be certain, it is possible that Hierocles was the first Stoic to connect primary *oikeiôsis* with the social kind—following in the footsteps of Chrysippus, to be sure—by way of a theory of how the representation that an animal has of itself evolves or develops. In any case, this idea of the progressive extension of *oikeiôsis* from oneself to others corresponds perfectly to the above-mentioned, well-known image of the concentric circles found in the Stobaean extracts.

5.2. In the Treatise *On Appropriate Acts*

In the treatise *On Appropriate Acts*, too, there are themes that belong to early Stoicism, although to a lesser degree than in the *Elements*; however, in *On Appropriate Acts* influences that are foreign to Stoicism are evident as well, for example in a passage exhibiting a negative valuation of matter that is certainly inconsistent with Stoic principles, as I indicate in the commentary.[112] Hierocles affirms the superiority of the highest regions of the cosmos, in virtue of the "extremely pure substance" of which they are composed. As opposed to the terrestial region (ἐπίγεια), events contrary to nature cannot occur there. Such a dichotomous vision of the cosmos does not seem to be inspired by Old Stoicism, which, although it grants a privileged status to the ether as the better kind of fire, does not imply a cosmological dualism or differentiation of substance; Hierocles' view would appear to be due rather to an "eclectic contamination" with ideas more at home in Platonism.[113]

---

111. Bastianini and Long, *CPF* 1.1.2:290.

112. See the commentary below on the Stobaean extracts from *On Appropriate Acts*, n. 11.

113. Isnardi, "Ierocle," 2221 n. 53.

There would seem to be a precedent, perhaps, for this kind of departure from the Old Stoic cosmology in Boethus of Sidon, according to whom the divine substance is drawn from the sphere of the fixed stars: "in respect to the substance of God, Zeno affirms that it is the entire world and heaven, and Chrysippus likewise does so in the first book of *On the Gods* (*De dis*), as Posidonius too does in the first book of his *On the Gods* (*De dis*). Antipater, in the seventh book of *On the Universe* (*De mundo*), maintains that his substance is similar to air; Boethus, however, in his work *On Nature* (*De rerum natura*), says that the substance of God is the sphere of the fixed stars" (*SVF* 3.3:265, from Diogenes Laertius, *Vit. phil.* 7.148). Above all, Boethus clearly distanced himself from the cosmological doctrine of the Old Stoa in denying the doctrine of a cosmic conflagration,[114] anticipating in this the Middle Stoic Panaetius: "Boethus of Sidon and Panaetius, men skilled in Stoic teachings, as though divinely inspired abandoned the theory of cosmic conflagrations [ἐκπυρώσεις] and universal palingenesis and advanced on their own to a more pious doctrine, namely, that of the incorruptibility [ἀφθαρσία] of the cosmos" (*SVF* 3.7:265). This fragment, drawn from Philo, *Aet.* 15, is the longest we have from Boethus, and it sets forth the arguments that he himself employed, which center chiefly on the following: if the cosmos were generated and corruptible, anything could be generated from nonbeing, since no cause, either external or internal, can be found for the destruction of the universe; so the genesis of the destruction would have to arise from nonbeing. Besides, Boethus wondered what God would do during the conflagration: his inactivity would, paradoxically, resemble death. But still earlier Diogenes of Babylon, a disciple of Chrysippus and head of the Stoic school, who is a transitional figure between the Old and Middle Stoa, exhibited, according to the same passage in Philo, over the course of his thinking a departure from the theory of cyclical conflagrations of the universe: "It is said that Diogenes too, when he was young, agreed with the doctrine of cosmic

114. Anthony A. Long, "The Stoics on World-Conflagration and Everlasting Recurrence," in *Recovering the Stoics* (ed. Ronald H. Epp; Supplement to the Southern Journal of Philosophy; Memphis: Dept. of Philosophy, Memphis State University, 1985), 13–58; Keimpe Algra, "Stoic Theology," in Inwood, *Cambridge Companion to the Stoics*, 163–78, esp. 173–74; and Ramelli, *Allegoria*, ch. 2. See also Michael Hillgruber, "Dion Chrysostomos 36 (53), 4–5 und die Homerauslegung Zenons," *MH* 46 (1989): 15–24. On Boethus, see Peter Steinmetz, "Die Stoa," in Ueberweg and Flashar, *Grundriss der Geschichte der Philosophie*, 4.2:635–36; Francesca Alesse, "Lo stoico Boeto di Sidone," *Elenchos* 18 (1997): 359–83.

conflagration [ἐκπύρωσις]; however, when he was older, he began to doubt it and modified his view" (*SVF* 3.27:215). Indeed, some late representatives of the Old Stoa, beginning with Diogenes of Babylon himself, are assigned to the Middle Stoa precisely because they anticipated some of its specific teachings.[115]

In the commentary on the Stobaean extracts I note *in extenso* various elements in Hierocles' account that go back to a transitional phase between Old and Middle Stoicism, such as, for example, the very close affinitities between Hierocles and Antipater of Tarsus in the treatise on marriage.[116]

Where Hierocles, however, explains that the cause of evil, far from residing with the gods, is located exclusively in human vice or κακία, he clearly situates himself in the tradition of strictly orthodox Stoicism, which

115. See Maximilian Schäfer, "Diogenes der Mittelstoiker," *Philologus* 91 (1936): 174–96. In addition, for Diogenes and his position in the history of the Stoa, see Jean-Paul Dumont, "Diogène de Babylone et la preuve ontologique," *RPFE* (1982): 389–95; idem, "Diogène de Babylone et la déesse Raison: La Métis des Stoïciens," *Bulletin de l'Association G. Budé* (1984): 260–78; Malcolm Schofield, "The Syllogisms of Zeno of Citium," *Phronesis* 28 (1983): 31–58; Dirk Obbink and Paul A. Vander Waerdt, "Diogenes of Babylon: The Stoic Sage in the City of Fools," *GRBS* 32 (1991): 355–96; Curzio Chiesa, "Le problème du langage intérieur chez les Stoïciens," *RIPh* 45 (1991): 301–21; Daniel Delattre, "Speusippe, Diogène de Babylone et Philodème," *CErc* 23 (1993): 67–86; David L. Blank, "Diogenes of Babylon and the *kritikoi* in Philodemus," *CErc* 24 (1994): 55–62. Specific aspects, such as Diogenes' interest in rhetoric and music, which conform nicely to the philosophical ideal of Chrysippus, rich and varied as it is thanks to his inclusion of scientific disciplines, are illuminated by David Sohlberg, "Aelius Aristides und Diogenes von Babylon: Zur Geschichte des rednerischen Ideals," *MH* 29 (1972): 177–200 and 256–77; Eduardo Acosta Méndez, "Diogenes Babylonius, fr. 104 *SVF* III, p. 238 von Arnim," *Lexis* 9–10 (1992): 155–61; Richard Janko, "A First Join between P. Herc. 411 + 1583 (Philodemus, *On Music* IV): Diogenes of Babylon on Natural Affinity and Music," *CErc* 22 (1992): 123–29; Daniel Delattre, "Une 'citation' stoïcienne des Lois (II, 669 B–E) de Platon dans les Commentaires sur la musique de Philodème?" *RHT* 21 (1991): 1–17; Andrew D. Barker, "Diogenes of Babylon and Hellenistic Musical Theory," in *Cicéron et Philodème: La polémique en philosophie* (ed. Clara Auvray-Assayas and Daniel Delattre; Études de Littérature Ancienne 12; Paris: Rue d'Ulm, 2001), 353–70; Teun L. Tieleman, "Diogenes of Babylon and Stoic Embryology: Ps. Plutarch, *Plac.* V 15. 4 Reconsidered," *Mnemosyne* 44 (1991): 106–25. For the chronology of Diogenes, who was the teacher of Antipater of Tarsus (who in turn was the teacher of Posidonius), see Tiziano Dorandi, "Contributo epigrafico alla cronologia di Panezio," *ZPE* 79 (1989): 87–92.

116. See the commentary below on the Stobaean extracts from *On Appropriate Acts*, nn. 17 and 29.

holds that the only good is virtue and the only evil vice.[117] Even before Chrysippus, indeed, Cleanthes in his *Hymn to Zeus* 11ff. had insisted that the cause of the evils that afflict human beings is certainly not God but rather human vice alone:[118]

> Without you, O God, nothing occurs on earth / nor in the divine and ethereal heaven nor in the sea, / apart from the plans that wicked people [κακοί] in their madness [ἄνοια] set in motion. / But you know how to reduce excesses to due measure, disorder to order, and to make what is inimical friendly. / Thus you have resolved all things in unity, both good and evil, / affirming a single eternal Logos for all things. / But some mortals, who are evil [κακοί], abandon and flee this Logos.... / Behold them, foolishly wandering from evil to evil [κακόν].... / But you, O Zeus, who dispense all gifts, who thicken the clouds, you of the bright lightning, / free humanity from its ruinous ignorance [ἀπειροσύνη], / chase it from the soul, and at last let that wisdom [γνώμη] be found, / trusting in which you yourself govern the world with justice."[119]

117. See the commentary below on the Stobaean extracts from *On Appropriate Acts*, nn. 4, 7, 9, and esp. 10, with full documentation.

118. For documentation on Cleanthes' *Hymn to Zeus*, see the commentary below on the Stobaean extracts from *On Appropriate Acts*, n. 25.

119. *SVF* 1.537. As is evident from the text, Zeus is far from being the cause of human misfortunes: it is human beings themselves who seek them out by virtue of their foolishness and from which they pray to the god to liberate them, since he is able to restore things to their just order, reduce excesses to their proper measure, and so on. For this latter idea in comparison with that expressed by Solon in his elegy to the Muses, see Eleonora Cavallini, "L'Elegia alle Muse di Solone e l'Inno a Zeus di Cleante," *RFIC* 117 (1989): 424–29. A commentary precisely on these verses of Cleanthes (11ff.) may be found in the appendix "Zu den Versen 11–14 des Zeusymnus des Stoikers Kleanthes," in Douwe Holwerda, *Sprünge in die tiefen Heraklits* (Groningen: Bouma, 1978). For Cleanthes' conception of Zeus, deriving principally from the Hymn, see also Marisa Ghidini Tortorelli, "Morfologia cleantea di Zeus," *Atti dell'Accademia Pontaniana* 22 (1973): 327–42. On Cleanthes' theology in the *Hymn to Zeus*, see also the commentary on the extracts from Stobaeus, n. 25, with documentation, and above all Johan C. Thom, *Cleanthes' Hymn to Zeus: Text, Translation, and Commentary* (STAC 33; Tübingen: Mohr Siebeck, 2005).

That god is not the cause of evil was probably also maintained by Cleanthes on the basis of a distinction between fate and divine Providence, which not all Stoics accepted, and which Chrysippus in particular rejected: see *SVF* 2.933, from Calcidius, *Comm. Tim.* 144: "Some maintain that one can allow a certain distinction between Providence and fate, although in fact they are a single thing. For Providence is the will of God [*Dei voluntas*], but that cannot be other than the chain of causes [*series causarum*]. Now, as for will, that is Providence; and as for the chain of causes, that has the name of fate. It follows that what occurs according to fate is also a product of Providence, and likewise, as Chrysippus

Chrysippus, for his part, reflected especially on the question of divine punishment and elaborated a theory of secondary evil, that is, of evil that is resolved in good, since it is directed by divine activity to the punishment of the wicked. Thus, in the first book of his *On Justice* (*De iustitia*) he writes that "Hesiod attributes to the gods this behavior," that is, of bringing about plagues, famines, and the like, "so that, when seeing the punishment of the wicked, others will profit from it and be less inclined to follow their example" (*SVF* 2.1175). Further, in the second book of his treatise *On the Gods* he writes that "evils are assigned according to Zeus's reason, whether for punishment [sc. of bad people] or for the economy of the whole" (*SVF* 2.1176).[120]

Again, a certain sacred sense of nature in Hierocles, according to which we are its "priests," does not seem beyond the influence of the Old Stoics. For if Hierocles says that "we must think of ourselves as ministers and priests in our own house as in a temple, chosen and consecrated to nature itself,"[121] Cleanthes already had, as has been indicated above, a

believes, what is in accord with Providence is in accord with fate. Others, however, like Cleanthes, do maintain that what occurs at the behest of Providence happens also by way of fate, and not vice versa." In this way one may affirm that misfortunes can derive from fate, in addition to human foolishness and vice, but nevertheless not from Providence. On this fragment, see Myrto Dragona-Monachou, "Providence and Fate in Stoicism and Prae-Neoplatonism: Calcidius as an Authority on Cleanthes' Theodicy," *Philosophia* 3 (1973): 262–306.

120. On the problem of human responsibility and punishment in Chrysippus, see Augusta Mattioli, "Ricerche sul problema della libertà in Crisippo," *RIL* 73 (1939–41): 161–201; Adrianus Jan Kleywegt, "Fate, Free Will, and the Text of Cicero," *Mnemosyne* 26 (1973): 342–49; Pier Luigi Donini, "Fato e volontà umana in Crisippo," *Atti dell'Accademia di Torino* 109 (1975): 187–230; Curzio Chiesa, "Le problème du mal concomitant chez les Stoïciens," *StudPhil* 52 (1993): 45–65; Giorgio Armato, "Possibilità, necessità e verità nella teoria deterministica di Crisippo," *PP* 53 (1998): 241–54; R. W. Sharples and M. Vegetti, "Fato, valutazione e imputabilità: un argomento stoico in Alessandro, *De fato* 35," *Elenchos* 12 (1991): 257–70; Mansfeld, "Chrysippus' Definition of Cause," 99–109. On the question of the connection between freedom and fate in Chrysippus and in the Old Stoa in general, see the documentation in the commentary below on the Stobaean extracts from *On Appropriate Acts*, n. 7.

121. This idea is related to the metaphor of parents as minor gods, in the image of the greater gods. Each of us is a priest of these minor gods, in the sense of ministering to and serving them. See the commentary below on the Stobaean extracts from *On Appropriate Acts*, nn. 30, 31, and 32. More generally, Plutarch too, in *Frat.* 479F, makes care of parents the thing most dear to the gods: "There is nothing that human beings can do that is more pleasing to the gods than to repay gladly and eagerly those old favors invested in their young to the ones who bore and raised them."

mystical and sacred conception of nature, which is identified, in the Stoic fashion, with the immanent divinity, and he conceived of the universe itself as a symbol of initiation: "Cleanthes affirms that the gods are initiatory forms [μυστικὰ σχήματα] and sacred names [κλήσεις ἱεραί], that the sun is a torch-bearer of the mysteries, that the universe is an initiatory device [μυστήριον], and that those who are possessed by the gods are priests who provide initiation into the mysteries [τελεσταί]."[122] Chrysippus, in turn,

122. *SVF* 1.538. See my *Allegoria*, ch. 2.3.1, with documentation and an analysis of the fragment that follows in the text. For the mystical or sacral aspect of Cleanthes' thought, including the descent of human beings from the highest divinity (*Hymn to Zeus* 4), which Hierocles too accepted (see the commentary below on the Stobaean extracts, n. 12), see Myrto Dragona-Monachou, "Ὁ ὕμνος στὸ Δία ... Ἡ ποιητικὴ θεολογία τοῦ Κλεάνθη καὶ ἡ ὀρφικο-πυθαγορικὴ παραδόση," *Philosophia* 1 (1971): 339–78; Robert F. Renehan, "Acts 17.28," *GRBS* 20 (1979): 347–53; A. Dirkzwager, "Ein Abbild der Gottheit haben und Weiteres zum Kleanthes-Hymnus," *RhM* 123 (1980): 359–60; Giuseppe Giangrande, "Cleanthes' *Hymn to Zeus*, line 4," *Corolla Londiniensis* 2 (1982): 95–97; Pieter A. Meijer, "Kleanthes' Loflied op Zeus: Kunt genog zingen, zing dan mee!" *Lampas* 16 (1983): 16–37; W. Appel, "Zur Interpretation des 4. Verses von Kleanthes' Hymnus auf Zeus," *Eranos* 82 (1984): 179–83; and above, n. 119. In light of these ideas, and thanks also to the possible allusion to the *Hymn to Zeus* in the famous speech of Saint Paul on the Athenian Areopagus, it is not surprising that Christian writers should have held Cleanthes in high esteem, on which see Johan C. Thom, "Cleanthes' Hymn to Zeus and Early Christian Literature," in *Antiquity and Humanity: Essays on Ancient Religion and Philosophy Presented to Hans Dieter Betz on His 70th Birthday* (ed. Adela Yarbro Collins and Margaret M. Mitchell; Tübingen: Mohr Siebeck, 2001), 477–99. Douglas Kidd, ed., *Aratus: Phaenomena* (Cambridge: Cambridge University Press, 1997), 72–73, 166, believes that Aratus is citing Cleanthes' *Hymn to Zeus*, 4: ἐκ σοῦ γὰρ γένος ἐσμέν, but see Jean Martin, ed., *Aratos: Phénomènes* (2 vols.; Paris: Belles lettres, 1998), 2:145 for difficulties in reconstructing this verse. According to Pohlenz, Paul is quoting Aratus; according to Schwabl and Wilamowitz, Cleanthes; see also Euripides, *Hipp.* 450: οὗ πάντες ἐσμὲν οἱ κατὰ χθόν' ἔκγονοι. See also Renehan, "Acts 17:28," 347–53; Günther Zuntz, "Vers 4 des Kleanthes-Hymnus," *RhM* 122 (1979): 97–98; Giangrande, "Cleanthes' *Hymn to Zeus*," 96–97; W. Appel, "Zur Interpretation des vierten Verses von Kleanthes' Hymnus auf Zeus," *Eranos* 82 (1984): 179–83; Ramelli, "Aspetti degli sviluppi," 103–35; Thom, *Cleanthes' Hymn to Zeus*, 3.1, *ad* v. 4. See also Mark J. Edwards, "Quoting Aratus," *ZNW* 83 (1992): 266–69, esp. 268–69, who argues that Paul's quotation of Aratus is indirect: v. 5 was already quoted by Aristobulus, frag. 4 (a quotation that seems to have escaped both Roberto Radice, *La filosofia di Aristobulo e i suoi nessi con il "De mundo" attribuito ad Aristotele* [Milan: Vita e pensiero, 1995]; and Carl R. Holladay, *Aristobulus* (vol. 3 of *Fragments from Hellenistic Jewish Authors*; SBLTT 39; Atlanta: Scholars Press, 1995]). David L. Balch, "The Areopagus Speech," in *Greeks, Romans and Christians: Essays in Honor of Abraham J. Malherbe* (ed. David L. Balch, Everett Ferguson, and Wayne A. Meeks; Minneapolis: Fortress, 1990), 52–79, notices parallels with Posidonius. For the recurrence of the specific idea of μυστήριον, as expressed in the passage by Cleanthes, in

conceived of the ceremony of the mysteries or τελετή in the same terms, as the science of nature that is also the science of the divine, simultaneously physical and theological, since theology is the highest form of physics: he asserted, indeed, that "in physics, the ultimate argument is that concerning the gods, and it is not for nothing that the traditions [παραδόσεις] in this matter are called 'initiatory ceremonies' [τελεταί]."[123] In authors contemporary with or a little later than Hierocles, such as Epictetus and Marcus Aurelius, similar ideas can be found, such as that of the sage as priest, minister, and servant of the gods (ἱερεύς, ὑπουργός, ὑπηρέτης; e.g., Epictetus, *Diss.* 3.22.82; Marcus Aurelius, *To Himself* 3.4).[124]

In the Stoic system, in fact, nature itself is a direct manifestation of God in his various aspects, which are identified with the traditional divinities of myth; it is understandable that in Stoicism, allegory, as Chrysippus theorizes it (*SVF* 2.1009), should turn out to be in perfect accord with Cleanthes' way of thinking, that is, a philosophical tool that is useful precisely for the transition from the physical to the theological plane and vice versa. If, in *SVF* 2.42 Chrysippus asserts that theological argument falls within physics, in 2.1009 he presents physics as one of the ways in which theology is transmitted: "Those who have handed down to us reverence for the gods have done so in three ways: first of all in a physical form [φυσικὸν εἶδος], second in a mythical form [μυθικόν], and third in a form that is manifested in norms [νόμοι]; the physical [or natural] form is given expression by philosophers, the mythical by poets, and that involv-

Clement of Alexandria, see my "Μυστήριον negli *Stromateis* di Clemente Alessandrino: Aspetti di continuità con la tradizione allegorica greca," in *Il volto del mistero* (ed. Angela Maria Mazzanti; Castel Bolognese: Itaca, 2006), 83–120.

123. *SVF* 2.42. For the union of theology and physics characteristic of Stoic immanentism and emphasized especially by Chrysippus in his important theoretical study of the forms of mythology (*SVF* 2.1002: it was part of his *Peri theôn*), see my discussion in *Allegoria*, chs. 2.1 and 4. On the sacral quality of Old Stoic cosmology, see Jaap Mansfeld, "Providence and the Destruction of the Universe in Early Stoic Thought," in *Studies in Hellenistic Religions* (ed. Maarten J. Vermaseren; ÉPRO 78; Leiden: Brill, 1979), 129–88. On Stoic theology, naturally connected with physics precisely by means of allegorical exegesis, apart from my *Allegoria*, chs. 2 and 9, see Long and Sedley, *The Hellenistic Philosophers*, 1:274–79, 323–33; 2:271–77, 321–32; David Furley, "Cosmology, III: The Early Stoics," in *The Cambridge History of Hellenistic Philosophy* (ed. Keimpe A. Algra et al., Cambridge: Cambridge University Press, 1999), 432–51; Jaap Mansfeld, "Theology," in Algra, *Cambridge History of Hellenistic Philosophy*, 452–78; and my "Saggio integrativo" in Ramelli, *Cornuto*, esp. for the Old Stoic allegoresis of myths of the gods in a cosmological sense.

124. Isnardi, "Ierocle," 2220.

ing norms by the ritual practices of individual cities." Nature, the object of physics, is on a par with myth and ritual traditions as one of the three modes of knowledge of the gods. This premise, indeed, grounds theological exegesis by way of allegory and confirms the degree to which, for the Stoics, allegory had philosophical and, above all, theological value: the philosophical allegorist has the job of discriminating, in myths and rites, truths of nature concealed in divine symbolism.[125]

---

125. Alongside the scientific method of philosophy, "physical" in the sense that it directly investigates nature or φύσις, the mythical is presumed to express allegorically the same φύσις that is simultaneously divine, since theology, in Stoicism, is reducible to physics, given that the divine is coextensive with the all-pervasive *pneuma* (on Chrysippus's conception of the *pneuma*, see Paul Hager, "Chrysippus' Theory of Pneuma," *Prudentia* 14 [1982]: 97–108). Myth is thus a vehicle for the veneration of the divine, just like the sacred rites of cities, since myth, ritual, figurative representations, and cultic epithets of the gods are all traced back, by way of allegorical exegesis, to underlying physical meanings. In the immediate follow-up to this passage, indeed, Chrysippus himself offers an allegorical exegesis, in physical terms, of the gods and heroes of myth, in which he has recourse to etymology and provides a systematic and programmatic foundation for the Stoic allegorical interpretation of myth. Full discussion and documentation may be found in my *Allegoria*, chs. 9, 2.1, and 4, with analysis of *SVF* 2.1009, on which see also George R. Boys-Stones, "The Stoics' Two Types of Allegory," in *Metaphor, Allegory, and the Classical Tradition: Ancient Thought and Modern Revisions* (ed. George R. Boys-Stones; Oxford: Oxford University Press, 2003), 189–216, esp. 194–96. On Stoic theology and the connection of the divine as a whole with other lesser divinities, which are understood as aspects of the whole, see Michael Frede, "Monotheism and Pagan Philosophy in Later Antiquity," in *Pagan Monotheism in Late Antiquity* (ed. Polymnia Athanassiadi and Michael Frede; Oxford: Oxford University Press, 1999), 41–68, and the entire volume for monotheism in the philosophy of the imperial period at the time of Hierocles; also, the discussion by Timothy D. Barnes, "Monotheists All?" *Phoenix* 55 (2001): 142–62; Hans-Josef Klauck, "Pantheisten, Polytheisten, Monotheisten—Eine Reflexion zur griechisch-römischen und biblischen Theologie," in idem, *Religion und Gesellschaft im frühen Christentum: Neutestamentliche Studien* (WUNT 152; Tübingen: Mohr Siebeck, 2003), 3–56. On the connection between philosophy and religion in the early imperial period, see also idem, *The Religious Context of Early Christianity: A Guide to Graeco-Roman Religions* (Minneapolis: Fortress, 2003), 331–428; Ilaria Ramelli, "Monoteismo," in *Nuovo Dizionario Patristico e di Antichità Cristiane* (ed. Angelo Di Berardino; 3 vols.; Genoa: Marietti, 2007), 2:3350–58; on Socrates' conception of religion and the role of religion in the city of Athens, in turn (in connection with the condemnation of Socrates for atheism), see Manuela Giordano-Zecharya, "As Socrates Shows, the Athenians Did Not Believe in Gods," *Numen* 52 (2005): 325–55, with a careful examination of the sources and of the concept of "belief in the gods" in the ancient world; on the latter, see also Ilaria Ramelli, "Alcune osservazioni su *credere*," *Maia* NS 51 (2000): 67–83. On Chrysippus, two comprehensive treatments still worth consulting are Émile Brehier, *Chrysippe et l'ancien stoïcisme* (3rd ed.; Paris:

From Chrysippus's theory comes that *theologia tripertita* that is found variously in Varro, in the Neo-Stoic Cornutus, in the Stoicizing Dio Chrysostom, who was probably a contemporary of Hierocles, and finally in Augustine and others.[126]

Hierocles does not openly indicate a commitment to philosophical allegory in what survives of his work; nevertheless, he surely knew the practice among his contemporaries and in the Stoic tradition right from its inception.[127] Besides, he displays a sacralized conception of nature in the passage noted above and does not hesitate to introduce the gods in his philosophical discussions as paradigms and repositories of morality and as the cause of goods and evils.

There are also other points in Hierocles' treatise *On Appropriate Acts* that can be traced back to the Old Stoa: obviously, the distinction itself between goods, evils, and indifferents, clearly expressed by Hierocles,[128] is part of orthodox Stoicism, even if it makes an appearance also in the treatise *On Appropriate Acts*, which smacks more, as I have said, of Middle than of Old Stoicism, though there too there is talk of *καθήκοντα*. The specific inclusion of the discussion of duties under the heading of "how one should behave" (*πῶς χρηστέον*) is probably due to Posidonius rather than the Old Stoa, for it seems that Posidonius proposed, at least in broad outline, a typology involving behavior toward the gods, toward people,

---

Presses Universitaires de France, 1971); and Josiah B. Gould, *The Philosophy of Chrysippus* (Leiden: Brill, 1970).

126. For Chrysippus's conception and the history of the *theologia tripertita*, see Ramelli, *Allegoria*, ch. 2.4.2; see also Godo Lieberg, "Die *theologia tripertita* in Forschung und Bezeugung," *ANRW* 1.4:63–115; Jean-Claude Fredouille, "La théologie tripartite, modèle apologétique," in *Hommages à Henri Le Bonniec: Res sacrae* (ed. Danielle Porte and Jean-Pierre Néraudau; Brussels: Latomus, 1988), 220–35; and, for the reappearance of the *theologia tripertita* in Dio Chrysostom, Paolo Desideri, "Religione e politica nell'*Olimpico* di Dione," *QS* 15 (1980): 141–61, esp. 145–51; Klauck, *Dion von Prusa*, 186–91; Ilaria Ramelli, "L'ideale del filosofo nelle orazioni dionee," in Amato, *Dione Crisostomo*, in the section "Saggi interpretativi." For the *theologia tripertita* of Varro and his sources, see Jean Pépin, "La théologie tripartite de Varron," *REAug* 2 (1956): 265–94; idem, *Mythe et allégorie* (2nd ed.; Paris: Études augustiniennes, 1976), 13–32 and 276–392; Yves Lehmann, *Varron théologien et philosophe romain* (Brussels: Latomus, 1997), 193–225; Ilaria Ramelli, "Varrone," in Melchiorre, *Enciclopedia Filosofica*, 12:12018–19.

127. For the presence of theological allegory already in Zeno, see my *Allegoria*, ch. 2.2; for antecedents prior to Stoicism, ch. 1.

128. See n. 68 to this introductory essay for my demonstration that the *μέσα* of which Hierocles speaks are in fact the *ἀδιάφορα* and that he is following here in the wake of Stoic tradition rather than contradicting it.

and toward things: "how the gods are venerated, how one should behave toward people, how one should use objects."[129] Hierocles appears to have developed and further subdivided this classification.

The duties or *καθήκοντα* of the sage, as they are delineated by Hierocles, are not strictly Old Stoic but echo a later tradition: Hierocles' sage, besides marrying, having children, and being loving and attentive toward ever-widening circles of people who are bound to him by kinship or other ties, will also be a good household manager and a good master of slaves, as well as, of course, a good citizen. As Isnardi notes,[130] Hierocles' insistence on the capacity for household management or *οἰκονομία* does not derive from the Old Stoa, and certainly not from Zeno, for whom the sage is indeed a good manager (*οἰκονομικός*: *SVF* 1.216), but only in a most general sense, insofar as the sage should be able to exercise every art and "do everything well, even cook lentils" (*SVF* 2.217). Zeno, in any case, in the political theory he developed in his famous and much-criticized *Republic* (*Respublica*), did not admit of any household or *οἶκος* that could be managed, since the wise were to live in conditions of complete communalism;[131] this theory went unrefuted by Chrysippus (*SVF* 3.743–746:185–86,

129. *Quomodo dii sint colendi, quomodo hominibus sit utendum, quomodo rebus sit utendum* ((Seneca, *Ep.* 95.47, 51, 54; cf. frag. 176 in Edelstein and Kidd, *Fragments 150–293*).

130. See Isnardi, "Ierocle," 2222, who, however, cites *SVF* 2.216 but not frag. 217.

131. See Radice, *Oikeiôsis*, 63–75, for the *Republic* of Zeno and the abolition of the family there, due to Cynic influence (for the latter's role in Stoicism, see Marie-Odile Goulet-Cazé, *Les Kynika du stoïcisme* [Wiesbaden: Steiner, 2003]); on 67, however, Radice observes that Zeno himself, not to speak of his successors, seems also to have found himself ill at ease with Cynicism, and at *SVF* 1.244, for example, he condemns adultery *διὰ τὸ κοινωνικόν*, asserting that "it is contrary to nature for a rational animal to cause a woman who has been previously wed to another man under the law to bear illegitimate children and to corrupt the household of another person." To reconcile the contradiction, Radice suggests that Zeno considered Cynic unscrupulousness as an *ἀδιάφορον*. In fact, as we shall see in the next note, for Zeno and particularly for Chrysippus, there is more than one source that attests that certain behaviors permitted by these two philosophers in their works entitled the *Republic*, such as incest or adultery, were considered indifferents, so not true evils, but it should be noted that neither are they goods; in any case, they did not recommend such behavior in established states.

On the *Republic* of Zeno, see Jan Janda, "Einige ethisch-soziale Probleme in der Philosophie des Zenon von Kition: Zur *Politeia* des Zenon," in *Soziale Probleme im Hellenismus und im römischen Reich: Akten der Konferenz (Liblice 10. bis 13. Oktober 1972)* (ed. Pavel Olivia and Jan Burian; Prague: CSAV, 1973), 99–116, who attempts to reconstruct the features of the Zenonian *Republic* and the objections that critics raised to it on the

728:183), whereas later Stoics flatly rejected it, as Philodemus attests in his work *De Stoicis* (*On the Stoics*) (XIV.4ff.).[132]

basis of book 7 of Diogenes Laertius, providing as well a comparison with Plato's *Republic* in order to underscore the fact that Zeno's ideal state was reserved for the wise alone; Jean-Paul Dumont, "Le citoyen-roi dans la *République* de Zénon," *CPhPJ* 4 (1983): 35–48; Paul A. Vander Waerdt, "Zeno's Republic and the Origins of Natural Law," in *The Socratic Movement* (ed. Paul A. Vander Waerdt; Ithaca, N.Y.: Cornell University Press, 1994), 272–308; Francesca Alesse, "La *Repubblica* di Zenone di Cizio e la letteratura socratica," *SIFC* 16 (1998): 17–38; George Boys-Stones, "Eros in Government: Zeno and the Virtuous City," *CQ* NS 48 (1998): 168–74; Andrew Erskine, "Zeno and the Beginning of Stoicism," *Classics Ireland* 7 (2000): 51–60, who, in the context of an investigation of the biography and writings of Zeno (for which contemporary sources are lacking, so that it is not always easy to determine whether major Stoic doctrines were already maintained by the founder), concentrates on the *Republic*, his most celebrated work, and on the polemics to which it gave rise; Gaca, *The Making of Fornication*, 44–45, 276–77. Édouard Des Places, "Des temples faits de main d'homme (Actes des Apôtres XVII, 24)," *Bib* 42 (1961): 217–23, finds already in Zeno's *Republic*, and indeed in Plato's *Leges* (*Laws*), an opposition between temples built by human hands and the site of God's spiritual presence, developed also in Paul's speech at the Areopagus, and evidenced also by Mark 14:58: both Paul's speech and the passages of the two philosophers were noted by Clement of Alexandria, who in *Strom.* 5.74–76 cites the latter two. For a comprehensive overview, Andreas Graeser, *Zenon von Kition: Positionen und Probleme* (Berlin: de Gruyter, 1975), continues to be important.

132. See Tiziano Dorandi, "Filodemo: Gli Stoici (PHerc 155 e 3339)," *CErc* 12 (1982): 91–133, esp. 101 and 93–96. The most relevant Chrysippean fragments in respect to the permissibility of incest are drawn from his *Republic*, which has—significantly—the same title as the work by Zeno. In *SVF* 3.744:185, Diogenes Laertius (*Vit. phil.* 7.188) reports that Chrysippus, "in his work *On the Republic*, says that one may sleep with mothers, daughters, and sons, and he says the same thing right at the beginning of his work *On Things That Are Not Choiceworthy in Themselves*." Similar is frag. 746, from Epiphanius, *Haer.* 3.39: "Chrysippus of Soli drew up godless laws, for he said that sons should have sex with their mothers and daughters with their fathers, and in other matters too he agreed with Zeno of Citium." So too frag. 745, drawn from Sextus Empiricus, *Math.* 11.192: "Chrysippus in the *Republic* literally says the following: 'In my view one may behave, as even now it is the custom—not wrongly [οὐ κακῶς]—among many: that a mother <may have children with her son, a father> with his daughter, or a brother with his full sister' "; and in *Pyr.* 3.246: "Chryippus too agrees with these views [of Zeno]; in his *Republic*, at any rate, he says: 'In my view one may behave, as even now it is the custom—not wrongly [οὐ κακῶς]—among many: that a mother may have children with her son, a father with his daughter, or a brother with his full sister.' " As is apparent, the argument here is based on the usages of various peoples, which are deemed permissible insofar as they are indifferents, as the third passage in frag. 745 makes clear, again drawn from Sextus, *Pyr.* 3.200: "What is there to wonder at, when even the Cynics and the followers of Zeno, Cleanthes, and Chrysippus say that this is an ἀδιάφορον," and as is confirmed again by frag. 743 (from Origen, *Cels.* 4.45): "They say that in its own right it is ἀδιάφορον to sleep with one's own daughters, even

The family that is founded on marriage, then, which is so much praised by Hierocles, was not strictly speaking an ideal for Zeno, who proposed as well the community of women and was followed in this once again by Chrysippus (*SVF* 3.728:183). Incidentally, Chrysippus also allowed love for boys (*SVF* 3.713:180, 719:181), without apparent contradiction between this and love for a woman, and he did allow the wise man to marry (*SVF* 3.727:183) and softened some of his more extreme statements insofar as he condemned incest and adultery in established cities (*SVF* 3.743:185, 729:183).[133]

Nevertheless, only Antipater of Tarsus, the successor to Diogenes of Babylon, who was in turn the disciple of Chrysippus, openly and unabiguously praised marriage and family life in two works, *On Marriage* and *On Cohabitation with a Woman*; the close parallels between these treatises and the Stobaean extracts of Hierocles are noted in the commentary.[134]

---

if one ought not to do such a thing in established states [ἐν ταῖς καθεστώσαις πολιτείαις].... These points, then, are roundly affirmed by the Greeks, and the by no means contemptible sect of the Stoics supports them."

133. The preceding note mentioned frag. 743; for Chrysippus's advice to the sage to marry, so as not to offend Zeus Gamelios and Genethlios (frag. 727), see the quotation and further documentation in the commentary to the Stobaean extracts below, n. 22, where I cite frag. 3.729 of Chrysippus (= *SVF* 1.244, under Zeno) against adultery. The community of women on the part of the wise is attested for Zeno by Diogenes Laertius, *Vit. phil.* 7.33 = *SVF* 1.269 ("in the *Republic* [Zeno] too affirms the community of women": see Reale, *Diogene Laerzio*, 760–61, with my n. 87), and in frag. 728 it is attested both for Zeno and for Chrysippus and is motivated, as in Plato, by the desirability of loving all children as one's own: "They hold the view too that women should be in common for the wise, so that any chance man may sleep with any chance woman, as Zeno says in the *Republic* and Chrysippus in his work *On the Republic*, and so too Diogenes the Cynic and Plato: 'Thus we will love all children just like fathers and jealousy over adultery will disappear'" (from Diogenes Laertius, *Vit. phil.* 7.131; see Reale, *Diogene Laerzio*, 848–49, with my n. 285). The overall significance of Eros in Zeno's *Republic* is underscored by Boys-Stones, "Eros in Government," 168–74, who shows that Eros in this work is given its full cosmological value, as is clear from Athenaeus, *Deipn.* 561CD: it keeps the city safe and sound, guaranteeing harmony with the entire cosmos and, within the city itself, among the citizens, since Eros, in its cosmic function, harmonizes all the elements and their parts among themselves, eliminating discord and chaos. In Zeno's view, apparently, the elimination of the friction and jealousy associated with adultery, and the extension of paternal affection to all children as possibly being one's own, could be relevant factors. Very different is the view of Hierocles and Musonius, who, as we shall see, do speak of harmony and concord, but among spouses, as something not incompatible with harmony in the city.

134. See §4 of this introductory essay, above, and the commentary below on the extracts from *On Appropriate Acts*, nn. 17 and 29, with documentation.

According to Antipater, indeed, marrying and bringing children into the world are a particularly important duty or καθῆκον, an action, in other words, that is highly to be preferred. He advises on the need to choose one's future spouse carefully, since she will be a valuable support in one's life: these are only a few examples of ideas that are likewise found in Hierocles. There are also profound analogies on this score (again highlighted in the commentary) with Musonius Rufus, who is chronologically later than Antipater and earlier than Hierocles by some decades:[135] many affinities, indeed, both of language and content between the two were already observed by Praechter.[136]

Isnardi has also called attention to certain terms that are employed by Hierocles, such as the verb ἐκλέγειν and its derivatives and the participle προηγούμενος, which are connected to the sphere of preferable indifferents and go back to expressions that Antipater of Tarsus seems to have endowed with philosophical dignity, thus anticipating, as I have said, Middle Stoic innovations.[137] A Stobaean fragment (*SVF* 1.192, under Zeno; 3.128:31, under Chrysippus, although he is not named there) reports the Stoic definition of a preferable indifferent as "that which we choose in accord with a criterion of preferability" (ὃ ἐκλεγόμεθα κατὰ προηγούμενον λόγον). It is likely, according to Isnardi, that this definition, which is quoted by Stobaeus in a general way immediately after the mention of Zeno as the first to have named προηγμένα or preferables and their opposites, ἀποπροηγμένα, goes back to Antipater of Tarsus, who defined the ethical end or τέλος as "always acting so as to achieve preferables according to nature" (προηγούμενα κατὰ φύσιν).[138] This participle is not yet a key term

135. See §4 of this introductory essay, above, and the commentary below on the extracts from *On Appropriate Acts*, nn. 12, 17, 18, 19, 22, 23, 26, 28, 29, 31, 35, 36, 39, 44, 45, 46, and 47, with full references.

136. Praechter, *Hierokles*, 90ff.

137. Isnardi, "Ierocle," 2224–25.

138. The double definition of the τέλος in Antipater is to be found in *SVF* 3.57:252–53: ζῆν ἐκλεγομένους μὲν τὰ κατὰ φύσιν, ἀπεκλεγομένους δὲ τὰ παρὰ φύσιν: "to live choosing things that are in accord with nature and refusing those things that are contrary to nature"; and πᾶν τὸ καθ' αὑτὸν ποιεῖν διηνεκῶς καὶ ἀπαραβάτως πρὸς τὸ τυγχάνειν τῶν προηγουμένων κατὰ φύσιν: "to do everything we can continually and inalterably to obtain those things that are preferable in accord with nature." Antipater's doctrine of the τέλος seems to bear witness to a certain departure from Old Stoic teachings; see Radice, *Oikeiôsis*, 202–5, who examines the doctrine of the τέλος in Antipater in connection with that of *oikeiôsis* and relates it to the Peripatetic idea of the τέλος. Marion Soreth, "Die zweite Telosformel des Antipater von Tarsos," *AGPh* 50 (1968): 48–72, analyzes frag. 57 of Antipater; see also

in Old Stoicism; even with regard to the verb ἐκλέγειν, which occurs in the definition of the preferable indifferent, we may note that, although it is securely attested for Chrysippus in *SVF* 3.191:46,[139] it is included in the definition of the ethical goal only by Antipater of Tarsus, again in fragment 57 (first definition): the τέλος is to live "preferring or choosing [ἐκλεγόμενοι] what is in accord with nature and rejecting [ἀπεκλεγόμενοι] whatever is contrary to nature." It is thus not unlikely that it was Antipater who coined the derivative nouns ἐκλογή, "preference or choice," and ἀπεκλογή, "rejection," in *SVF* 3.118:28; in fact, in the same fragment, classified under Chrysippus but referred by the source Stobaeus to Stoics in general, there appears also the expression ἀξία ἐκλεκτική,[140] which is typical of Antipater, as may be seen from *SVF* 3.52:251: "Antipater calls it ἐκλεκτική, 'preferable.'" After him, Archedemus of Tarsus—an Athe-

---

Gisela Striker, "Antipater or the Art of Living," in Schofield and Striker, *The Norms of Nature*, 185–204; Anthony A. Long, "Carneades and the Stoic *Telos*," *Phronesis* 12 (1967): 59–90, esp. 76–77; and especially Margaret E. Reesor, *The Nature of Man in Early Stoic Philosophy* (London: Duckworth, 1985), 110ff.; and Brad Inwood, "Goal and Target in Stoicism," *JPh* 10 (1986): 547–56, esp. 551, who notes that Antipater runs the risk of making *sapientia* subject to error. See above n. 59 to this introductory essay, with discussion of Antipater's connection to the Middle Stoa.

139. From Epictetus, *Diss.* 2.6.9: "Chrysippus rightly says: 'So long as what is to come remains obscure to me, I stick continually to the best means of achieving what is in accord with nature [κατὰ φύσιν]: for God himself has made me such as to prefer [ἐκλεκτικός] these things.'"

140. *SVF* 3.118:28, from Stobaeus, *Anth.* 2.7.7 (2:79,4–17 Wachsmuth and Hense): ἀδιάφορα δ' εἶναι λέγουσι τὰ μεταξὺ τῶν ἀγαθῶν καὶ τῶν κακῶν, διχῶς τὸ ἀδιάφορον νοεῖσθαι φάμενοι, καθ' ἕνα μὲν τρόπον τὸ μήτε ἀγαθὸν μήτε κακὸν καὶ τὸ μήτε αἱρετὸν μήτε φευκτόν· καθ' ἕτερον δὲ τὸ μήτε ὁρμῆς μήτε ἀφορμῆς κινητικόν … κατὰ τὸ πρότερον δὴ λεκτέον τὰ μεταξὺ ἀρετῆς καὶ κακίας ἀδιάφορα λέγεσθαι … οὐ μὴν πρὸς ἐκλογὴν καὶ ἀπεκλογήν· δι' ὃ καὶ τὰ μὲν ἀξίαν ἐκλεκτικὴν ἔχειν, τὰ δὲ ἀπαξίαν ἀπεκλεκτικήν, συμβλητικὴν δὲ οὐδαμῶς πρὸς τὸν εὐδαίμονα βίον: the Stoics "say that things that are between goods and evils are indifferents, affirming that 'indifferent' is understood in two ways: in one sense, it is what is neither good nor bad, neither to be chosen nor avoided; in another sense, it is what motivates neither an impulse toward nor repulsion from…. According to the former, one must say that things that are between virtue and vice are called indifferents … but not with respect to preference and rejection. That is why some things have a value that is to be preferred, while others have a disvalue that is to be rejected, but neither has a value that contributes in any way to a happy life." In cases where ἐκλέγω and its derivatives refer to preferable indifferents as technical terms, I render them as "to prefer" and/or "to select" and cognate words, in order to avoid confusion with αἱρέω, "choose," the technical term that refers to the choice of true goods and not of preferable indifferents, which is equivalent to saying that it pertains to the sphere of κατορθώματα rather than of καθήκοντα.

nian who, after he moved to the territory of the Parthians, left behind a Stoic school in Babylon (*SVF* 3.2:262)—will define the ethical goal as "to live choosing [ἐκλεγόμενος] the greatest and most important things in accord with nature" (*SVF* 3.21:264). Diogenes of Babylon, generally located between the Old and Middle Stoa, had already expressed himself in a similar fashion, using the corresponding substantive in his definition of the ethical goal as "think carefully in the choice [ἐκλογή] of what is in accord with nature" (*SVF* 3.46:219). Archedemus, moreover, in an alternative definition of the τέλος or goal of ethics, for the first time connected this closely and explicitly with duty or καθῆκον, when he affirmed that the end is "to live fulfilling all one's duties" (*SVF* 3.18–19:264). Attention, as we see, is entirely on the domain of the preferable indifferents, to which these duties pertain. The focus, in sum, seems to have shifted to the καθήκοντα rather than being on the κατορθώματα, which derive from choosing (αἱρέω) absolute goods (ἀγαθά).

Here, then, one may truly mark a transition, at last, from the Old to the Middle Stoa. And Hierocles sometimes follows this line, even in his terminology: he indicates the preferability of married life—which, in fact, in Stoic theory is neither a true good nor a true evil but a preferable indifferent that entails precisely duties—not by the term προηγμένος but rather with προηγούμενος, specifying that the celibate life is chosen only if it is imposed by some particular circumstance (κατὰ περίστασιν). It is significant that the opposition between "preferable" versus "because of some particular circumstance" (προηγουμένως versus κατὰ περίστασιν) is found also in other Neo-Stoics, such as Epictetus (*Diss.* 3.14.7), who also regards marriage as a "preferable."[141] So, too, the verb ἐκλέγειν in a technical sense, in reference to the choice of preferables and in the specific instance of duties, is widespread in the Neo-Stoics. Hierocles himself uses the substantive ἐκλογή in the Stobaean extracts to indicate the "choice of duties"

141. Hierocles is a particularly valuable witness for *oikeiôsis* and for the conception of interpersonal ties in Epictetus, who is not far distant in time from Hierocles, among other things because Hierocles consciously accepts the Old Stoic heritage, but in a way that is nevertheless responsive to developments in Neo-Stoicism. Brad Inwood demonstrates this well in "L'οἰκείωσις sociale chez Épictète," where he argues that Epictetus, with his return to the Old Stoa, returned also to Socrates: Socrates forced him to reconsider the tension between the emphasis on individual perfection, which implies a certain distance from one's neighbor, and duties toward others, the καθήκοντα emphasized in Stoic ethics and above all in Middle and Neo-Stoicism. Epictetus seeks to resolve the tension by placing the accent mainly on the relationship between parents and children.

or the preference given to these, and in the *Elements of Ethics* he employs the corresponding adverb ἐκλεκτικῶς to designate *oikeiôsis* "based on the choice of preferables" in regard to external things: thus, he posited, as I make clear in the commentary,[142] an ἐκλεκτική *oikeiôsis* in respect to external objects, one that appropriates those things that are preferable, alongside a αἱρετική *oikeiôsis* that involves the rational choice of true goods and that pertains only to human beings and not to animals.

Another indication of an apparent distance on the part of Hierocles from the ancient Stoic line may be found in the fact that, in the abovementioned figure of concentric circles designating duties toward others in order of increasing inclusiveness and decreasing intensity, the circle representing the city comes well after that of the family—although, at least in the *Republics* of Zeno and Chrysippus, the family was abolished, as we have seen. The circles indicate, in expanding order: mind, body, parents, siblings, wives, children—thus the nearest relatives—and then grandparents, uncles and aunts, and cousins, that is, more distant relations, then those still further removed, such as members of the same deme and tribe, and finally fellow citizens, followed by members of neighboring cities, those of the same *ethnos* or people, and the human race in general.[143] Thus, one may suppose that for Hierocles the family was more important than the city. However, in the complex structure of the Stobaean fragments of *On Appropriate Acts*, subdivided into various rubrics πῶς χρηστέον ("How we ought to behave toward…"), the order of which is reproduced in the edition of Hierocles that goes back to von Arnim, we find, in succession, gods, country, and family, and within this last, wife, children, parents, and siblings. One's country thus comes before the family, thanks to the priority of the whole in respect to the parts, since the destruction of the whole would entail as well the destruction of the parts. In addition, Hierocles is also aware that the whole consists of the parts, so that if the parts were missing, the whole too would perish, and thus its priority is only relative.[144]

Another problem, moreover, is that of the greater importance of parents as opposed to wife and children. For if, in the Stobaean extracts, the

142. See the commentary below on the *Elements of Ethics*, n. 54, with discussion and documentation.

143. See the commentary below on the Stobaean extracts from *On Appropriate Acts*, nn. 37–41.

144. For documentation and the contextualization of this question in Stoic thought generally, see the commentary below on the extracts from *On Appropriate Acts*, n. 14.

argument concerning wife and children precedes that concerning parents, the latter argument, nevertheless, begins by pointing out that one's duties toward parents must be treated immediately after those due to country, and so before those due to wife and children: "After the discourse concerning gods and country, what other person could one mention first if not one's parents? Hence we must speak about these, whom one would not err in calling as it were second and terrestrial gods, and indeed because of their nearness, if it is lawful to say so, even more to be honored than the gods."[145] Further, at the end of the discussion of duties toward one's country, a kind of parity in rank seems to be recognized between country and parents, in that one is supposed to honor the former more than the latter but venerate the latter more than the former: "This reasoning, indeed, suggests that we honor our country, which is one, on a par with our two parents, so as in fact to prefer our country to either one of those who bore us, and not even to honor the two together more than it, but rather to hold them in equal respect" (Stobaeus, *Anth.* 3.39.34 [3:731,7–11 Wachsmuth and Hense]). Yet Hierocles alters the terms immediately afterwards, affirming the priority of country over the entire family, thanks to the above-mentioned priority of the whole in respect to the part: "But there is also another argument, which exhorts us to honor our country more than both our parents together, and not only more than them, but also more than our wife together with them, and our children and our friends and, in a word, more than all other things, apart from the gods" (ibid.). The priority of parents or of wife is difficult to establish, since, alongside assertions that parents come immediately after the gods (or at least right after country), there is also a tribute to marriage as the primary communal bond bar none: "A discussion of marriage is most necessary. For our entire race is naturally disposed to community, and the first and most elementary of the communities is that in accord with marriage. For there would not be cities if there were not households."[146] We could continue to illustrate difficulties that lie in the way of reconstructing the precise hierarchy that Hierocles might have had in mind.

145. Stobaeus, *Anth.* 4.79.53 (3:95,30–99,9 Meineke; cf. *Anth.* 4.25.53 = 4:640,4–644,15 Wachsmuth and Hense). See the commentary below on the extracts, n. 30. As we see, in a certain sense Hierocles assumes as well that parents can even come before the gods in respect to reverence, because of their nearness: there is a recurrent change of perspective, involving the creation and re-creation of ever-varying hierarchies.

146. Stobaeus, *Anth.* 4.67.21 (Meineke 3:7,13–19; cf. *Anth.* 4.22a.21 = 4:502,1–7 Wachsmuth and Hense). See the commentary below on the Stobaean extracts, n. 17.

In reality, however, rather than actual contradictions, these divergences would seem to result from the different perspectives from which the question is considered, which make clear how difficult it is to establish a true, proper, and univocal hierarchy among country, parents, and the nuclear family that includes wife and children. The gods come first, no doubt about that (even if their priority, too, as we have seen, can be upstaged by parents, those minor gods, "because of their nearness"!), and it is unarguable that the more remote relationships come afterwards. But among the first three objects of our duties—gods, country, and immediate family—it is difficult to establish an unambiguous order, and any one such will depend on the perspective one adopts. Thus, the sequence of circles follows the order of proximity to the subject, in decreasing degree, and here country comes after family and even after neighbors. The criterion in the arrangement πῶς χρηστέον, however, seems that of rank and importance, and here country, thanks to the priority of the whole over the parts, comes immediately after the gods and before parents, even if it is specified that, from another point of view, that of reverence, parents come before country and immediately after the gods, inasmuch as they are lesser gods. The same obtains also in respect to the priority of father or mother: each has primacy from a certain point of view, since "one should grant more love to his mother but more honor to his father."[147]

Moreover, even though Hierocles treats interpersonal relationships in detail and theorizes them, he does not emphasize the bond that obtains among the wise themselves, which, on the contrary, played such an important role in the thinking of the Old Stoa, for which true friendship is exclusively that between the wise and the virtuous, as attested in *SVF* 3.631:161 (located under Chrysippus but ascribed to Stoics in general by Diogenes Laertius, *Vit. phil.* 7.124):

> They say, then, that even friendship exists only among the virtuous [σπουδαῖοι], thanks to their resemblance to one another; and they say that it is a kind of commonality of life [κοινωνίαν κατὰ τὸν βίον], since we behave with friends as we do with ourselves. They show that a friend is choiceworthy [αἱρετός] in himself and that having many friends is

147. Stobaeus, *Anth.* 4.84.23 (3:134,1–136,2 Meineke; cf. *Anth.* 4.27.23 = 4:671,3–673,18 Wachsmuth and Hense). See the commentary below on the Stobaean extracts, n. 43.

> a good [ἀγαθόν]. Among the vicious, however, there exists no form of friendship, nor does any vicious person have a friend.[148]

I would call attention to the use of the verbal adjective derived from αἱρέω, which indicates that the choice of a friend is precisely the choice of a good, not simply of a preferable (for which the technical term would have been the verb ἐκλέγω),[149] as we see confirmed by the statement that to have many friends is not a duty or a preferable but a true and proper good in itself, an ἀγαθόν, which is eloquent testimony to the value of friendship in Old Stoicism. Further confirmation derives also from *SVF* 3.633.3:161 (= Seneca, *Ep.* 81.12), where it is flatly stated that *solus sapiens amicus est.* Further, in *SVF* 3.627:160 (= Plutarch, *Comm. not.* 22.1069a), we find a straight-out eulogy of "the marvelous joy that sages provide each other, from the mere fact of behaving toward one another in accord with virtue [κατ' ἀρετήν], even when they are far apart and do not even know each other."[150] Here, indeed, the quality of virtue, which in Stoicism pertains directly to the good, is the basis of friendship and of the behavior of the wise and virtuous (the σοφοί or σπουδαῖοι), who are friends and behave as such even if they are unacquainted with each other, thanks to their virtue and their capacity to do good.

Praise of the friendship among the wise in such exalted terms as to border on paradox is not found, in fact, in Hierocles. Of course, given that the remainder of his work is lost (i.e., all that is not published in this volume), we cannot assert that he did not treat the friendship among sages in some other part: one cannot appeal here to the *argumentum ex silentio*. It is nevertheless certain that in his model of the concentric circles Hierocles insists above all on family ties and duties to them, which come second only to duties to the gods. If we take into account the passages in which Hierocles mentions friends and friendship, we may note that in the discussion "How One Should Behave toward One's Country" (Stobaeus, *Anth.* 3.39.34 [3:730,17–731,15 Wachsmuth and Hense) he locates friends after family, and in three other passages that we shall examine in a moment he seems to place the bond of friendship among the wise or aspirants to wisdom on the same level as that between spouses, siblings, and parents and children. For the rest, in various other places he mentions

148. See Reale, *Diogene Laerzio*, 840–43, with my nn. 264 and 265.

149. See my proof of this in commentary below on the *Elements of Ethics*, n. 54.

150. Τὴν θαυμαστὴν ὠφέλειαν ἣν οἱ σοφοὶ κινουμένων κατ' ἀρετὴν ἀλλήλων ὠφελοῦνται, κἂν μὴ συνῶσιν μηδὲ γινώσκοντες τυγχάνωσιν.

in a general way and only *en passant* friends alongside relatives, without conferring on the former any particular preeminence.[151]

Just as for Musonius, in his way, so also for Hierocles friendship among the wise, as a means of pursuing virtue in common, is placed on a par with marriage, which for the Roman Stoics tended to acquire an importance that in an earlier epoch was ascribed only to friendship among the virtuous or those on the path to virtue, as Reydams-Schils has recently argued.[152] It is necessary, nonetheless, to spell out this idea further in light of Stoic theory and ethical terminology: we have seen that in the passages of the Old Stoics cited above, friends are counted among the true goods worthy of being chosen (αἱρεῖν), not among the preferable indifferents (προηγμένα) in regard to which there is simply ἐκλογή and attendant duties (καθήκοντα). Now, friends and family are both important to Hierocles, as they are for Musonius; the criterion of choice for a wife is, in Musonius even more than in Hierocles, virtue in addition to physical health, just as in the case of a friend; so too a sharing of the road to virtue and harmony that can occur only among the virtuous is, in addition to procreation, the goal of marriage, just as it is of friendship itself.[153]

151. In Stobaeus, *Anth.* 4.67.23 (3:8,19–24 Meineke; cf. *Anth.* 4.22a.23 = 4:503,11–16 Wachsmuth and Hense). Hierocles speaks of "worries over friends and family" as being among the problems that can afflict us; at *Anth.* 4.75.14 (3:72,4–74,3 Meineke; cf. *Anth.* 4.24a.14 = 4:603,8–605,16 Wachsmuth and Hense) he again puts friends and relatives on the same plane: "we beget children not only for ourselves but also for those thanks to whom we ourselves were born, and then also for our friends and relatives. For it is pleasing for them too to see children born of us, because of their goodwill and relationship and more particularly for the sake of safety.... Hence, eagerness for marriage and children accords with someone who is loving of his relatives and friends." The priority of the family over friends is found also in a contemporary writer such as Plutarch, who in his treatise *On Brotherly Love* (see the commentary below on the Stobaean extracts *On Appropriate Acts*, n. 42) establishes a precise hierarchy of honor (τιμή, δόξα) in which brothers come before friends: "even if one accords an equal goodwill to a friend, one must always reserve pride of place for one's brother ... in all matters that are visible to the public and pertain to honor [δόξα]" (491B).

152. The greater dignity that is conferred upon marriage among the Roman Stoics, and the promotion of the marriage bond to the level of friendship among the *sapientes* or σοφοί, is underscored especially, although without a close analysis of the texts, by Reydams-Schils, *The Roman Stoics*, ch. 5. See the commentary below on the Stobaean extracts from *On Appropriate Acts*, nn. 19, 23, 36, with detailed documentation.

153. See *Diss.* 13B of Musonius: "Therefore those who marry should not look to lineage and whether they descend from noble ancestors, nor to money and whether they possess many things, nor to the body and whether theirs is beautiful; for neither wealth

Now, virtue is nothing but the true good and the source of true goods, not simply a preferable; accordingly, a marriage that leads to it would seem no longer to pertain only to preferable indifferents that are to be selected (ἐκλέγειν) but to acquire, at least to the degree that it does tend toward virtue, an element of the true good as well, and so is to be chosen rationally (αἱρεῖν) for its own sake, just as the Old Stoics advised that one must choose a friend.

If this assimilation, even on the terminological level, is present in Musonius,[154] the vocabulary adopted by Hierocles remains that of preferables and καθήκοντα: in an important passage Hierocles defines marriage as "preferable" (προηγούμενος) for the sage and places it explicitly within the sphere of "duties" (καθήκοντα).[155] But one must also recall that Hierocles

---

nor beauty nor lineage is of a nature to increase community [κοινωνία], nor again concord [ὁμόνοια], nor do these things make for better procreation. Rather, those bodies suffice for marriage that are healthy, middling in beauty, and up to working and that are less subject to attack by intemperance.... And one must consider those souls more adapted to marriage that are naturally disposed to moderation [σωφροσύνη] and justice [δικαιοσύνη] and virtue [πρὸς ἀρετήν] in general. For what kind of marriage is beautiful, without concord [ὁμόνοια]? What kind of community useful [κοινωνία χρηστή]? How could people who are bad [πονηροί] be in accord with one another [ὁμονοήσειαν ... ἀλλήλοις]? Or how could a good person [ἀγαθός] be in accord with a bad? No more might a crooked piece of wood accord with one that is straight"—the example of a crooked or straight piece of wood was employed already by the Old Stoics to show that there can be only virtuous or vicious people, without a middle ground (as we have seen in Diogenes Laertius, *Vit. phil.* 7.127 = *SVF* 3.536:143). It is significant that Musonius ends by speaking of friendship among the virtuous in a discourse that is devoted to marriage, for he proceeds: "For what is crooked cannot be fitted with another crooked piece similar to it, and still less with its opposite, something straight. So too a bad person, then, is not a friend to or in accord with a bad person [ὁ πονηρὸς τῷ πονηρῷ οὐ φίλος οὐδ' ὁμονοεῖ], and still less with a good one." The assimilation of the marriage bond to that of friendship among the wise or virtuous, even at the level of vocabulary, is evident; see Ramelli, *Musonio Rufo*, 176–79. Compare also Statius, *Silvae* 2.2.154–45 [*sic*], on the Epicurean couple Pollius Felix and Polla: "No other hearts adhere under a better divinity, no other minds has Concord instructed. Learn from her in security: your marriage torches, intertwined in your hearts, have coalesced forever, and a sacred love [*sanctus amor*] preserves the laws of chaste friendship [*pudicae amicitiae*]."

154. See the preceding note.

155. Stobaeus, *Anth.* 4.67.21 (3:7,13–19 Meineke; cf. *Anth.* 4.22a.21 = 4:502,1–7 Wachsmuth and Hense): "for a wise man a life with marriage is preferable [προηγούμενος], whereas that without a wife is so depending on circumstance. Thus, since it is right to imitate someone who has sense, in matters where we can, and marrying is preferable for the latter, it is clear that it should be a duty [καθῆκον] for us too, unless in fact some circumstance gets in the way.... when our reason is intent on nature as on a target that is well

places friends too among the several categories of people toward whom one has duties and does not differentiate between friendship and marriage by applying αἱρεῖν and ἀγαθόν to the former, as the Old Stoics did. Thus, the distance between these two types of relationship would seem actually to be reduced in his texts. In Stobaeus, *Anth.* 4.67.23 (3.8,19–24 Meineke; cf. *Anth.* 4.22a.23 = 4:503,11–16 Wachsmuth and Hense), Hierocles undertakes to show that marriage is not only in conformity with divine law and nature and is not only pleasant, but that it is also καλόν, a term that, if it is not exactly equivalent to ἀγαθόν, which designates the only object that is worthy of αἵρεσις, nevertheless comes very close to it, since it signifies something fine in the moral sense: "But I myself consider married life to be also beautiful [or fine: καλός]…, the union of a husband and wife who share each other's destinies and are consecrated to the gods of marriage, generation, and the hearth, in concord [ὁμονοεῖν] with each other and setting everything in common up to their very bodies, or rather up to their very own souls."[156] The conception of marriage as κοινωνία and ὁμόνοια, commonality in spiritual life and concord, seems here in Hierocles to be very similar to the conception of friendship as κοινωνία κατὰ τὸν βίον (*SVF* 3.631:161). So, too, the concord that Hierocles associates with the ideal of marriage[157] fully corresponds to that which enters into the Old Stoic definition of friendship, where once again it is connected with goods and not simply with preferable indifferents.[158]

---

lit and fixed, it chooses preferentially everything that is in harmony with nature and can make us live in the way one ought."

156. See also the commentary below on the Stobaean extracts, n. 23.

157. In addition to the passage from Hierocles just mentioned, see, e.g., in the same section of *Anth.* 4.67.23 (3:8,19–24 Meineke; cf. *Anth.* 4.22a.23 = 4:503,11–16 Wachsmuth and Hense), with a quotation from Homer: "what could be 'stronger and better than when a husband and wife, like-minded in their thoughts, maintain a home' "?

158. *SVF* 3.630:160–61, from Stobaeus, *Anth.* 2.7.11m (2:108,5 Wachsmuth and Hense): "Only among the wise do the Stoics admit friendship, since only among them is there concord [ὁμόνοια] concerning the way of life [περὶ τῶν κατὰ τὸν βίον]: for concord is the science of goods in common [κοινῶν ἀγαθῶν ἐπιστήμη]." See frag. 625, again from Stobaeus, *Anth.* 2.7.11b (2:93,19 Wachsmuth and Hense): the Stoics "say that the virtuous have all goods [ἀγαθά] in common, insofar as one who benefits another who is like him benefits himself as well. Concord [ὁμόνοια] is the science of goods in common [κοινῶν ἀγαθῶν ἐπιστήμη], which is why the virtuous are all in accord with one another, on account of their agreement concerning the way of life [ἐν τοῖς κατὰ τὸν βίον]" (see also frag. 626, in the same vein). This is why the wise are all friends of each other, as we saw earlier in the paradox of the sages who are friends and do each other good without even knowing one another, since there is always concord among them.

At the end of the same section on marriage in Hierocles, moreover, there is a very close alignment—one that I think is worthy of consideration—precisely between friendship and marriage, both of which are conceived of as providing defenses against chance: "For in any case it would be irrational to seek opportunities for friendships from every quarter and to acquire friends and comrades to be our allies in the face of the difficult things in life, and not to seek and acquire that alliance and assistance that is given to men by nature, the laws, and the gods—that is, the one that comes from a wife and children." In the same way, the relationship between siblings is brought in line with that between friends, to all appearances on one and the same level, at the end of the extract from Stobaeus (*Anth.* 4.84.20 [3:128,21–129,4 Meineke; cf. *Anth.* 4.27.20 = 4:664,9–18 Wachsmuth and Hense):

> Reason, too, is a great aid, which appropriates strangers and those wholly unrelated to us by blood and provides us with an abundance of allies. For this reason, we are eager by nature to win over and make a friend of everyone. Thus, that act is the most complete kind of madness: to wish to be joined with those who bear no affection toward us by nature and deliberately, to the greatest extent possible, to confer the family bond on them, but to neglect those helpers and caretakers who are at hand and have been bestowed upon us by nature, such as it happens that our brothers are.

So, too, at the end of the discussion of duties toward siblings, Hierocles repeats, employing the words of Socrates, the equivalence between the fraternal and the amicable bond.[159] Again, friends are assimilated by Hierocles not only to spouses or siblings but also to parents: "our parents are images of gods and, by Zeus, domestic gods, benefactors, relatives, creditors, masters and *most reliable friends*.... And no less, they are also constant *friends and assistants*, who come unsummoned at every crisis and are helpers in every circumstance" (Stobaeus, *Anth.* 4.79.53 [3:95,30–99,9 Meineke]; cf. *Anth.* 4.25.53 = 4:640,4–644,15 Wachsmuth and Hense);

159. "Thus, in the case of every human being, but especially in the case of a brother, one should imitate that famous saying of Socrates: for to someone who said to him, 'I shall die if I do not take revenge on you,' he replied: 'I shall die, if I do not make a friend of you!'"

correspondingly, a little later in the same section children are held to be the best friends of their parents.[160]

In sum, it appears that Hierocles, at the very least, does not elevate to the highest position the friendship among sages, contrasting it as a true good with marital and family ties that are relegated to an inferior status; on the contrary, at least to the extent that one can judge on the basis of what has survived, family and friends seem to hold for Hierocles the same importance. All the ties analyzed by Hierocles are embraced in the theory of the *kathêkonta* and *oikeiôsis*, in a consistent and continuous argument. It does not seem an accident that friendship and country—the topic covered in the Stobaean extracts—form the subject of the last, fragmentary column (XI) of the *Elements of Ethics* focused on *oikeiôsis*, where, in the new edition, it is now possible to read:

> of one's country ... of nature ... first, [15] it is necessary to consider that we are an animal, but a sociable one and in need of others. Because of this we dwell in cities: for there is no human being who is not part of a city. Then, we easily form friendships; for from having dined together or having sat together in the theater or having been in the same situation, friendships arise. And this is the most wondrous of all: for often ... for having taken from a battle ... they manifest ... goodwill ... by power ... teach ... toward others....[161]

There would thus seem to be a thoroughgoing continuity of treatment.

Hierocles, according to Isnardi, "gives us a good idea of how much the traditional legacy of the Old Stoa was alive and how much was dead in the official teaching of the Stoa in the imperial age."[162] The doctrine of *oikeiôsis*, at least in its primary form, remained practically identical; that concerning duties, on the other hand, reveals how certain harsh doctrines

160. "For just as, for those who are being sent on a long trip abroad, the company of their relatives and dearest friends, in a sort of send-off, contributes to their good cheer, in the same way too for parents, who are by now inclining toward departure, the attentions of their children are among the things that are most pleasing and dear to them." Finally, by transitivity, one should love the friends of one's parents as our own friends, just as we love the friends of our friends: "it is necessary to cherish their [sc. parents'] relatives and deem them worthy of care, and so too, indeed, their friends and everyone who is dear to them" (Stobaeus, *Anth.* 4.79.53 [3:95,30–99,9 Meineke]; cf. *Anth.* 4.25.53 = 4:640,4–644,15 Wachsmuth and Hense).

161. See the commentary below on the *Elements of Ethics*, n. 55.

162. Isnardi, "Ierocle," 2226.

of the Old Stoa in the area of ethics were softened over time. The treatment of sociable, deontological, and rational *oikeiôsis* was consciously developed by Hierocles, in the tracks of Chrysippus but also in light of later gains. I believe that this complex approach is important also insofar as it allows us to reconstruct a further segment of the mosaic of Neo-Stoicism.

From a formal point of view, as Bastianini and Long observe, Hierocles differs from other Neo-Stoics insofar as he does not preach or exhort, in the manner of Musonius Rufus, Epictetus, or Marcus Aurelius, but rather maintains the expository tone of a treatise, apparently shorn of any personal emotion, in this probably approaching "the professional style of the Great pre-Christian Stoics"; von Arnim had already illustrated the way in which Stoic doctrine in Hierocles is expressed "in a strictly scientific form."[163] At the same time, on the other hand, Hierocles' prose is not extremely technical, even if, as the commentary in particular makes clear, various tehnical terms of Stoicism are well-represented: it is important to identify them, I believe, in order to achieve a fuller understanding of his thought. Yet, though he locates himself decidedly in the wake of Old Stoic tradition, Hierocles tends to avoid esoteric terminology and an abstruse and skeletal exposition and adopts rather a style that is fairly polished even from a literary point of view. For this reason, Long and Bastianini rightly criticize the harsh judgment of Albin Lesky, who opined that "this popularization of Old Stoic ethics has little to say to us."[164]

Nevertheless, one relatively popular feature may be attributed Hierocles, it would seem: that is that he does not seem to reveal in his work, whether in the *Elements of Ethics* or in the Stobaean extracts, a huge interest in the most technical aspects of the topics he treats, even though, in all likelihood, he was a professional philosopher, here again like the Neo-Stoics Musonius Rufus, who, however, in the spirit of Socrates, left no writings of his own, or Annaeus Cornutus, who taught the philosophy of Cleanthes and Chrysippus to youngsters and who was also a refined man of letters, the author of various philosophical works, very likely technical treatises among them, and of an allegorical manual for students as well.[165]

163. Bastianini and Long, *CPF* 1.1.2:282; von Arnim, *Ethische Elementarlehre*, xvi: "in strictly scientific form."

164. Bastianini and Long, *CPF* 1.1.2:282; my translation of the quotation from Albin Lesky, *Geschichte der griechischen Literatur* (Munich: Taschenbuch, 1993), 980.

165. On Musonius, I provide full documentation in the commentary below on the Stobaean extracts, nn. 2, 12, 17, and *passim*. For the teachings and writings of Annaeus Cornutus, see Ramelli, *Cornuto*, ch. 6.1–3.

According to Bastianini and Long, this choice of a relatively less technical presentation was surely not due to Hierocles' incompetence as a philosopher but rather to a literary stance: the *Elements of Ethics* in particular will have had the purpose of making Stoic ethics readable, perhaps even pleasurable, while in the works of Chrysippus it was especially dry and unattractive from a literary point of view.[166] Hierocles, then, reworked the thought of Chrysippus in the light of later gains and simultaneously presented it in a form that was more elegant, accessible, and fluent.

166. Bastianini and Long, *CPF* 1.1.2:283.

HIEROCLES, *ELEMENTS OF ETHICS*

The Greek text contained in this volume as well as the following translation are based on the critical edition by Guido Bastianini and Anthony A. Long in *CPF* 1.1.2:296–362; I have taken into account the twenty-one corrigenda that are noted in *CPF* 4.1, "Indici (1.1)" (Florence: Olschki, 2002), viii–xi, incorporating them in the translation and indicating them in the notes. Roman numerals in square brackets indicate columns of the papyrus, arabic numerals every fifth line. I also translate the titles in the papyrus. Occasionally there are minor textual displacements in the papyrus edited by Bastianini and Long. So as to indicate the state of the papyrus, they have retained them in their edition. In such cases (e.g., pages 8–9) the translation disregards these displacements and seeks to present Hierocles' own sequence of thought. Finally, the superscripted numbers refer to discussions in the separate commentary section.

Ἱεροκλέους
Ἠθικ[ὴ] Στοιχείωσις

[I] [1a] Εἰ αἰσθάν[ε]ται τὸ ζῷον ἑαυτοῦ

[1] Τῆς ἠθικῆς στοιχειώσεως ἀρχὴν ἀρίστην ἡγοῦμαι τὸν περὶ τοῦ πρώτου οἰκείου τῷ ζῴῳ λόγον, ἀλλὰ θῶ οὐ χεῖρον ἐνθυμηθῆναι μᾶλλον ἄνωθεν ἀρξάμενος ὁποία τις ἡ γένεσις τῶν ἐμψύχων καὶ τίνα τὰ πρῶτα συμβαίνοντα τῷ ζῴῳ.

Τὸ τοίνυν σπέρμα καταπεσὸν εἰς ὑστέραν ἔν τε καιρῷ τῷ προσήκοντι καὶ ἅμα ὑπ᾽ ἐρρωμένου τοῦ ἀγγείου συλληφθὲν οὐκέτι ἠρεμεῖ καθάπερ τέως, ἀλλ᾽ ἀνακινηθὲν ἄρχεται τῶν ἰδίων ἔργων, παρά τε τοῦ κυοφοροῦντος σώματος ἐπισπώμενον τὴν ὕλην διαπλάττει τὸ ἔμβρυον κατά τινας ἀπαραβάτους τάξεις, ἕωσπερ οὗ πρὸς τέλος ἀφίκηται καὶ πρὸς ἀπότεξιν εὐτρεπὲς ἀπεργάσηται τὸ δημιούργημα. Τοῦτον μέντοι πάντα τὸν χρόνον—λέγω δὲ τὸν ἀπὸ συλλήψεως μέχρι ἀποτέξεως—διαμένει φύσις, τοῦτό δ᾽ ἐστι πνεῦμα, μεταβεβληκὸς ἐκ σπέρματος καὶ ὁδῷ κεινούμενον ἀπ᾽ ἀρχῆς εἰς τέλος· ἤδη δὲ κατὰ μὲν τὰ πρῶτα τοῦ χρόνου παχύτερόν πώς ἐστι πνεῦμα ἡ φύσις καὶ μακρὰν ἀφεστηκυῖα ψυχῆς, κατόπιν δὲ τούτων κἀπειδὰν σχεδὸν ἥκῃ τῆς ἀποτέξεως, ἀπολεπτύνεται ῥιπιζομένη τοῖς συνεχέσιν ἔργοις καὶ κατὰ τὸ ποσόν ἐστι ψυχή· διὸ δὴ καὶ θύραζε χωρήσασα ἱκανοῦται τῷ περιέχοντι, ὥστε οἷον στομωθεῖσα πρὸς αὐτοῦ μεταβάλλειν εἰς ψυχήν. καθάπερ γὰρ τὸ ἐν τοῖς λίθοις πνεῦμα ταχέως ὑπὸ πληγῆς ἐκπυροῦται διὰ τὴν πρὸς ταύτην τὴν μεταβολὴν ἑτοιμότητα, τὸν αὐτὸν τρόπον καὶ φύσις ἐμβρύου πέπονος ἤδη γεγονότος οὐ βραδύνει τὸ μεταβαλεῖν εἰς ψυχὴν ἐμπεσοῦσα τῷ περιέχοντι. ταύτῃ δὲ πᾶν τὸ ἐκπεσὸν ὑστέρας εὐθέως ἐστὶ ζῷον, κἂν τἄλλα τῶν οἰκείων ἀπολείπηται ῥυθμῶν, οὕτω δὲ δὴ μυθολογεῖται περὶ τῶν τῆς ἄρκτου ἐκγόνων καὶ ἄλλων ὁμοίων.

Hierocles
Elements of Ethics[1]

[I] [1a] "Whether an animal has perception of itself"

[1] I consider the best starting point for the elements of ethics to be a discussion of the "first thing that is one's own and familiar" [πρῶτον οἰκεῖον] for an animal, but I maintain that it is no worse to begin further back and consider what the generation of living things is like and what are the primary attributes of an animal.[2]

Thus, the seed that drops into the uterus at the right moment and at the same time is received by a healthy[3] womb no longer stays inert as it was until then but rather, now set in motion, begins its proper activities and, drawing to itself the matter of the body that bears it, forms the embryo in accord with certain arrangements that cannot be trangressed, until it arrives at the limit and has rendered the creature ready for birth.[4] However, during all this time—I mean that which goes from conception to birth—it remains as a nature [φύσις], that is a *pneuma* (breath), transformed from the status of a seed and proceeding from the beginning to the end in a preestablished order.[5] Now, in the first phases of this period of time the "nature" is a kind of particularly dense *pneuma* and far removed from soul; following this, however, and once it has nearly arrived at birth, it thins out, buffeted as it is by continuous doings, and, in respect to quantity, it is soul. Thus, once it arrives at the exit it is adapted to the environment, so that, toughened, so to speak, by this, it changes into soul.[6] For, just as the *pneuma* that is in stones[7] bursts into flame as a result of a blow, because of its disposition to this alteration, in the same way, too, the nature of the embryo, when it has become mature, is not slow to change to soul, when it comes out into the surrounding environment. For this reason, everything that comes out of the uterus is immediately an animal, even if, at times, it should lack the appropriate proportions, as is fabled to occur with the offpring of bears and other cases of the sort.[8]

Ταύτῃ δὲ ἐντεῦθεν ἐνθυμητέον ἐστίν, ὅτι τὸ ζῷον τοῦ μὴ ζῴου δυοῖν ἔχει διαφοράν, αἰσθήσει τε καὶ ὁρμῇ· ὧν θατέρου μὲν οὐδὲν πρὸς τὸ παρὸν δεόμεθα, βραχέα δὲ δοκεῖ γε περὶ τῆς αἰσθήσεως εἰπεῖν· φέρει γὰρ εἰς γνῶσιν τοῦ πρώτου οἰκείου, ὃν δὴ λόγον ἀρχὴν ἀρίστην ἔφαμεν ἔσεσθαι τῆς ἠθικῆς στοιχειώσεως.

Οὐκ ἀγνοητέον ὅτι τὸ ζῷον εὐθὺς ἅμα τῷ γενέσθαι αἰσθάνεται ἑαυτοῦ· καὶ δεῖ μὲν ἕνεκα τῶν βραδυτέρων λεχθῆναί τινα πρὸς ὑπόμνησιν τούτου· παρεμπίπτων δ᾽ ἕτερος λόγος ἐφ᾽ ἑαυτὸν ἡμᾶς καλεῖ πρότερον· οὕτω γὰρ αὖ βραδεῖς καὶ πόρρω συνέσεως ἔνιοι τυγχάνουσιν ὥστε καὶ τοῖς ὅλοις ἀπιστεῖν εἰ τὸ ζῷον αἰσθάνεται ἑαυτοῦ. Δοκοῦσι γὰρ τὴν αἴσθησιν ὑπὸ τῆς φύσεως αὐτῷ δεδόσθαι πρὸς τὴν τῶν ἐκτὸς ἀντίληψιν, οὐκέτι δὲ καὶ πρὸς τὴν ἑαυτοῦ. Διὰ δὴ τοὺς οὕτως ἀποροῦντας ὅπως τοιοῦτ᾽ ἂν γένοιτο, χρὴ προκαταστησασθαι μὲν τὸ τῶν μερῶν ἑαυτῶν αἰσθάνεσθαι τὰ ζῷα, πειρᾶσθαι δ᾽ ἐπαγαγεῖν ὅτι καὶ ἄνωθεν αὐτοῖς τοῦτο γίνεται.

Δεῖ τοίνυν συννοεῖν ὅτι τὰ ζῷα πρῶτον μὲν μερῶν τῶν ἰδίων αἰσθάνεται. ταύτῃ δὲ καὶ τὰ μὲν πτηνὰ τῆς τῶν πτερύγων πρὸς τὸ ἵπτασθαι παρασκευῆς κἀπιτηδειότητος ἀντιλαμβάνεται, τῶν δὲ χερσαίων ἕκαστον τῶν ἑαυτοῦ μερῶν, καὶ ὅτι ἔχει καὶ πρὸς ἣν ἔχει χρείαν, ἡμεῖς τε αὐτοὶ ὀφθαλμῶν καὶ ὤτων καὶ τῶν ἄλλων. τῇδε γοῦν κἀπειδὰν μὲν ἰδεῖν ἐθέλωμέν τι, τοὺς ὀφθαλμοὺς ἐντείνομεν ὡς ἐπὶ τὸ ὁρατόν, οὐχὶ δὲ τὰ ὦτα, κἀπειδὰν ἀκοῦσαι, τὰ ὦτα παραβάλλομεν καὶ οὐχὶ τοὺς ὀφθαλμούς, καὶ περιπατῆσαι μὲν ἐθέλοντες οὐ χερσὶν ἐπὶ τοῦτο χρώμεθα, ποσὶν δὲ καὶ τοῖς ὅλοις σκέλεσιν, καὶ κατά γε τὰ αὐτὰ δὴ οὐ σκέλεσιν ἀλλὰ ταῖς χερσίν, ἐπειδὰν λαβεῖν [II] ἢ δοῦναί τι βουλώμεθα. διὸ πρώτη πίστις τοῦ αἰσθάνεσθαι τὸ ζῷον ἅπαν ἑαυτοῦ ἡ τῶν μερῶν καὶ τῶν ἔργων, ὑπὲρ ὧν ἐδόθη τὰ μέρη, συναίσθησις·

δευτέρα δὲ ὅτι οὐδὲ τῶν πρὸς ἄμυναν παρασκευασθέντων αὐτοῖς ἀναισθήτως διάκειται. καὶ γὰρ ταῦροι μὲν εἰς μάχην καθιστάμενοι ταύροις ἑτέροις ἢ καί τισιν ἑτερογενέσι ζῴοις τὰ κέρατα προΐσχονται, καθάπερ ὅπλα συμφυᾶ πρὸς τὴν ἀντίταξιν. οὕτω δ᾽ ἔχει καὶ τῶν λοιπῶν ἕκαστον πρὸς τὸ οἰκεῖον καί, ἵν᾽ οὕτως εἴπω, συμφυὲς ὅπλον. τὰ μὲν γὰρ ὁπλαῖς, τὰ δὲ ὀδοῦσι, τὰ δὲ χαυλιοδοῦσι, τὰ δὲ κέντροις, τὰ δὲ ἰοῖς οἷον ὠχυρωμένα τούτοις ἐν ταῖς πρὸς ἕτερα διαμίλλαις ἐπὶ τὴν ἄμυναν χρῆται. τὸ δὲ δὴ τῆς πτυάδος καλουμένης ἀσπίδος

One must therefore understand that, from this moment, an animal differs from a nonanimal in two respects, that is, in perception [or sensation: αἴσθησις] and in impulse [ὁρμή]. For the present, we do not need to discuss the latter, but it is necessary, I believe, to speak, at least briefly, about pereception. For it contributes to a knowledge of the "first thing that is one's own and familiar," which is the subject that we in fact said would be the best starting point for the elements of ethics.[9]

One must know that an animal immediately, as soon as it is born, perceives itself,[10] and, for the benefit of those who are rather slow, it is necessary to say a few things as a reminder of this. Another argument, however, intrudes upon us and bids us turn to it first: for there are some people so slow and far from any understanding as to disbelieve utterly that an animal perceives itself.[11] For they believe that perception [αἴσθησις] is given by nature for apprehending [ἀντίληψις] external objects and not for apprehending oneself as well. For those who are in such a quandary about how something like this could occur, it is necessary to establish first of all that animals perceive their own parts and to attempt to show that this happens in them from the very beginning.

We must, then, understand first of all that animals perceive their own parts. Thus, winged creatures, on the one hand, are aware of the readiness and aptness of their wings for flying, and, on the other hand, every land animal is aware both that it has its own members and of their use; and we ourselves are aware of our eyes and ears and other parts. Thus, when we wish to see something, we direct our eyes toward the visible object, not our ears, and when we want to hear, we extend our ears and not our eyes, and when we wish to walk, we do not use our hands for this but rather our feet and our entire legs, and in the same way we do not use our legs but rather our hands when we desire to take [II] or give something. Therefore, the first confirmation that the entire animal perceives itself is the conscious perception [συναίσθησις] of its parts and of the activities for which the parts were given.[12]

The second confirmation is the fact that animals are not, by condition, unperceiving of the things with which they have been equipped for their defense.[13] For bulls, when they are readying themselves for a fight with other bulls or with animals of a different species, thrust their horns forward, like weapons that grow naturally for battle.[14] And every other animal is similarly disposed toward its own and, so to speak, inborn weapon. For some are fortified with hooves, others with teeth, others with tusks, others with spikes, still others with poisons, and they employ these for defense in clashes with other animals. In particular, that of the

οὐδ' ἱστορίας ἀπάξιον· τοσαύτῃ γὰρ ἄρα χαλεπότητι περίεστι τὸ θηρίον τῶν ὁμωνύμων τε καὶ ὁμογενῶν, ὥστε ἄνευ δήγματος, οἷον βέλος ἀφιεῖσα τὸν ἰὸν ἐφ' ὅτι ἂν θέλῃ τῶν ζῴων, οὐκ ἔλαττον τῶν ἑτέρων ἀναιρεῖν ἀσπίδων· ᾗ δὴ καὶ πόρρωθεν, ἐπειδὰν κατά τινος παροξυνθῇ, προσπτύουσα τὸν ἰὸν οὐδὲν δεῖται δήγματος ἐμβολῆς.

Καὶ μὴν τίνα τε ἀσθενῆ τῶν ἐν αὑτοῖς καὶ τίνα ῥωμαλέα καὶ δυσπαθῆ συναισθάνεται τὰ ζῷα. Ταύτῃ καὶ ταῦρος μέν, ὁπότε φράττοιτο πρὸς τὴν ἐπιβουλήν, τάττει πρὸ παντὸς τοῦ λοιποῦ σώματος τὰ κέρατα· χελώνη δὲ συναισθανομένη τινὸς ἐπιθέσεως τὴν κεφαλὴν καὶ τοὺς πόδας τῷ ὀστρακώδει μέρει ἑαυτῆς ὑποστέλλει, τῷ σκληρῷ καὶ δυσμεταχειρίστῳ τὰ εὐάλωτα· τὸ δὲ παραπλήσιον ποιεῖ καὶ ὁ κοχλίας κατειλούμενος εἰς τὸ κερατῶδες, ὁπότε κινδύνου συναίσθοιτο. Ἥ γε μὴν ἄρκτος οὐκ ἀμαθὴς ἔοικεν εἶναι τῆς περὶ τὴν κεφαλὴν εὐπαθίας, ὅθεν, παιομένη ξύλοις ἤ τισιν ἑτέροις, θραῦσαι τοῦτο δυναμένοις τὸ μέρος, ταύτῃ ἐπιτίθησι τὰς χεῖρας ἀποδεξομένας τὴν τῶν πληγῶν βίαν· κἂν εἴποτε διωκομένη δεηθείη τοῦ βαλανείου ἑαυτὴν [±15] κρημνοῦ, πάλιν ὑπ..[.].[..] τ[±12] ἀσφαλῶς ἐφίησιν ἑαυτήν. Ποιεῖ δὲ τὸ τοιόνδε καὶ ἡ φρύνη· πηδῆσαι μὲν γάρ ἐστιν εὐπρετέστατον ζῷον, οὐδενὸς δήπου λειπόμενον ἑτέρου τῶν ἰσομεγεθῶν ἐν τῷ ἅλλεσθαι· καὶ δῆτα καὶ αὐτοῦ τοῦ πόσον ἐκτείνεται διάστημα συναισθάνεται· εἰ δ' οὖν διωκομένη κατὰ ῥήγματος μὴ θαρρήσειεν ἑαυτῇ ὡς εἰς τὸ καταντικρὺ δυνησομένη διαλέσθαι, ῥιπτεῖ ἑαυτὴν εἰς τοὖδαφος, ῥιπτεῖ δ' οὐχ ὡς ἔτυχεν, ἀλλ' ἐμφυσήσασα γὰρ ἑαυτὴν ἐφ' ὅσον οἵα τ' ἐστί, κατὰ τὸ ἐνδεχόμενον ἀσκῷ ποιήσασα πεπνευματωμένῳ παραπλησίαν, καταφέρεται, τὰ σκέλη καὶ τὴν κεφαλὴν ἐπαίρουσα καὶ τοῖς ἐμπεφυσημένοις μέρεσι μηχανωμένη τὰ χαλεπὰ τοῦ πτώματος ἐκλῦσαι. Τὰ δὲ τῆς ἐλάφου τίς οὐκ ἂν θαυμάσειεν; δῶμεν γὰρ ἀνίσως ἔχειν κατά τε τὰ σκέλη καὶ τὰ κέρατα, καὶ ταῦτα μὲν ὑπερφυῶς εὐμεγέθη καὶ θαυμάσια τὴν ὄψιν εἶναι, τὰ δὲ σκέλη κομιδῇ λεπτὰ καὶ ῥᾴδια καταφρονηθῆναι· ἀλλ' ὅμως, κρείττονα τῆς ὄψεως διδάσκαλον τῶν καθ' ἑαυτὴν ἔχουσα τὴν φύσιν, τοῖς μέν, καίπερ οὖσι λεπτοῖς, πιστεύει καὶ οὔτε πρὸς ὑπερβολὰς τάχους οὔτε πρὸς μεγέθη πηδημάτων ἀπέγνωκεν αὐτῶν· τῶν δὲ κεράτων καὶ μάλα σφόδρα τῆς ἀσυμμετρίας κατέγνωκεν, ὡς παρ' αὐτὸ τοῦτο δυσχρήστων πρός τε τὴν ἄλλην διάζησιν καὶ πολὺ δὴ διαφερόντως, ὁπότε κατεπείγοι τὸ φεύγειν. ὺ δὴ διαφερόντως, ὁπότε κατεπείγοι τὸ φεύγειν. ταύτῃ μὴν καὶ τῆς αὐξήσεως τῶν κεράτων τὴν ἀμετρίαν ἐπιτίνουσ' ἀφικομένη πρὸς κρημνοὺς ἤ τινας πέτρας ἐξόχους, ἐκ διαστήματος ἐπιφερομένη

so-called "spitter" asp is worth recounting, for this beast so far exceeds in dangerousness others of the same name and species as to kill without a bite, projecting its poison like a missile at whatever it wishes, and no less effectively than other asps. In this way, indeed, even from a distance, whenever it is enraged at something it spits forth its poison and has no need to inject a bite.

Furthermore, animals also perceive which of their parts are weak and which are strong and hard to affect.[15] In this way, for example, the bull, when it is getting ready to defend itself against an attack, positions its horns in front of the entire rest of its body. The tortoise, in turn, when it becomes aware of an assault, withdraws its head and feet beneath its shell-like part, that is, those parts that are easily seized beneath the part that is hard and more difficult to get a handle on. The snail too does something similar, rolling itself up in its horny part when it perceives danger. The bear, for its part, does not seem to be unaware[16] of the vulnerability of its head, which is why, when it is beaten with sticks or with other objects that can strike this part, it puts its paws over it to take the force of the blows. Even when it is pursued, if it sometimes has to hurl itself *** down a cliff, it flings itself (safely by drawing its head back under [?]).[17] The toad too does something of the sort, for it is an animal extremely well suited to leaping and is truly not outdone in jumping by any other animal of its size, and on top of this it even perceives how far the interval stretches. If, then, it is pursued along a precipice and is not confident that it can leap to the opposite side, it throws itself to the bottom but does not throw itself in just any old way but inflates itself as much as it is able, and, making itself as similar as possible to a wineskin that has been filled with air, it raises its legs and head as it drops and with the inflated parts manages to eliminate the worst of the fall. And who can fail to be amazed at the stratagem of the deer? For let us grant that there is a disproportion between its legs and horns and that the latter are exceptionally grand and amazing to see, whereas its legs are extremely skinny and easy to despise; yet, nevertheless, it has, in nature, a teacher for what pertains to it that is greater than what sight reveals. Thus, it trusts in its legs even though they are skinny and does not give up on them whether for exceptional bursts of speed or for long leaps. But it scorns its horns, and most especially their lack of proportion, since they are a hindrance precisely for this, both in the other business of life and to a much greater degree when it is urgent to flee. In this way, it recognizes the lack of proportion in the growth of its horns, and when it comes upon cliffs or some outcroppings of rock, it races from a distance and shatters its horns,

περιρράσσει τὰ κέρατα, οὐ τοῖς μέσοις

[III] [1a] Εἰ αἰσθάνεται τὰ ζῷα τῶν ἐν ἑτέροις δυνάμεων
[1b] εἰ διηνεκῶς αἰσθάνεται ἑαυτοῦ τὸ ζῷον.

τῆς βίας χρωμένη, μετὰ δὲ πάσης σφοδρότητος, ἔστ' ἂν ἀποκαυλίσῃ τὰ πλεονάζοντα. Πρὸς τούτοις τοίνυν ἡ ἀσπὶς ὅτι μὲν εὐπαθέσι καὶ τῆς τυχούσης ἐπιβουλῆς ἥττοσι κέχρηται τοῖς οὐραίοις μέρεσι, ὅπλον δ' ἐπὶ τὴν ἑαυτῆς σωτηρίαν πεπόρισται τὸ στόμα, σαφῶς εὑρεθήσεται κατειληφυῖα. διωκομένη γοῦν εἴ τινι φωλειῷ προστυχὴς γένοιτο, τῆς καταδύσεως ἀπὸ τῶν κατ' οὐρὰν ἄρχεται μερῶν, ὑστάτην ἀποκρύπτουσα τὴν κεφαλήν, τέως δ' αὐτὴν ἐπ' ἀσφαλείᾳ τῶν λοιπῶν προϊσχομένη. τὸ δὲ τοῦ κάστορος ἔτι θαυμασιώτερον· ζῷον δ' ἐστὶ ποτάμιον ἐπιεικῶς τε περὶ τὸν Νεῖλον πλεονάζον. οὗτος γὰρ δοκεῖ μοι μηδ' ὧν εἵνεκα διώκεται μορίων ἀγνοεῖν. πρόφασις γὰρ αὐτοῦ τῆς θήρας ἀνθρώποις οἱ ὄρχεις, ἐπειδὴ τὸ παρὰ τοῖς ἰατροῖς περιβόητον καστόρειον ταῦτ' ἐστὶ τοῦ ζῴου τὰ μόρια. διωκόμενος δὲ πρὸς πολὺ μάλιστα μέν ἐστι ἀποδρᾶναι μηχανώμενος ὑγιὴς καὶ ἄρτιος· εἰ δὲ φαίνοιτο κρείττων ἡ ἀνάγκη, τοῖς ὀδοῦσι τοῖς αὐτὸς αὑτοῦ τοὺς ὄρχεις σχίσας ῥίπτει· καὶ τοῦτο γίνεται τοῖς μὲν διώκουσι πέρας τῆς θήρας, ἐκείνῳ δὲ αἴτιον σωτηρίας.

Ἦ μὴν ἔδει ταῦτα λέγειν, ὅπου γε τὰ ζῷα καὶ τῶν ἐν ἑτέροις ἀσθενειῶν καὶ δυνάμεων ἀντίληψιν ἔχει, καὶ τίνα μὲν αὐτοῖς ἐπίβουλα, πρὸς τίνα δὲ αὐτοῖς ἀνοχαὶ καὶ οἷον σύμβασις ἀδιάλυτος. λέων μὲν γοῦν, εἰ μὲν ταύρῳ μάχοιτο, εἰς τὰ κέρατα δέδορκεν αὐτοῦ, τῶν δ' ἄλλων τοῦ ζῴου μερῶν καταπεφρόνηκεν· ἐν δὲ ταῖς πρὸς τὸν ὄναγρον διαμίλλαις παντοῖός ἐστι προσέχων τοῖς λακτίσμασι καὶ τὰς ὁπλὰς φεύγειν σπεύδων. ὅ γε μὴν ἰχνεύμων τὸν πρὸς τὴν ἀσπίδα πόλεμον οὐκ ἀστρατηγήτως διατίθεται, τό τε τῶν δηγμάτων τοῦ θηρίου φυλαττόμενος ὀλέθριον καὶ ὥς ἐστι [......]..[..]α[±12]αυτόν· εἶθ' ἡ [..

α.[±21]σας πλεονάκις, ὥστε ..[..].. [±16].() καθίησίν τισιν [....]λα [±18]τησας ἐπῆρε [...]υρα [±13]τὴν ἀσπίδα ἀντορθιάσαι τω... ερεω [.] ζ. [±9] τοῦ ἰχν]εύμονος μέρει, μένου δὲ τοῦ [±13].ον ἐπὶ τὸν τράχηλον τοῦ θηρίου καὶ[±8]ου [.....] διὰ τὸ περὶ τὸν τράχηλον διατ[....] η[.]εικησ[....]ενόμενος τούτου ῥᾷστα τ..... θηρί παρα....... ας· ἀλλὰ δήπου

καὶ τὰ κατοικίδια νεόττια περιχωρήαντος μὲν ἁλλομένου ταύρου κατευνᾶται οὐδὲ πτοιεῖται, γαλῆς δὲ ἢ ἱέρακος, τέτριγέν τε καὶ ὡς ἔχει τάχους ὑπὸ τὰς μητρῴας καταδύεται πτέρυγας. καὶ μὴν ὁ λέων γυμνοῦ μὲν ἀνδρὸς ῥᾷον καταφρονεῖ, σιβύνην δ' ἐν χεροῖν ἔχοντι μεθ' ἥττονος ἐπιτίθεται θράσους.

not with [III] a moderate amount of force but with all its energy, until it has snapped off the oversized parts.

Furthermore, the asp will be found to have understood clearly that it has at its disposal tail parts that are vulnerable and not up to any chance attack, whereas it is furnished with a weapon for its safety, namely, its mouth. Thus, if, when it is being pursued, it should happen to come upon a hole, it begins its descent with the tail parts and hides its head last of all, sticking it out the whole time for the safety of its other parts. The stratagem of the beaver is even more amazing. It is a riverine animal that is fairly abundant around the Nile. For this creature, it seems to me, is not ignorant even of the parts for which it is pursued. For the reason human beings have for hunting it is its testicles, since castoreum, which is renowned among physicians, is just this part of the animal. And so, when it is being pursued, for a good while it contrives to run away healthy and intact; but if necessity should be too strong, it cuts off its testicles with its own teeth and tosses them away. And this puts an end to the hunt for those who are pursuing it, whereas for the animal it is the cause of its deliverance.[18]

[1a] "Whether animals perceive the capacities that are in other animals"
[1b] "Whether an animal perceives itself continuously"

It was necessary, of course, to speak about this: when and where animals have apprehension [ἀντίληψις] as well of the weaknesses and strengths in others: which ones are aggressive toward them; and toward which they enjoy rather a truce and, as it were, an indissoluble pact.[19] When a lion, for example, fights with a bull, it watches its horns but disdains the other parts of the animal; in battles with the wild ass, however, it is entirely focused on kicks and is keen to avoid the hooves. The ichneumon, for its part, gets ready for war against the asp with no lack of strategy but rather guards against the deadliness of the beast's bites and, as is

*** many times, so as to … it drops on some … it raises itself against the asp … a part of the ichneumon … on the throat of the beast and … on the part around the throat … quite easily …. ***[20]

But of course household chicks, if a bull circles them and jumps around, continue sleeping and do not go all aflutter, but if it is a weasel or a falcon they screech and duck under the mother's wings as quickly as possible.[21] And, for its part, the lion the more easily shows contempt for an unarmed man, whereas he attacks one who holds a hunting spear in his hands with less confidence.

Δοκεῖ δέ μοι καὶ σύμπαν τὸ γένος τῶν ἀλόγων, οὐ τῶν ἀφυεστέρων μόνον, ἀλλὰ καὶ τῶν τάχεσιν ἢ μεγέθεσιν ἢ δυνάμεσιν ὑπερφερόντων ἡμᾶς ὅμως αἰσθόμενον τῆς περὶ τὸν λόγον ὑπεροχῆς, ἀποτρέπεσθαι καὶ ἐκκλίνειν τὸν ἄνθρωπον, οὐκ ἂν εἰ μὴ καὶ τῶν ἐν ἑτέροις προτερημάτων ἀντιληπτικῶς εἶχε τὰ ζῷα τούτου οὕτω γενομένου. Ἀλλὰ γὰρ λοιπὰ μέν ἐστιν, ἃ συνηγορεῖ τῷ τὸ ζῷον αἰσθάνεσθαι ἑαυτοῦ, ἐφ' ὅσα δὲ εἰς τὸ παρὸν ἥρμοττεν, ἀποχρήσει τὰ λεγόμενα·

καὶ ἐφεξῆς οὐ χεῖρον ὀλίγα καὶ περὶ τοῦ διανεκῆ καὶ ἀδιάλειπτον εἶναι τῷ ζῴῳ τὴν ἑαυτοῦ συναίσθησιν ἐπελθεῖν.

Πρῶτον μὲν τοίνυν οὐκ ἀγνοητέον ὡς, καθάπερ τὸ σῶμα τοῦ ζῴου θικτόν ἐστιν, ἵν' οὕτως εἴπω, καὶ ἁπτόν, οὕτως ἐστὶ καὶ ἡ ψυχή· καὶ γὰρ αὐτὴ τοῦ γένους ἐστὶ τῶν σωμάτων—ἀλλ' ἐν τοῖς οἰκείοις τοῦτο παρίσταται λόγοις, ἀνηκέστους ἀποφαίνουσι τὰς τῶν ἄλλων ὑπὲρ τῆς ψυχῆς ἀτοπίας λεγόντων φοράς. σῶμα [IV] δὲ οὖσα θίξιν, ὡς ἔφην, καὶ προσέρεισιν καὶ ἀντίβασιν καὶ βολὴν καὶ πρόσβλησιν καὶ πᾶν εἴ τι τούτοις παραπλήσιόν ἐστιν ἐπιδέχεται.

Δεύτερον δὲ ἐπὶ τῷδε προσενθυμητέον ὡς οὐχὶ καθάπερ ἐν ἀγγείῳ τῷ σώματι περιείργεται ἡ ψυχὴ κατὰ τὰ περιισχόμενα ταῖς πιθάκναις ὑγρά, συμπεφύραται δὲ δαιμονίως καὶ συγκέκραται κατὰ πᾶν, ὡς μηδὲ τοὐλάχιστον τοῦ μίγματος μέρος τῆς ὁποτέρου αὐτῶν ἀμοιρεῖν μετοχῆς· προσφερεστάτη γὰρ ἡ κρᾶσις τοῖς ἐπὶ τοῦ διαπύρου σιδήρου γινομένοις· ἐκεῖ τε γὰρ ὁμοίως κἀνταῦθα δι' ὅλων ἐστὶν ἡ παράθεσις. ταύτῃ καὶ τὰ τῆς συμπαθίας ἐστὶν ἀμφοῖν κατακορῆ. θάτερον γὰρ τῷ ἑτέρῳ συμπαθὲς καὶ οὔτε τῶν σωματικῶν παθῶν ἀνήκοος ἡ ψυχὴ οὔτε αὖ τέλεον ἐκκεκώφηται πρὸς τὰ τῆς ψυχῆς δεινὰ τὸ σῶμα. διὰ τοῦτο καθάπερ φλεγμοναῖς τῶν καιρίων τοῦ σώματος τόπων ἕπεται παρακοπὴ καὶ ἀλλόκοτος φορὰ τῆς διανοίας ἢ καὶ πάσης τῆς φανταστικῆς παραποδισμὸς ἕξεως, οὕτως καὶ λύπαις φόβοις τε καὶ ὀργαῖς καὶ ὅλως τοῖς τῆς ψυχῆς πάθεσι συνδιατίθεται τὸ σῶμα μέχρις ἑτεροχροίας καὶ τρόμου σκελῶν προέσεώς τε οὔρου καὶ συγκρύσεως ὀδόντων ἔτι δὲ φωνῆς ἐπισχέσεως καὶ τοῦ ὅλου καταπληκτικῆς μεταμορφώσεως. οὐ γὰρ ἂν οὕτως ἦν εὐτρεπῆ πρὸς μετάδοσιν καὶ μετάληψιν παθῶν, εἰ μὴ τρόπον ἀλλήλοις, ὃν ἔφαμεν, συνεκέκρατο.

τρίτον γε μὴν ἐπὶ τούτοις οὐκ ἂν οὐδὲ τὸν Μαργίτην ἀντειπεῖν νομίζω, ὡς οὐκ ἔστιν ἡ ψυχὴ δύναμις αἰσθητική· ταύτῃ γὰρ καὶ φύσεως πλεονάζει καὶ προσέτι τῷ ὁρμητικὴ τυγχάνειν· ἐπεί τοι λελείψεται φύσις μόνον ἀντὶ ψυχῆς ὁρμῆς καὶ αἰσθήσεως στερομένη.

In my opinion, moreover, the entire class of irrational animals, not just those that are less endowed by nature but also those that exceed us in speed, size, and strength, nevertheless when they perceive our superiority in respect to reason [λόγος], run away from and avoid humans; but this would not happen in this way if animals were not perceptive of the advantages in other creatures as well. Indeed, there are further points that support the case that an animal perceives itself, but insofar as suits the present purpose, what has been said will suffice.

Next, it is not amiss to go briefly into the fact that an animal's perception of itself is continuous and uninterrupted.[22]

First, then, it is necessary to know that, just as the body of an animal is touchable, if I may put it this way, and tangible, so too is the soul;[23] for in fact it is of the class of bodies[24]—but this is available in our own treatises, which demonstrate that the arguments of those who speak about the exceptional status of the soul are fatally flawed. [IV] Since it is body, then, it admits of touch, as I have said, and of pressure and resistance, blow and counterblow, and whatever else is similar to these.[25]

Second, and in addition to this, one must consider that the soul is not enclosed in the body as in a bucket, like liquids surrounded by jars, but is wondrously blended and wholly intermingled, so that not even the least part of the mixture fails to have a share in either of them.[26] For the mixture is most similar to those that occur in the case of red-hot iron.[27] For there, just like here, the juxtaposition is by wholes. Thus, too, what pertains to shared affect [συμπάθεια] is total for both. For each shares the affects of the other, and neither is the soul heedless of bodily affects, nor is the body completely deaf to the torments of the soul. That is why, just as there follow upon inflammations of the vital spots of the body delirium and strange driftings of thought and even the obstruction of the entire imaginative faculty, so too the body is affected by the griefs, fears,[28] rages, and, in sum, all the passions of the soul, to the point of changes of color, trembling of the legs, emission of urine, knocking of the teeth, and right up to the blocking of the voice and a shocking transformation of the body as a whole. For they would not be so easily exposed to the transmission and reception of affects, if they were not mixed together in the way we have said.

Third, in addition to this, I think that not even Margites would claim in contra that the soul is not a perceptive [αἰσθητική] faculty. For this is why it surpasses a mere "nature," and also by virtue of becoming endowed with impulse; since it would have remained just a "nature" rather than a soul if it were deprived of impulse [ὁρμή] and pereception [αἴσθησις].[29]

Τίνος μὴν ἔτι δεῖ τετάρτου τὰ παρόντα; ἦ δῆλον ὡς ὃν τρόπον εἴληχεν ἡ ψυχὴ τῆς κινήσεως παραστῆσαι. κινδυνεύει δ' οὐκ ἰδία αὐτῆς κατά γε τὴν πιθανωτάτην δόξαν εἶναι τῆς αἱρέσεως οὐδὲ ἄφετος, ἀλλὰ κοινὴ ψυχῇ τε καὶ σώματι οὐ γὰρ ἐκ τῶν μέσων ἀν' ἄκρον συνείχετ' ἂν πάντα τὰ σώματα διὰ τόνον δὴ καὶ τὴν τονικὴν κίνησιν, εἰ μὴ πάντως ὑπῆρχε τρόπος οὗτος τῆς κινήσεως πασῶν συνεκτικῶν δυνάμεων. ἦν δ' ἄρα καὶ ἡ ψυχὴ δύναμις συνεκτικὴ καὶ κινοῖτ' ἂν καὶ αὐτὴ τὴν τονικὴν κίνησιν [±9] ἐφ' ἑκάτερα .... υσι ...... αυ. δ....... ιδίους καθηρημένων α. ην ...... ται . την [±10]. κινήσεις. Ἐπεὶ τοίνυν γένος οὐδὲν ἕτερον ἐστὶ τὸ ζῷον ἢ τὸ σύνθετον, ἐκ σώματος καὶ ψυχῆς, ἄμφω δ' ἐστὶ θικτὰ καὶ πρόσβλητα καὶ τῇ προσερείσει δὴ ὑπόπτωτα, ἔτι δὲ δι' ὅλων κέκραται, καὶ θάτερον μέν ἐστιν αὐτῶν δύναμις αἰσθητική, τὸ δ' αὐτὸ τοῦτο καὶ τρόπον, ὃν ὑπεδείξαμεν, κινεῖται, δῆλον ὅτι διανεκῶς αἰσθάνοιτ' ἂν τὸ ζῷον ἑαυτοῦ. τεινομένη γὰρ ἔξω ἡ ψυχὴ μετ' ἀφέσεως προσβάλλει πᾶσι τοῦ σώματος τοῖς μέρεσιν, ἐπειδὴ καὶ κέκραται πᾶσι, προσβάλλουσα δὲ ἀντιπροσβάλλεται· ἀντιβατικὸν γὰρ καὶ τὸ σῶμα, καθάπερ καὶ ἡ ψυχή· καὶ τὸ πάθος συνερειστικὸν ὁμοῦ καὶ ἀντερειστικὸν ἀποτελεῖται. καὶ ἀπὸ τῶν μερῶν τῶν ἄκρων εἴσω νεῦον ἐπὶ τὴν ἡγεμονίαν τοῦ στήθους εἰσαναφέρεται, ὡς ἀντίληψιν γίνεσθαι μερῶν ἁπάντων τῶν τε τοῦ σώματος καὶ τῶν τῆς ψυχῆς· τοῦτο δέ ἐστιν ἴσον τῷ τὸ ζῷον αἰσθάνεσθαι ἑαυτοῦ.

Μαρτύρια δ' οὐκ ἄπιστα τῶν λόγων τὰ συμβαίνοντα· πιθανὸν μὲν γάρ, εἴπερ ὅλως ποθ' ἑαυτοῦ γίνεται τὸ ζῷον ἀνεπαίσθητον, ἐν τῳ ὕπνου πάντως χρόνῳ μάλιστα τοῦτο συμβαίνειν. ὁρῶμεν δ' ὡς καὶ τότε, οὐ μάλα μὲν τοῖς πολλοῖς εὐπαρακολουθήτως, συναισθάνεται δ' οὖν ἑαυτοῦ τὸ ζῷον. ἀπόχρη δὲ πρὸς τὴν ὑπὲρ παντὸς τοῦ γένους διάληψιν τὰ ἐφ' ὃν διάγομεν βίον ἀπαντῶντα παραθέσθαι· καὶ γὰρ περὶ χειμῶνος ὥραν παραγυμνωθέντες μέρη τινὰ τοῦ σώματος, [V] εἰ καὶ βαθυτάτῳ πεπιεσμένοι τύχοιμεν ὕπνῳ, ὅμως ἐφελκόμεθα τὰ ἐνεύναια καὶ περισκέπομεν τὰ ψυχόμενα, τά τε ἕλκη φυλάττομεν ἀπρόσκρουστα καὶ ἄθλιπτα κοιμώμενοι βαθέως, ὡς ἂν ἐγρηγορυίᾳ, ἵν' οὕτω φῶ, χρώμενοι τῇ προσοχῇ, τῇ τε προτεραίᾳ συνταξάμενοί τισι νύκτωρ ἐπαναστήσεσθαι διεγρόμεθα τῆς ὡρισμένης ὥρας ἡκούσης. ἴδοις δ' ἂν καὶ τὰς σπουδὰς τὰς περί τινα μέχρι τῶν ὕπνων ἐπακολουθούσας· ὁ μέν γε φίλοινος καταδαρθάνει πολλάκις οὐκ ἀφιεὶς ἐκ τῆς χειρὸς τὴν λάγυνον· ὁ δὲ φιλάργυρος ἀπρὶξ ἐχόμενος τοῦ βαλλαντίου κοιμᾶται· τῇδε μέντοι καὶ

What, then, do the present considerations still require as a fourth point? It is clear, surely, that it is to present how the soul attains movement. Now, this last runs the risk of not being specific to the soul, at least according to the most convincing doctrine of our school, but neither is it independent of it, but rather it is common to both soul and body. For bodies would not all cohere from mid-parts to extremity by tension [τόνος] and tensive [τονική] movement, unless this kind of movement of all the cohesive forces existed throughout.[30] Thus, the soul too is a cohesive force, and it too must move in a tensive movement *** to both … their specific … destroyed … *** movements. Since, then, an animal is no other kind of thing than a composite of body and soul, and both of these are touchable, able to deliver blows and subject to pressure, and since furthermore they are mixed by wholes, and one of them is a perceptive faculty, and this itself too moves in the way that we have shown, it is clear that an animal must continuously perceive itself. For the soul extends outward with an expansion and strikes all the parts of the body, since it is also mixed with all of them, and when it strikes them it is struck back in turn. For the body too offers resistance, just like the soul: and the affect ends up being simultaneously characterized by pressure and counterpressure. And, tilting inward from the outermost parts, the affect is borne in toward the hegemonic faculty [ἡγεμονία] in the chest,[31] so that there is apprehension [ἀντίληψις] of all the parts, both of the body and of the soul:[32] and this is equivalent to the animal perceiving [αἰσθάνεται] itself.[33]

Things that actually happen are not implausible witnesses to these arguments, for it is plausible that, if ever an animal becomes wholly insensible [ἀνεπαίσθητον] of itself, this invariably happens above all in time of sleep. But we see that even then—in a way not very easy for most people to follow—an animal nevertheless perceives itself.[34] Now, for a grasp of the entire [animal] genus, it suffices to lay out what we encounter in our daily life. For in fact, in the winter season if some parts of our body are exposed, [V] even if we happen to be gripped in the deepest sleep we nevertheless draw up the bedsheets and cover those parts that are cold, and we keep wounds free of blows and pressure, even if we are sleeping profoundly, as though we were employing, if I may put it this way, a fully awake attention, and if, the day before, we have agreed with some others to get up at night, we awaken when the hour we set arrives. You can see that even the pursuits that concern a person follow him right into sleep. Thus, a winebibber often falls asleep without releasing the flask from his hand, whereas the miser naps with a tight grip on his purse.[35] In this

τὸν ἱκανῶς ἔχοντα πρὸς ἐπίκρισιν ἠθῶν οὐκ ἀπελπίζω κοιμωμένοις ἐπιστάντα δυνατῶς ἕξειν ἐκ τοῦ τρόπου τῆς κοιμήσεως γνῶναι, ποία τις ἡ τοῦ καθεύδοντος διάθεσις, πότερον ἐρρωμένη καὶ τόνου πλήρης ἢ μαλθακωτέρα τοῦ δέοντος. οὐ γὰρ δὴ τεθνήξεσθαι μὲν προσδοκῶντες οἱ βραχεῖς χ[ρόνους ἔχοντες] πρόνοιαν ποιοῦνται τοῦ καὶ νεκροὶ πεσεῖν εὐσχημόνως, κατὰ τὴν τραγικὴν παρθένον, οὐχὶ δὲ πολλῷ μᾶλλον εἰς τὰ τῶν κοιμωμένων σώματα διΐξεται τὰ τεκμήρια τῆς διαθέσεως· οὕτω δὴ καὶ ὁ Ἡρακλῆς εὕδει πιέζων χειρὶ δεξιᾷ ξύλον. ταῦτ᾽ οὖν ἅπαντα καὶ τὰ τούτοις ἐοικότα—μυρία δ᾽ ἐστὶ τὸ πλῆθος—ἐχεγγυωτάτη πίστις εἶναί μοι δοκεῖ τοῦ κἀν τοῖς ὕπνοις αἰσθάνεσθαι ἡμᾶς ἑαυτῶν. καὶ οὐκ ἐφ᾽ ἡμῶν μὲν ἀληθὴς ὁ λόγος, οὐχὶ δὲ κἀπὶ τῶν ἄλλων ζῴων·

μὴ γὰρ καὶ λεπτοτέρων ἐκεῖνα προσδεᾶ εὕροιμεν ἂν ὕπνων, ἅτε ῥώμῃ σωμάτων πρὸς πέψιν εὐφυεστέρως ἔχοντα καὶ διὰ τοῦθ᾽ ἧττον μακρῶν καὶ βαθέων ὕπνων χρῄζοντα· ἵνα μὴ πλαγχυ λέγω τὸ συχνόν· ἀλλὰ γὰρ καὶ ὁ τοῦ κοιμᾶσθαι τρόπος πίστις οὐχὶ τῆς λεπτότητος μόνον τῆς αὐτῶν, ἀλλὰ καὶ τῆς ἑαυτῶν ἐν τῷ καταδαρθάνειν ἀντιλήψεως.

ἀπὸ γὰρ [±13] θεῖναι καιρ...
[±25]όμενον π....
[±25]μαλεν....
[±25]τοοῦ τοιούτου ζῴου αἰσθή—
[±23 αἰσθά]νεται ἑαυτοῦ
[.....]π [±18]καιρω
... και ......σ αν...[±10]διο..

...σαι πρῶτον μέντοι [±10] τὰ πρῶτα διαλεχθέντα ἡμῖν καὶ αἰσθάνεται τῶν μερῶν καὶ τῶν ἔργων τὸ ζῷον ἅπαν ἀδιαλίπτως, δῆλον ὅτι τὸ ζῷον ἑαυτοῦ αἰσθάνεται καὶ ἀπ᾽ ἀρχῆς· καὶ γὰρ αὐτὴ μέρος ἐστὶ τοῦ χρόνου τὸ πρῶτον· δι᾽ ὅ. τοῦτο μὲν ἰσχυρότατον ὂν ἐξ ἑτοίμου φαίνεται πρὸς συνηγορίαν εἰλῆφθαι.

φέρε δὲ μετὰ τοῦτο ἐννοηθῶμεν, τίνι τῶν χρόνων ἀναθεῖναι πρέποι ἂν τὸ συμβαῖνον, ἀφελομένους τοῦ πρώτου· καί μοι τῶν ἀντιλεγόντων τις ἀποκρινάσθω, ἐν τίνι τῶν χρόνων ἄρχεται τὸ ζῷον τῆς ἑαυτοῦ ἀντιλήψεως; ὃν γὰρ ἂν εἴπῃ τις, οὐδὲν ἐρεῖ περιττότερον ἔχοντα τοῦ πρώτου· τὴν γοῦν αἰσθητικὴν δύναμιν, ἧς δεῖ πρὸς τὸ αἰσθάνεσθαι τὸ ζῷον ἑαυτοῦ, οὐκ ἐν μὲν τῷ δευτέρῳ τῶν χρόνων ἢ τῷ τρίτῳ ἤ τινι τῶν ἄλλων ἔχει τὸ ζῷον, ἐν δὲ τῷ πρώτῳ ταύτης ἐστέρηται, ἀλλ᾽ ἀφ᾽ οὗ ἂν ᾖ χρόνου ζῷον, εὐθὺς αἰσθητικόν ἐστι.

μετὰ ταῦτα τοίνυν οὐκ ἄν μοι δοκεῖ τις ἀντειπεῖν, ὡς οὐχὶ πάντως τινὸς τῶν ἐκτὸς αἰσθάνεται τὸ ζῷον· καὶ γὰρ ὁρᾷ, ὅσα γε μὴ ὑπότυφλα τίκτεται, καὶ ἀκούει· εἰ δὲ μή, γεύεται μὲν καὶ ἅπτεται· διὰ τοῦτο καὶ τὰ μὲν ἐπὶ θηλὰς

way, indeed, I fully expect that someone who is good at judging characters, if he stands next to people in their sleep, will be able to recognize, on the basis of his manner of sleeping, what kind of disposition the sleeper has—whether it is strong and full of tension or else softer than it should be. For if in fact people who expect to die and have a brief time left take thought for falling down gracefully as corpses, like the virgin in the tragedy,[36] then much more so will signs of their disposition filter through the bodies of those who are sleeping. Thus, for example, Heracles too sleeps grasping his club in his right hand.[37] All these examples, then, and others that resemble them—they number in the tens of thousands—seem to me to be a most reliable confirmation of the fact that even in sleep we perceive ourselves.

Nor is the argument true for us but not for other animals.[38] For we shall find that they are in need of lighter sleep, since, thanks to the strength of their bodies, they are better equipped by nature for digestion and therefore require periods of sleep that are less long and deep—but so as not to speak at too great length: their manner of sleeping too, in fact, is a confirmation not only of the lightness of their sleep but also of their perception of themselves during sleep.

For, from the *** such an animal … perceives itself … at the right time … first, nevertheless …

the first things that were discussed by us, and an animal as a whole perceives its parts and their functions uninterruptedly. It is clear that an animal perceives itself, and from the beginning: for in fact this latter [i.e., the beginning] is a part of time—the first part. This is why this point, since it seems the strongest available, has been adopted in support.[39]

After this, come let us consider to which stage [of life] it would be appropriate to ascribe this event, if we were denied the first stage.[40] Let one of those who object answer me: In which stage does the animal initiate perception of itself? For whichever one a person may name, he will not mention any that is more important than the first. Indeed, as far as the perceptive faculty goes, which an animal needs in order to perceive itself, an animal will not have it in the second stage or the third or any other, if it is deprived of it in the first, but rather from that stage on—whichever it may be—in which it is an animal, it is immediately endowed with perception [αἰσθητικόν].

After this, then, I do not believe that anyone could object that an animal does not at all perceive anything that is external. For in fact all animals see [sc. as soon as they are born], at least if they are not born practically blind, and hear; and if not, in any case they taste and feel. It

μητρῴας ὁρμήσαντα ἀποσπᾷ τὸ γάλα, τὰ δ' ὑπὸ πτέρυξι τῆς γειναμένης καταδύεται, τὸ ἀπηνὲς ἐκτρεπόμενα τοῦ περιέχοντος, τὰ δὲ κλαυμυρίζεται οἷον τυπτόμενα καὶ βαλλόμενα ὑπὸ τοῦ ἀέρος. εἰς τί ποτ' οὖν φέρει οὗτος ὁ λόγος; εἰς πάνυ καλὴν καὶ ἀναντίλεκτον ὑπόμνησιν [VI]

[1a] εἰ αἰσθανόμενον ἑαυτοῦ χαίρει τὸ ζῷον
[1b] καὶ οἰκειοῦται ἑαυτῷ.

τοῦ προκειμένου· καθόλου γὰρ οὐ συντελεῖται τῶν ἐκτός τινος ἀντίληψις δίχα τῆς ἑαυτῶν αἰσθήσεως. μετὰ γὰρ τῆς τοῦ λευκοῦ φέρε εἰπεῖν αἰσθήσεως καὶ ἑαυτῶν αἰσθανόμεθα λευκαινομένων καὶ μετὰ τῆς τοῦ γλυκέως γλυκαζομένων καὶ μετὰ τῆς τοῦ θερμοῦ θερμαινομένων κἀπὶ τῶν ἄλλων τἀνάλογον· ὥστ' ἐπειδὴ πάντως μὲν γεννηθὲν εὐθὺς αἰσθάνεταί τινος τὸ ζῷον, τῇ δ' ἑτέρου τινὸς αἰσθήσει συμπέφυκεν <ἡ> ἑαυτοῦ, φανερὸν ὡς ἀπ' ἀρχῆς αἰσθάνοιτ' ἂν ἑαυτῶν τὰ ζῷα.

τοῖς δ' ὅλοις οὐκ ἀγνοητέον, ὡς ἡγεμονικὴ πᾶσα δύναμις ἀφ' ἑαυτῆς ἄρχεται· ταύτῃ καὶ ἡ μὲν ἕξις, συνέχουσα τὸ καθ' ἑαυτήν, πρότερον ἑαυτῆς ἐστι συνεκτική· καὶ γὰρ οὐδ' ἂν συνεῖχε ἄλλο τι πρᾶγμα, τὰ μόρια προσπαραδεδεγμένη, εἰ μὴ τοῖς ἑαυτῆς τοῦτο προπαρεῖχε μορίοις· ἥ τε φύσις, δή, συνέχουσα καὶ σῴζουσα καὶ τρέφουσα καὶ αὔξουσα τὸ φυτόν, αὐτῶν τούτων πρότερον αὐτὴ μετέχει παρ' αὑτῆς. ὁ δὲ παραπλήσιος λόγος κατὰ πάσης ἀρχῆς, ὥστε καὶ ἡ αἴσθησις, ἐπειδὴ καὶ αὐτὴ δύναμίς ἐστιν ἀρχική, καὶ συνεχέστερον δεῖ χρῆμα ἢ ἕξις τε καὶ φύσις εἶναι, δῆλον ὅτι ἄρχοιτ' ἂν ἀφ' ἑαυτῆς καὶ πρὶν ἢ ἑτέρου τινὸς ἀντιλαβέσθαι, ἑαυτῆς αἰσθάνοιτο.

παντὸς οὖν τοῦ προγεγονότος λόγου κοινὸν θώμεθα κεφάλαιον, ὡς ἅμα τῇ γενέσει τὸ ζῷον αἰσθάνεται ἑαυτοῦ. Μετὰ ταῦτ' οὖν δῆλόν ἐστιν ὅτι φαντασίας τινὸς ἑαυτοῦ γενομένης αὐτῷ τὸ πιθανὸν ἴσχει—πῶς γὰρ ἂν ἄλλως δύναιτο;—περὶ τῆς φαντασίας καὶ τούτῳ συγκατατίθεται.

Δεῖ γε μὴν περὶ τριῶν ἐπιστῆσαι πάντως· ἢ μέντοι εὐαρεστεῖ τῇ φαντασίᾳ, ἣν ἑαυτοῦ εἴληφεν, ἢ δυσαρεστεῖ ἢ ἀρρεπῶς ἴσχει· τὴν γὰρ α[±10]ν οὐδέν ἐστι ....

is because of this that some rush to the mother's breast and suck out the milk, whereas others hide under the wings of their mother, escaping the severity of the environment, and still others cry, as though they were struck [60] and beaten by the air. To what, then, is this argument leading? To a very beautiful and incontrovertible cue [VI] to the thesis proposed above. For, in general, the apprehension [ἀντίληψις] of some external thing is not realized without perception [αἴσθησις] of oneself. For, together with the perception [αἴσθησις] of white, we may say, we perceive [αἰσθανόμεθα] ourselves too being whitened, and together with [5] that of something sweet, we perceive ourselves sweetened, with that of something hot ourselves heated, and similarly with the rest. Thus, since an animal invariably perceives something as soon as it is born, and perception of itself is naturally joined to the perception of something else, it is clear that animals must perceive [αἰσθάνοιτο] themselves right from the beginning.[41]

[10] In general, one must not be ignorant of the fact that every hegemonic faculty begins with itself. In this way a cohesive structure [ἕξις], which binds together what pertains to it, is first binding of itself. For indeed it could not bind together any other thing, when it has attached its parts to itself, if it had not previously provided this [15] to its own parts. A "nature" too, indeed, when it binds together, preserves, nourishes and increases a plant, first shares in these very things itself. There is a similar argument for every beginning; thus, pereception [αἴσθησις] too, since it too is an initiating [ἀρχική] faculty, must be a thing even more binding [20] than a cohesive structure and a "nature," obviously because it must begin from itself and, before apprehending [ἀντιλαβέσθαι] something else, must perceive [αἰσθάνοιτο] itself.[42]

Let us, then, set down as the chief point common to the entire preceding argument the fact that an animal, simultaneous with its birth, perceives [αἰσθάνεται] itself.[43] After this, then, it is obvious [25] that when there occurs in it some representation of itself, it [the animal] holds onto the persuasive aspect—for how could it do otherwise?—of the representation, and assents to it.

[1a] "Whether an animal, when it perceives itself,
[1b] also becomes its own and familiar [οἰκειοῦται] to itself"

It is necessary, however, to pause over three points in total: either the animal is pleased with the representation that it has received of itself, or it is displeased, [30] or else it remains indifferent. *** For ... nothing ... its

[±26]ας τῶν ἐκ τ....
[±26]ζῳ τῇ ἑαυτοῦ
[±24 εὐ]αρεστοῦν γ....
[±26] ἠλλοτρίωται δὲ
[±28]διαμένει χρόνον
[±26]ρτε..κάτης
[±26]τι οι.α ..
.εο [±10].θο.... ἀλλ' ἐκ τῶν ε
..τ.......μεν... ἐρ.μενο... σώζειν δύναται
[±8]· ἔχοι δ' ἂν τὴν αἰτίαν καὶ ἡ φύσις, ὡς μάτην τὰ τοιαῦτα καμοῦσα πρὸ γενέσεως, εἰ μὴ μέλλει τὸ ζῷον εὐθὺ γενόμενον ἀρέσειν ἑαυτῷ. διὰ ταῦτα οὐκ ἄν μοι δοκεῖ τις, οὐδὲ Μαργίτης ὤν, εἰπεῖν ὥς τε γεννηθὲν τὸ ζῷον ἑαυτῷ τε καὶ τῇ φαντασίᾳ τῇ ἑαυτοῦ δυσαρεστεῖ· καὶ μὴν οὐδ' ἀρρεπῶς ἴσχει· οὐχ ἧττον γὰρ τῆς δυσαρεστήσεως καὶ αὐτὸ τὸ μὴ εὐαρεστεῖν πρός τε ὄλεθρον τοῦ ζῴου καὶ πρὸς κατάγνωσιν φέρει τῆς φύσεως· ὅθεν ὁ συλλογισμὸς οὗτος ἀναγκάζει ὁμολογεῖν ὅτι τὸ ζῷον, τὴν πρώτην αἴσθησιν ἑαυτοῦ λαβόν, εὐθὺς ᾠκειώθη πρὸς ἑαυτὸ καὶ τὴν ἑαυτοῦ σύστασιν.

φαίνεται δ' ἔμοιγε καὶ αὐτὰ τὰ γινόμενα βεβαιοῦν τὸν λόγον. τί γάρ; οὐχὶ κατὰ τὴν ἑαυτοῦ δύναμιν ἕκαστον ποιεῖ τὸ ἐπιβάλλον ὑπὲρ τῆς ἑαυτοῦ συντηρήσεως, ἐκκλεῖνον μὲν πᾶσαν ἐπιβουλὴν πόρρωθεν καὶ διαμένειν μηχανώμενον ἀπαθὲς ἐκ τῶν σφαλερῶν, ᾄττον δ' ἐπὶ τὰ σωτήρια καὶ πάνταχόθεν ποριζόμενον τὰ πρὸς διαμονήν. οὐ γὰρ δὴ τὰ θαυμαστοῖς κάλλεσι καὶ μεγέθεσιν ὑπερέχοντα μόνα καί τισιν ἀλκαῖς ἢ τάχεσι δια [VII] φέροντα τοιαῦτα περὶ τὴν ἑαυτῶν ὄντα συντήρησιν εὕροιμεν ἄν, ἀλλὰ καὶ τὰ μικρὰ καὶ εὐτελῆ καὶ τὴν ἄλλως εἰδεχθῆ. δεινὴ γὰρ ἡ φύσις καὶ τοῖς τοιοῖσδε σφῶν αὐτῶν ἐντῆξαι σφοδρὸν ἵμερον, τῷ τὴν σωτηρίαν ἄλλως ἄπορον ὑπάρχειν. ταύτῃ ἄρα δοκεῖ μοι καὶ τὰ νεαρὰ παιδάρια μὴ ῥᾳδίως φέρειν κατακλειόμενα ζοφεροῖς οἴκοις καὶ πάσης φωνῆς ἀμετόχοις. ἐντείνοντα γὰρ τὰ αἰσθητήρια καὶ μηδὲν μήτ' ἀκοῦσαι μήτ' ἰδεῖν δυνάμενα φαντασίαν ἀναιρέσεως αὑτῶν λαμβάνει καὶ διὰ τοῦτο δυσανασχετεῖ. διὸ καὶ φιλοτέχνως αἱ τίτθαι παρεγγυῶσιν αὐτοῖς ἐπιμύειν τοὺς ὀφθαλμούς· παρηγορεῖ γὰρ τὸν φόβον τὸ ἐθελουσίᾳ καὶ μὴ ὑπ' ἀνάγκης στερεῖσθαι τῆς ἀ[ντιλήψεως] τῶν ὁρατῶν. τινὰ δὲ αὐτῶν καὶ δίχα παρεγγυήσεως τοὺς ὀφθαλμοὺς ἐπιμύει, τῷ πληκτικῷ ἀντίσθα[σθαι τοῦ σκότους] οὐκ ἐξαρκοῦντα.

Τοσαύτη δ' ἄρα περιουσία τεκμηρίων ἐστὶ τῷ τὸ ζῷον οἰκειοῦσθαι ἑαυτῷ, ὥστ' ἤδη καὶ ἀπὸ τῶν παρὰ φύσιν ἔξεστιν ὑπομιμνήσκειν ὑγιὲς ὂν τὸ ἀξιούμενον. .....φιλ....πρᾶγμα χαλεπόν καὶ τοῦ μὴ θεραπευ ... τοὺς αἰτιώτατον· ὅμως τὴν καταρχήν γε ἡ πρὸς ἑαυτοὺς οἰκείωσις παρέχει, δι' ἣν οἷστός ἐστιν ἕκαστος

own… being content… it is estranged… it remains for a time… but from the … to save ***

But nature would also be subject to the charge of making these kinds of effort in vain prior to birth, if an animal were not going to be pleased with itself as soon as it is born. Because of this, no one, it seems to me, not even if he were Margites, could say that an animal, when it has been born, is displeased with itself and with its representation of itself. And, in fact, it does not remain indifferent: for not being pleased, no less than displeasure, leads both to the destruction of the animal and to a contempt for its own nature. Consequently, this reasoning compels us to agree that an animal, when it has received the first perception [αἴσθησις] of itself, immediately becomes its own and familiar to itself [ᾠκειώθη πρὸς ἑαυτῷ] and to its constitution [σύστασις].[44]

It seems to me, at all events, that the facts themselves support the argument.[45] What, then? Is it not the case that, in accord with its own ability, each animal does what contributes to its own preservation, avoiding every attack even from afar and contriving to remain unharmed by dangers, while it leaps toward whatever brings safety and provides for itself from far and wide whatever tends toward its survival?[46] For, in truth, we can find that not only those that excel for the wondrous beauty and size and are outstanding in their particular strength or speed [VII] are such in respect to their own preservation, but also those that are small and of no account and in some other way unsightly. For nature is cunning at instilling even in such creatures a powerful passion for themselves, because their survival would otherwise be impossible. For this reason, indeed, it seems to me that even newborn infants do not readily tolerate being enclosed in dark rooms that are deprived of all sound, for they extend their sense organs, and if they are unable to hear or see anything, they receive a representation of their own annihilation, and for this reason they can scarcely endure it. This is why nurses cleverly urge them to close their eyes: for the fact that they are deprived of the apprehension of what is visible by their own choice and not under compulsion allays their fear. And some of them close their eyes without urging, since they are unable to withstand the jolt of darkness.[47]

So great, then, is the superabundance of signs that an animal becomes its own and familiar to itself [οἰκειοῦσθαι ἑαυτῷ] that it is even possible to show that the proposition is sound on the basis of things that are contrary to nature. *** a difficult thing even for what is not … most responsible. Nevertheless, becoming their own and familiar to themselves [οἰκείωσις πρὸς ἑαυτούς] provides them with a starting point, thanks

ἑαυτῷ, κἂν ἄλλοις ἀφόρητος ᾖ. ἕλκη γοῦν τὰ δυσοσμώτατα καὶ πρὸς τὴν ὄψιν ἀπηνέστατα φέρομεν ἑαυτῶν καὶ τὴν ἄλλην ἀηδίαν ὑπὸ τῆς φιλαυτίας ἐπισκοτουμένην. τὸ δὲ θαυμασιώτατον· τί γάρ ἐστιν εἰδεχθέστερον .ακίας; εἴγε καρκινώματα μὲν καὶ ὀχθώδεις ἐπαναστάσεις σαρκῶν, μελανίαι τε καὶ σηπεδόνες [καὶ λοιπ]ὰ πρὸς ὄψιν ἀτερπῆ .....το...ει....

......π.ειανε.αλ ....σουτ...

...... περὶ τούτων ὥστε ο.......ατὸν εἶναι τῶν

.......ν............ οὖν ἃ ῥέπει ...

........................την γε .....

........................αι σφῶν αὐ

[τῶν .... ἡ]δοναῖς.

.... φιλαυτί

..........................μεν

....

........................βεβαιω

..........ν..........χουν φη

........................ον..των ἤδη

.... ζωτης κατεστηκότος

.... ἅμα τῇ γενέσει

τὸ ζῷον ο.............. κ .ην ἂν ὅτι ....

το...γα .ν............. πρώτους χρόνους ἀπὸ.

γενέσεως ὑπὲρ τοῦ διασώζειν καὶ συντηρεῖν ἑαυτὸ προβῆναι ...α........ τὴν εἰρημένην οἰκείωσιν, εὐθὺς α ..το........... ὁρμὴ, καὶ τοῦ πρὸς τὸ σωτήριον ἑαυτοῦ συν αἴσθησίς ἐστὶν ἡ λελεγμένη οἰκείωσις· διὸ φαίνεται τὸ ζῷον ἅμα τῇ γενέσει αἰσθάνεσθαί τε αὑτοῦ καὶ οἰκειοῦσθαι ἑαυτῷ καὶ τῇ ἑαυτοῦ συστάσει·

ἐνταῦθα δὴ τοῦ λόγου γενόμενος οὐκ ἂν ἀκαίρως διασαφησαίμην τῆς φαντασίας τὸν τρόπον. οὕτως οὖν ἐπειδὰν πολὺ αὐξάνηται τὸ ζῷον ἀνὰ χρόνον μὲν .. και ο .. τ....... ς ἤδη τῆς διαρθρώσεως, τρανὴς ἡ φαντασία γίνεται καὶ διηκριβωμένη ητ...

..ου.........οτητα τρανότητος μόνον ἀλλὰ καὶ....... μετὰ ῥώμης διατετορευμένη πως καὶ διὰ σαφῶν τύπων ἡ ἀντίληψις τῶν ἰδιωμάτων ἀποτελεῖται·

τὸ δὲ κατ' ἀρχὰς κἂν τῇ πρώτῃ γενέσει οὐχ οὗτος ἐστιν ὁ τρόπος τῆς φαντασίας οὔτε τῆς αἰσθήσεως ἀλλὰ ....καὶ συγκεχυμένος ὁλοσχερεῖ

to which each is bearable to itself even if it is unbearable to others. For example, we endure the most malodorous wounds, those most repulsive to the sight, if they are our own, and every other unpleasantness, since it is overshadowed by our self-love.[48] But this is most amazing of all: for what is uglier than … ? [25] Surely, if carcinomas and tuber-like excrescences of the flesh, and black splotches and putrefactions and the rest are unpleasant to the sight … concerning these, so that … [30] then, those that incline … of their own … to pleasures … self-love … [35] firm … then …

[40] simultaneous with its birth … that an animal, during the first stages after its birth, moves forward so as to survive and preserve itself, [45] … the so-called becoming one's own and familiar, immediately … impulse, and the above-mentioned becoming one's own and familiar [οἰκείωσις] is the self-conscious perception [συναίσθησις] of what tends to one's own safety. That is why an animal is seen, simultaneous with its birth, to perceive itself and to become its own and familiar to itself [οἰκειοῦσθαι ἑαυτῷ] and to [50] its own constitution.[49]

Having arrived at this point in our argument, it would not be inopportune for me to clarify the manner of representation [φαντασία].[50] So, when an animal has, in this way, grown considerably over time … and by now the representation of its articulation is clear and precise …

[55] … not only of clarity but also … sculpted as it were with strength, and through clear impressions an apprehension [ἀντίληψις] of its properties is achieved.[51]

But from its beginnings, even in the first moments of birth, this is not the manner of representation, nor of perception [αἴσθησις], but rather *** [60] both being confused and employing a generic impression; and

τε τῇ τ[υπώσει χρώμεν]ος· καὶ μάλ᾽ εἰκότως· αὐτή τε γὰρ

[1a] .... θ ....
[1b] εὐνοητικῶς ἑαυτῳ το ζῷον

[VIII] ἡ ἐκτύπωσις ἔτι παχεῖα καὶ .... οὖσα τα
.... οὐκ ἰσχυράν· δεύτερον δὲ ..... σκαθ .
........μάτων διὰ τὴν σύγχυσιν ....στησις ἀτριβὴς καὶ ἀγύμναστος ως ... α ...σην τὸ αἰσθητὸν .... αὐτοῦ περιδράξασθαι ὡς ἀκριβῶς ἐντὸς γενέσθαι πραγμάτων· διὰ ταῦτα τοίνυν ἡ φαντασία ἀοριστώδης [μένει]. τηνικαῦτα η ....νυ... αἴσθησις ἀνὰ μέσον ἔχουσα καὶ δίχ[α ἐπιρρέπει ὡ]ς τοιάδε καὶ ὡς πρὸς τοιόνδε.

εἰκασίαις δὲ διαφόροις περὶ τούτου τοῦ συμβαίνοντος ἐμβαλοῦσι δύ᾽ ἄνδρες γενναῖοι τῆς αἱρέσεως, Χρύσιππός τε καὶ Κλεάνθης, ὧν ὁ μὲν Χρύσιππος ....

ἂν μέρος τι τῶν ἑαυτοῦ ....
μὲν γὰρ ἀλεεινὸν ....
. η σαρκινο .. η ....
....ερ δε ... αι πουση ετε[
. τούτων ἀοριστώδης ἥ τε φαντασία καὶ ἡ ἀντίληψις
. με ..υστ .....εται τὸν .... τὴν πρώτην
.....ν· ὁ δὲ .....εγα .... καθάπερ
γὰρ ....τυγχαν
..........................ωσιν τοῦ
...................................νεοττὸς
.... ενη .... ησ .ς ἰδέαν καὶ μορφὴν
..μ........πρὸς .... κατ᾽ ἀρχὰς ἡ
... φαντασία τε καὶ ἀντίληψις ὁλοσχερής τις
ἐστι .. δια .... καὶ ὡς ἔθος ἡμῖν ὀνομάζειν δ..
ο .κ ....τα ..ἐπὶ τοσον ....νο...
.... ἀοριστώδους ....α ..
.... α ....
.... εχ[
.... ε[
lines 31–37 wholly missing
οσ[
.... [
..δ ....
τησ .... [
μεν .... [

very plausibly: for [VIII] the same imprint, which is still thick and ... not strong. Secondly, then, ... because of its confusion ... without exercise and without practice... [5] the perceptible thing ... to grasp it so as to become inside things in a precise way. Because of this, then, the representation remains indefinite. At that time ... perception, being in an intermediate condition, tilts this way and that insofar as it is such-and-such and in relation to such-and-such a thing.[52]

Now, with different conjectures [εἰκασίαι] concerning this [10] event, two noble men of our sect, Chrysippus and Cleanthes, of whom the first, Chrysippus ...[53]

some part of one's own things ... for in the sun ... fleshy [15] ... of these, the representation is indefinite and the apprehension ... the first ... for just as .... [20] a baby bird ... idea and form ... at the beginning, the ... the representation and apprehension [ἀντίληψις] is somewhat generic [25] ... and, as it is our custom to name ... indefinite ... [30] ... [40] ...

[1b] "An animal being well-diposed toward itself"

σθ .... [
α .... [
ὁ αὐτὸς και .. [
..ιν...... [
.... αυ .... χεν
ἄρχειν ουσ .... ων ......
της με .... ουτης .....
αδ .... γεγενε ......ο
τηε .....φ ....ασυστη ... πρὸς
δὲ τὰ απ .... α .... ἄρχεται
ἑαυτ .... φ .... οἰκείων .....
τυγχαν .... οτι ... καὶ οι ..ν
τε .. λ .... σιν ... ταύτην ἀπο
.... δευτερ .... τῆς οἰκειώσεως
η .ωμεν .ν ...... ρια ... τεισιν
τ .α ....ἐνθυμηθῇ τι
ω .... οι οἰκειοῦται
καὶ .... οικε ....
.... γὰρ ω ....

[1a] τί τὸ τέλος

[IX] σωτηρίων τῆς συστάσεως .... . ιστ ... α ... οις καὶ ὅλοις γένεσι ... οἰκεῖον ... τι ἡ μὲν πρὸς ἑαυτὸ εὐνοητική, στερκτικὴ δὲ ἡ συγγενική· καλεῖται γὰρ ἡ οἰκείωσις πολλοῖς ὀνόμασιν. ἡ δὲ πρὸς τὰ ἐκτὸς χρήματα αἱρετική. καθάπερ οὖν στερκτικῶς μὲν καθόλου οἰκειούμεθα τοῖς τέκνοις, αἱρετικῶς δὲ τοῖς ἐκτὸς χρήμασιν, οὕτω καὶ τὸ ζῷον ἑαυτῷ μὲν εὐνοητικῶς, τοῖς δὲ πρὸς τήρησιν τῆς συστάσεως συμφέρουσιν ἐκλεκτικῶς ... ανη κοινὸν ....
μ‍ατος .. αισε ... σ ....ν ... ε ....
... να .... καὶ γὰρ ἡ μέν ἐστι κ........
.... κ ....την, ἡ δὲ πρὸς ....
... υ .. τ ...... ἀγωγήν πω ....
..θ ... οισ ...... σιτων ἐστιν .. μ ....
προ ...... ομεν ....
του .... προτ ....
ζη .... αστικ ....
σ[
.[
γει[
τογ[

[45] the same too … begin … [50] begins … itself … of its own … [55] this … second … of becoming one's own and familiar [οἰκείωσις] … consider something … if it makes its own … [60] and … for …

[IX] … of things that preserve one's constitution … and for all kinds … one's own … a becoming one's own and familiar [οἰκείωσις] toward oneself is [called] "well-disposed" [εὐνοητική], while that toward one's family is "loving" [στερκτική]; for becoming one's own and familiar is called [5] by many names: that toward external things is "by choice" [αἱρετική]. Just as, then, we generally make our children our own and familiar in a loving way, and with external things do so by choice, so too an animal does so in a well-disposed way in respect to itself and by way of a preferential selection [ἐκλεκτικῶς] toward those things that tend to the preservation of its constitution. [10] … common … for in fact one is … but the other, in respect to … a leading …[54]

[1a] "What the goal is"

[15] … is … [20–50] …

...ρ[
... μεν[
lines 31–37 wholly missing
.
..
[40] ....ων ....
δ .... ω ....
α ....
.
. .
[45] .
. .
.. ετοσ ....
... ιον ἑαυτ ....
.... ονδε....
[50] .... τ....
.... εὐαρεστ ....
........καὶ ....
οδ ...... ων .... ει....
....
[55] .... ντ ....
... ν .... το ....
.... ται ταῦται αἱ φύσεις ν ....
.... ω .... α ....
.... σε ....
[60] .... ο ....
....
[X] minuscule traces of approximately 24 lines
[47] .... ολ ...ιασε ....
.... ειν .. ν.............
.... τρ...........
[50] .... δε ταυ...........
.... υ .υ ....
.... ὀνομάζεται καὶ ..... ντης ....
.... τῆς ποιήσεως ....
.... π .. τινυτ............
[55?] .... ταμεν τῷ ....
.... ς ἀπορίαν ....
.... ἀπο ....

[IX] [55] … these natures … [X] … is named … of making … puzzle …

[1a] .φ....... αλ.......
[1b] ... σα .ο ...... ν ....

[XI] .... σι .... καὶ
.... στ .... α
.... ασ .ν ... ἐστι ... ο .λου .... δε
.... α ... φε .... χασ ......α
.... εσουδ ...... π ...τοι
...............λ ....
.... θ ....ισ ...το
...δ ....δ.........μ.........οι .... τρε
..............ο ......ε .. παραπ ....ο
.. τ .... εω .... υτων ..χόντων ...το γὰρ
παλι....κ ....η .... τοῦ τῆς πατρίδος
....καλῶ ....φως κ .... τῆς φύσεως
η ....ρισθαι λοι .... τον ὑπο
..η .. λε ......κ . αφωνια ....ον .... πρῶτον μὲν

ἐνθυμητέον ὅτι ἐσμὲν ζῷον, ἀλλὰ συναγελαστικὸν καὶ δεόμενον ἑτέρου· διὰ τοῦτο καὶ κατὰ πόλεις οἰκοῦμεν· οὐδεὶς γὰρ ἄνθρωπος ὃς οὐχὶ πόλεώς ἐστι μέρος· ἔπειτα ῥᾳδίως συντιθέμεθα φιλίας· ἐκ γὰρ τοῦ συνεστιαθῆναι ἢ τοῦ συγκαθίσαι ἐν θεάτρῳ ἢ εἰς τὸ αὐτὸ καταστῆναι [αἱ φιλίαι γιγνονται·] τὸ δὲ θαυμασιώτατον· πολλάκις γὰρ ...τουδ ...ε .... λαβόντες γὰρ παρὰ τῆς μάχης. ..δηλοῦσιν ....ν εὐνοίας κατα ....

no legible letters from lines 24–44

... κ ....
... προ ....ττο .
... ἀπο ....διδασκε
...................πρὸς ἄλλους
α .... σεως αο
... εσ .... αμησ
.... σανα
............υ .... αι φα
... ο ....
..δε .α. ο ....
..χενε .ε ....
.... αυτων .... καὶ τ ....
.... π.ν ...... λ ... μενου ...
.... αυτ ..... ν ..ε ...των . ξ ...α
..............απ ..
.... μ ..... ξ .....ταδε

[XI] … and … [5] … [10] … for the … of one's country … of nature … first, [15] it is necessary to consider that we are an animal, but a sociable one and in need of others. Because of this we dwell in cities: for there is no human being who is not part of a city. Then, we easily form friendships; for from having dined together or having sat together in the theater or having been in the same situation, [20] friendships arise. And this is the most wondrous of all: for often … for having taken from a battle … they manifest … goodwill … by power … [25–45] … teach … toward others … [50–60] …[55]

.... ε .....τῳ[56]

[1a] ει αι

[XII] ....
.... ων ἀρχῆς[
.... τῶν λοιπῶν[
τατων ἐν ἡμ[
τοῖς αλ .ν[
.αντων περιτ[
κενῶς ὕλη[
ως ἐνταῦθα[
δὸν ἔτεμε[
αις ἔτι καὶ τ[
τοῖς φιλοσόφ[οις
δὲ μία μὲν φύσ[ις
ἀντίπραξιν [
τὸν ἀκαρῆ δ[
μένη τὴν κατάλυσι[ν
ἔχουσα καὶ προσκα[
ἀνατεταμένη [
μὴ καλῶν ὡς ἀγ[........... μεγα—]
λόψυχον καὶ κατ[
τοτε τῶν πράξεων[
τι καὶ λαμπηδ[
κατε αἰρῶ ηα[
σ ..ασμοστε[
ἀλλ' οὖν ...οσ[
.....λ ..ω[
no legible letters from lines 26–35
[36] κω[
μεν[.
μεν[
...τε τέχνης α[
...ω ἵνα μὲν οδο[
καὶ τοῦ βουλήματ[ος
η ... γασαμε τ[
ν..... τέρου[
μ .... οδ[

[XII] … beginning … of the rest … in … [5] vainly … here … [10] philosophers … one nature … resistance … the tiny … [15] dissolution … having … lifted up … not fine … high-spirited and … [20] of the actions … brilliance … I take … but … [25–35] of skill [40] so that … and of the intention ….

η ....[
αὐτὴ τονα ..[
εὑρεθῆναι δ .. [............. ἀν—]
θρώπων καὶ ..το .[
κατεσκεύασεν[
κρωματ ...[
ηφ ....[
ως τέλος ....[
το προσενθυμητέ[ον
τὸ τέλος ἡμῖν κ[
τέλος καὶ ....ατ[
δ' ἐπίνοιαν .ν .[
ου ἐπειδὴ καὶ[
κρατιστ[
βαλεῖν ....[
.τησεπ ....[
σιως ορχησ .[

... it ... discovered ... human beings and ... prepared ... ... end ... the end for us must be considered further ... end and ... by thought ... since also ... strongest ... [pro]ject ... ...

Elements of Ethics: Commentary

1. Greek ἠθικῆς στοιχειώσεως: another Stoic, Eudromus, probably in the second century A.D. (see Hans Friedrich August von Arnim, "Eudromos," PW 6.1:950), had written a work with this title, as Diogenes Laertius, *Vit. phil.* 7.39, attests. From the context there it appears that he discussed the division of philosophy and the order of its three parts, which he listed as logic first, then physics, and ethics third; evidently this treatise was an "elementary" account in the sense of "basic" rather than "simple" (see Reale, *Diogene Laerzio*, 767–69 and notes). Von Arnim translated the Greek title as *Ethische Elementarlehre* and explained (xiii) that the title may be understood as meaning not a simple overview of ethics as a whole but rather an exposition of the elements of ethics in the sense of the basics. Margherita Isnardi Parente ("Ierocle," esp. 2203) renders it as *Elementi di dottrina etica*; Bastianini and Long, the editors whose text I follow, give *Elementi di etica* and explain (*CPF* 1.1.2:286) that it consists of an account and proof, point for point, of the principles of ethics according to Stoic doctrine. For the use of στοιχείωσις and related terms in Stoicism and in Greek philosophy, see Hermann Diels, *Elementum: Eine Vorarbeit zum griechischen und lateinischen Thesaurus* (Leipzig: Teubner, 1899); 8, 38 and 46; Diskin Clay, *Lucretius and Epicurus* (Ithaca: Cornell University Press, 1983), 55–72. On the various forms of philosophical texts in the time of Hierocles, see Pier Luigi Donini, "Testi e commenti, manuali e insegnamento: la forma sistematica e i metodi della filosofia in età post-ellenistica," *ANRW* 36.7:5027–5100.

In the papyrus, in the line following the title, there appears θεός, "god," perhaps an augural formula placed at the beginning, as is found occasionally in Greek epigraphs, whether as θεός or as θεοί. See Robert L. Pounder, "The Origin of θεοί as Inscription-Heading," in *Studies Presented to Sterling Dow on His Eightieth Birthday* (ed. Alan L. Boegehold; Durham, N.C.: Duke University, 1984), 243–50; Bastianini and Long, *CPF* 1.1.2:274, support this hypothesis with additional arguments.

2. That the *πρῶτον οἰκεῖον*, the "first thing that is one's own"—that is, what a being senses to be most proper and most familiar to itself—is the highest ethical principle, as Hierocles repeats in I.35–37, is a thesis that undoubtedly derives from Chrysippus:

> They say that an animal has its first impulse in the direction of preserving itself, since nature adapts it to itself from the beginning; this according to what Chrysippus says in book 1 of *On Ends*, where he says that for every animal what is first its own [πρῶτον οἰκεῖον] is its constitution [σύστασις] and its consciousness of its constitution.... What remains, then, is to affirm that [nature] has constituted it to make it [sc. the animal] its own and familiar to itself, for thus it avoids harmful things and pursues those that are proper to it. (*SVF* 3.178:43, from Diogenes Laertius, *Vit. phil.* 7.85)

For the phrase *πρῶτον οἰκεῖον*, see also Stobaeus, *Anth.* 2.7.3c (2:47,12 Wachsmuth and Hense), discussed in Pembroke, "*Oikeiôsis*," 114–149, esp. 116 and 141 n. 8; also *SVF* 3.183:44 (from Alexander of Aphrodisias, *An.* 150.25): "Indeed, the question of what is first our own [πρῶτον οἰκεῖον] has been investigated by philosophers, and not all have had the same view.... The Stoics, though not all, say that an animal is first own [πρῶτον οἰκεῖον] to itself: for every animal, as soon as it exists, is adapted [or appropriated] to itself, and especially human beings." For the doctrine of οἰκείωσις see the introductory essay above, with relevant bibliography, and Radice, *Oikeiôsis*, esp. 189–95 for the doctrine as it appears in Hierocles. Alongside this Old Stoic doctrine we find inserted here a treatment of embryology and of the primary attributes of animals, introduced by the expression "to begin further back," which by its position seems to be an original contribution by Hierocles, according to Bastianini and Long (*CPF* 1.1.2:368), although in many respects it goes back to Stoic doctrines, as we shall see. Hierocles' discussion of embryology is longer than any other testimonies on the subject, which are included under *SVF* 2.804–808 (with the addition of the passages adduced by F. W. Kohnke, "Γαστὴρ ἐργαστήριον φύσεως: Ein Chrysippzitat," *Hermes* 93 [1965]: 383–84), and it differs from these above all in the emphasis that is placed on the goal of the process, which extends from conception to birth, as is clear from I.9–11 and 14–15 (see Bastianini and Long, 1.1.2:370).

3. For the Stoic doctrines on the seed and the forms of conception, see Pseudo-Galen's *De optima secta ad Thrasybulum liber* in Karl Gottlob Kühn, *Claudii Galeni opera omnia* (20 vols.; Leipzig: Knobloch, 1821–33), 19:165; Aristotle, *Hist. an.* 8.4, 583b29; and *SVF* 2.741–751.

4. On the Stoic notion that it is the paternal seed that instigates the entire developmental process of the new creature, see *SVF* 2.743: "for them [the Stoics], the seed is the very craftsman: according to some, it is the entire seed, while for others it is the *pneuma* contained in it." Hierocles indeed maintains that the *pneuma* is that into which the seed is transformed (see *Elements* I.10–15, where the transformation of the seed into *pneuma* is mentioned).

5. The process systematically organized by the *pneuma* into which the seed is transformed is a close echo of the Old Stoic definition of *pneuma* as "the productive fire that proceeds systematically toward creation" (*SVF* 2.1027): the phrase ὁδῷ κινούμενον in Hierocles is analogous to the Old Stoic ὁδῷ βαδίζων; so too the Stoic connection between *pneuma* and seminal reasons (λόγοι σπερματικοί) recalls the identification of *pneuma* as an advanced stage of the paternal seed, precisely in its creative function.

6. That the fetus in the pregnant woman, before it is born, is characterized simply by the term φύσις, as though it were merely a vegetable and without a soul (unlike a complete animal), is a doctrine that goes back, in general terms and also in many specifics, to Chrysippus *SVF* 2.806 (see the notes below for more on the implications of this text):

> He believes that the fetus in the womb is naturally nourished like a plant. But when it is born, the *pneuma*, cooled [ψυχόμενον] and tempered by the air, changes and becomes an animal: thus it is not inappropriate that it is called soul [ψυχή] in relation to cooling [ψύξις].... (2) He says that the soul is produced when the fetus is born, as the *pneuma* changes because of cooling, as if by tempering.... (3) The Stoics say that *pneuma* in the bodies of fetuses is tempered by cooling and that as it changes from a "nature" [φύσις] it becomes a soul.... (4) The *pneuma* yields the soul itself ... when, by cooling and, as it were, immersion in the air, it is kindled or tempered.

As we see, Chryippus shows that the transformation of the φύσις of the fetus into a soul is the result of a process of the cooling of the former—which the Stoics explained as a consequence of the first inhalation of air on the part of the newborn infant (Tieleman, "Diogenes of Babylon and Stoic Embryology," 106–25, esp. 117–22). This change seems only implicit in the treatise of Hierocles, who speaks of the "toughening" of the soul by the environment, without explicitly stating that this happens because of cooling; according to *SVF* 2.787, the Stoics held that the *pneuma* of the φύσις was colder and more humid that that of the ψυχή, but the fetal φύσις was probably imagined as hot, given that it cools off precisely in

order to become ψυχή. The point is attested also in *SVF* 2.805, in which we find exactly the same metaphor of tempering ("like incandescent iron immersed in cold water") that is used by Hierocles. From this it is clear that cooling was implicit in the idea of tempering. Thus too *SVF* 2.756–757: "The Stoics say that it [the embryo] is part of the belly, and not an animal [ζῷον]. For just as fruits are parts of the plants [φυτά] and fall off only when they are ripe, so too the embryo"; "They say that [the embryo] is not an animal but is nourished and grows like trees [δένδρα]: they do not have impulses and aversions as animals do." For the Stoic assimilation of the embryo to a plant, see also Long, "Soul and Body in Stoicism," 34–57, esp. 43–44. It is worth noting that Hierocles reaches back to Old Stoicism when he adopts the theory that φύσις in fetuses is transformed into ψυχή. For, in Middle Stoicism, Panaetius had abandoned this notion, probably because—as Teun Tieleman supposes—he assimilated the physiological side of reproduction to the processes of digestion and growth (Tieleman, "Panaetius' Place," 105–42, esp. 129). For a comparison with other, non-Stoic embryologies, such as that of Aristotle (who also considered the active life of a fetus in the womb to be similar to that of a plant) and Galen, see Bastianini and Long, 371–73. See also Galen, *Foet. form.* 6 (Kühn, *Claudii Galeni opera omnia*, 4:700), who assimilates the Stoic φύσις, which is characteristic of fetuses before they become ψυχαί, to Aristotle's vegetative soul and Plato's appetitive soul, although he is well aware that the Stoic φύσις is not soul. As for the expression in I.20, "arrives at the exit" (θύραζε), this may be at the basis of a curious misunderstanding on the part of Aetius (*Placita* 4.5.11), who ascribes to Cleanthes the doctrine that the soul is introduced into the body "by the door" (θύραθεν; noted in *SVF* 1.523; Isnardi, "Ierocle," 2203 n. 11).

7. See *SVF* 3.370:90: "For if a *pneuma* pervades even stones and plants, so as to unite us with them, there is nevertheless no justice for us toward plants and stones, nor do we do wrong when we cut and saw such kinds of bodies"; and above all Chrysippus again, from Galen: "According to the ancients there are two *pneuma*s: the psychic [ψυχικόν] and the natural [φυσικόν]. But the Stoics introduce a third, the cohesive [ἐκτικόν], which they call 'cohesion' [ἕξις]." "There is a double form of connatural *pneuma*: the natural and the psychic; but there are those who introduce a third, the cohesive. The cohesive [ἐκτικόν] *pneuma* is that which holds stones together; the natural [φυσικόν] *pneuma* is that which makes animals and plants grow; and the psychic [ψυχικόν] *pneuma*, in the case of animated creatures, makes animals able to perceive and to move with every kind of motion" (*SVF* 2.716).

8. There was a widespread belief, from which Hierocles distances himself, that newborn bears were shapeless and that their mothers licked them into shape: see Aristotle, *Hist. an.* 6.30, 579a24; Aelian, *Nat. an.* 2.19; Pliny the Elder, *Nat.* 8.126; Sextus Empiricus, *Pyr.* 1.42; Arthur L. Peck, *Aristotle: Historia Animalium IV–VI* (LCL; Cambridge: Harvard University Press, 1970), 376. In line 29 I take account of the improvement in the text adopted in *CPF* 4.1:viii of ὡς δή to οὕτω δὲ δή.

9. Characterizing "animal" by means of perception and impulse is in conformity with the orthodox Stoic line. However, it seems peculiar to Hierocles to leave aside impulse at the beginning of the discussion of the πρῶτον οἰκεῖον (which ends at VI.51–53), according to which an animal, when it acquires the first perception of itself, suddenly becomes "adapted" (or "appropriated") to itself and to its constitution—a conclusion perfectly in accord with Stoic tradition; see Diogenes Laertius, *Vit. phil.* 7.85 (in Reale, *Diogene Laerzio*, 808–9 and my nn. 178–79); Cicero, *Fin.* 3.4.16. Nevertheless, another peculiarity of Hierocles lies in the role that perception assumes in his argument; see Bastianini and Long, 379.

The argument is articulated in five stages: (1) animals perceive themselves (I.51–III.54); (2) they perceive themselves continually (III.54–V.38); (3) they perceive immediately upon being born (V.38–VI.24); (4) they are favorably disposed toward themselves and toward the representation of themselves right from birth (VI.24–49); (5) finally, certain behaviors confirm that animals love themselves (VI.53–VII.50). On the last point, see Brunschwig, "The Cradle Argument," esp. 130–40. For a comparison with the parallel treatments in Seneca, *Ep.* 121.4; Diogenes Laertius, *Vit. phil.* 7.85; and Cicero, *Fin.* 3.4.16, see Bastianini and Long, 381–85, who, distancing themselves in this from Brad Inwood, show that Hierocles' argumentation is similar to that elaborated in these parallel sources, even if it proceeds in a different order, beginning with the self-perception of animals from birth and deducing from this the thesis of οἰκείωσις, which Hierocles then confirms empirically by means of behavior in animals that demonstrates self-love. The importance of sense perception (αἴσθησις) to the proof of οἰκείωσις in Stoic thought is indicated by Plutarch, *Stoic. rep.* 1038C (*SVF* 2.724): "appropriation [οἰκείωσις] seems to be the perception and apprehension [αἴσθησις, ἀντίληψις] of what is one's own [οἰκεῖον]"; and by Porphyry, *Abst.* 3.19 (*SVF* 1.197): "perception [αἰσθάνεσθαι] is the principle of every appropriation [οἰκείωσις]." Bastianini and Long (385) maintain that Hierocles, omitting impulse and privileging perception in his proof of οἰκείωσις, did not separate himself significantly from the tradition but rather adhered to the basic Stoic line that, from Chrysip-

pus onward, considered self-perception and not impulse as the basis of οἰκείωσις. But see Inwood, "Hierocles," 155–56. Inwood maintains that Hierocles was substantially faithful to Chrysippus's theories and ready to defend them against criticizers, although he was more than a simple divulger and was capable of innovations of his own.

10. The doctrine of self-perception, which is developed in practically all that remains of the present work by Hierocles, could not be maintained for the prenatal existence of an animal as well, and least not by a Stoic, since Stoicism, or at least the Old Stoa, which Hierocles, as I have mentioned, follows here, assimilated the fetus in the womb to a plant—characterized by φύσις alone, by mere nature and not by a soul—rather than to an animal: only at the moment of birth is its vital principle transformed into ψυχή or soul, which is what makes it an animal; the fundamental perceptive trait of the soul had already been stipulated by Zeno, when he defined it as αἰσθητικὴ ἀναθυμίασις, "a perceptive exhalation" (*SVF* 1.141). That, in Hierocles' time, the question whether the fetus that is formed in the mother's womb is already animal was being debated seems confirmed by the discussion of this doxographical issue already in Pseudo-Plutarch, *Plac. philos.* 907C. See Jaap Mansfeld, "Doxography and Dialectic: The Sitz im Leben of the 'Placita,'" *ANRW* 36.4:3186–90; Tieleman, "Diogenes of Babylon," 106–25.

11. Rightly Bastianini and Long, 390–91, who show how the two groups of "slow people" of whom Hierocles speaks respectively at I.39 and 42 must be kept distinct. The first "slow people," in fact, who are perhaps to be identified with Antiochus of Ascalon and his followers in the Academy, believe only that self-perception begins for the animal immediately after birth; the second group of "slow people," perhaps the Peripatetics of whom Stobaeus speaks at *Anth.* 2.7.13–26 (2:116,19–152,25 Wachsmuth and Hense), must, however, be persuaded that sensibility in animals is directed not only toward external objects but also toward themselves. In respect to the first group, that there was a difference of opinion between the Academics of Antiochus and the Stoics concerning immediate self-perception is proved by Cicero, *Fin.* 5.9.24–27 on animals, and Seneca, *Ep.* 121, since Antiochus believed that self-perception, which he called "self-awareness," was a faculty that developed gradually (*Fin.* 5.15.41). See Inwood, "Hierocles," 173–77; Giusta, "Antioco di Ascalona," 29–49; Prost, "L'éthique d'Antiochus d'Ascalon," 244–68. As for the second group of "slow people," the belief that animal sensibility is directed only toward external things is not found in Aristotle himself so much as in some commentators on him, for example, Philoponus in his commentary on the treatise

De an. 417a2: "the object of perception [αἰσθητόν] is external." Of course, Hierocles does not explicitly identify his opponents, nor does he discuss the reasons and purposes of their positions; on this, see von Arnim, *Ethische Elementarlehre*, xxi–xxii, who criticizes a certain "superficiality" in Hierocles and an ignorance of the technique of refutation. According to Badalamenti ("Ierocle stoico," 53–97), the emphasis that Hierocles places on the priority of self-perception in relation to the perception of external things might be due to an antiskeptical thrust.

12. Hierocles begins to prove empirically that animals have self-perception (that is, perception of all their bodily parts and of the soul in relation to the body). Passages by other Stoics proceed in the same way, emphasizing the interest that animals evince in the parts of their own bodies; see Cicero, *Fin.* 2.5.17; Seneca, *Ep.* 121.6–8.

There are four stages to the argument: (1) Hierocles first shows, in the passage under analysis, that animals perceive their own parts and their respective functions; (2) he shows that animals are aware of the weapons that nature has given them for their self-defense; (3) he shows that they perceive which of the parts that constitute their bodies are strong and which are weak (II.18–III.19); and (4) he shows that they perceive which are the strong points and which the weak points of the animals that are their enemies, and which animals represent a danger for them (III.19–54). With this Hierocles refutes the second group of "slow people" (on whom see the preceding notes), who maintained that the perceptive faculty of animals was directed exclusively to external things and not also to themselves; he will next refute the first group.

In connection with συναίσθησις, which I have translated as "self-conscious (or conscious) perception," we may note, with Bastianini and Long (295, 399–400), that the terminology employed by Hierocles is nevertheless not exceedingly rigid, and often the verbs αἰσθάνομαι, συναισθάνομαι, ἀντιλαμβάνομαι, and the substantives derived from them (αἴσθησις, συναίσθησις, ἀντίληψις), are used as synonyms.

13. This is the second proof that animals have self-perception; see the preceding notes. This second proof is based on the perception, on the part of animals, of the weapons of self-defense that are native to them and congenital. That these are congenital weapons and not just chance is important for Hierocles, since his argument aims to prove οἰκείωσις, and so it turns on what is proper or "own" to the animal by nature. See the formulation in Aelian, *Nat. an.* 9.40: "Every animal knows in which part it has its strength, and it has confidence in this, and when it attacks it uses it as a weapon, but when it is in danger as defense."

14. The example of bulls is one that, in Hierocles' time, was a particular favorite of Epictetus; see, for example, his *Diss.* 3.1.22; 22.6; 22.99.

15. This is the third proof that animals perceive themselves; see the preceding notes. It is the longest of the proofs, but, like the rest, it consists simply of a series of empirical examples. Bastianini and Long (404), however, stress the importance of the present demonstration, insofar as, "in proving that animals have perception of their strengths and their weaknesses, Hierocles connects self-perception with the capacity to evaluate one's own environment in terms of safety and danger (see that argument at III.19–54), and in this way he prepares the ground for the following proof that what primarily concerns an animal (τὸ πρῶτον οἰκεῖον) is its own self-preservation." A little earlier, in II.13, I adopt the correction, recorded by Bastianini and Long in *CPF* 4.1:viii, of ἀνάξιον to ἀπάξιον: the meaning "unworthy of" remains unchanged.

16. Hierocles' terminology, alongside that pertaining to perception or sensation, presents some items that appear to be new in connection with cognition and knowledge, here in II.27 as again in II.39, 41, 52, 53, 55; III.5–6, 12–13. According to Bastianini and Long (404), however, the words καταγιγνώσκω, μὴ ἀγνοέω are not clearly differentiated from terms indicating perception, such as αἰσθάνομαι, συναισθάνομαι, and ἀντιλαμβάνομαι.

17. For credence in this story about bears, see Pliny the Elder, *Nat.* 8.130: "the weakest part of the bear is its head … which is why if bears are forced of necessity to hurl themselves off a cliff, they do so covering their heads with their paws." In II.32, the reading κατὰ with unmarked *kappa* is corrected by Bastianini and Long in *CPF* 4.1:ix, where the *kappa* is marked as uncertain: the translation, of course, remains unchanged, but in II.33–34, in the same place, the reading ὑπάγουσα τὴν κεφαλήν has disappeared and what remains is just ἀσφαλῶς, which is why I have put in brackets (with the addition of a question mark) the translation proposed in the previous edition. A little later, in II.37, in the same location in the line, an editorial change is again proposed, this time minimal, however, and not affecting the translation: in πόσον, the final *nu* is given simply as an uncertain letter, whereas in *CPF* 1.1.2 it was presented as certain.

18. For this belief concerning beavers, see also Aelian, *Nat. an.* 6.34; Pliny the Elder, *Nat.* 8.109; both texts insist as well, like Hierocles, on the beaver's knowledge of the reason why it is being pursued by hunters; see also Aesop, *Fab.* 153; Apuleius, *Metam.* 1.9; Horapollo, *Hier.* 2.65.

19. This is the fourth proof of the thesis that animals perceive themselves, and it consists of the fact that they have perception of the strong

points and weak points in others. This fact is criticized as nonprobative by von Arnim, *Ethische Elementarlehre*, xxi, whereas Bastianini and Long, 408, defend Hierocles' argumentation, observing that it is necessary to connect the first part of his claim, that concerning the perception of the capacities of other animals, with the second part, which turns on the perception of hostile or friendly animals, since the perception on the part of an animal of the capacities of another animal immediately implies self-perception, given that the strong and weak points of the other animal are not perceived in themselves but always in relation to the "self" of the perceiving subject.

20. The text is lacunose. For the ichneumon, a mammal, see Nicander, *Ther.* 190; Aelian, *Nat. an.* 3.22; 6.38; Isidore, *Etym.* 12.2.37. Its name derives from ἰχνεύω, "to track," for it sought out the eggs of crocodiles. It was venerated by the ancient Egyptians precisely for this reason. For military terminology applied to the ichneumon, see Plutarch, *Soll. an.* 966D; also Nicander, *Ther.* 200–208; Pliny the Elder, *Nat.* 8.87; Aristotle, *Hist. an.* 9.6, 612a15. See also Jacques Aymard, "La querelle du cobra et de la mangouste dans l'antiquité," *Mélanges de l'École Française de Rome* 71 (1959) : 227–62, with analysis of the ancient literary and iconographical evidence. The ancient and modern synonyms of "ichneumon" are investigated by D. Martínková, "Neomon," *Zpravy Jednoty Klassickych Filologuring* 9 (1967): 1–4; a recent archaeological and faunistic study is Lorenza Campanella and Barbara Wilkens, "Una mangusta egiziana ('Herpestes ichneumon') dall'abitato fenicio di Sant'Antioco," *Rivista di Studi Fenici* 32 (2004): 25–48.

21. See Seneca, *Ep.* 121.19: "Why do chicks fear a cat but not a dog?" Von Arnim (*Ethische Elementarlehre*, xxi–xxii) aptly discusses the present passage in Hierocles and the epistle of Seneca, which in the section immediately preceding the sentence just quoted, runs: "'How,' he says, 'can a newborn animal have knowledge of whether a thing is safe or lethal?' The first thing to inquire is whether it knows, not how it knows. That they have knowledge is evident from the fact that they would do nothing additional if they did know. Why is it that a hen does not flee a peacock or a goose but does flee a falcon, which is so much smaller and not even known to it?" Note that the argument deals with empirical behavior, just as in Hierocles, and note too the example of the falcon, which again is the same as in Hierocles.

22. Having finished the refutation of the second group of "slow people," now that he has proved that all animals have self-perception, Hierocles proceeds to the refutation of the first group of "slow people,"

proving from this point up to V.41 that animals have self-perception continually from their birth. The proof here does not consist any longer of a series of empirical examples, such as we have seen in the preceding section, but has rather the form of a theoretical argument focusing on the constant interaction between body and soul; only toward the end will there be an empirical illustration of the fact that self-perception is uninterrupted, even in sleep.

For the argument that follows, relative to the reciprocal ties between body and soul, see von Arnim, *Ethische Elementarlehre*, xxi–xxviii; Inwood, "Hierocles," 161–64; Bastianini and Long, 409ff. In itself, the psychological doctrine expounded by Hierocles derives from Chrysippus and finds many parallels in other Stoic sources; nevertheless, there are not lacking some aspects peculiar to Hierocles. The structure of the argument seems due to him: he proves that animals have self-perception continually on the basis of four premises: (1) the soul is corporeal and tangible and able to exert and undergo pressure (III.56–IV.3); (2) body and soul are completely mixed with one another (IV.3–22); (3) the soul is a perceptive faculty (IV.22–27); and (4) soul and body participate in tensive movement (IV.27–38).

23. This is the first premise of the argument dedicated to demonstrating continual self-perception on the part of animals (see the preceding notes). The tangibility and graspability of the soul are necessary properties of any body, according to the Stoics; see Cicero, *Acad. pr.* 39; Nemesius of Emesa, *Nat. hom.* 78.7–79.2. For III.56, in *CPF* 4.1:ix, Bastianini and Long add μὲν between πρῶτον and τοίνυν; the translation is not affected. In III.58 they no longer read οὖν, "therefore," but ἐστί.

24. The inclusion of the soul among corporeal entities is typical of Stoic materialism, as it is also of Epicureanism, both of which are opposed to the dualism of immanence and transcendence that is the basis of Platonic metaphysics; the latter locates the soul among immaterial, intelligible entities. The materiality of the soul is well-attested as early as Zeno, particularly in *SVF* 1.137–139, and also in 1.134–136, where the soul is defined as fire and *pneuma*, given that the latter is conceived of as corporeal by the Stoics. The opposition between the Platonic view and that of the Stoics in respect to the soul and its metaphysical or physical status is explicit in *SVF* 1.136, from Galen: "Some, like Plato, maintained that its [sc. the soul's] substance was incorporeal, but others, like Zeno and his followers, said that it moves bodies. For they supposed too that the soul was *pneuma*," on which see Jaap Mansfeld, "Some Stoics on the Soul (*SVF* I 136)," *Mnemosyne* 37 (1984): 443–45. For the Stoic view that only material entities exist, see, e.g., Jacques Brunschwig, "Stoic Metaphysics,"

in Inwood, *Cambridge Companion to the Stoics*, 206–32; Michael J. White, "Stoic Natural Philosophy (Physics and Cosmology)," in Inwood, *Cambridge Companion to the Stoics*, 124–52. The "reasons" mentioned in what follows are Stoic doctrines.

25. For the sense of the verbs προσβάλλειν, ἀντιπροσβάλλεσθαι, συνερείδειν, and ἀντερείδειν, see von Arnim, *Ethische Elementarlehre*, xxvii. For IV.1, in *CPF* 4.1:ix Bastianini and Long no longer read οἷον but rather καί; thus the translation too changes from "of touch, as I have said, like pressure" to "of touch, as I have said, and of pressure." The difference in meaning is that "touch" is distinct from "pressure," whereas in the earlier version pressure was a subspecies of touch.

26. This is the second premise of the argument intending to prove continual self-perception on the part of animals; at the end Hierocles illustrates this premise with cases of bodily affects that involve the soul and emotions that have a reflex in the body. The doctrine of the complete mixture of soul and body (κρᾶσις δι' ὅλου) was already espoused by Chrysippus, according to Alexander of Aphrodisias (*SVF* 2.473; see also 2.471–472, 474), for Chryippus distinguished simple mingling from fusion and explained the mixture of body and soul as follows:

> the soul, although it has its own subsistence, just as the body that contains it does, pervades the entire body, and yet in the mixture with it it preserves its own substance; for there is no part of a body possessing soul that is without a share in soul. The nature of plants is similar, and also the cohesion in those things that are held together by cohesion [i.e., stones and the like].

The refutation of the idea that the soul is contained in the body καθάπερ ἐν ἀγγείῳ ("as in a bucket or container") is characteristic of Old Stoicism: οὐδὲ ὡς ἐν ἀγγείῳ ("but not as in a bucket"), as Alexander of Aphrodisias attests as well in *An.* 115.32 (*SVF* 2.797). For a comparison between Hierocles' view of the connection between soul and body and that of the Old Stoa, see the discussion in von Arnim, *Ethische Elementarlehre*, xxiii–xxiv. The definition of "mixture" (κρᾶσις) in Old Stoicism is examined by Jaap Mansfeld, "Zeno and Aristotle on Mixture," *Mnemosyne* 36 (1983): 306–10. See also §3 in the introductory essay above, with further documentation.

27. For this example, see Alexander of Aphrodisias, *Mixt.* 218.1–2 (*SVF* 2.473 [p. 155, lines 30ff.]): "But they also say that fire as a whole penetrates the whole of iron, although each preserves its own substance." See also *SVF* 2.475 (p. 156, lines 16ff.):

> The same argument [holds] concerning the principles, god, the unification of the cosmos and its sympathetic interaction with itself. For god pervading matter is all these things for them. This claim, that a body penetrates throughout a body, on which the plausibility of practically their entire physical theory depends, although it is affirmed contrary to common intuitions [προλήψεις] and to the doctrines of all other philosophers, gains confirmation for them from the fact, as though it were self-evident, that when (they say) iron is fired it is not ignited and made to burn like those things on whose matter fire feeds, but rather (they suppose) the fire pervades all of it, together with that matter which the fire, when it is upon it and has neared the iron, heats and ignites [i.e., the iron].

28. In *CPF* 4.1:ix Bastianini and Long correct the reading in the previous edition λύπαις καὶ φόβοις (IV.16) to λύπαις φόβοις τε; the translation remains practically unchanged, except for a tighter coordination between the two terms.

29. Margites is the protagonist of a poem of the same name attributed to Homer, which Aristotle, *Poet.* 4, considered the forerunner of comedy, whereas the *Iliad* and the *Odyssey* were the precursors of tragedy. Margites represents the fool by antonomasia, who is nevertheless clever enough, in his way; he returns in VI.44.

This is the third premise of the argument designed to prove continual self-perception on the part of animals: the soul is a δύναμις αἰσθητική, a "perceptive faculty." Von Arnim (*Ethische Elementarlehre*, xxiv) observes that, strictly speaking, this was not so for the Old Stoa; it was not a faculty or power but rather a corporeal entity (as noted above in n. 24) endowed with faculties: "It is not at all a *dynamis* but a substantial and corporeal entity that, on the one hand, possesses different properties as qualities, on the other hand, parts": see *SVF* 2.826.1–2:

> The followers of Chrysippus and Zeno and all those who believe that the soul is a body treat its faculties as though they were qualities [ποιότητες] in the substrate and posit the soul as the substance that underlies the faculties. … There is a single mode of their presence [sc. of soul and body], which is in participation or in mixture with the entire animal [κεκρᾶσθαι τῷ ὅλῳ ζῴῳ]. How, then, are they distinguished? According to the Stoics, some mixtures are distinguished by a difference in the underlying bodies. For they say that the *pneuma*s extend from the *hêgemonikon* to various items, some to the eyes, some to the ears, some to the other senses. Some mixtures, in turn, are distinguished by the individual quality [ποιότης] of their substrate: for just as an apple has sweetness and

fragrance in the same body, so too the *hêgemonikon* gathers together in the same body representation, assent, impulse, and reason.

Now, that the soul is a perceptive faculty is a premise that Hierocles considers to be self-evident and that is accordingly not demonstrated. What interests Hierocles in connection with the present proof is the presupposition that this perceptive faculty extends to every point via the distribution of the soul throughout the body. That is why the soul, thanks to its contact with the body in its entirety, "makes of the entire organism a sensitive field whose various conditions are registered in the soul" (Bastianini and Long, 415). This point will be made again in the summary at IV.45–52 and has a clear Old Stoic ancestry, above all in Chrysippus: see *SVF* 2.879:

> The soul, he [Chrysippus] says, is found to be divided into eight parts: for it consists of the ruling part, the five senses, the vocal faculty and the power of inseminating the procreating. Further, the parts of the soul, as though from a fountainhead, flow from their seat in the heart and extend *to the entire body*, and fill all its members everywhere with vital spirit [i.e., *pneuma*].... The *entire* soul, extending from its ruling part [i.e., *hêgemonikon*] as from a tree trunk, opens up the senses, which are its instruments, like branches.... Just as the spider, in the middle of its web, holds the tips of all the threads in its feet, so that it immediately perceives when any tiny animal falls into its trap from any direction, so too the ruling part of the soul, located in its seat in the middle of the heart, holds the tips of the senses, so that it recognizes from close up when they announce anything.

See also *SVF* 2.836:

> From the *hêgemonikon* seven parts of the soul grow out and extend to the body like the tentacles of an octopus. Of the seven parts of the soul, five are the senses.... Vision is *pneuma* extending from the *hêgemonikon* to the eyes; hearing is *pneuma* extending from the *hêgemonikon* to the ears; smell is *pneuma* extending from the *hêgemonikon* to the nostrils; taste is *pneuma* extending from the *hêgemonikon* to the tongue; and touch is *pneuma* extending from the *hêgemonikon* to the surface, for the readily perceptive feeling of what lands on it. Of the rest, one is said to be seed, which itself is *pneuma* extending from the *hêgemonikon* to the testicles; the part called "vocal" by Zeno ... is *pneuma* extending from the *hêgemonikon* to the throat, tongue, and related organs.

On pereception and impulse as faculties that distinguish the soul from mere φύσις, which is characteristic of plants, see what Hierocles says at I.13–33. Programmatically, Hierocles set himself only the topic of perception and not that of impulse, as the object of his discussion; we have seen that this decision was not, in reality, a departure from the strictures of the Stoics.

30. This is the fourth premise of the argument intended to demonstrate continual self-perception on the part of animals: tensive movement—that is, the internal movement that confers cohesiveness on an individual creature—is a property of soul and body. See *SVF* 2.407, where the cohesive force is attributed to tension (*τόνος συνεκτικός*, "the tension that holds something together"). According to von Arnim (*Ethische Elementarlehre*, xxiv and note to IV.38), because the three preceding premises do not in fact prove that an animal has self-perception in a way that is strictly continuous, this aspect was probably to be found in the present, fourth premise, which is lacunose in the papyrus (see xxiv–xxvi). Bastianini and Long (418–19) are unsure whether continuity was treated in these lost bits; however, they remark that Hierocles could count in any case on Old Stoic theory, for which "the continuous, double course of cohesiveness is imperishable [ἄφθαρτος]" (*SVF* 2.458): the course is double since the cohesiveness "is *pneuma* which turns back on itself: for it begins from the middle and extends to the limits [of the body], and when it touches the extreme surface it turns back again, until it comes back to the same place from which it first was launched" (ibid.). For IV.28, Bastianini and Long emend *τὰ λεγόμενα* to *τὰ παρόντα*, "the discourse" to "the present considerations" (*CPF* 4.1:ix).

31. The location of the *hêgemonikon* in the chest is Chrysippean; see, for example, *SVF* 3.33:217 (under Diogenes of Babylon: "Chrysippus says that the *hêgemonikon* is in the chest"); see also the documentation in Teun L. Tieleman, *Galen and Chrysippus on the Soul: Argument and Refutation in the* De placitis, *Books II–III* (PhAnt 68; Leiden: Brill, 1996). Its location either in the chest (apart from the fragment quoted, see also *SVF* 2.837–839, 848, 879–881, 885–886, 889, 894–896, 898, 901, 908) or in the head (*SVF* 2.836, 910–911) is a much-debated problem in Stoicism, to which Chrysippus had dedicated an extended and prolix treatment in his *On the Soul* (*De anima*), supported also by numerous poetic citations that drew the criticism of Galen; see Ramelli, *Allegoria*, chs. 2.4.9 and 11.5.1. The Stoics identified the *hêgemonikon* of the world with the ether, with the Logos, and with the highest deity, Zeus (e.g., in *SVF* 2.605, 837, 1021, 1077); see the index in Radice, *Stoici antichi*, s.v. "Egemonico (ἡγεμονικόν),"

1571–72, and Isnardi, "Ierocle," 2221, for the connection between the ether and the *hêgemonikon* in Stoicism. I have already mentioned the Stoic identification of the soul with *pneuma* and fire, and the ether is the igneous element par excellence and the highest as well, where the *pneuma* is manifested in its purest form (since the *hêgemonikon* is itself *pneuma*: *SVF* 1.484; 2.96, 841), without ceasing, on this account, to be a body. The corporeality of the *hêgemonikon* is clearly stated in *SVF* 2.132, from Sextus Empiricus: τὸ ἡγεμονικὸν σῶμα ὑπῆρχεν. The Stoics held that, at the time of the universal conflagration, the cosmos was reduced to its *hêgemonikon*, a fiery substance and supreme divinity, the only thing that does not perish in the total destruction of the rest, as is attested esp. in *SVF* 2.605, in which Plutarch cites Chrysippus, *Prov.* book 1: "for when the cosmos is wholly fiery, it is at once its own soul and ruling part [ἡγεμονικόν]; but when it changes to the moist and into a contained soul, it somehow changes into body and soul, so as to be composed of these, but it retains Logos as something other." For IV.49–50, in *CPF* 4.1:ix Bastianini and Long emend the text from ἀπὸ τῶν ἔξω τῶν μερῶν to ἀπὸ τῶν μερῶν τῶν ἄκρων, with which the translation changes from "from external parts" to "from the outermost parts." For IV.51 there is proposed, in the same place, the emendation of συναναφέρεται to εἰσαναφέρεται, "is equivalent to."

32. This is due to the above-mentioned total interaction of body and soul, which was certainly the easier for their material homogeneity in the Stoic system; the Stoics represented the perception of internal processes as "internal touch" (ἐντὸς ἁφή; see von Arnim, *Ethische Elementarlehre*, xxviii), described in Cicero, *Acad. pr.* 20, as the faculty of the soul that receives all the various states of the organism that are different from those mediated by the five senses. It is significant for Hierocles' argument that in *SVF* 2.852 "internal touch" is presented as that "thanks to which we are able to perceive and apprehend [ἀντιλαμβανόμεθα] ourselves as well."

33. Hierocles has here recapitulated the four premises that lead to the conclusion that there exists in animals continual self-perception. For, if the soul is a perceptive faculty and it interacts constantly with the body, it derives from this the perception of all the parts of the body and the soul, and this means that an animal perceives itself. See von Arnim, *Ethische Elementarlehre*, xxvii–xxix (esp. "perception [αἴσθησις] perceives itself"), and Bastianini and Long, who incidentally propose the formula "intraspecific receptivity," since, according to Hierocles, animals "are receptive of their own specific nature—for example, bulls, the asp, etc.—and are also receptive, as bull, etc., of every affect that is transmitted from their particular perceptions.... The entire organism is continually receptive,

in an 'autospecific' way, in respect to everything that it is able to receive via its constitution, for example, that it will react to a painful stimulus aimed at any part of its body" (420–21). For a discussion of the continuity of self-perception in Hierocles, see the entire section on the question in the introduction to von Arnim, *Ethische Elementarlehre*, xxiiff. Von Arnim speaks of "Selbstwahrnehmung," although the term "self-perception" is perhaps a bit too loaded with implications that it does not have in Hierocles. For this reason critics today, and especially Bastianini and Long, prefer to speak only of "perception of onself"; Isnardi translates αἰσθάνεται ἑαυτοῦ both ways: "percepisce se stesso" and "ha coscienza di sé" ("Ierocle," 2204).

34. From here to the end of V.38, Hierocles, in confirmation of the preceding conclusion concerning the continual self-perception of animals, adduces an empirical argument: even at the time when one might suppose that an animal does not have self-perception, that is, during sleep, it nevertheless does perceive itself; thus, there is no time in which an animal does not perceive itself. For a discussion of the validity of the examples, see Bastianini and Long, 423–25.

Hierocles' incidental observation on the difficulty that some have in believing that animals perceive themselves during sleep can be explained by the fact that the Stoics identified sleep with a relaxation of perceptive tension (τόνος) or perceptive *pneuma*; see *SVF* 2.766–767: "Sleep occurs when the perceptive tension [τόνος αἰσθητικός] around the *hêgemonikon* is slackened. … Sleep occurs via the relaxation of the perceptive [αἰσθητικόν] *pneuma*," although a total relaxation leads rather to death (ibid.).

A correction in the new edition, indicated by Bastianini and Long at *CPF* 4.1:ix, does not have an impact on the translation: in IV.54–55, instead of reading γάρ ἐστιν, εἴπερ, with ἐστίν in brackets, they prefer to read γάρ, εἴπερ.

35. These two examples are particularly interesting with regard to the general purpose of the entire argument, which concerns οἰκείωσις and the doctrine of self-love, since the alcoholic and the miser tend to "appropriate for themselves" the wineflask and the purse; they consider them to be parts of themselves and hence hold on to them during sleep.

For IV.60, Bastianini and Long propose a new reading that is decidedly better: in place of εἰς ὃν διάγομεν βίον, which introduces a sense of purpose that is out of place here, they now read ἐφ' ὃν διάγομεν βίον (*CPF* 4.1:ix).

36. It is probably Iphigenia, whose dignity at the moment of her sacrifice is recalled also by Lucretius at the beginning of his poem *De rerum*

natura (On Nature) in order to show that *tantum religio potuit suadere malorum*, "such crimes superstition could induce people to commit!" (1.101). For V.16, Bastianini and Long propose a supplement that contributes importantly to the sense: whereas earlier they limited themselves to reading οἱ βραχε-, indicating that the next eight letters or so had fallen out, they now read οἱ βραχεῖς χρόνους ἔχοντες, "have a brief time left" to live (*CPF* 4.1:ix).

37. See *TrGF* 2.416,2, cited also by Plutarch, *Soll. an.* 967C, who compares the behavior of Heracles in his sleep, during which he grasped his club tightly, with that of storks, who attempt to keep themselves awake by supporting themselves on one foot and holding onto a stone with the other.

Hierocles is availing himself in this passage of principles derived from physiognomy, a science that has recently begun to receive special attention on the part of classicists: in Diogenes Laerius it is already attributed to the Old Stoic Cleanthes (*Vit. phil.* 7.173 = *SVF* 1.204):

> It is said that, when he claimed that, according to Zeno, one could grasp a person's character from his aspect, some witty young men brought a cinaedus before him who had been hardened from work in the fields and asked him to pronounce concerning his character. Cleanthes, at a loss, ordered the man to depart. And when the man, as he departed, sneezed, Cleanthes said: "I've got him! He's an effeminate."

Physiognomy is, indeed, a science that long had a place in Stoic ethics. In *SVF* 2.10a, included among the fragments of Chrysippus (= Dio Chrysostom, *Or.* 33.53–55), there is a reference to a past figure, not further specified, who was competent in this area:

> They say that one of the cleverest men from these parts came to a city practicing just this occupation. Thus he knew the character of each person and could describe his particularities, and he never failed with anyone. But, just as we recognize animals upon seeing them, that this is a sheep, for instance, and that a dog, and this other a horse or cow, so he recognized human beings upon seeing them and was able to say that this one was courageous, this one cowardly, this one a braggart, that other violent or a cinaedus or an adulterer. Thus, since he became famous for his displays and was never wrong, they brought to him a certain man who was hardy in body and with eyebrows joined together, squalid and shabby and with calluses on his hands, covered in a dark, rough cloak, hairy down to his legs and badly shaven, and they asked him to say what type he was. He looked at him for quite a while, and finally, hesitating, I

> think, to say what occurred to him, he announced that he did not know and bade the man to walk. Just as he was leaving, he sneezed, and the other shouted out at once that he was a cinaedus: in the case of this man, then, a sneeze proved his character and prevailed over all the rest so that it did not deceive him.

As we see, the anecdote, though more fully elaborated in Dio, is nevertheless of the same stamp as that related by Diogenes. Physiognomy was, in fact, further developed in works subsequent to the Old Stoa, for example by Pseudo-Aristotle, Polemo, Adamantius, and the Anonymous Latinus (the fragments of these treatises are edited in Richard Förster, *Scriptores physiognomonici graeci et latini* [2 vols.; Berlin: Teubner, 1893]; the Anonymous Latinus has been more recently edited as well by Jacques André, *De Physiognomonia liber* [Paris: Belles Lettres, 1981]). Especially in the first period of the Empire, at the time of Hierocles, physiognomy achieved an extended application; see Elizabeth C. Evans, "The Study of Physiognomics in the I Century A.D.," *TAPA* 72 (1941): 96–108; Tamsyn Barton, *Power and Knowledge: Astrology, Physiognomics and Medicine under the Roman Empire* (Ann Arbor: University of Michigan Press, 2003); Simon Swain, ed., *Seeing the Face, Seeing the Soul: Polemon's Physiognomy from Classical Antiquity to Medieval Islam* (Oxford: Oxford University Press, 2007). For a recent attempt to apply it to New Testament texts, see Mikeal C. Parsons, *Body and Character in Luke and Acts: The Subversion of Physiognomy in Early Christianity* (Grand Rapids: Baker, 2006). On Dio Chrysostom, see Cécile Bost-Pouderon, "Dion de Pruse et la physiognomonie dans le Discours XXXIII," *REA* 105 (2003): 157–74. In *Or.* 4.88, Dio refers to the "discipline and prophesying skill of the so-called physiognomists" (τῆς τῶν λεγομένων φυσιογνωμόνων ἐμπειρίας καὶ μαντικῆς). The four fundamental indications on the basis of which physiognomy identified character were general comportment, gaze, manner of speaking, and manner of walking. Hierocles here applies above all the first of these, relative to the general attitude of body and gestures, to the case of people immersed in sleep, thereby putting the principles of physiognomy to work in the service of his own argument.

38. In the section that begins here, severely damaged in the papyrus, Hierocles showed that animals too, and not only human beings, have self-perception during sleep.

39. Now that he has demonstrated that animals have continual self-perception, Hierocles can reach the conclusion that he had set for the argument in I.38–39, that is, that animals perceive themselves immedi-

ately after birth (von Arnim, *Ethische Elementarlehre*, xxx, summarizes the stages of the argument as follows: simple self-perception, or *Selbstwahrnehmung überhaupt* → uninterrupted self-perception, or *ununterbrochene Selbstwahrnehmung* → original self-perception beginning with birth, or *ursprüngliche Selbstwahrnehmung seit der Geburt*). The arguments that Hierocles adopts are four in number, as Bastianini and Long, 428–29, perspicaciously remark: (1) the first is the one expounded here: continual perception implies perception from the very beginning, because the beginning itself is part of the continual period of time; (2) an elenchic or refutational demonstration, based on a *reductio ad absurdum*: if the beginning of life were not characterized by self-perception, one would be taking as the initial moment of self-perception a time that has less significance or authority than the beginning of life itself (V.43–52); (3) because perception of external things implies perception of oneself, and because the former occurs from birth, the second too must begin with birth itself (V.52–VI.10); and (4) self-perception must precede the perception of any other entity that is other than the perceiving subject (VI.10–24).

In *CPF* 4.1:ix, Bastianini and Long propose for V.40–41 a correction to the first edition that has a certain bearing on the translation: in place of αἰσθάνεται ἀπ' ἀρχῆς, they read αἰσθάνεται καὶ ἀπ' ἀρχῆς, "an animal perceives itself, and from the beginning," so that the two stages in the demonstration are kept distinct.

40. This is the second elenchic argument, in support of self-perception from birth; see the preceding note.

41. Here we have the third argument in support of the thesis of self-perception on the part of animals from the beginning. See the preceding notes and Brunschwig, "The Cradle Argument," 142–43. As opposed to Pembroke ("Oikeiôsis," 142) and Badalamenti ("Ierocle stoico," 68, 70), Bastianini and Long (433) maintain that the expressions "we perceive ourselves being whitened," "sweetened" (λευκαινόμενοι, γλυκαζόμενοι), and the like do not imply here an epistemological argument directed against skepticism but rather signify that we never perceive an external object without perceiving also our own internal conditions while we perceive it; the use of verbs such as λευκαίνομαι and the like to indicate the subjective aspect of sensible impression is attested for this period by Sextus Empiricus, *Math.* 7.293, 367; 8.211. For self-perception as implied by the perception of external objects, see Seneca, *Ep.* 121.12: "for it is necessary that they perceive that by means of which they perceive other things as well."

42. This argument, the fourth and last in support of self-perception from birth, is based on the Stoic theory concerning unified bodies

(ἡνωμένα): inanimate bodies, in which *pneuma* appears as a mere cohesive principle or *habitus* (ἕξις); plants, in which it appears as "nature" (φύσις); and animals, in which it appears as "soul" (ψυχή). Each of these three degrees of cohesion transcends and at the same time subsumes the preceding: thus perception (αἴσθησις), which in Hierocles has its place in the soul and is characteristic of animals, is endowed with a degree of cohesiveness greater than that of *habitus* and of nature. Because these latter also have their beginning or principle in themselves, there is all the more reason why perception should begin from itself and thus perceive itself before perceiving other things. For the idea of a lexical slide from ἡγεμονικὴ δύναμις to ἕξις in Hierocles' vocabulary in this passage, see Isnardi, "Ierocle," 2204 n. 12, and already von Arnim, *Ethische Elementarlehre*, note to 28–29.

A notable improvement to the text is proposed in *CPF* 4.1:ix for VI.15: in place of ἥ τε φύσις, ἡ συνέχουσα, "A nature too, which binds together," the editors now read ἥ τε φύσις, δή, συνέχουσα, "A nature too, indeed, when it binds together...." For it is not a question of distinguishing a nature that keeps something cohesive from some other that does not do so, but simply of underscoring this function of *physis* and its consequences. At VI.21, where I render "before apprehending something else," I am taking into account the correction indicated in *CPF* 4.1:ix, of πρὶν τῶν ἑτέρων τινὸς ἀντιλαβέσθαι to πρὶν ἢ ἑτέρου τινὸς ἀντιλαβέσθαι.

43. Here is the conclusion to all the preceding arguments: an animal, immediately after birth, perceives itself. From here on, Hierocles engages in two further arguments designed to show that, immediately after birth, an animal "becomes its own and familiar" (οἰκειοῦται) to itself and to its own constitution (VI.52–53; VII.49–50), which is nothing other than the "first appropriation and familiarization" (πρῶτον οἰκεῖον) that Hierocles, at the very beginning of his essay, defined as the "best principle or starting point" for the elements of ethics. One linguistic point: the expression οἰκειοῦσθαι ἑαυτῷ is sometimes translated as "appropriate itself to itself," but it is more accurate to translate "render itself its own (and familiar) to itself," which I personally prefer, or else "be rendered its own to itself" ("essere reso proprio a se stesso"), as Bastianini and Long prefer, 286 and *passim*.

44. First argument in support of the thesis of appropriation to oneself and to one's own constitution on the part of animals from birth (see above). Brunschwig ("The Cradle Argument," 139) and then Bastianini and Long (436–37) observe the deep similarities between this argument of Hierocles' and the thesis of Chrysippus reported in Diogenes Laertius, *Vit.*

phil. 7.85: "For it is not plausible that it [sc. nature] would estrange it from itself [ἀλλοτριῶσαι] or that, having made it, that it would neither estrange it [ἀλλοτριῶσαι] nor appropriate it [οἰκειῶσαι] to itself." The pairing in Diogenes "estrange it/appropriate it" corresponds to Hierocles' "be pleased/be displeased" (δυσαρεστεῖν/εὐαρεστεῖν). That the self-perception an animal possesses is already also perception of its own constitution seems to be confirmed by Seneca, *Ep.* 121, who speaks of "perception of its own constitution" (*constitutionis suae sensus*), although he also says that an animal "perceives that it is an animal" (*animal esse se sensit*, 121.11). Seneca also defines the "constitution" of an animal as "the ruling faculty of the soul disposed in a certain way toward the body" (*principale animi quodam modo se habens erga corpus*, 121.10). For Hierocles, too, although he is less explicit, when an animal perceives itself, it perceives the disposition of its own soul in relation to its body, as is clear from IV.51–53. See Bastianini and Long, 387–89, who agree with Brunschwig, "The Cradle Argument," 137, on the affinity between this perception of self and of one's own constitution, which Hierocles and Seneca discuss, and the "proprioperception" discovered by Sherrington and analyzed by the neurologist Oliver Sacks (see introductory essay above). The Stoics, who knew nothing about neurology—and seem rather to have rejected even the Hellenistic discovery of nerves (see Friedrich Solmsen, "Greek Philosophy and the Discovery of the Nerves," *MH* 18 [1961]: 150–97)—displaced functions of the nervous system onto the interaction between the soul and the body, which Hierocles indicates with the expressions "perception" and "perceiving oneself" (αἴσθεσις, συναίσθησις, αἰσθάνεσθαι ἑαυτοῦ), and which we could render as "self-consciousness," if this did not load the term with modern connotations of reflection on one's own thoughts and the like (see n. 33 above). Rather, it is a matter here of the perception of one's own organism and its distinctness from external entities, which implies an "appropriation" (οἰκείωσις) of oneself that manifests itself in tendency to self-preservation. It is probable that Hierocles specifically treated self-perception on the part of human beings in that part of the papyrus, now lost, that was dedicated to the moral end (τέλος) in column IX. See, on this section, von Arnim, *Ethische Elementarlehre*, xxxiii–xxxvi, who also suggests that it contained an anti-Epicurean polemic.

45. Second argument, this time empirical and illustrative, for the thesis that, immediately at birth, an animal "makes its own and familiar" (οἰκειοῦται) both itself and its own constitution. The argument is based on the observable fact that each animal seeks invariably to preserve itself and infers that this could not be the case if animals did not love themselves.

Other Stoic versions of this argument are found in Cicero, Diogenes Laertius, and Aulus Gellius:

> They believe that, as soon as an animal is born (this is the point of departure), it is conciliated with itself [*conciliari* = οἰκειοῦσθαι] and is led to preserve itself and its own condition, and to loving those things that preserve its condition; it is estranged, moreover, from its destruction and those things that appear to bring on destruction. They prove that this is so on the grounds that small creatures [*parvi*] seek what is salubrious and avoid the contrary before pleasure or pain has touched them. This would not be the case if they did not love their stable condition [*status*] and fear destruction. Nor would it be possible, in turn, that they desired something if they had no sense of themselves and consequently loved themselves. From this one should understand that the principle [or origin] is derived from loving oneself [*a se diligendo*]. (Cicero, *Fin.* 3.5.16 [*SVF* 3.182])

> They maintain that the first impulse an animal has is toward preserving itself, since nature appropriates it [or makes it its own] to itself [οἰκειοῦν αὐτῷ] from the beginning. This is according to what Chrysippus says in book 1 of *On Ends* [Περὶ τελῶν], where he says that the first appropriation [πρῶτον οἰκεῖον] for every animal is its own constitution and an awareness of it. For it is not plausible that it [sc. nature] would estrange it from itself [ἀλλοτριῶσαι] or, having made it, that it would neither estrange it [ἀλλοτριῶσαι] nor appropriate it [οἰκειῶσαι] to itself. What remains, then, has constituted it to make it [sc. the animal] its own and familiar to itself [οἰκειῶσαι πρὸς ἑαυτό]. (Diogenes Laertius, *Vit. phil.* 7.85 [*SVF* 3.178:43])

> The nature of all things, which gave birth of us, inculcated and developed in us from the very moment in which we were born love and affection for ourselves, in such a way that nothing is dearer and more important to us than we ourselves; and she decided that this was fundamental to preserving the continuity of human beings, namely if each of us, as soon as he emerged into the light of day, acquired an awareness and affection for those things which were called 'first according to nature' [πρῶτα κατὰ φύσιν] by the ancient philosophers: thus he would find pleasure in all the things that were favorable to his body and flee those that were unfavorable. Afterwards, with increase in age, reason arises from these its seeds … and there stands forth and shines the nobility of what is decent and honest. (Aulus Gellius, *Noct. att.* 12.5.7 [*SVF* 3.181:43–44])

46. See analogous Stoic arguments concerning the fact that animals, from very early on, avoid danger and seek their own preservation: Cicero, *Fin.* 3.4.16; Diogenes Laertius, *Vit. phil.* 7.85; Seneca, *Ep.* 121.21.

47. Because sensible external objects, for Hierocles, imply self-perception (VI.1–10), infants, if they are deprived of the perception of external things, also lose self-perception and thus fear that they are dead or on the point of dying. This is the explanation offered by Hierocles of the fear of the dark that infants often manifest.

For VII.12, Bastianini and Long propose no longer reading *γενέσθαι τὴν ἀποστέρησιν τῶν ὁρατῶν*, "the deprivation of what is visible occurs," but rather *στερεῖσθαι τῆς ἀντιλήψεως τῶν ὁρατῶν*, "deprived of the apprehension of what is visible," which much improves the sense (*CPF* 4.1:ix).

48. A similar argument is found in Cicero, *Fin.* 5.11.32: "But the force of nature is most evident in this kind of thing: when many people … endure even what we see that Philoctetes did in the myth." See also Cicero, *Fin.* 2.29.94; *Tusc.* 2.19; Plutarch, *Mor.* 18C, 674A; *SVF* 3.196:47, among the ethical fragments of Chrysippus, from a letter of Fronto to Marcus Aurelius: "If you ask me whether I desire good health, I would deny it, if I were a philosopher. For it is not right for a sage to desire or seek what he might perchance desire in vain; nor must he desire what he sees is in the hands of fortune. Nevertheless, if one or the other must be chosen, I would choose the swiftness of Achilles over the debility of Philoctetes" (here, however, the point is not so much the nature of *oikeiôsis* as exemplified in Philoctetes as the question of indifferents).

49. We have here a recapitulation of the reasoning and a reassertion of the thesis. On VII.47 Bastianini and Long indicate in *CPF* 4.1:ix an improvement that does not affect the translation: in place of λελεγμένη (with final *eta* uncertain), they now place the *nu* and final *eta* in square brackets.

50. Here begins a further development of Hierocles' argument, which seems to continue up to VIII.27. The extremely lacunose state of the text makes it very difficult to follow the train of thought; it is probable, however, that Hierocles introduced at this point, alongside primary οἰκείωσις directed to oneself, another form of οἰκείωσις, the social, directed toward other people, which according to Stoicism is a development in human beings of the love for their own children that is characteristic of all animals; see Cicero, *Fin.* 3.19.62–20.68; Chrysippus in *SVF* 3.179:43: "As soon as we are born we are made familiar to ourselves, to our parts, and to our offspring"; Engberg-Pedersen, *The Stoic Theory of* Οἰκείωσις, 122–26, and Blundell, "Parental Nature and Stoic *Oikeiôsis*," 221–42; Radice,

Oikeiôsis, 195–234, on the movement in Stoic thought from preservative to deontological *oikeiôsis*, and from this latter to rational *oikeiôsis*, and on the value of sociable *oikeiôsis* in Stoicism. The importance of the faculty of representation in Stoicism is clear in Epictetus, for whom representation explains every type of knowledge in every living creature; see Anthony A. Long, "Representation and the Stoic Self," in *Psychology* (ed. Stephen Everson; vol. 2 of *Companions to Ancient Thought*; Cambridge: Cambridge University Press, 1991), 102–20, esp. 105–6; also María del Carmen García de Sola, "La representación en el estoicismo antiguo," *Estudios de Filosofía Griega* 2 (1986): 247–52; Noël Aujoulat, "De la phantasia et du pneuma stoïciens, d'après Sextus Empiricus, au corps lumineux néo-platonicien (Synésios de Cyrène et Hiéroclès d'Alexandrie)," *Pallas* 34 (1988): 123–46.

51. Representation (φαντασία), according to the Stoics, is precisely an imprint upon the soul, and more specifically on the hegemonic or ruling function, like the similar impression of fingers on wax, and is received by thought (νοουμένη τύπωσις). See, e.g., *SVF* 2.56, 59, 458, 847; see also n. 53 below.

52. See von Arnim, *Ethische Elementarlehre*, xviii; Bastianini and Long, 445–47. In this section, unfortunately very damaged, three factors are invoked to explain why representation (φαντασία) is undeveloped at the beginning of life, whether of a young animal or an infant child: (1) the density or thickness of the imprint (παχεῖα, "thick"); (2) confusion (σύγχυσις), probably pertaining to the representation itself; and (3) the lack of practice and hence of experience: ἀτριβὴς καὶ ἀγύμναστος, adjectives perhaps referring to the soul. Because of these three factors, there cannot be a representation that permits one to "become inside things," that is, to receive objects in a precise way. The reference at the end to tilting, which is typical of metaphors involving a scale or balance (see also VII.30; VI.46), is part of the Hellenistic epistemological lexicon, on which see Sextus Empiricus, *Math.* 1.280: "human beings are disposed to tilt…." Hierocles' argument is that, in the first stages of an animal's life, the senses are not sufficiently developed to permit it to identify objects in a determinate way. One may thus suppose that he denied to infants the ability to have a "catalectic representation," on which see R. J. Hankinson, "Stoic Epistemology," in Inwood, *Cambridge Companion to the Stoics*, 59–84.

For VIII.4, Bastianini and Long propose an emendation, although unfortunately it is of little help here, since it pertains to a damaged portion of the text: the change is from τρίτον δὲ ἀγύμναστος, "in third place, not exercised," to ἀτριβὴς καὶ ἀγύμναστος, "without exercise and without

practice," perhaps to be taken as feminine and referring to the soul (see above), since these are two termination adjectives (*CPF* 4.1:ix).

53. Here Hierocles apparently refers to two distinct views held by two heads of the Stoic school. The lacunose state of the passage creates problems of interpretation concerning just what the conjectures or images (εἰκασίαι) of the two early Stoics concerning a certain event (περὶ τοῦ συμβαίνοντος) might be. We know from Sextus Empiricus, *Math.* 7.228–231 (*SVF* 2.56), that the two disagreed on the interpretation of Zeno's "imprint" (τύπωσις): for Cleanthes, it will have been an imprint like that of fingers in wax; for Chrysippus, however, it was a metaphor for "alteration" or ἑτεροίωσις:

> For them [sc. the Stoics], then, representation is an imprint in the soul; but they immediately disagreed concerning this: Cleanthes understood the imprint as dip and rise, like the impression made by fingers in wax. But Chrysippus believed that such a thing was absurd. For, he said, first of all, when the mind has a representation simultaneously of a triangle and a quadrilateral, then it must happen that the same body at the same time has in itself the different figures of a triangle and a quadrilateral.... He therefore supposed that the term "imprint" had been used by Zeno in place of "alteration."

Von Arnim, however, in *Ethische Elementarlehre*, xvii–xviii, with whom Bastianini and Long, 448, are in agreement (except that they accidentally cite xxviii), observes that this divergence does not seem to have a direct bearing on the present discussion in Hierocles relative to "indeterminate representation" and that it is more likely that the disagreement between the two masters looked rather to a question concerning perception on the part of those who are "not yet practiced." Isnardi, "Ierocle," 2205 and n. 14, suggests that one ought to speak not so much of a true polemic here as a different account of a process of representation that both alike recognized. See also Isnardi, "Ierocle," 2222, and §5 in the introductory essay above.

54. In column IX Hierocles apparently treats the various forms of οἰκείωσις, perhaps making it the basis of his discussion of the τέλος or "end," which is clearly to be understood as the moral end (see Long, "Carneades and the Stoic Telos," 59–90; for the connection with the σκοπός, in turn, in Stoicism, see Roswitha Alpers-Gölz, *Der Begriff Skopos in der Stoa und seine Vorgeschichte* [Spoudasmata 8; Hildesheim: Olms, 1976]; for both concepts, see Inwood, "Goal and Target in Stoicism," 547–56); on the connection between the discussion of the moral τέλος and that of pref-

erables and of οἰκείωσις in the Middle Stoa and its immediate precursors, see §5b and the relevant notes in the introductory essay above.

A differentiation among the forms of *oikeiôsis* similar to that of Hierocles, but less complex, is found in the anonymous author of the commentary on Plato's *Theaetetus*, column VII, which employs in part the same vocabulary as Hierocles, in a way that does not have parallels in any other source and hence leads Bastianini and Long (292) to suppose that the authors are not far distant in time from one another. See n. 57 in the introductory essay, with documentation on this text and a possible dating. The anonymous author, who would seem to be associated with Middle Platonism, though with Stoic and Peripatetic influences, and who in the matter of epistemology denies that knowledge can be founded on the senses and opinion, distinguishes between οἰκείωσις αἱρετική, "appropriation resulting from choice," which I believe is to be understood as a rational choice of what is good or ἀγαθόν, and οἰκείωσις κηδεμονική, "appropriation characterized by concern or care."

In Hierocles, this latter is further divided into two types: that which everyone directs toward oneself, called "benevolent" or εὐνοητική, and that directed to one's own dear ones, called "loving" or "affectionate" (στερκτική). In addition, in Hierocles it is unclear whether there is also a fourth form, that suggested by the adverb ἐκλεκτικῶς, in reference to the οἰκείωσις of an animal in respect to itself, although one cannot exclude the possibility that it is rather a case of simple *variatio* or synonymy, ἐκλεκτική = αἱρετική: both cases involve an *oikeiôsis* characterized by choice, as Isnardi, "Ierocle," 2205, too seems to take it, among other reasons because the behavior of human beings in respect to *oikeiôsis*—in four forms—is compared with that of animals. Nevertheless, one ought to recall, I believe, that if the most elementary forms of *oikeiôsis* are shared with animals, the higher forms, and certainly any rational form, cannot be shared with animals. In technical Stoic terminology, the verb αἱρέω and its cognates refer to the choice of goods, that is, of virtue and whatever derives from it, and in a negative sense with avoiding evils, that is, vices and their consequences; the verb ἐκλέγω refers to the selection (ἐκλογή) of preferables (προηγμένα or προηγούμενα) among the indifferents or ἀδιάφορα, that is, things that are neither good nor evil, since they do not in themselves lead either to virtue or to vice, but that, on the basis of a kind of value (ἀξία) or lack of value, are divided among things that are preferable or to be rejected (ἀποπροηγμένα). The former pertain to duties or καθήκοντα, whereas κατορθώματα are actions that result from a rational choice (αἵρεσις strictly speaking, not ἐκλογή) of the good. For

this technical terminology, see, e.g. *SVF* 3.118:28; Diogenes Laertius, *Vit. phil.* 7.98–109. Thus, unless Hierocles is using the two terms in a nontechnical sense, which is certainly possible but extremely unlikely, when he speaks of οἰκείωσις ἐκλεκτική he would seem to be referring to *oikeiôsis* based on the selection of preferables, which is the *oikeiôsis* of duties, for instance, that which comes into play with regard to the various classes of people with whom we enter into relationships. When he speaks of οἰκείωσις αἱρετική, on the other hand, he should be indicating an *oikeiôsis* based on the rational choice of goods, that is, of virtue. One might have thought, taking into consideration the context and the passage in which Hierocles employs the terms οἰκείωσις αἱρετική, οἰκείωσις ἐκλεκτική, and οἰκείωσις στερκτική, of a semitechnical use of the adjectives αἱρετική and ἐκλεκτική; in the parallel between human beings and animals, Hierocles attributes οἰκείωσις στερκτική toward offspring to both, whereas he changes the vocabulary for *oikeiôsis* directed to external things: for animals it is οἰκείωσις ἐκλεκτική, while for human beings it is οἰκείωσις αἱρετική. In fact, bearing in mind that αἵρεσις is strictly speaking the rational choice of true goods, Hierocles could not have attributed it to animals devoid of reason; in their case it is only a matter of preference or selection of preferables (this is what ἐκλογή technically refers to in Stoic ethical vocabulary), because for them there is no moral good or evil, which depends on reason. I believe that in this way we can discern a certain coherence in the use of these adjectives in Hierocles and the retention of the technical Stoic terminology on his part, without supposing its dilution or reduction to synonyms.

This passage on the forms of "appropriation" is very important for Hierocles' theory: the various kinds of οἰκείωσις are not, however, different "appropriations" but rather different aspects of a single tendency toward appropriation, according to the difference in its objects, not just the self but also others. This frees the doctrine of οἰκείωσις from possible charges of egoism—for instance, the above-mentioned commentator on the *Theaetetus* (*CPF* 1.1.2:291) criticizes οἰκείωσις as a possible ground of justice—and at the same time summons up the famous fragment of Hierocles, preserved by Stobaeus, *Anth.* 4.84.23 (3:134,1–136,2 Meineke; cf. *Anth.* 4.27.23 = 4:671,3–673,18 Wachsmuth and Hense) and translated here, in which the relationships of the human subject—we might say, his or her appropriative tendencies—are described metaphorically as a series of concentric circles around a point that represents the "I" (and, still more narrowly, the hegemonic function); the smallest circle is given by one's own body, with which the soul first enters into relation, but the others suc-

cessively include other people, from those who are most dear and closely related up to all of humanity.

55. This last part is extremely fragmentary: from the title over column IX we know that the topic was the τέλος, that is, the ethical end, one of the principal points of Stoic ethics according to Diogenes Laertius, *Vit. phil.* 7.84, although it is not certain that this is still the theme of XI.15ff., where Hierocles speaks of the social nature of human beings. Nevertheless, this argument could well have been included in the discussion of the ethical end. According to Cicero's account of Stoic ethics in *Fin.* 3.19.62ff., the sociability of human beings has its ground in the love of parents for their children, which Hierocles included (see above) among the forms of οἰκείωσις.

We do not know for sure what that "most wondrous [thing] of all" is, of which Hierocles speaks. On the basis of the few legible words that follow, von Arnim, in his commentary *ad loc.*, hypothesized that it was friendship between members of enemy armies. Bastianini and Long (297) suppose that Hierocles, in the part of the papyrus that is lost, after having treated the ethical end, went on to discuss some classical topics in Stoic ethics, such as virtues, goods, evils, and indifferents, and among these preferables and the duties (καθήκοντα) that are bound up with them: these are the main theme of the Stobaean extracts. Thus, there would be a clear continuity between the *Elements of Ethics* and the Stobaean extracts from *On Appropriate Acts*. See Long, "Arius Didymus," 41–65.

56. Here I depart from Bastianini and Long in preferring the iota subscript, reading τῳ rather than τωι.

Stobaeus's Extracts from Hierocles, *On Appropriate Acts*

The present translation is based on the edition of Hans Friedrich August von Arnim, *Ethische Elementarlehre (Papyrus 9780): Nebst den bei Stobaios erhaltenen ethischen Exzerpten aus Hierokles* (Berliner Klassikertexte 4; Berlin: Weidmann, 1906), 48–64. I have made use of von Arnim's edition only for the extracts from Stobaeus, since, as indicated above, there is now available the new *CPF* edition for the *Elements of Ethics*.

Stobaeus, *Anthology* 1.3.53 (1:63,6–27 Wachsmuth and Hense)
Ἱεροκλέους ἐκ τοῦ Τίνα τρόπον θεοῖς χρηστέον.

Ἔτι προσδιαληπτέον καὶ ταῦθ' ὑπὲρ τῶν θεῶν, ὡς εἰσὶν ἄτρεπτοι καὶ ἀραρότες τοῖς κρίμασιν, ὥστε τοῦ δόξαντος μηδέποτε <τοῦ> ἀπ' ἀρχῆς ἐξίστασθαι. μία γάρ τις ἦν τῶν ἀρετῶν καὶ ἡ ἀμεταπτωσία καὶ βεβαιότης, ἣν εἰκὸς οὐχ ἥκιστα κἀν θεοῖς εἶναι παρέχουσαν τὸ ἱδρυμένον καὶ ἔμπεδον τῶν ἅπαξ αὐτοῖς δοξάντων. ἐξ οὗ δῆλον, ὡς οὐδὲ τὰς κολάσεις, ἃς ἔκρινέ τισιν ἐπιθεῖναι τὸ δαιμόνιον, πιθανὸν παρίεσθαι. καὶ γὰρ ἀναλογίσασθαι ῥᾴδιον, ὡς εἰ μεταβάλλουσιν οἱ θεοὶ τὰς αὐτῶν κρίσεις καὶ ὃν ἔγνωσαν κολάσαι παριᾶσιν ἀκόλαστον, οὔτε καλῶς καὶ δικαίως διοικοῖεν <ἂν> τὰ κατὰ τὸν κόσμον, οὔτε ἀπολογισμὸν εἰκότα φέρειν ἂν δύναιντο μετανοίας. καὶ τὰ τοιαῦτα ἔοικεν αὐτοσχεδίως καὶ μετ' οὐδενὸς λέγειν ἡ ποιητική

> καὶ θυσίαισι καὶ εὐχωλῆς ἀγανῇσι
> λοιβῇ τε κνίσῃ τε παρατρωπῶσ' ἄνθρωποι
> λισσόμενοι, ὅτε κέν τις ὑπερβαίῃ καὶ ἁμάρτῃ

καὶ τὸ

> στρεπτοὶ δέ τε καὶ θεοὶ αὐτοί,

συνόλως τε πᾶν εἴ τι τούτοις εἴρηται παραπλησίως.

Stobaeus, *Anthology* 1.3.54 (1:64,1–14 Wachsmuth and Hense)
Ἐν ταὐτῷ.

Ἀλλ' οὐ μὴν οὐδὲ ἐκεῖνο παρετέον, ὡς εἰ καὶ μὴ κακῶν αἴτιοι τυγχάνουσιν οἱ θεοί, τῶν γε τοιούτων ἔνια προσάπτουσί τισι καὶ περιβάλλουσιν ἀξίους σωματικαῖς τε ἐλαττώσεσι καὶ ταῖς τῶν ἐκτός, οὐ κακοηθείᾳ χρώμενοι κἀξεπίτηδες δυσχρηστῆσαι ἄνθρωπον οἰόμενοι δεῖν, ἀλλ' ἐν τρόπῳ κολάσεως. καθάπερ γὰρ λοιμοὶ καὶ αὐχμοί, ἔτι δὲ ἐπομβρίαι καὶ σεισμοὶ καὶ πᾶν τὸ τοιόνδε τὰ μὲν πολλὰ γίγνεται δι' αἰτίας ἑτέρας τινὰς φυσικωτέρας, ἔστι δ' ὅτε καὶ ὑπὸ θεῶν, ἐπειδὰν καιρὸς ᾖ δημοσίᾳ καὶ κοινῇ τὰ πολλῶν ἀμπλακήματα κολασθῆναι, τὸν αὐτὸν τρόπον καὶ πρὸς ἕνα χρῶνταί ποτε θεοὶ σωματικοῖς

Of Hierocles, from the Treatise *How Should One Behave toward the Gods?*

Furthermore, it is necessary to affirm this too concerning the gods, that they are immutable and fixed in their judgments, so as never to depart from their initial decision. For changelessness and firmness too was one of the virtues, and it is reasonable that this provides among the gods too the stability and immovability of what they have once decided. From this it is clear that it is plausible that not even the chastisements that a divinity has determined to inflict on some people should be remitted. For in fact it is easy to draw the analogy, that if the gods changed their judgments and left unchastised one whom they decided to chastise, they could neither govern the world well and justly nor produce a reasonable justification for their change of mind. And yet epic poetry seems to say things of this sort off the cuff and without any <argument>:[1]

> people supplicate with sacrifices and pleasing prayers, libations
> and the scent of smoke, if someone should transgress and err,[2]

and this:

> Even the gods themselves are pliable,[3]

and in general all that is said that is similar to these [statements].

In the same treatise.

But in fact one must not overlook this either: that even if the gods are not responsible for evils,[4] they nevertheless inflict some things of this kind on some people and wrap those who deserve them in both bodily and external defects, not because they practice malevolence[5] or because they spitefully believe that a human being should suffer but rather as a form of chastisement. For just as famines and droughts and also floods and earthquakes and every such thing mostly occur because of other, physical causes, but sometimes are also caused by the gods, when it is time for the faults of many people to be chastised publicly and collectively, in the same way the gods sometimes make use of bodily and external defects against a

ἐλαττώμασι καὶ τοῖς ἐκτός, <ἐς> αὐτοῦ μέντοι κόλασιν, ἐπιστροφὴν δὲ καὶ προαίρεσιν ἀμείνω τῶν ἄλλων.

Stobaeus, *Anthology* 2.9.7 (2:181,8–182,30 Wachsmuth and Hense)
Ἱεροκλέους ἐκ τοῦ Τίνα τρόπον θεοῖς χρηστέον.

Πολὺ δέ μοι δοκεῖ συμβάλλεσθαι πρὸς τὸ καλῶς χρῆσθαι θεοῖς καὶ τὸ διειληφέναι, ὡς οὐδενός ποτε κακοῦ γίγνεται θεὸς αἴτιος, ἀλλὰ ταῦτα μὲν ἐκ τῆς κακίας ἀπαντᾷ μόνης, οἱ δὲ θεοὶ τὸ ἐφ' ἑαυτοῖς ἀγαθῶν τέ εἰσιν αἴτιοι καὶ τῶν εὐχρήστων, ἡμεῖς δέ ἐσμεν οἱ τὰς εὐεργεσίας αὐτῶν οὐ προσιέμενοι, περιβάλλοντες δ' ἑαυτοὺς κακοῖς αὐθαιρέτοις. ἤδη καιρὸν ἔχειν μοι τὸ ποιητικὸν ἐκεῖνο δοκεῖ κατὰ τὸν τόπον τοῦτον, ὡς δὴ οἱ «βροτοὶ» τοὺς «θεοὺς αἰτιόωνται» ὡς ἐξ αὐτῶν ἐπιπεμπομένων τῶν κακῶν,

οἱ δὲ καὶ αὐτοὶ
σφῇσιν ἀτασθαλίῃσιν ὑπὲρ μόρον ἄλγε' ἔχουσιν.

ἐπεί τοί γε ὡς ὁ θεὸς οὐδαμῇ οὐδαμῶς κακῶν αἴτιός ἐστιν, ἐκ πολλῶν <ἂν> νοήσειέ τις, πρὸς δὲ τὸ παρὸν ἀποχρήσειεν ἂν ἴσως ὁ Πλάτωνος ἐκεῖνος λόγος. οὐ γὰρ θερμοῦ φησι τὸ ψύχειν ἀλλὰ τοῦ ἐναντίου, οὐδὲ ψυχροῦ τὸ θερμαίνειν ἀλλὰ τοῦ ἐναντίου· οὕτως οὖν οὐδὲ ἀγαθοποιοῦ τὸ κακοποιεῖν, ἀλλὰ τοὐναντίου. καὶ μὴν ἀγαθὸς ὁ θεός, πεπληρωμένος εὐθὺς ἀπ' ἀρχῆς ταῖς ἁπάσαις ἀρεταῖς, ὥστ' οὐκ ἂν κακοποιητικὸς ὁ θεὸς εἴη οὐδέ τινι κακῶν αἴτιος, πάντα δὲ τοὐναντίον παρέχων ἀγαθὰ τοῖς λαβεῖν βουλομένοις ἅπασι, χαριζόμενος δὲ σὺν τοῖς ἀγαθοῖς καὶ τῶν μέσων, ὅσα κατὰ φύσιν ἡμῖν ἐστι [τὰ] ποιητικά τε τῶν κατὰ φύσιν. ἓν δὲ καὶ μόνον αἴτιον τῶν κακῶν <ἡ κακία>. ***

Ταῦτα χρὴ διειληφέναι, ὡς τῶν μὲν ἀγαθῶν αἰτίων ὄντων τῶν θεῶν, τῶν δὲ κακῶν τῆς κακίας. τίνα οὖν ἡμῖν τοῦ κακῶς πάσχειν αἴτια; ἐπειδὴ τῶν μέσων ἐστί τινα παρὰ φύσιν καὶ δύσχρηστα ἢ νὴ Δία ποιητικὰ τῶν τοιούτων, ἄξιον καὶ περὶ τούτων τὴν νυνὶ διάληψιν ἔχειν, οἷον νόσου λέγω, πηρώσεως, θανάτου, πενίας, δόξης καὶ τῶν παραπλησίων. πολλὰ τοίνυν πέφυκεν αὐτῶν περαίνειν καὶ ἡ κακία· καὶ δι' ἀκρασίαν καὶ λαγνείαν πολλαὶ μὲν γίνονται νόσοι, πολλαὶ δὲ πηρώσεις· διά τε ἀδικίαν πολλοὶ μὲν ἐχειροκοπήθησαν καὶ ἄλλας τοιαύτας ἀνεδέξαντο λώβας, πολλοὶ δὲ καὶ ὅλως ἀπέθανον. ἐμποδίζεται δὲ πυκνὰ καὶ ἡ

single person too, for his chastisement, to be sure, but also for his conversion and a better choice than his other [choices].[6]

Of Hierocles, from the treatise *How Should One Behave toward the Gods?*

I believe that it contributes much to behaving well toward the gods also to consider that a god is never the cause of any evil but that evils befall us as a result of vice alone, whereas the gods, in themselves, are responsible for good and useful things: but we do not welcome their benefactions but rather wrap ourselves in evils freely chosen.[7] I think that well-known poetic passage is opportune here, in connection with this topic: "mortals blame the gods"[8] as though evils were sent by them,

> whereas they themselves, by their own faults, have sufferings beyond what is fated.

For that a god, in fact, is never in any way responsible for evils one may realize on the basis of many things, but for the present, perhaps, that famous argument of Plato may suffice.[9] For he says that cooling is not a property of heat but rather of the opposite, and warming is not a property of cold but rather of the opposite; so too, then, doing evil is not a property of a benefactor but rather of the opposite. Now, a god is good, filled right from the beginning with all the virtues; thus a god cannot be a doer of evil nor a cause of evils for anyone: on the contrary, he furnishes good things to all who are willing to receive them, delighting in good things and, among those that are indifferent, in all those that are in accord with nature in regard to us and productive of things in accord with nature. But vice [κακία] is the one and only thing that is responsible for evils [κακά]: ***[10]

It is necessary to consider the following, given that gods are the cause of good things but vice of evils: What, then, is the reason for our faring badly? Since, of indifferents, some are contrary to nature and adverse or, by Zeus, productive of such things, it is worth making a distinction here among these too: I mean, for example, illness, disability, death, poverty, reputation, and similar things. Now vice, too, is naturally so constituted as to bring about many of these things. Many illnesses and many disabilities arise as a result both of lack of self-control and libertinism. And because of injustice many have had a hand cut off or endured other such mutilations, and many have died outright. Even medicine, kindly to men, is

φιλάνθρωπος ἰατρικὴ πρὸς τὴν ἑαυτῆς πρόθεσιν ὑπὸ τῆς κακίας· ἄπρακτα γὰρ γίνεται τὰ βοηθήματα τῆς τέχνης δι' ἀπείθειαν καὶ ἀκρασίαν καὶ φυγοπονίαν τῶν νοσούντων. καὶ μὴν πολλοὺς μὲν ἀπειργάσατο πτωχοὺς καὶ ἀπόρους ἀσωτία καὶ πολυτέλεια, πολλοὺς δὲ ἀδόξους αἰσχροκέρδεια καὶ μικροπρέπεια.

μετά γε μὴν τὴν κακίαν δευτέρα τῶν τοιούτων πρόφασις ἡ ὕλη. τὰ μὲν γὰρ μετέωρα καὶ ὑπὲρ ἡμᾶς, ὡς ἂν ἐκ τῆς εἰλικρινεστάτης οὐσίας γεγονότα, δι' ὁμαλοῦ πορεύεται, πάντων ἐν αὐτοῖς κατὰ τοὺς τῆς φύσεως λόγους περαινομένων, τὰ δ' ἐπίγεια καθάπερ ὑποστάθμην καὶ ἰλὺν ἔχοντα τὴν ὅλων τὴν οὐσίαν ****

Stobaeus, *Anthology* 3.39.34 (3:730,17–731,15 Wachsmuth and Hense)
Ἱεροκλέους ἐκ τοῦ Πῶς πατρίδι χρηστέον.

Μετὰ τὸν περὶ θεῶν λόγον εὐλογώτατόν ἐστιν ὑποθέσθαι πῶς πατρίδι χρηστέον. ἔστι γὰρ ὡσανεὶ δεύτερός τις θεὸς αὕτη <ἢ> νὴ Δία πρῶτος καὶ μείζων γονεύς· παρ' ὃ δὴ καὶ ὁ τοὔνομα τῷ πράγματι θέμενος οὐκ ἀνεντρεχὲς ἔθετο, παρασχηματίσας μὲν τῷ πατρί, θηλυκῶς δ' ἐξενεγκών, ἵν' οἷον μῖγμα τυγχάνοι τῆς τε τοῦ πατρὸς καὶ τῆς μητρῴας <ἀξίας>. καὶ δὴ οὗτος μὲν ὁ λόγος ὑπαγορεύει πατρίδα τιμᾶν ἐπίσης τοῖς δυσὶ γονεῦσι τὴν μίαν, ὥστε θατέρου μὲν τῶν γειναμένων ὁποτερουοῦν καὶ δὴ προκρίνειν τὴν πατρίδα, προτιμᾶν δ' αὐτῆς μηδ' ἅμα τοὺς δύο, δι' ἴσης δὲ μοίρας ἄγειν. ἀλλ' ἕτερος αὖ λόγος ἐστίν, ὃς παρακαλεῖ καὶ προτιμᾶν αὐτὴν τῶν γονέων ἅμα τοῖν δυεῖν, καὶ οὔτοι μόνον τούτων, ἀλλὰ καὶ γυναικὸς σὺν αὐτοῖς καὶ τέκνων καὶ φίλων καὶ ἁπαξαπλῶς μετὰ θεοὺς τῶν ἄλλων ἁπάντων.

Stobaeus, *Anthology* 3.39.35 (3:731,16–733,6 Wachsmuth and Hense)
Ἐν ταὐτῷ.

Ὥσπερ οὖν ἀνόητος μὲν ὁ τῶν πέντε δακτύλων τὸν ἕνα προκρίνων, εὐλόγιστος δὲ ὁ τοὺς πέντε τοῦ ἑνός· ὁ μὲν γὰρ ἀτιμάζει καὶ τὸν προκεκριμένον, ὁ δ' ἐν τοῖς πέντε καὶ τὸν ἕνα περισῴζει· τοῦτον δ' αὖ τὸν τρόπον καὶ ὁ μὲν ἑαυτὸν τῆς πατρίδος πλέον σῴζειν βουλόμενος πρὸς τῷ δρᾶν ἀθέμιτα καὶ ἄλλως ἀνόητος ἱμείρων ἀδυνάτων, ὁ δὲ ἑαυτοῦ προτιμῶν τὴν πατρίδα θεοφιλής τε

often impeded in its application by vice: for the benefits of the art are rendered useless by the disobedience, lack of self-control, and avoidance of effort on the part of those who are sick. Indeed, profligacy and prodigality have made many men beggars and destitute, while a shameful avarice and niggardliness have made many infamous.

After vice, however, the second cause of such things is matter. For things in the heavens and above us proceed uniformly as though they were made of the purest substance, since everything that is in them is accomplished in accord with nature's reasons, whereas terrestrial things, insofar as they have sediment and slime as the substance of their whole [selves] ****[11]

Of Hierocles, from the treatise *How Should One Behave toward One's Country?*

After the discourse on the gods, it is most reasonable to take up how one should behave toward one's country. For it is, as it were, a kind of second god, or, by Zeus, a first and greater parent;[12] indeed, he who gave its name to the thing [i.e., πατρίς, that is, "fatherland"] did not do so ineptly, since he modeled it on father [πατήρ] but produced it in the feminine, so that, like a mixture, it should acquire both a paternal and a maternal <dignity>.[13] This reasoning, indeed, suggests that we honor our country, which is one, on a par with our two parents, so as in fact to prefer our country to either one of those who bore us, and not even to honor the two together more than it, but rather to hold them in equal respect. But there is also another argument, which exhorts us to honor our country more than both our parents together, and not only more than them, but also more than our wife together with them, and our children and our friends and, in a word, more than all other things, apart from the gods.

In the same treatise.

Just as, then, a person would be senseless who preferred one finger over the five, whereas he would be reasonable in preferring the five to just one—for the former ends up discrediting even the preferred finger, whereas the latter, amidst the five, saves also the one—in the same way a person who wishes to save himself more than his country, in addition to doing what is unlawful, is also senseless, since he desires things that

καὶ τοῖς λογισμοῖς ἀραρώς. εἴρηται δ' ὅμως, ὡς κἂν εἰ μὴ συναριθμοῖτό τις τῷ συστήματι, κατ' ἰδίαν δ' ἐξετάζοιτο, καθήκειν τῆς ἑαυτοῦ σωτηρίας τὴν τοῦ συστήματος προκρίνειν, ὅτι τὴν ὡς πολίτου σωτηρίαν ἀνύπαρκτον ἀπέφαινεν ἡ τῆς πόλεως ἀπώλεια, καθάπερ καὶ τὴν [ὡς] δακτύλου, ὡς μέρους χειρός, ἡ τῆς χειρὸς ἀναίρεσις. καὶ δὴ κατὰ τούτων ἡμῖν συγκεκεφαλαιώσθω, διότι χρὴ τὸ κοινῇ συμφέρον τοῦ ἰδίᾳ μὴ χωρίζειν, ἀλλ' ἓν ἡγεῖσθαι καὶ ταὐτόν· τό τε γὰρ τῇ πατρίδι συμφέρον κοινόν ἐστι καὶ τῶν κατὰ μέρος ἑκάστῳ (τὸ γὰρ ὅλον δίχα τῶν μερῶν ἐστιν οὐδέν) τό τε τῷ πολίτῃ συμφέρον προσήκει καὶ τῇ πόλει, ἐάν γε ὡς πολίτῃ συμφέρον λαμβάνηται. καὶ γὰρ <τὸ> τῷ χορευτῇ ὡς χορευτῇ λυσιτελὲς καὶ τῷ ὅλῳ χορῷ κερδαλέον ἂν εἴη. τοῦτον οὖν τὸν λόγον ἐνθέμενοι πάντα ταῖς διανοίαις πολὺ φῶς ἕξομεν ἐν τοῖς κατὰ μέρος, ὥστε ἐν μηδενὶ παραλιπεῖν καιρῷ τὸ πρὸς τὴν πατρίδα καθῆκον.

Stobaeus, *Anthology* 3.39.36 (3:733,7–734,10 Wachsmuth and Hense)
Ἐν ταὐτῷ.

Ὧν οὕνεκά φημι δεῖν ἀποικονομεῖσθαι πᾶν καὶ πάθος καὶ νόσημα τῆς ἑαυτοῦ ψυχῆς τὸν πατρίδι χρησόμενον καλῶς. δεῖ δὲ καὶ τοὺς νόμους τῆς πατρίδος καθάπερ τινὰς θεοὺς δευτέρους συντηρεῖν αὐτόν τε βιοῦντα κατὰ τὴν τούτων ὑφήγησιν, κἂν εἰ παραβαίνειν τις αὐτοὺς ἢ νεοχμοῦν ἐπιχειροίη, σπουδῇ πάσῃ κωλύοντα καὶ πάντα τρόπον ἐναντιούμενον. οὐ γὰρ ἀγαθὸν ἐπιτήδευμα πόλει δι' ἀτιμίας ἀγόμενοι νόμοι καὶ τὰ νέα προκρινόμενα τῶν παλαιῶν. ὅθεν καὶ τῶν ψηφισμάτων καὶ τῆς παραθέρμου ταύτης καινουργίας εἱρκτέον τοὺς αὐθαδέστερον ἐπὶ τοῦτ' ἰόντας. ἀποδέχομαι δ' οὖν ἔγωγε καὶ τὸν τῶν Λοκρῶν νομοθέτην Ζάλευκον, ὃς ἐνομοθέτησε τὸν καινὸν εἰσοίσοντα νόμον βρόχου περικειμένου τῷ τραχήλῳ τοῦτο ποιεῖν, ὡς ἀκαρὴς οἴχοιτο πνιγείς, εἰ μὴ μάλα σφόδρα λυσιτελῶς τῷ κοινῷ παραδιατάττοιτο τὴν ἐξ ἀρχῆς τῆς πολιτείας κατάστασιν. οὐδὲν δ' ἧττον τῶν νόμων καὶ τὰ ἔθη φυλακτέον τά γε ὄντως πάτρια καὶ τάχα που πρεσβύτερα καὶ τῶν νόμων αὐτῶν· ἐπεὶ τά γε χθιζὰ ταῦτα καὶ πρωιζά, τὰ νῦν εἰς ἅπασαν εἰσηγμένα πόλιν οὔτε πάτρια ἡγητέον καὶ τάχ' οὐδὲ ἔθη τὸ σύνολον. εἶτα τὸ μὲν ἔθος ἄγραφός τις εἶναι

are impossible, whereas one who honors his country more than himself is both dear to the gods and is furnished with rational arguments. It has been said, nevertheless, that even if one does not count himself in the whole [σύστημα], but rather reckons himself individually, it is appropriate for him to prefer the safety of the whole to his own, because the destruction of the city renders the safety of the citizen impossible, just as the elimination of the hand renders impossible the safety of the finger, as part of the hand. In these matters, then, let us sum up as follows: that one must not separate the collective advantage from the individual but rather consider them one and the same thing. For what is advantageous to one's country is common also to each of its parts—for the whole is nothing without its parts—and what is advantageous to the citizen is useful also to the city, if at all events it is understood as advantageous to him as citizen.[14] For in fact what is profitable to a chorus member as chorus member is a gain for the entire chorus as well. Thus, by fixing this overall argument in our thoughts, we shall obtain much light also in individual cases, so as never to neglect at any critical moment our duty to our country.

In the same treatise.

For these reasons I claim that whoever behaves rightly toward his country must rid himself of every passion and illness of the soul.[15] He must also observe the laws of his country as though they were second gods, by living in accord with their guidance and, if anyone should attempt to transgress or change them, by making every effort to prevent him and opposing him in every way. For it is not good practice for a city that the laws be held in disesteem and that innovations be preferred to old ways. This is why one must keep those who approach it in too arrogant a manner away from decrees and from this kind of overheated innovation. Therefore, I for my part welcome Zaleucus, the lawgiver of the Locrians, who made it law that anyone who proposed a new law should do it with a noose around his throat, so that he should be instantly strangled and die, unless he rearranged the original constitution of the state in a way that was most emphatically profitable to the community. No less than the laws, customs must also be preserved, those that are truly ancestral and perhaps more ancient than the laws themselves. For indeed those of yesterday and the day before—those that have now been introduced into every city—must not be considered either ancestral or, perhaps, even customs at all. Besides, custom aims to be a kind of unwritten law, which has enrolled as

βούλεται νόμος, καλὸν ἐπιγεγραμμένος νομοθέτην τὴν τῶν χρωμένων ἁπάντων εὐαρέστησιν, ἴσως δέ που καὶ τοῖς φύσει δικαίοις ἐγγὺς βάλλων.

Stobaeus, *Anthology* 4.67.21 (3:7,13–19 Meineke; cf. *Anth.* 4.22a.21 = 4:502,1–7 Wachsmuth and Hense)
Ἱεροκλέους ἐκ τοῦ περὶ γάμου.

Ἀναγκαιότατός ἐστιν ὁ περὶ τοῦ γάμου λόγος. ἅπαν μὲν γὰρ ἡμῶν τὸ γένος ἔφυ πρὸς κοινωνίαν, πρώτη δὲ καὶ στοιχειωδεστάτη τῶν κοινωνιῶν ἡ κατὰ τὸν γάμον. οὔτε γὰρ πόλεις ἂν ἦσαν μὴ ὄντων οἴκων, οἶκός τε ἡμιτελὴς μὲν τῷ ὄντι ὁ τοῦ ἀγάμου, τέλειος δὲ καὶ πλήρης ὁ τοῦ γεγαμηκότος.

Stobaeus, *Anthology* 4.67.22 (3:7,20–8,18 Meineke; cf. *Anth.* 4.22a.22 = 4:502,8–503,10 Wachsmuth and Hense)
Ἐν ταὐτῷ.

Οὐκοῦν ἔχομεν ἐν τοῖς περὶ οἴκων ἀποδεδειγμένον, ὡς τῷ σοφῷ προηγούμενος μέν ἐστιν ὁ μετὰ γάμου βίος, ὁ δ' ἄνευ γυναικὸς κατὰ περίστασιν· ὥστ' ἐπειδὴ χρὴ μὲν ἐν οἷς γε δυνάμεθα μιμεῖσθαι τὸν ἔχοντα νοῦν, τούτῳ δὲ προηγούμενόν ἐστι τὸ γαμεῖν, δῆλον ὅτι καὶ ἡμῖν ἂν εἴη καθῆκον, εἴ γε μή τις εἴη περίστασις ἐμποδών. καὶ δὴ τοῦτο μὲν πρῶτον·ἔοικε δὲ καὶ πρὸ τοῦ σοφοῦ παρακαλεῖν ἡμᾶς ἡ καὶ αὐτὸν τὸν σοφὸν ἐπὶ τὸν γάμον ἐξοτρύνουσα φύσις, ἥ τις οὐ συναγελαστικοὺς ἡμᾶς ἀπειργάσατο μόνον, ἀλλὰ καὶ συνδυαστικούς, μετὰ τοῦ ἕν τε καὶ κοινὸν ἔργον ὑποθεῖναι τῷ συνδυασμῷ· λέγω δὲ τὴν παίδων γένεσιν καὶ βίου διεξαγωγὴν εὐσταθοῦς.

δικαία δὲ διδάσκαλος ἡ φύσις, ὅτι τῇ παρ' αὐτῆς κατασκευῇ σύμφωνον τὴν ἐκλογὴν χρὴ γίνεσθαι τῶν καθηκόντων. ζῇ γοῦν ἕκαστον τῶν ζῴων ἑπομένως τῇ ἑαυτοῦ φυσικῇ κατασκευῇ, καὶ νὴ Δία τὸ φυτὸν ἅπαν ὡσαύτως κατὰ τὸ ἐπὶ αὐτῶν λεγόμενον ζῆν, πλὴν οὐκ ἐκλογισμῷ καὶ ἀριθμήσει τινὶ χρώμενα καὶ ταῖς ἀπὸ τῶν βασανιζομένων ἐκλογαῖς, ἀλλὰ τὰ μὲν φυτὰ τῇ φύσει ψιλῇ (ψυχῆς γάρ ἐστιν ἀμέτοχα), τὰ δὲ ζῷα φαντασίαις τε σπώσαις ἐπὶ τὰ οἰκεῖα καὶ ἐξελαυνούσαις προθυμίαις. ἡμῖν δὲ ἡ φύσις ἔδωκε τὸν λόγον τά τε ἄλλα πάντα καὶ σὺν πᾶσι, μᾶλλον δὲ πρὸ πάντων αὐτὴν κατοψόμενον τὴν φύσιν, ὅπως ὡς πρός τινα σκοπὸν εὐφεγγῆ τε καὶ ἀραρότα τεταμένος ταύτην, ἐκλεγόμενός τε

its noble law-giver the satisfaction of all who make use of it, thereby perhaps putting it [i.e., custom], I suppose, close also to things that are just by nature [i.e., natural law].[16]

By Hierocles, from the treatise *On Marriage*.

A discussion of marriage is most necessary.[17] For our entire race is naturally disposed to community, and the first and most elementary of the communities is that in accord with marriage. For there would not be cities if there were not households,[18] and the household of an unmarried man is in truth only half complete, but that of a man who is married is complete and full.

In the same treatise.

We have demonstrated, then, in our discourses on households that for a wise man a life with marriage is preferable, whereas that without a wife is so according to circumstance. Thus, since it is right to imitate someone who has sense, in matters where we can, and marrying is preferable for this latter person, it is clear that it should be a duty for us, too, unless in fact some circumstance gets in the way. But indeed the following comes first: even prior to the wise man, nature, it seems, which motivates the wise man himself to marriage, summons us to it as well—that nature which fashioned us not only as social beings but also as living in couples, along with setting out the single, common function for a couple: I mean the generation of children and the leading of a stable life.[19]

Nature is a just teacher, since, by the instruction that comes from her, there necessarily occurs a harmonious choice of duties. In fact, each of the animals lives in a way that follows its own natural constitution: every plant, too, by Zeus, lives similarly in accord with what is called "living" in their case, except that they do not make use of reasoning or any calculation or choices based on things that are tested, but rather plants make use of bare nature—for they are without a share of soul—whereas animals make use both of representations that draw them and of desires that drive them toward what is appropriate to them [οἰκεῖον].[20] To us, nature gave reason as well as all those other things, and along with all of them or rather in place of all of them, to see nature itself, so that, when our reason is intent on nature as on a target that is well lit and fixed, it chooses pref-

τὸ σύμφωνον αὐτῇ πᾶν καθηκόντως βιοῦντας ἡμᾶς ἀπεργάζοιτο.

Stobaeus, *Anthology* 4.67.23 (3:8,19–24 Meineke; cf. *Anth.* 4.22a.23 = 4:503,11–16 Wachsmuth and Hense)
Ἐν ταὐτῷ.

Ὅθεν καὶ οὐκ ἂν ἁμάρτοι τις ἀτελῆ φήσας οἰκίαν τὴν ἄνευ γάμου, τῷ μήτε τὸ ἄρχον ἄνευ τοῦ ἀρχομένου δύνασθαι νοηθῆναι μήτ' ἄνευ τοῦ ἄρχοντος τὸ ἀρχόμενον· οὗτος γὰρ ὁ λόγος εὖ μάλα μοι δοκεῖ δυσωπεῖν τοὺς ἠλλοτριωμένους πρὸς γάμον.

Stobaeus, *Anthology* 4.67.24 (3:8,25–11,27 Meineke; cf. *Anth.* 4.22a.24 = 4:503,17–507,5 Wachsmuth and Hense)
Ἐν ταὐτῷ.

Φημὶ τοίνυν καὶ σύμφορον εἶναι τὸν γάμον πρῶτον μὲν ὅτι θεῖον ὡς ἀληθῶς φέρει καρπὸν τὴν παίδων γένεσιν, οἳ παραστάται μὲν ἡμῖν οἷον συμφυεῖς ἔτι καὶ αὐτοῖς ἐρρωμένοις ἐν ἁπάσαις γίγνονται πράξεσιν, ἀγαθοὶ δὲ ἐπίκουροι κάμνουσιν ὑφ' ἡλικίας καὶ γήρᾳ πιεζομένοις, οἰκεῖοι μὲν ἐν εὐπραγίαις εὐφροσύνης κοινωνοί, συμπαθεῖς δὲ ἐν τοῖς ἐναντίοις καιροῖς διάδοχοι τῶν ἀνιαρῶν.

ἔπειτα καὶ πρὸς γένεσιν τέκνων λυσιτελὴς ἡ μετὰ γυναικὸς συμβίωσις. πρῶτον μὲν γὰρ ἀποτετρυμένους τοῖς θυραίοις καμάτοις ὑποδέχεται θεραπευτικῶς ἀναλαμβάνουσα καὶ μετ' ἐπιμελείας ἀνακτωμένη πάσης· ἔπειτα τῶν ὄντων δυσχερῶν ἐν τῇ διανοίᾳ λήθην ἐντίθησι. τὰ γὰρ σκυθρωπὰ τοῦ βίου περὶ μὲν τὴν ἀγορὰν ἢ τὸ γυμνάσιον ἢ τὸ χωρίον ἢ καθόλου πάσης μερίμνης ἀσχολίας καὶ περὶ τοὺς φίλους τε καὶ συνήθεις διατρίβουσιν ἡμῖν οὐκ ἔστι πρόχειρα τοῖς ἀναγκαίοις ἐπιπροσθούμενα περισπασμοῖς· ἀνεθεῖσι δ' ἐκ τούτων εἴς τε τὴν οἰκίαν ἐπανελθοῦσι καὶ οἷον εὐσχόλοις τὴν ψυχὴν γενομένοις ἐμπελάζει καιρῷ χρώμενα τούτῳ τοῦ ἀνιᾶν ἡμᾶς, ὅταν γε ἔρημος εὐνοίας καὶ μονήρης ὁ βίος ᾖ. γυνὴ δὲ παροῦσα μεγάλη γίνεται καὶ πρὸς ταῦτα παρηγορία, πυνθανομένη τι περὶ τῶν ἐκτὸς ἢ περὶ τῶν ἔνδον ἀναφέρουσα καὶ συνδιασκεπτομένη καί τινα διάχυσιν κἀξ ἀπλάστου προθυμίας εὐφροσύνην παρέχουσα. καὶ μὴν οἷα μέν ἐστιν ἐν ἑορταῖς συνεπιμεληθῆναι θυσιῶν καὶ ἱερουργιῶν, οἷα δ' ἐν ἀνδρὸς ἀποδημίαις εὐσταθῆ διατηρῆσαι καὶ μὴ παντάπασιν ἀπροστάτητον τὸν οἶκον, οἷα δὲ κηδεμὼν οἰκετῶν, οἷα δὲ ἐν νόσοις [οἷα δὴ] παραστάτις, μακρὸς ἂν

erentially everything that is in harmony with nature and can make us live in the way one ought.[21]

In the same treatise.

Hence, one would not err in saying that a household without marriage is incomplete, since neither can what governs be conceived without that which is governed nor what is governed without that which governs. This argument, thus, seems to me to put quite out of countenance those who are hostile to marriage.

In the same treatise.

I say, then, that marriage is also useful, first of all because it is divine,[22] since it truly brings as its fruit the generation of children, who, inasmuch as they are naturally part of us, become our helpers in all activities even when we are well and become good caretakers when we are laboring under our years and weighed down by old age, family members who share our joy in good fortune, whereas in contrary moments they are sympathetic relievers of our pains.

Next, a shared life with a wife is profitable also for the generation of children. For, first of all, she welcomes us when we are worn out with troubles outside the home, restoring us with her healing and refreshing us with every attention. Then she instills in our minds forgetfulness of disagreeable things. For while we are busy, the irritations of life associated with the marketplace or gymnasium or our plot of land or in general with occupations involving any worry, whether about friends or about companions, are not easily occluded by the necessary diversions. Rather, when we have got away from these things and returned to our home and become, as it were, leisured in our soul, they come near again, taking advantage of this opportunity to cause us pain, at least when our life is barren of goodwill and solitary. But if a wife is there, there is a great comfort even for these things: she asks us about affairs outside or inside the home, takes them up and examines them together with us, and provides some relief and joy out of her sincere eagerness. And in truth, in festivals she can take care of sacrifices and rites along with us; during her husband's trips abroad she can maintain the house in order and not altogether without a manager; she can take charge of the slaves; she can be an assistant during illnesses—it

γένοιθ' ὁ λόγος πάντ' ἐπεξιὼν τὰ κατὰ μέρος. ἀρκεῖ γὰρ κεφάλαιον εἰπεῖν, ὡς δεῖ μὲν ἅπασιν ἀνθρώποις πρὸς μετρίαν τοῦ βίου διεξαγωγὴν δυοῖν, συγγενικῆς ἐπικουρίας καὶ συμπαθοῦς εὐνοίας· οὔτε δὲ συμπαθέστερόν τι γυναικὸς εὕροιμεν ἂν οὔτε τέκνων συγγενέστερον. παρέχει δ' ἑκάτερον ὁ γάμος. πῶς οὖν οὐχὶ λυσιτελέστατον ἡμῖν;

ἀλλ' ἔγωγε καὶ καλὸν ἡγοῦμαι τὸν μετὰ γάμου βίον. τίς γὰρ ἕτερος τοιοῦτος γένοιτ' ἂν οἰκίας κόσμος οἷός ἐστιν ὁ κατὰ τὴν ἀνδρὸς καὶ γυναικὸς κοινωνίαν; οὐ μὲν δὴ πολυτελεῖς οἶκοι καὶ ὀρθόστρωτοι τοῖχοι καὶ περίστοα τοῖς ὑπὸ τῆς ἀπειραγαθίας θαυμαζομένοις λίθοις διακεκοσμημένα οὐδὲ ζωγραφία καὶ ψαλιστοὶ μυῤῥινῶνες οὐδ' ἄλλο τι τῶν ἐκπληττόντων τοὺς ἠλιθίους κάλλος ἐστὶν οἰκίας, ἀλλὰ ζεῦγος ἀνδρὸς καὶ γυναικός, συγκαθειμαρμένων ἀλλήλοις καὶ καθιερωμένων θεοῖς γαμηλίοις γενεθλίοις ἐφεστίοις, συμφωνούντων μὲν ἀλλήλοις καὶ πάντα κοινὰ πεποιημένων μέχρι καὶ τῶν σωμάτων, μᾶλλον δὲ καὶ αὐτῶν τῶν ψυχῶν, καὶ περὶ προστασίαν μὲν ἐχόντων τὴν ἐπιβάλλουσαν τοῦ οἴκου καὶ τῶν θεραπόντων, ἀνατροφὴν δὲ καὶ κηδεμονίαν τῶν τέκνων, ἐπιμέλειαν δὲ οὔτε σύντονον οὔτε μὴν ῥᾴθυμον, ἀλλ' ἐμμελῆ καὶ καθηρμοσμένην τῶν πρὸς τὸ ζῆν ἀναγκαίων. τί γὰρ ἂν γένοιτο «κρεῖσσον καὶ ἄρειον» κατὰ τὸν θαυμασιώτατον Ὅμηρον «ἢ ὅθ' ὁμοφρονέοντε νοήμασιν οἰκί' ἔχητον ἀνὴρ ἠδὲ γυνή;»

διὸ καὶ πολλάκις ἐθαύμασα τοὺς ὡς βαρὺν ἡγουμένους τὸν μετὰ γυναικὸς βίον. οὐ γὰρ δὴ γυνὴ μὰ Δία βάρος ἢ φορτίον ἐστί, καθάπερ οὗτοι δοκοῦσιν· ἀλλ' ἥδε μὲν κἀκ τῶν ἐναντίων κοῦφόν τι καὶ ῥᾷστα φέρεσθαι δυνάμενον, μᾶλλον δὲ καὶ τῶν ὄντως ἐπαχθῶν καὶ βαρέων κουφιστικόν. οὐδὲν γὰρ οὕτω φορτικόν ἐστι τῶν ὄντων, ὥστε μὴ ῥᾷστον εἶναι συμφρονοῦσί γε ἀνδρὶ καὶ γυναικὶ καὶ κοινῇ φέρειν αὐτὸ βουλομένοις. βαρὺ δέ ἐστιν ὡς ἀληθῶς ἀφροσύνη καὶ δύσοιστον τοῖς αὐτὴν κεκτημένοις, ὑφ' ἧς δὴ καὶ τὰ φύσει κοῦφα γίνεται βαρέα, τά τε ἄλλα καὶ γυνή. τῷ ὄντι γὰρ καὶ συχνοῖς [γὰρ] δή τισιν ἀφόρητος ἐγένετο ὁ γάμος, ἀλλ' οὐχὶ παρ' ἑαυτοῦ οὐδὲ τῷ φύσει τοιάνδε τὴν μετὰ γυναικὸς εἶναι κοινωνίαν· ἀλλ' ὅταν γαμῶμεν ἃς μὴ δεῖ, μετὰ τοῦ καὶ αὐτοὶ παντάπασιν ἀπειροβίως διακεῖσθαι καὶ ἀπαρασκεύως ἔχειν πρὸς τὸ ἀγαγεῖν ὡς χρὴ τὴν ἐλευθέραν ἄγεσθαι, τὸ τηνικαῦτα συμβαίνει χαλεπὴν καὶ ἀφόρητον γίνεσθαι τὴν κοινωνίαν.

ἀμέλει καὶ ταύτῃ χωρεῖ τοῖς πολλοῖς ὁ γάμος. οὐ γὰρ ἐπὶ παίδων γενέσει καὶ βίου κοινωνίᾳ ἄγονται γυναῖκας, ἀλλ' οἳ μὲν διὰ προικὸς ὄγκον, οἳ δὲ δι' ἐξοχὴν μορφῆς, οἳ δὲ δι' ἄλλας τινὰς τοιουτοτρόπους αἰτίας, αἷς

would be a long story to go through everything one by one. For it suffices to mention the chief point, that for all people two things are needed for a tolerable way of life: succor from relations and affectionate goodwill; but we cannot find anyone more affectionate than a wife, or more closely related than children—and marriage provides both. How, then, can it not be most useful to us?

But I myself consider married life to be also beautiful.[23] For what other adornment of the home could there be like the community between a husband and wife? For the beauty of a home is not expensive buildings and marble walls and porticoes adorned with stones that are admired by poor taste, nor painting nor trimmed myrtle groves, nor any other of the things that amaze the foolish, but the union of a husband and wife who share each other's destinies and are consecrated to the gods of marriage, generation, and the hearth, in concord with each other and setting everything in common up to their very bodies, or rather up to their very own souls, and who take thought for the management that is incumbent on them of their household and their servants, and the rearing and care of their children, and a concern for the necessities of life that is neither strained nor slack, but is balanced and attuned. For what could be "stronger and better," in the words of the most marvelous Homer,[24] "than when a husband and wife, like-minded in their thoughts, maintain a home"?

This is why I have often wondered at those who consider that life with a wife is burdensome. For, in fact, a wife, by Zeus, is not a weight or a load, as they believe; she is rather, on the contrary, something light that can be easily borne, but rather she is able to lighten even things that really are onerous and heavy. For there is nothing so burdensome among real things that it is not easy to bear for a husband and wife who think alike and are willing to bear it together. What is truly heavy and difficult to bear for those who have it is foolishness, as a result of which, in fact, even things that are by nature light become heavy—and among these, even a wife.[25] For marriage has really been unbearable for many, indeed, but not of itself, nor because community with a wife is such by nature. Rather, when we marry women we ought not, together with the fact that we ourselves are altogether inexperienced in life and unprepared to wed as one ought to wed a free woman—then life in common turns out to be difficult and unbearable.

This is actually the reason why marriage comes about for many men. For they do not wed women for the generation of children or for a community of life, but rather some do so for the size of their dowry, others for their extraordinary beauty, and still others for other motives of this type,

χρώμενοι κακοῖς συμβούλοις, οὐδὲν περὶ τῆς διαθέσεως καὶ τοῦ ἤθους τῆς νύμφης πολυπραγμονήσαντες, ὄλεθρον αὑτῶν θύουσι τὸν γάμον, καὶ θύραις κατεστεμμέναις τύραννον ἀντὶ γυναικὸς ἐπεισάγουσιν ἑαυτοῖς, καὶ ταῦτα μηδὲ ἐφ' ὁποσονοῦν ἀνταρκέσαι δυνάμενοι καὶ τὴν περὶ τῶν πρωτείων ἅμιλλαν ἀγωνίσασθαι. φανερὸν οὖν ὡς οὐ δι' αὐτὸν, ἀλλὰ διὰ ταῦτα πολλοῖς βαρὺς καὶ ἀφόρητος ὁ γάμος γίνεται. χρὴ δ' οὔτ' ἀναίτια, φησίν, αἰτιᾶσθαι οὔτ' ἔγκλημα πραγμάτων ποιεῖσθαι τὴν αὑτῶν ἀσθένειαν καὶ περὶ τὴν χρῆσιν αὐτῶν <ἄγνοιαν>· ἐπεί τοι καὶ ἀλόγιστον ἄλλως πανταχόθεν μὲν ἀφορμὰς ζητεῖν φιλιῶν καί τινας προσποιεῖσθαι φίλους καὶ ἑταίρους οἷον συμμάχους ἐσομένους πρὸς τὰ τοῦ βίου δυσχερῆ, τὴν δὲ καὶ παρὰ τῆς φύσεως καὶ παρὰ τῶν νόμων καὶ παρὰ τῶν θεῶν διδομένην ἀνδράσιν συμμαχίαν τε καὶ βοήθειαν, τουτέστι τὴν ἐκ γυναικὸς καὶ τέκνων, μὴ ζητεῖν τε καὶ προσποιεῖσθαι.*

Stobaeus, *Anthology* 4.75.14 (3:72,4–74,3 Meineke; cf. *Anth.* 4.24a.14 = 4:603,8–605,16 Wachsmuth and Hense)

Ἐν δὲ τῷ περὶ τοῦ γάμου καὶ τῆς παιδοποιΐας τόπῳ θετέος ἐστὶ καὶ ὁ <περὶ> τῆς πολυτεκνίας λόγος. κατὰ φύσιν γάρ πως καὶ ἀκόλουθον τῷ γάμῳ τὸ πάντα ἢ τά γε πλεῖστα τῶν γεννωμένων ἀνατρέφειν· ἀλλ' ἐοίκασιν οἱ πλείους ἀπειθεῖν τῇ παραινέσει δι' αἰτίαν οὐ μάλα πρεπώδη. διὰ γὰρ φιλοπλουτίαν καὶ τὸ πάμμεγα κακὸν ἡγεῖσθαι τὴν πενίαν τοῦτο πάσχουσι. πρῶτον μὲν δὴ λογιστέον, ὡς οὐχ ἑαυτοῖς μόνον παραστάτας καὶ γηροβοσκοὺς καὶ πάσης τύχης τε καὶ περιστάσεως κοινωνοὺς γεννῶμεν, οὐδ' ὑπὲρ ἑαυτῶν μόνον, ἀλλὰ καὶ ὑπὲρ τῶν γονέων ἡμῶν κατὰ πολλά γε. καὶ γὰρ εὐχαριστίαν ἔχει πρὸς αὐτοὺς ἡ παιδοποιΐα τῷ, κἂν εἴ τι πάθοιμεν ἡμεῖς πρότερον, καταλείπειν ἐκείνοις ἀνθ' ἡμῶν αὐτοὺς γηροβοσκούς· καλὸν δὲ πάππος ὑπὸ σφετέρων ἐκγόνων χειραγωγούμενός τε καὶ τῆς ἄλλης ἐπιμελείας ἀξιούμενος· ὥστε πρῶτον μὲν εὐχάριστα πράττοιμεν ἂν εἰς γονέας τοὺς ἑαυτῶν, παίδων ἐπιμελούμενοι γενέσεως. εἶτα καὶ ταῖς εὐχαῖς τε καὶ σπουδαῖς τῶν ἡμᾶς γειναμένων συνεργήσομεν· εὐθὺ γὰρ ὅτε πρῶτον περὶ τὴν ἡμετέραν εἶχον

---

* Wachsmuth and Hense (4:507,3–5) reads: ἐπεί τοι καὶ ἀλόγιστον ἄλλως πανταχόθεν μὲν ἀφορμὰς ζητεῖν φιλιῶν καί τινας προσποιεῖσθαι φίλους καὶ ἑταίρους οἷον συμμάχους ἐσομένους πρὸς τὰ τοῦ βίου δυσχερῆ, τὴν δὲ καὶ παρὰ τῆς φύσεως καὶ παρὰ τῶν νόμων καὶ παρὰ τῶν θεῶν διδομένην μισεῖν συμμαχίαν τε καὶ βοήθειαν, τουτέστι τὴν ἐκ γυναικὸς καὶ τέκνων.

and they use these things as bad counselors, not busying themselves at all about the disposition and character of their bride:[26] and so they celebrate a marriage that is their own ruin, and at doors hung with garlands they lead in a tyrant for themselves rather than a wife, since they cannot hold out against these things to any extent or struggle in competition for first prize. It is obvious, accordingly, that for many marriage is burdensome and unbearable for these reasons, and not in itself. People should not blame what is blameless, as he says,[27] nor turn their own weakness and ignorance concerning the use of things into a complaint about the things themselves. For it would indeed be irrational to seek opportunities for friendships from every quarter and to acquire friends and comrades to be our allies in the face of the difficult things in life, and not to seek and acquire that alliance and assistance that is given to men by nature, the laws, and the gods—that is, the one that comes from a wife and children.*

In the section concerning marriage and procreation, a discussion about having many children should also be included. For it is, somehow, in accord with nature and consequent upon marriage to rear all or at least most of those that have been begotten. But most people seem to disobey this advice for a reason that is not very seemly: for they feel this way on account of their love of wealth and because they believe that poverty is a huge evil.[28] But first we must consider that we do not beget assistants and caretakers of old age and partners of every fortune and circumstance for ourselves alone nor only in our own behalf, but also at least much of the time in behalf of our parents. For, in fact, procreation encompasses gratitude toward them, because, even if we ourselves should pass away first, we leave them our children in our place as caretakers of their old age: a grandfather who is led by the hand of his own grandchildren and considered worthy of every other attention is a lovely thing. Thus, first of all, we would be doing something thankful toward our own parents by taking care for the generation of our children; next, we shall collaborate also with the prayers and concerns of those who begot us. For immediately, as soon

* For it would indeed be irrational to seek opportunities for friendships from every quarter and to acquire friends and comrades to be our allies in the face of the difficult things in life, and to hate that alliance and assistance that is provided by nature, the laws, and the gods—that is, the one that comes from a wife and children.

γένεσιν, διανοίᾳ χρώμενοι τοῦ χύσιν αὐτῶν εἰς πλεῖστον λαβεῖν τὴν διαδοχὴν καὶ παῖδας ἐκ παίδων ὑπολιπέσθαι, καὶ γάμου προὐνόησαν καὶ τῆς ἡμετέρας σπορᾶς καὶ ἀνατροφῆς. ὅθεν γαμοῦντες μὲν καὶ παιδοποιούμενοι πράττοιμεν ἂν οἷον μέρη τῆς ἐκείνων εὐχῆς· τὰ δ' ἐναντία φρονήσαντες ἐγκόπτοιμεν ἂν αὐτῶν τῇ προαιρέσει. καὶ μὴν κινδυνεύει πᾶς ὁ θελοντὴς καὶ περιστάσεως ἄνευ γάμον ἐκκλίνων καὶ παιδοποιΐαν παρανοίας κρίνειν τοὺς ἑαυτοῦ γονέας, ὡς οὐ σὺν ὀρθοῖς λογισμοῖς περὶ γάμου πεπραγματευμένους. ἔνθα δὴ καὶ τὴν ἀνομολογίαν φωράσειεν ἄν τις εὐπετῶς. πῶς γὰρ οὐ μάχης πλῆρες εὐαρεστεῖν μὲν τῷ ζῆν καὶ μένειν ἐν αὐτῷ, ὡς καθηκόντως εἰς τὸν βίον ὑπὸ τῶν σπειράντων παρηγμένον, τὸ δ' αὐτὸν ἑτέρους γεννῆσαι τῶν ἀδοκίμων ὑπολαμβάνειν;

ἀλλὰ γὰρ πρῶτον μέν, ὡς ἔφην, ἐντεθυμῆσθαι χρή, διότι γεννῶμεν οὐχ ἑαυτοῖς μόνον, ἀλλὰ καὶ τοῖς δι' οὓς γεγόναμεν αὐτοί· ἔπειτα καὶ ὑπὲρ φίλων τε καὶ συγγενῶν. κεχαρισμένον γὰρ καὶ τούτοις ἐστὶ παῖδας ἐξ ἡμῶν ἰδεῖν, διά τε τὴν εὔνοιαν καὶ οἰκειότητα καὶ δὴ καὶ διὰ τὴν ἀσφάλειαν. διορμίζεται γὰρ ὑπὸ τοῦ τοιούτου τοῖς προσήκουσιν ὁ βίος ἀνὰ λόγον ταῖς ἐπὶ πολλῶν ἀγκυρῶν σαλευούσαις ναυσίν. ὅθεν κατὰ τὸν φιλοσυγγενῆ καὶ φιλεταῖρόν ἐστιν ἡ περὶ γάμον καὶ τέκνα σπουδή.

παρακαλεῖ δ' εὖ μάλα καὶ ἡ πατρὶς ἐπὶ ταὐτόν. καὶ σχεδὸν οὐδ' ἑαυτοῖς οὕτως ὡς τῇ πατρίδι φυτεύομεν παῖδας, τῆς μεθ' ἡμᾶς προνοούμενοι τάξεως καὶ τῷ κοινῷ παρέχοντες τοὺς διαδεξομένους ἡμᾶς. ὅθεν ὁ μὲν ἱερεὺς ἴστω τῇ πόλει τῇ ἑαυτοῦ ἱερέας ὀφείλων, ὁ δ' ἄρχων ἄρχοντας, ὁ δὲ δημηγόρος δημηγόρους, καὶ ὡς ἁπλῶς εἰπεῖν ὁ πολίτης πολίτας. καθάπερ οὖν χορῷ μέν ἐστι κεχαρισμένη ἡ τῶν χορευτῶν διαμονή, στρατεύματι δὲ ἡ τῶν στρατιωτῶν, οὕτω καὶ πόλει ἡ τῶν πολιτῶν. ἀλλ' εἰ μὲν ἦν ὀλιγοχρόνιόν τι σύστημα πόλις, ὅ τε βίος αὐτῆς κατὰ βίον ἀνθρώπου τὴν συμμετρίαν ἐλάμβανεν, οὐδὲν ἔδει διαδοχῆς. ἐπεὶ δ' εἰς πολλὰς γενεὰς ἐξικνεῖται, δαίμονι δὴ εὐδαιμονεστέρῳ χρησαμένη, καὶ εἰς μακροὺς αἰῶνας πόλις, φανερὸν ὡς οὐ τοῦ παρόντος ἐστοχάσθαι δεῖ μόνον, ἀλλὰ καὶ τοῦ μετέπειτα, τήν τε ἰδίαν μὴ περιορᾶν χώραν ἔρημον, ἀλλ' ἐπ' ἐλπίσιν ἱδρυμένην ταῖς ἀπὸ τῶν ἡμετέρων τέκνων.

as they took thought for our birth, with the idea of acquiring the greatest diffusion of themselves in their posterity and of leaving behind the children of our children, they planned ahead for our marriage, our offspring, and their rearing. Hence, in marrying and procreating we realize, as it were, a part of their prayer, but if we should contemplate the opposite, we would be opposing their preference. And, in fact, whoever voluntarily avoids both marriage and procreation, independently of circumstance, is in danger of accusing his own parents of insanity, on the grounds that they did not trouble themselves about marriage with the right kinds of reasoning. But here one can in fact easily discover their incoherence, too. For how is it not full of contradiction to be content in one's life and remain in it, once one has been dutifully brought into life by one's parents, but suppose that for oneself to beget others is among the things that are disreputable?

But first of all, as I said, one must consider that we beget children not only for ourselves but also for those thanks to whom we ourselves were born, and then also for our friends and relatives. For it is pleasing for them too to see children born of us, because of their goodwill and relationship and more particularly for the sake of safety. For life is brought into harbor by such a person for his kin, just like sea-tossed ships that rest on many anchors. Hence, eagerness for marriage and children is fitting for someone who is loving of his relatives and friends.

Our country, too, encourages us strongly to the same end.[29] For by and large we sow children not so much for ourselves as for our country, taking forethought for the situation that will come after us and providing the community with those who will succeed us. Hence, let the priest know that he owes priests to his city, the ruler that he owes rulers, the orator orators, and, in a word, the citizen citizens. Thus, just as the continuity of its chorus members is pleasing to a chorus and that of its soldiers to an army, so too that of its citizens is pleasing to a city. Now, if a city were a short-lived entity, and if its life had commensurability with the life of a human being, there would be no need of succession. But since a city goes on for many generations and, indeed, if it enjoys a happier fate, even for long epochs, it is clear that one must not set one's sights only on the present but rather also on what comes after, and not gaze on one's own land as barren but rather as founded upon the hopes that derive from our children.

Stobaeus, *Anthology* 4.79.53 (3:95,30–99,9 Meineke; cf. *Anth.* 4.25.53 = 4:640,4–644,15 Wachsmuth and Hense)

Μετὰ τὸν περὶ θεῶν καὶ πατρίδος λόγον τίνος μᾶλλον ἂν προσώπου μνησθείη τις πρῶτον ἢ γονέων; ὅθεν λεκτέον περὶ τούτων, οὓς δευτέρους καὶ ἐπιγείους τινὰς θεοὺς εἰπὼν οὐκ <ἂν> ἁμάρτοι τις, ἕνεκά γε τῆς ἐγγύτητος, εἰ θέμις εἰπεῖν, καὶ θεῶν ἡμῖν τιμιωτέρους. προλαβεῖν δ' ἀναγκαῖόν ἐστιν, ὡς μόνον μέτρον τῆς πρὸς αὐτοὺς εὐχαριστίας ἡ διηνεκὴς καὶ ἀνένδοτος προθυμία πρὸς τὸ ἀμείβεσθαι τὰς εὐεργεσίας αὐτῶν· ἐπεί τοί γε πολὺ καταδεέστερα, κἂν πάνυ πολλὰ πράξωμεν ὑπὲρ αὐτῶν. ἀλλ' ὅμως κινδυνεύει καὶ ταῦτ' ἐκείνων ἔργα τυγχάνειν, ὅτι καὶ ἡμᾶς τοὺς ταῦτα πράττοντας ἐκεῖνοι πεποιήκασιν. ὥσπερ οὖν τὰ ὑπὸ Φειδίου καὶ τῶν ἄλλων τεχνιτῶν ἀπεργασθέντα, εἴπερ καὶ αὐτὰ ἕτερά τινα κατεσκεύαζεν, οὐκ ἂν ὀκνήσαιμεν καὶ ταῦτα τῶν τεχνιτῶν ἔργα φάσκειν· οὕτως εἰκότως καὶ τὰ ὑφ' ἡμῶν δρώμενα λέγοιμεν ἂν εἶναι τῶν γονέων ἡμῶν ἔργα, δι' οὓς καὶ ἡμεῖς γεγόναμεν, καὶ οὐχὶ τἆλλα μέν, οὐχὶ δὲ καὶ τὰ ὑπὲρ αὐτῶν πραττόμενα τῶν γονέων. πρὸς οὖν τὴν εὐμαρῆ τῶν ἐπ' αὐτοὺς καθηκόντων αἵρεσιν κεφαλαιώδη τινὰ χρὴ προβαλλομένους λόγον, τοῦτον ἐν προχείρῳ διηνεκὲς ἔχειν, ὡς οἱ γονεῖς ἡμῶν θεῶν εἰκόνες καὶ νὴ Δία θεοὶ ἐφέστιοι καὶ εὐεργέται καὶ συγγενεῖς δανεισταί τε καὶ κύριοι καὶ φίλοι βεβαιότατοι. θεῶν τε γὰρ εἰκόνες ὁμοιόταται καὶ ὑπὲρ τὰς τῶν τεχνῶν δυνάμεις καθιγμέναι τῆς ἐμφερείας. θεοί τε <γὰρ> ἐστιοῦχοι καὶ συνδίαιτοι ἡμῖν, ἔτι δ' εὐεργέται μέγιστοι καὶ παρεσχημένοι τὰ μέγιστα καὶ μὰ Δί' οὐχὶ μόνον ἃ ἔχομεν, ἀλλὰ καὶ ὁπόσα παρέχειν ἐβουλήθησαν ἅ τε κἂν εὔξαιντο. πρὸς δὲ τούτοις συγγενεῖς ἔγγιστα καὶ τῆς πρὸς ἑτέρους αἴτιοι συγγονῆς. δανεισταὶ δὲ τῶν τιμιωτάτων, μόνα ἀπαιτοῦντες ὧν καὶ ἡ ἀπόδοσις πάλιν ἐστὶν ἡμῶν εὐεργεσία. τί γὰρ τηλικοῦτον παιδὶ κέρδος, ἡλίκον ἐστὶ τὸ πρὸς τοὺς γειναμένους εὐσεβὲς καὶ εὐχάριστον; κύριοί γε μὴν δικαιότατα. τίνος γὰρ <ἂν> κτῆμα μᾶλλον εἴημεν ἢ ἐκείνων δι' οὓς ἐσμέν; οὐ μὴν ἀλλὰ καὶ φίλοι καὶ παραστάται διηνεκεῖς καὶ αὐτόκλητοι παντὸς καιροῦ καὶ πάσης περιστάσεως ἐπίκουροι.

ἐπεὶ δὲ τῶν προκατηριθμημένων ἁπάντων τὸ ἐξοχώτατον ἦν ὄνομα γονεῦσι, καθὸ θεοὺς αὐτοὺς ἀπεκαλοῦμεν, τῇ τοιᾷδε ἐπινοίᾳ προσθετέον ἕτερον καὶ νομιστέον ἑαυτοὺς καθάπερ ἐν ἱερῷ τῇ οἰκίᾳ ζακόρους τινὰς καὶ ἱερέας, ὑπ' αὐτῆς κεχειροτονημένους καὶ καθιερωμένους τῆς φύσεως, ἐγκεχειρίσθαι τὴν τῶν γονέων θεραπείαν. ὅθεν καὶ διελόντες τῆς ἐπιμελείας τὸ μὲν εἰς σῶμα τὸ δ'

[Parents]

After the discourse concerning gods and country, what other person could one mention first if not one's parents? Hence we must speak about these, whom one would not err in calling as it were second and terrestrial gods, and indeed because of their nearness, if it is lawful to say so, even more to be honored than the gods.[30] It is necessary to posit first, as the only measure of gratitude toward them, a continual and unremitting eagerness to repay their benefaction, for even if we do very many things in their behalf, they will always prove too little. But nevertheless, there is the risk that even these will turn out to be their acts, since they created us who do these things. Just as, if the works fashioned by Pheidias and other artists should themselves produce other such works, we would not hesitate to say that these too were the artists' works, so too we may reasonably call the things done by us the works of our parents, through whom we ourselves came into being—and not some things yes, but not those done in behalf of our parents themselves. Thus, to make the choice of our duties toward parents easy, it is best that we propose a summary argument and keep it continually at hand: that our parents are images of gods and, by Zeus, domestic gods, benefactors, relatives, creditors, masters, and most reliable friends. For they are images of gods that are supreme likenesses, achieving a resemblance that is beyond the capacity of the arts. <For> they are domestic gods, dwelling with us, and beyond this they are our greatest benefactors who have provided the greatest things and, by Zeus, not only those we have but also all those that they wished to provide and for which they might have prayed. Moreover, they are our closest relatives and responsible for our kinship with others. They are also our creditors for the most valuable things and ask in return only for those things, the return of which is again a benefaction for us. For what profit for a child is so great as piety and gratitude toward his parents? And they are most justly our masters. For whose possessions could we be, more than theirs, though whom we exist? And no less, they are also constant friends and assistants, who come unsummoned at every crisis and are helpers in every circumstance.

But since, of all those we have listed above, the most excellent name for our parents was when we called them gods, to this idea we must add another, that we must consider ourselves as kinds of ministers and priests in our home as in a temple, elected and consecrated by nature itself and entrusted with the tendance of our parents. For this reason, if within this care we separate what pertains to the body and what pertains to the soul,

εἰς ψυχήν, καθ' ἑκάτερον αὐτῶν μεθ' ἑκάστης προθυμίας, πείθεσθαί γε τῷ λόγῳ τι βουλόμενοι, τὸ καθῆκον ἐκπληρώσομεν. τοῦ μὲν οὖν σώματος ἕνεκα βραχὺς ὁ λόγος, εἰ καὶ ἀναγκαῖος· προνοήσομεν γὰρ τροφῆς αὐτῶν ἐλευθερίου καὶ πρὸς τὴν ἀσθένειαν τοῦ γήρως ἡρμοσμένης· ἔτι δὲ κοίτης καὶ ὕπνου ἀλείμματός τε καὶ λουτροῦ καὶ ἐσθῆτος καὶ ἁπαξαπλῶς τῶν ἕνεκα τοῦ σώματος ἀναγκαίων, ὡς κατὰ μηδὲν τούτων ἐνδείας ποτὲ πειραθεῖεν, μιμούμενοι τὴν αὐτῶν ἐκείνων περὶ τὴν ἡμετέραν ἀνατροφήν, ὅτ' ἦμεν νεογνοί, κηδεμονίαν· ὥστε προσαναγκάζειν ἑαυτοὺς καὶ μαντικόν τι προσφέρεσθαι <πρὸς τὴν> θεραπείαν, κἀξευρίσκειν, εἴπερ αὐτοὶ μὴ λέγοιεν, πρὸς τίνα μάλιστα ῥέπουσιν αὐτοῖς αἱ προθυμίαι τῶν τῷ σώματι προσαγομένων. πολλὰ γὰρ αὖ κἀκεῖνοι περὶ ἡμῶν ἐμαντεύσαντο, πολλάκις ἀνάρθροις ἔτι καὶ κλαυθμώδεσι φωναῖς ὅτι μὲν δεόμεθα τινῶν σημηνάντων, τίνα δ' ἐστὶν ὧν δεόμεθα διασαφῆσαι μὴ δυνηθέντων. κἂν εἰ ἡμῖν καὶ αὐτῶν τούτων τῶν καθ' ἡμᾶς γεγονότων διδάσκαλοι γεγόνασιν, ὧν ἄξιοι τυγχάνειν εἰσὶ παρ' ἡμῶν, ταῦθ' ἡμᾶς διὰ τοῦ προπαρασχεῖν ἡμῖν διδάξαντες.

ταῖς δὲ ψυχαῖς αὐτῶν παρασχετέον πρῶτον μὲν τὴν εὐθυμίαν, ἣ μάλιστα γένοιτ' ἂν ἐκ τοῦ συναναστρέφεσθαι νύκτωρ τε καὶ μεθ' ἡμέραν αὐτοῖς, εἰ μή τι κωλύοι, συμπεριπατοῦντας συναλειφομένους συνδιαιτωμένους. καθάπερ γὰρ τοῖς μακρὰν στελλομένοις ἀποδημίαν πρὸς εὐθυμίαν εἰσὶν ἐν τρόπῳ γινόμεναι προπομπίας τῶν οἰκειοτάτων τε καὶ φιλτάτων συναναστροφαί, τὸν αὐτὸν τρόπον καὶ τοῖς γονεῦσιν νενευκόσιν ἤδη πρὸς τὴν ἄφοδον ἐν τοῖς μάλιστα κεχαρισμέναι καὶ προσφιλεῖς εἰσιν αἱ τῶν τέκνων προσεδρίαι. καὶ μέντοι κἂν εἴ τί που γένοιντο παραμαρτάνοντες (ὁποῖα δὴ πολλὰ φιλεῖ γενέσθαι περὶ τοὺς πλείονας καὶ ἰδιωτικώτερον ἠγμένους), ἐπανορθωτέον μέν, ἀλλ' οὐ μετ' ἐπιπλήξεως μὰ Δία, καθάπερ ἔθος πρὸς τοὺς ἐλάττονας ἢ ἴσους ποιεῖν, ἀλλ' ὡς μετὰ παρακλήσεως, καὶ οὐχ ὡς δι' ἀμαθίαν ἁμαρτάνοντας, ἀλλ' ὡς παρορῶντας τῷ μὴ ἐφεστακέναι, πάντως δ' ἂν ἰδόντας εἴπερ ἐπέστησαν. ἀνιαραὶ γὰρ τοῖς τηλίκοις καὶ μάλιστα αἱ ἐκτενῶς νουθετήσεις, ἀναγκαία δὲ μετὰ παρακλήσεως καί τινος φιλοτεχνίας ἴασις τῶν παρορωμένων. φέρει δ' ἐπὶ τὴν εὐθυμίαν αὐτοῖς καὶ τὸ τῶν θητικωτέρων εἶναι δοκούντων ὑπηρετημάτων ἅπτεσθαί ποτε τοὺς παῖδας, ὥστε καὶ πόδας ὑπονίψαι καὶ κλίνην στορέσαι καὶ παραστῆναι διακονουμένους. εὐφραίνοιντο γὰρ οὐκ ὀλίγως παρὰ τῶν φιλτάτων χειρῶν τὰς ἀναγκαίας ὑπηρεσίας λαμβάνοντες καὶ διακόνοις χρώμενοι τοῖς σφετέροις ἔργοις. μάλιστα δ' ἂν εἴη γονεῦσι κεχαρισμένον καὶ τὸ φαίνεσθαι τιμῶντας τοὺς παῖδας, οὓς ἂν ἐκεῖνοι στέργωσιν καὶ περὶ πολλοῦ ποιῶνται. διὸ συγγενεῖς

we will fulfill our duty in each of these with all eagerness, if at least we wish to obey reason to some extent. Concerning the body, now, our discourse is brief, albeit necessary: for we shall take thought for nourishment for them that is liberal and adapted to the weakness of old age and, further, for their bed and sleep, unguents, baths, clothing, and, in a word, the needs of the body, so that they may never experience a lack of any of these things, imitating their own concern for our rearing, when we were newborns. Thus, we oblige ourselves to apply a certain divination to their tendance and to discover, even if they themselves do not tell us, toward which of the things that apply to the body their wishes most incline. For they too had to divine many things concerning us, as we often indicated with inarticulate and plaintive sounds that we needed something but were unable to make clear what it was that we needed.[31] And if they were our teachers in the very things that happened in our case, then they deserve to obtain these things from us, since they taught us these things by providing them for us first.

For their souls there must first of all be provided good cheer, which can most of all come about by keeping them company night and day, if nothing should prevent it: taking walks with them, oiling them down, dining with them. For just as, for those who are being sent on a long trip abroad, the company of their relatives and dearest friends, in a sort of send-off, contributes to their good cheer, in the same way too for parents, who are by now inclining toward departure, the attentions of their children are among the things that are most pleasing and dear to them. And indeed, even if they should err in something—the kind of thing that tends often to occur with most people who have been brought up rather vulgarly—they should be corrected, to be sure, but not with a rebuke, by Zeus, as it is customary to do with those who are our inferiors or equals, but rather with exhortation, and not as though they had erred through ignorance, but as though they overlooked it because they did not pay attention but would certainly have seen it if they had been paying attention. For admonitions are painful to people of that age, and especially when given sharply: the necessary cure for their oversights is with encouragement and a kind of art.[32] What also contributes to their good cheer is for their children occasionally to assume what seem like rather menial services, such as washing their feet, making their bed, and standing by to attend to them. For they are delighted in no small measure when they receive necessary services from the dearest of hands and have as their attendants their own creation. But what would be above all pleasing to parents is that their children, whom they love and value so highly, should

αὐτῶν στερκτέον καὶ ἐπιμελείας ἀξιωτέον, φίλους θ' ὡσαύτως καὶ δῆτα καὶ ἑκάστους τοὺς ἐκείνοις κεχαρισμένους.

ἀφ' ἧς ἀφορμῆς εὕρεσις ἡμῖν ὑπογράφεται καὶ ἑτέρων πλειόνων καθηκόντων οὐ σμικρῶν οὐδὲ τῶν τυχόντων. ἐπεὶ γὰρ χάρις ἐστὶ γονεῦσι τῶν στεργομένων ὑπ' αὐτῶν κηδεμονία, μάλιστα δ' ἔχουσι πρὸς ἡμᾶς οὕτως, δῆλον ὡς οὐ τὰ τυχόντα ἂν αὐτοῖς χαριζοίμεθα προνοοῦντες αὐτῶν.

Stobaeus, *Anthology* 4.84.20 (3:126,11–129,4 Meineke; cf. *Anth.* 4.27.20 = 4:660,15–664,18 Wachsmuth and Hense)

Πρώτη μὲν οὖν ὑποθήκη μάλα σαφὴς ἐπιεικῶς τε εὔπορος, πρὸς δὲ καὶ κοινή. κατὰ παντὸς μὲν γὰρ εἰπεῖν προσώπου ὑγιὴς ὁ λόγος, ὡς σαφὴς ἡ ὁτουοῦν χρῆσις ἒκ [τε] τοῦ ἑαυτὸν μὲν ἐκεῖνον, ἐκεῖνον δὲ ἑαυτὸν ὑποθέσθαι. καὶ γὰρ οἰκέτῃ χρῷτ' ἄν τις καλῶς, ἐνθυμηθεὶς πῶς ἂν ἠξίωσεν ἐκεῖνον αὑτῷ προσφέρεσθαι, εἴπερ ἐκεῖνος μὲν ἦν δεσπότης, αὐτὸς δὲ δοῦλος· ὁ δ' ὅμοιος λόγος καὶ γονεῦσι περὶ τέκνων καὶ παισὶ περὶ τῶν γειναμένων καὶ συνόλως πᾶσι περὶ πάντων.

ἐξαιρέτως δ' ἐστὶν εὔπορος ἡ παραίνεσις κατὰ τὸν τῶν ἀδελφῶν τόπον· ἐπειδήπερ οὐδὲν δεῖ προϋποθέσθαι τὸν σκεπτόμενον πῶς ἀδελφῷ χρηστέον, λαβεῖν δ' ἐξ ἑτοίμου παρὰ τῆς φύσεως <τὴν> τοῦ προσώπου ταυτότητα. καὶ δῆτα καὶ πρῶτος οὗτος εἰρήσθω λόγος, ὡς τοῦτον χρὴ προσφέρεσθαι τὸν τρόπον ἀδελφῷ, ὅνπερ ἄν τις ἐκεῖνον ἀξιώσειεν [ἂν] ἑαυτῷ. νὴ Δία, φήσει τις, ἀλλ' ἐγὼ μέν εἰμι μέτριος καὶ ἐπιεικής, ὁ δ' ἀδελφὸς σκαιὸς καὶ δυσομίλητος. οὐκ ὀρθῶς δὲ ἐρεῖ. πρῶτον μὲν ἴσως οὐδ' ἀληθεύσει. ἱκανὴ γὰρ ἡ φιλαυτία τὰ μὲν ἴδια μεγαλοποιῆσαι καὶ ἀποκυδᾶναι, τὰ δὲ τῶν ἄλλων κατασμικρῦναι καὶ διαφαυλίσαι· πολλὰ γοῦν διὰ ταύτην οἱ κακίους σφᾶς αὐτοὺς προκρίνουσι τῶν κατὰ πολὺ βελτιόνων. ἔπειτα, κἂν ὄντως τοιοῦτος ᾖ <ὁ> ἀδελφός, ἀλλὰ σύ γε, φαίην ἄν, ἀμείνων εὑρέθητι καὶ νίκησον αὐτοῦ τὴν ἀγριότητα ταῖς εὐποιΐαις. ἐπεί τοί γε οὐδὲ πολλὴ χάρις τοῖς εὐγνώμοσι προσενεχθῆναι μετρίως· ἀλλ' ἀνδρὸς ἔργον καὶ πολλῆς ἄξιον ἀποδοχῆς, τὸν ἀβέλτερον καὶ σκαιὸν πραῢναι τοῖς ἐς αὐτὸν πραττομένοις. καὶ γὰρ οὐδὲ πάμπαν ἐπ' ἀδύνατον ἡ παράκλησις·ἀλλ' ἔνεστι γὰρ κἀν τοῖς ἀτοπώτατα διακειμένοις σπέρματα μεταβολῆς τῆς ἐπὶ τὸ κρεῖττον τιμῆς τε καὶ ἀγαπήσεως τῶν εὐεργετησάντων.

be seen to honor them. That is why it is necessary to cherish their relatives and deem them worthy of care, and so too, indeed, their friends and everyone who is dear to them.

From this point of departure, the discovery of many other duties, neither slight nor casual, suggests itself to us. For since concern on the part of those who are loved by them is gratifying to our parents, and they are above all so disposed toward us, it is clear that we would be pleasing them in no ordinary way by providing for them.

[Siblings]

Now, the first recommendation is very clear and quite simple, and besides it is also common. For, for pretty much every role, this argument is sound: that the treatment of anyone is clear from supposing that one is oneself that person and that that person is oneself.[33] For, in fact, a person would treat a slave well, if he considered how he would think the other should behave toward himself, if the other were the master and he himself the slave. And the argument is similar for parents in respect to children and children in respect to parents and, in a word, for all in respect to all.

This advice is particularly simple for the case of brothers, since a person who is contemplating how one should treat a brother does not need to make such a supposition in advance but to take immediately from nature the identity of the role. So, then, let this be stated as the first argument: that one should behave in such a way toward one's brother as one would think that he should behave toward oneself. By Zeus, someone will say, but I am a balanced and decent person, whereas my brother is crude and unsociable. But he will not be speaking correctly. First of all, perhaps he will not even be telling the truth, for self-love is able to magnify and glorify one's own qualities and to diminish and cheapen those of others. It is on account of this, in fact, that those who are worse often judge themselves superior to those who are much better. Second, even if your brother really should be such, then at all events you, I would say, must show yourself to be better and to conquer his cruelty with your good deeds.[34] For it is no great grace to behave decently toward those who are well-disposed, but it is the task of a man and worthy of great approbation to make a crude and stupid person gentle by what you do toward him. For, in fact, such encouragement is not at all aimed at the impossible. Rather, even in people with the most terrible disposition there are seeds of a change for the better in honor and affection for those who have done

οὐ γὰρ δὴ ζῷα μὲν ἄγρια καὶ φύσει πρὸς τὸ γένος ἡμῶν ἐκπεπολεμωμένα, πρὸς βίαν ἀχθέντα καὶ τὴν πρώτην κατασχεθέντα δεσμοῖς ἢ γαλεάγραις, χρόνοις ὕστερον τιθασὰ γίγνεται καθημερούμενα ποιαῖς τημελείαις καὶ τῇ καθ' ἡμέραν τροφῇ· ἄνθρωπος δὲ οὐχ ὅπως ἀδελφός, ἀλλὰ κἂν μηδὲν προσήκων τύχῃ, οὐ τῷ παντὶ μᾶλλον ἐπιμελείας ἀξιούμενος μεταβάλλει πρὸς τὸ ἡμερώτερον, κἂν ὑπερβολὴν μὴ ἀπολίπῃ σκαιότητος. μιμητέον οὖν ἐπὶ παντὸς μὲν ἀνθρώπου, πολὺ δὲ διαφερόντως ἐπ' ἀδελφοῦ τὸ τοῦ Σωκράτους· ἐκεῖνος γὰρ πρὸς τὸν εἰπόντα «ἀποθανοῦμαι εἰ μή σε τιμωρησαίμην» ἔφη «ἀποθανοῦμαι εἰ μή σε φίλον ποιήσω».

ἀλλὰ γὰρ ταῦτα μὲν ταύτῃ. μετὰ ταῦτα δ' ἐνθυμητέον, ὅτι τρόπον τινὰ οἱ ἀδελφοὶ ταὐτοῦ μέρη τυγχάνουσιν, ὥσπερ οἱ ἐμοὶ ὀφθαλμοὶ ἐμοῦ καὶ ὡσαύτως σκέλη τε καὶ χεῖρες καὶ τὰ λοιπά. καὶ γὰρ οὗτοι τοῦτον ἔχουσιν τὸν τρόπον, εἴ γε πρὸς τὸν οἶκον ἐξετάζοιντο. ὥσπερ οὖν οἱ ὀφθαλμοὶ καὶ αἱ χεῖρες, εἴπερ ἕκαστον ἰδίαν ψυχὴν καὶ νοῦν λάβοι, περιέποι ἂν τὰ λοιπὰ πάσῃ μηχανῇ διὰ τὴν εἰρημένην κοινωνίαν, τῷ μηδ' αὐτὰ τὸ ἴδιον ἔργον οἷάτε εἶναι παρέχειν καλῶς δίχα τῆς τῶν ἑτέρων παρουσίας· οὕτως δεῖ καὶ ἡμᾶς, ἀνθρώπους γε ὄντας καὶ ψυχὴν ὁμολογοῦντας ἔχειν, μηδὲν παριέναι σπουδῆς ὑπὲρ τοῦ δεόντως προσφέρεσθαι τοῖς ἀδελφοῖς. καὶ γὰρ αὖ καὶ πλεῖόν τι παρὰ τὰ μέρη συλλαμβάνειν ἀλλήλοις ἀδελφοὶ πεφύκασιν, εἴ γε ὀφθαλμοὶ μὲν <συν>ορῶσιν ἀλλήλοις παρὼν παρόντι καὶ χεὶρ συνεργάζεται παροῦσα χειρὶ παρούσῃ· ἡ δ' ἀδελφῶν σύμπραξις ἀλλήλοις πολυχουστέρα πώς ἐστι. πράττουσι γὰρ τὰ κοινῇ διαφέροντα καὶ διεστηκότες τοῖς τόποις πάμπαν, μέγα θ' ὑπάρχουσιν ἀλλήλων ὄφελος κἂν μυρίον ᾖ τὸ διάστημα. ὅλως δὲ ἐνθυμητέον ὡς ὁ βίος ἡμῖν κινδυνεύει μακρός τις εἶναι καὶ πολυετὴς πόλεμος, τοῦτο μὲν διὰ τὴν αὐτῶν τῶν πραγμάτων φύσιν ἐχόντων τι ἀντίτακτον, τοῦτο δὲ διὰ τὰς ἐξαιφνιδίους καὶ ἀπροσδοκήτους ἐπιδρομὰς τῆς τύχης, πολὺ δὲ μάλιστα δι' αὐτὴν τὴν κακίαν οὔτε βίας τινὸς ἀπεχομένην οὔτε δόλου καὶ κακῶν στρατηγημάτων. ὅθεν καλῶς ἡ φύσις, ὡς ἂν ἐφ' ἃ γεννᾷ μὴ ἀγνοοῦσα, παρήγαγεν ἡμῶν ἕκαστον τρόπον τινὰ μετὰ συμμαχίας. οὐδεὶς οὖν ἐστι μόνος οὐδ' ἀπὸ δρυὸς οὐδ' ἀπὸ πέτρης, ἀλλ' ἐκ γονέων καὶ μετ' ἀδελφῶν καὶ συγγενῶν καὶ ἄλλων οἰκείων. μέγας δὲ βοηθὸς ὁ λόγος, καὶ τοὺς ὀθνείους καὶ μηδὲν καθ' αἷμα προσήκοντας ἐξιδιούμενος ἀφθονίαν τε παρέχων συμμάχων. διὰ τοῦτο κατὰ φύσιν ἡμῖν

them a service. For they are not savage animals and by nature at war with our race, that are captured by force and at first restrained by chains and cages, and later become tame when they have been made gentle by certain kinds of handling and by daily food: a human being, not just insofar as he is a brother but even if he should be no relation of ours, and even though he is not considered more worthy of concern in every respect, still changes for the gentler, although he may not get over an excessive degree of contrariness. Thus, in the case of every human being, but especially in the case of a brother, one should imitate that famous saying of Socrates: for to someone who said to him, "I shall die if I do not take revenge on you," he replied: "I shall die, if I do not make a friend of you."

Such, then, is how these matters stand. After these, one must consider that, in a certain way, one's brothers are parts of oneself, just as my eyes are parts of me and so too my legs and hands and the rest.[35] For in fact they do have this character, at least if they are judged in relation to the household. Just as eyes and hands, accordingly, if each should obtain its own soul and mind, would respect the other parts in every possible way for the sake of their declared communality, since they are not even able to perform their own function well without the presence of the other parts, so too we, who are human beings and confess to having a soul, should not omit any effort in behaving toward our brothers as one ought. For, in fact, brothers are by nature such as to cooperate with each other even more, in comparison with bodily parts, since eyes see together with each other when each is in the presence of the other, and hand works together with hand when each is in the presence of the other. But the collaboration of brothers with each other is, in a way, more bountiful. For they do things that are in their common interest even when they are utterly separated in their locations and are a great benefit to one another even if the distance is enormous. In general, one must consider that life for us runs the risk of being a long and perennial battle, and this, on the one hand, because of the very nature of things, which have something contrary about them, and, on the other hand, because of the sudden and unexpected assaults of fortune, but most of all because of vice itself, which does not refrain from any kind of violence or treachery or evil schemes.[36] Hence, nature has, as though it were not ignorant of why it creates us, nicely brought each of us into the world with, in a way, an ally. Thus, no one is alone, or born from an oak or a rock,[37] but rather from parents and with brothers and relatives and other members of the household. Reason, too, is a great aid, which appropriates strangers and those wholly unrelated to us by blood and provides us with an abundance of allies. For this reason, we are eager by nature to win over

σπουδῇ καὶ ὁντινοῦν προσαγαγέσθαι καὶ φιλοποιήσασθαι. γίγνεται οὖν ἤδη τὸ πρᾶγμα τελεωτάτη μανιῶν, τοῖς μὲν οὐδὲν ἐκ φύσεως ἔχουσι φίλτρον πρὸς ἡμᾶς ἐθέλειν συγκραθῆναι καὶ τῇ γνώμῃ εἰς ἐφ' ὅσον ἐνδέχεται πλεῖστον χέαι τὴν οἰκειότητα, τῶν δὲ ἐξ ἑτοίμου καὶ παρ' αὐτῆς χορηγουμένων τῆς φύσεως κατημεληκέναι βοηθῶν κἀπικούρων, οἵους δὴ συμβέβηκεν εἶναι τοὺς ἀδελφούς.

Stobaeus, *Anthology* 4.84.23 (3:134,1–136,2 Meineke; cf. *Anth.* 4.27.23 = 4:671,3–673,18 Wachsmuth and Hense)
Ἱεροκλέους ἐκ τοῦ πῶς συγγενέσι χρηστέον.

Τοῖς εἰρημένοις περὶ γονέων χρήσεως καὶ ἀδελφῶν γυναικός τε καὶ τέκνων ἀκόλουθόν ἐστι προσθεῖναι καὶ τὸν περὶ συγγενῶν λόγον, συμπεπονθότα μέν πως ἐκείνοις, δι' αὐτὸ δὲ τοῦτο συντόμως ἀποδοθῆναι δυνάμενον. ὅλως γὰρ ἕκαστος ἡμῶν οἷον κύκλοις πολλοῖς περιγέγραπται, τοῖς μὲν σμικροτέροις, τοῖς δὲ μείζοσι, καὶ τοῖς μὲν περιέχουσι, τοῖς δὲ περιεχομένοις, κατὰ τὰς διαφόρους καὶ ἀνίσους πρὸς ἀλλήλους σχέσεις. πρῶτος μὲν γάρ ἐστι κύκλος καὶ προσεχέστατος, ὃν αὐτός τις καθάπερ περὶ κέντρον τὴν ἑαυτοῦ γέγραπται διάνοιαν· ἐν ᾧ κύκλῳ τό τε σῶμα περιέχεται καὶ τὰ τοῦ σώματος ἕνεκα παρειλημμένα. σχεδὸν γὰρ ὁ βραχύτατος καὶ μικροῦ δεῖν αὐτοῦ προσαπτόμενος τοῦ κέντρου κύκλος οὗτος. δεύτερος δὲ ἀπὸ τούτου καὶ πλέον μὲν ἀφεστὼς τοῦ κέντρου, περιέχων δὲ τὸν πρῶτον, ἐν ᾧ τετάχαται γονεῖς ἀδελφοὶ γυνὴ παῖδες. ὁ δ' ἀπὸ τούτων τρίτος, ἐν ᾧ θεῖοι καὶ τηθίδες, πάπποι τε καὶ τῆθαι, καὶ ἀδελφῶν παῖδες, ἔτι δὲ ἀνεψιοί. μεθ' ὃν ὁ τοὺς ἄλλους περιέχων συγγενεῖς. τούτῳ δ' ἐφεξῆς ὁ τῶν δημοτῶν καὶ μετ' αὐτὸν ὁ τῶν φυλετῶν, εἶθ' ὁ πολιτῶν, καὶ λοιπὸν οὕτως ὁ μὲν ἀστυγειτόνων, ὁ δὲ ὁμοεθνῶν. ὁ δ' ἐξωτάτω καὶ μέγιστος περιέχων τε πάντας τοὺς κύκλους ὁ τοῦ παντὸς ἀνθρώπων γένους. τούτων οὖν τεθεωρημένων, κατὰ τὸν ἐντεταμένον ἐστὶ περὶ τὴν δέουσαν ἑκάστων χρῆσιν τὸ ἐπισυνάγειν πως τοὺς κύκλους ὡς ἐπὶ τὸ κέντρον καὶ τῇ σπουδῇ μεταφέρειν ἀεὶ τοὺς ἐκ τῶν περιεχόντων εἰς τοὺς περιεχομένους. κατὰ τὸν φιλοίκειον γοῦν ἐστὶ γονέας μὲν καὶ ἀδελφοὺς .... οὐκοῦν κατὰ τὴν αὐτὴν ἀναλογίαν καὶ τῶν συγγενῶν τοὺς μὲν πρεσβυτέρους καὶ <τὰς> πρεσβυτέρας ὡς πάππους <ἢ> θείους ἢ τηθίδας, τοὺς δ' ὁμήλικας ὡς ἀνεψιούς, τοὺς δὲ νεωτέρους ὡς παῖδας ἀνεψιῶν.

and make a friend of everyone. Thus, that act is the most complete kind of madness: to wish to be joined with those who bear no affection toward us by nature and deliberately, to the greatest extent possible, to confer the family bond on them, but to neglect those helpers and caretakers who are at hand and have been bestowed upon us by nature, such as it happens that our brothers are.

Of Hierocles, from the treatise *How Should One Behave toward One's Relatives?*

It goes along with what has been said concerning behavior toward parents and brothers and wife and children, to add also a discussion of relatives, which feels more or less like those others and for this very reason can be expounded concisely.[38] For each of us, most generally, is circumscribed as though by many circles, some smaller, some larger, some surrounding others, some surrounded, according to their different and unequal relations to one another.[39] The first and closest circle is that which each person draws around his own mind, as the center: in this circle is enclosed the body and whatever is employed for the sake of the body. For this circle is the shortest and all but touches its own center. The second after this one, standing further away from the center and enclosing the first, is that within which our parents, siblings, wife, and children are ranged. Third, after these, is that in which there are uncles and aunts, grandfathers and grandmothers, the children of one's siblings, and also cousins. After this comes the one that embraces all other relatives. Next upon this is the circle of the members of one's deme, then that of the members of one's tribe, next that of one's fellow citizens, and so, finally, that of those who border one's city and that of people of like ethnicity. The furthest out and largest one, which surrounds all the circles, is that of the entire race of human beings.[40] Once these have been thought through, accordingly, it is possible, starting with the most stretched-out one, to draw the circles—concerning the behavior that is due to each group[41]—together in a way, as though toward the center, and with an effort to keep transferring items out of the containing circles into the contained. For example, in respect to love of one's family it is possible to *** parents and siblings *** and therefore, in the same proportion, among one's relatives, <to treat> the more elderly men and women as grandparents or uncles and aunts, those of the same age as cousins, and the younger ones as children of one's cousins.

ὥστε εἴρηται διὰ συντόμων ὑποθήκη σαφὴς πῶς χρὴ προσφέρεσθαι συγγενέσιν, ἐπειδὴ προεδιδάχθημεν πῶς τε χρηστέον ἑαυτοῖς καὶ πῶς γονεῦσι καὶ ἀδελφοῖς, ἔτι δὲ γυναικὶ καὶ τέκνοις, πρόσκειται δ' ὅτι καὶ τούτοις μὲν ὁμοίως τιμητέον τοὺς ἐκ τοῦ τρίτου κύκλου, τούτοις δ' αὖ πάλιν τοὺς συγγενεῖς. ἀφαιρήσεται μὲν γάρ τι τῆς εὐνοίας τὸ καθ' αἷμα διάστημα πλέον <ὄν>· ἡμῖν δ' ὅμως σπουδαστέα περὶ τὴν ἐξομοίωσίν ἐστιν. ἥκοι μὲν γὰρ ἂν εἰς τὸ μέτριον, εἰ διὰ τῆς ἡμετέρας αὐτῶν ἐνστάσεως ἐπιτεμνόμεθα τὸ μῆκος τῆς πρὸς ἕκαστον τὸ πρόσωπον σχέσεως.

τὸ μὲν οὖν συνέχον καὶ πραγματικώτερον εἴρηται· χρὴ δ' ἐπιμετρεῖν καὶ κατὰ τὴν τῶν προσηγοριῶν χρῆσιν, τοὺς μὲν ἀνεψιοὺς καὶ θείους καὶ τηθίδας ἀδελφοὺς ἀποκαλοῦντας πατέρας τε καὶ μητέρας, τῶν δὲ συγγενῶν τοὺς μὲν θείους, τοὺς δὲ ἀδελφιδοῦς, τοὺς δὲ ἀνεψιούς, ὡς ἂν καὶ τὰ τῆς ἡλικίας παρήκῃ ἕνεκα τῆς ἐν τοῖς ὀνόμασιν ἐκτενείας. οὗτος γὰρ τῆς προσρήσεως ὁ τρόπος ἅμα μὲν ἂν σημεῖον οὐκ ἀμαυρὸν εἴη τῆς οὔσης ἡμῖν σπουδῆς περὶ ἑκάστους, ἅμα δ' ἂν ἐποτρύνοι καὶ προσεντείνοι πρὸς τὴν ὑποδεδειγμένην οἷον συνολκὴν τῶν κύκλων.

ἐνταῦθα μέντοι γενομένοις οὐκ ἄκαιρος τοῦ ῥηθέντος ἐπὶ γονέων διορισμοῦ φαντάζεται μνήμη. ἐλέγομεν γὰρ αὖ κατ' ἐκεῖνον ἡνίκα τὸν τόπον ἦμεν, ἔνθα μητέρα πατρὶ συνεκρίναμεν, ὡς χρὴ τῇ μὲν μητρὶ τῆς στοργῆς, τῆς δὲ τιμῆς τῷ πατρὶ πλέον ἀπονέμειν· οἷς ἑπομένως καὶ δεῦρο τιθεῖμεν ἄν, ὡς τοὺς μὲν μητρόθεν προσήκοντας στέργειν πλέον πρέπει, τοὺς δ' αὖ κατὰ πατέρα συγγενεῖς διὰ μείζονος ἄγειν τιμῆς.

Stobaeus, *Anthology* 4.85.21 (3:150,6–152,3 Meineke; cf. *Anth.* 4.28.21 = 5:696,21–699,15 Wachsmuth and Hense)
Ἱεροκλέους ἐκ τοῦ Οἰκονομικοῦ.

Πρὸ πάντων γε περὶ τῶν ἔργων, ὑφ' ὧν οἶκος συνέχεται. ταῦτ' οὖν διαιρετέον μὲν κατὰ τὸ πλεῖστον, <ὥστε> τῷ μὲν ἀνδρὶ τὰ κατ' ἀγρὸν καὶ τὰ περὶ τὰς ἀγορὰς καὶ τὰ περὶ τὴν ἀστυπολίαν ἀνακεῖσθαι, τῇ δὲ γυναικὶ τὰ περὶ τὴν ταλασίαν καὶ σιτοποιίαν καὶ ὅλως τὰ κατοικίδια τῶν ἔργων. οὐδὲ μὴν ἀγεύστους ἀξιωτέον εἶναι τοὺς ἑτέρους τῶν ἑτέρων. γένοιτο γὰρ ἄν ποτε καὶ γυναικὶ κατ' ἀγρὸν γενομένῃ καθῆκον τὸ τοῖς ἐργαζομένοις ἐπιστῆναι καὶ τὴν τοῦ οἰκοδεσπότου τάξιν ἐκπληρῶσαι, καὶ ἀνδρὶ περὶ τῶν κατὰ τὴν οἰκίαν ἐπιστροφὴν ποιήσασθαι καὶ τὰ μὲν διαπυθέσθαι, τὰ δὲ καὶ ἐπιδεῖν τῶν γινομένων. οὕτω γὰρ ἂν ἐπισυνδέοιτο μᾶλλον τὰ τῆς κοινωνίας, εἰ συμμετέχοιεν

Thus, a clear recommendation has been set forth, in concise terms, for how one should treat relatives, since we had already taught how people should behave toward themselves, and how toward parents and siblings, and further toward wife and children: the charge is that one must honor, in a way similar to these last, those from the third circle, and must in turn honor relatives in a way similar to these latter. Indeed, a greater distance in respect to blood will subtract something of goodwill, but, nevertheless, we must make an effort about assimilating them.[42] For it would arrive at fairness if, through our own initiative, we cut down the distance in our relationship toward each person.

The principal and most practical point has been discussed. But it is necessary to add in also usage in regard to modes of address, calling cousins, uncles, and aunts "brothers," "fathers," and "mothers," and among further relatives calling some "uncles," others "nephews," and still others "cousins," in whatever way their ages may run, for the sake of the affection in the names. For this kind of address is a by no means faint sign of the concern that we feel for each and at the same time can excite and intensify the above-indicated contraction, as it were, of the circles.[43]

Now that we have got this far, the recollection of the distinction that was affirmed concerning parents comes opportunely to mind. For we said, when we were discussing that topic, where we were comparing a father with a mother, that one should grant more love to his mother but more honor to his father.[44] Consequent upon this, here too we may set down that it is appropriate to cherish relatives on the mother's side more but treat with greater honor those relations associated with the father.

Of Hierocles, from *Household Management.*

First of all, indeed, concerning the tasks by which a household is sustained.[45] These, then, should be divided according to what is most [pertinent to each spouse]: thus, to the husband are referred tasks concerning fields, marketplaces, and city business, whereas to the wife are referred those relating to the spinning of wool, breadmaking, and, in general, domestic tasks. But one must not think that the one group should be without a taste of the other tasks. For the duty of overseeing the laborers, and thereby fulfilling the role of the master of the household, may also sometimes fall to the wife, if she happens to be in the field, and to the husband to pay attention to household matters, informing himself of some things and superintending others. For thus what belongs to the communality [of

ἀλλήλοις τῶν ἀναγκαίων φροντίδων.

δεῦρο μέντοι τοῦ λόγου γενόμενος οὐκ ἂν ὀκνῆσαί μοι δοκῶ καὶ τῆς αὐτουργίας ποιήσασθαί τινα μνήμην, ἐπεὶ εἰκὸς τοῖς ὑπὲρ τῶν ἔργων εἰρημένοις καὶ τοῦτο προστεθῆναι. ὡς μὲν τοίνυν τἀνδρὶ καθήκει τῶν γεωργικῶν ἅπτεσθαι πόνων, τί καὶ λέγειν δεῖ; οὐ πολὺς γὰρ ὁ κατὰ τοῦτο δυσπειθής, ἀλλὰ καίπερ τοσαύτης τρυφῆς καὶ ἀπονίας τὸν νῦν κατεχούσης βίον, ὅμως σπάνιός ἐστιν <ὁ> μὴ καὶ δι' ἑαυτοῦ προθυμούμενος ἔργων κοινωνῆσαι τῶν ὑπὲρ σπόρου καὶ φυτείας καὶ τῶν ἄλλων τῶν κατὰ γεωργίαν. δυσπειθέστερος δ' ἴσως ὁ πρὸς θάτερα τῶν ἔργων, ὅσα γυναιξὶν ἀπονενέμηται, παρακαλῶν τὸν ἄνδρα λόγος. καὶ πάσχουσί γε οὐκ ἀπεικὸς οἱ καθαρειότεροι, μὴ καθ' ἑαυτοὺς εἶναι τοπάζοντες ἅψασθαι ταλασίας. ἐπεὶ γὰρ ὡς ἐπὶ τὸ πλῆθος εὐτελεῖς ἀνθρωπίσκοι καὶ τὸ τῶν κατεαγότων καὶ γυννίδων φῦλον ὡς τὴν ἐρίων ἐργασίαν καταφέρεται ζήλῳ θηλύτητος, οὐ δοκεῖ κατὰ τὸν ἀληθινώτερον ἄνδρα τυγχάνειν τὸ εἰς ταῦτα συγκαθιέναι· ὥστ' ἔγωγε τάχ' ἂν οὐδ' ἂν αὐτὸς συμβουλεύσαιμι τοῖς μὴ τελείαν παρεσχημένοις πίστιν ὑπὲρ τῆς ἑαυτῶν ἀῤῥενότητος καὶ σωφροσύνης ἅπτεσθαι τοιοῦδέ τινος. εἰ μέντοι διὰ τοιοῦδε βίου πεποιήκοι τις [ἂν] ἑαυτὸν πάσης ὑπονοίας ἀτόπου καθαρεύοντα, τί κωλύσει καὶ κατὰ ταῦτα τῇ γυναικὶ κοινωνῆσαι τὸν ἄνδρα; τῶν μὲν γὰρ ἄλλων κατοικιδίων ἔργων μὴ καὶ τὸ πλέον ἀνδράσι προσήκειν ἡγητέον ἤπερ γυναιξίν. ἔστι γὰρ καματωδέστερα καὶ ῥώμης δεόμενα σωματικῆς, οἷον ἀλέσαι καὶ σταῖς μάξαι διασχίσαι τε ξύλα καὶ ὕδωρ ἀνιμῆσαι καὶ σκεύη μεταθεῖναι καὶ διατινάξαι στρώματα καὶ πᾶν τὸ τούτοις παραπλήσιον. καὶ τὰ μὲν ὑπὲρ ἀνδρῶν ἀποχρῴη ἄν· ἐπιμετρῆσαι δέ τι καὶ τὴν γυναῖκα πρέπον, ὥστε μὴ τῆς ταλασίας κοινωνεῖν μόνον ταῖς θεραπαίναις, ἀλλὰ καὶ τῶν ἄλλων ἔργων τῶν ἐπανδροτέρων. καὶ γὰρ σιτοπονίας ἅψασθαι κατὰ τὴν ἐλευθέραν εἶναί μοι δοκεῖ καὶ ὕδωρ ἀνιμῆσαι <καὶ> πῦρ ἀνακαῦσαι καὶ κλίνην καταστρῶσαι καὶ πᾶν τὸ τούτοις ἐοικός. πολὺ δ' ἂν ἀνδρὶ φαίνοιτο καλλίων τῷ γε ἑαυτῆς, καὶ μάλιστα νεᾶνις οὖσα καὶ μηδέπω τετρυμένη κυοφορίαις, εἰ καὶ τρύγης ἀμπέλων αὐτουργοῦσα συμμετάσχοι καὶ συλλογῆς ἐλαῶν, εἰ δὲ παρείκοι, καὶ σπόρου καὶ ἀρόσεως καὶ παραδόσεως ἐργαλείων τοῖς σκάπτουσιν ἢ φυτεύουσι. τοῦτον γὰρ τὸν τρόπον ἕνεκα τῶν ἔργων οἶκος προστατούμενος ὑπ' ἀνδρὸς καὶ γυναικὸς ἄριστ' ἄν μοι δοκεῖ κατά γε ταῦτα διεξάγεσθαι.

the two] can be all the more bound together, if they share one another's concerns about necessities.[46]

Having reached this point in my discourse, I think I should not hesitate to make some mention also of personal labor,[47] since it is reasonable to add this also to what has been said about tasks. Since, then, it is the duty of the husband to take up agricultural work, what need one say? For the argument about this is not very hard to accept; rather, even though so great a fastidiousness and laziness has seized upon life nowadays, nevertheless it is a rare person who is not eager on his own to share the tasks of sowing and planting and the other things relating to agriculture. Harder to accept, perhaps, is the argument that summons the husband to the other set of tasks, namely, all those that have been assigned to wives. Men who are too respectable feel something not unreasonable, indeed, in imagining that taking up weaving is not for them. For since for the most part shabby little manikins and a tribe of effeminate and womanish types rush headlong into wool-working in their zeal for femininity, stooping to these things does not seem to be in line with a true man. Thus I myself would not advise any men who did not exhibit complete confidence in their own masculinity and restraint to touch such a thing. If, however, through a life of this kind he should have rendered himself free of every absurd suspicion, what will prevent a husband from sharing in these things too with his wife?[48] For of other domestic tasks should not one believe that most, indeed, are suitable to husbands rather than to wives?[49] For some are very tiring and require bodily strength, such as grinding, kneading flour, splitting wood, drawing water, moving furniture, shaking out bedding, and all that is similar to these things. And she might even be up to some tasks in behalf of her husband: it is appropriate for a wife, too, to add something, so as not only to share in spinning with her slave girls but also in other, more masculine tasks. For in fact undertaking breadmaking, drawing water, lighting the fire, making beds, and everything like this is, I believe, entirely suitable for a free woman. She would seem much more beautiful to her husband by means of herself, indeed—above all if she is still young and has not yet been worn out by pregnancies—if she, working personally, shared also in the harvesting of the vines and the gathering of the olives and, if it should be practical, even in sowing and plowing and distributing tools to the diggers or planters. For in this way, I believe, through their tasks, a household presided over by a husband and wife can best be administered, at least in these respects.

The Stobaean Extracts: Commentary

1. I adopt Meineke's conjecture μετ' οὐδενὸς <λόγου>. See the *apparatus criticus* in von Arnim, *Ethische Elementarlehre*, 48.

2. *Il.* 9.499–501. Hierocles cites Homer here, but not in support of his own theory, which was often the case on all fronts on account of his *auctoritas* (see the following note) but rather, on the contrary, to adduce an example of distorted and fallacious thinking. For the gods are, for the Stoics, models of virtue, as Musonius Rufus emphasizes more than any other of the Neo-Stoics, ascribing this paradigmatic status to Zeus, the supreme deity, and at the same time also the function of supervising the moral behavior of humans (see Ramelli, "La concezione di Giove," 292–320; idem, *Musonio Rufo*, 23–25).

Thus, consistency and stability in their decisions, which are not made casually but rather thoughtfully, are an essential feature of the gods' lives, which are in turn the model for ours. For, if the decisions made by the *sapiens*, like those made by God, are best inasmuch as they conform to right reason, they must remain stable and cannot change, for otherwise they would become worse (see the definition of virtue as "steadfast and immutable" already in Zeno [see *SVF* 1.202], as noted in the introductory essay, §4): hence, too, the much-discussed and misunderstood rejection of pardon on the part of the Stoics, which in Roman Stoicism remained a subject of debate, as shown by Maria Scarpat Bellincioni, *Potere ed etica in Seneca*: Clementia *e* voluntas *amica* (Brescia: Paideia, 1984); idem, "Clementia liberum arbitrium habet," *Paideia* 39 (1984): 173–83, repr. in idem, ed., *Studi senecani e altri scritti* (Brescia: Paideia, 1986) 113–25; Ilaria Ramelli, "Il tema del perdono in Seneca e in Musonio Rufo," in *Responsabilità, perdono e vendetta nel mondo antico* (ed. Marta Sordi; CISA 24; Milan: Vita e pensiero, 1998), 191–207. See also Terrence H. Irwin, "Stoic Inhumanity," *The Emotions in Hellenistic Philosophy* (ed. Juha Sihvola and Troels Engberg-Pedersen; Dordrecht: Kluwer Academic, 1998), 219–41; Charles L. Griswold, *Forgiveness: A Philosophical Exploration* (Cambridge: Cambridge University Press, 2007), 1–19.

3. *Il.* 9.497. Apparently Hierocles does not consider Homer to be a sage who is invariably infallible, as did a long tradition of Stoic allegorizers and *Homerapologeten*, often associated more or less closely with the Stoic line; see Ramelli, *Allegoria*, chs. 2 (Old Stoics and their attitude toward Homer), 3 (the Stoicizing Crates of Mallus, for whom Homer was a πολυμαθής), 6 (Cornutus), 7 (Pseudo-Plutarch, *De vita et poesi Homeri*, for whom Homer was a philosopher and the founder of every science), and 8 (by G. Lucchetta) on the *Homeric Problems* (*Quaestiones Homericae*) of Heraclitus, who not only seeks to demonstrate Homer's wisdom but also defends him against accusations of impiety, making use of Stoic styles of allegorical exegesis of his epics. On Heraclitus as heir to this tradition, though not himself a strictly observant Stoic, see the new edition, with introduction, translation, and notes, by Donald A. Russell and David Konstan, *Heraclitus*: Homeric Problems (SBLWGRW 14; Atlanta: Society of Biblical Literature, 2005); my section on Heraclitus in *Opere e frammenti: Allegoristi dell'età classica* (Il Pensiero occidentale; Milan: Bompiani, 2007). For the diverse attitudes of Roman Stoics toward the wisdom of the ancients, and of Homer in particular, and the divergences between the views of Cornutus and Seneca, see my introductory essay in Ramelli, *Cornuto*, and *Allegoria*, chs. 6.4 and 9 (treatment of the significance and purposes of the allegorizing Stoic exegeses of Homer). In the ongoing debate among the Roman Stoics, Hierocles seems to line up more with the critical posture of Seneca than with that of the allegorist Annaeus Cornutus and the *Homerapologeten*, who considered Homer infallible and irreproachable in every detail in his poems.

4. The idea that the gods are not responsible for evil was famously affirmed by Plato at the end of his *Republic*, in the context of the myth of Er, with the celebrated formula θεὸς ἀναίτιος. God, as Plato explains there, is not responsible for the evils that afflict humans; human beings themselves, since they are endowed with free will, choose their own kind of life and whether or not to adhere to virtue. As the Fates state in *Resp.* 10.617E: "A *daimôn* will not choose you, but you will choose a *daimôn*. Let him whose lot is first be first to choose the life with which he will be associated by necessity. Virtue has no master: as each person values it or denies it value, so will he have more or less of it. *The responsibility is his who chooses: God is blameless* [αἰτία ἑλομένου: θεὸς ἀναίτιος]" (see also *Resp.* 2.379BC; *Tim.* 42DE; *Leg.* 10.904C). Plato's formula will be adopted, for example, by Porphyry, *Marc.* 12, and even in *Corp. Herm.* 4.8 (see the commentary *ad loc.* in Ilaria Ramelli, *Corpus Hermeticum* [Milan: Bompiani, 2005]). But in Stoic circles, too, Cleanthes, in his *Hymn to Zeus*, had already pro-

claimed the same idea (for the religious drift in Cleanthes' hymn, see Thom, *Cleanthes' Hymn to Zeus*, introduction); on its further development, see Silvia Lanzi, *Theos Anaitios: Storia della teodicea da Omero ad Agostino* (Rome: Il calamo, 2000); Ilaria Ramelli, "La colpa antecedente come ermeneutica del male in sede storico-religiosa e nei testi biblici," in *Origine e fenomenologia del male: Le vie della catarsi vetero-testamentaria: XIV Convegno di Studî vetero-testamentarî dell'Associazione Biblica Italiana, Roma-Ciampino, Il Carmelo, 5–7.IX.2005* (ed. Innocenzo Cardellini; Bologna: Dehoniane, 2007) = *Ricerche Storico-Bibliche* 19 (2007): 11–64. In Christian texts, the idea is forcefully reasserted by several Platonizing church fathers, such as Bardaisan, Clement of Alexandria (*Paed.* 1.8.69.1; *Strom.* 1.1.4.1; 1.17.84; 2.16.75; 4.23.150; 5.14.136, where the myth of Er is explicitly mentioned; 7.2.12), and Origen, followed thereafter by Gregory of Nyssa (see the philosophical essay in my *Gregorio di Nissa: Sull'anima e la resurrezione* [Milan: Bompiani, 2007]). Human freedom and responsibility, however, are in general defended in patristic philosophy, where it is pretty much a commonplace, since it appears to be supported by biblical texts; see, e.g., Theophilus, *Autol* 2.27; Irenaeus, *Haer.* 4.4.3, 37.1–6, 39.1; the apologist Athenagoras, who was well-informed about Greek philosophical doctrines; and others (see Claudio Moreschini, *Storia della filosofia patristica* [Brescia: Morcelliana, 2004], 81 and the entire chapter devoted to the apologists). Among the various expounders of patristic thought, however, some provide it with a better theoretical foundation than others, and one of the most lucid and consistent defenders of the idea is Origen, who deepens it in the course of his antignostic polemic and reconciles it admirably with the doctrine of the ontological insubstantiality of evil and with that of apocatastasis and universal salvation. See my "La coerenza della soteriologia origeniana: Dalla polemica contro il determinismo gnostico all'universale restaurazione escatologica," in *Pagani e cristiani alla ricerca della salvezza: Atti del XXXIV Incontro di Studiosi dell'Antichità Cristiana, Roma, Augustinianum, 5–7.V.2005* (Studia ephemeridis Augustinianum 96; Rome: Institutum patristicum Augustinianum, 2006), 661–88. This theme of human rather than divine responsibility for evil will be treated also in the next fragment of Hierocles and seems to have been particularly dear to him.

5. The gods, indeed, are impassive and are the epitome of ἀπάθεια or complete absence of the passions, the moral ideal of the Stoics as opposed to the μετριοπάθεια or moderation of the passions defended in Peripatetic circles; see Brad Inwood and Pier Luigi Donini, "Stoic Ethics," in *The Cambridge History of Hellenistic Philosophy* (ed. Keimpe A. Algra et al.;

Cambridge: Cambridge University Press, 1999), 675–738; Richard Sorabji, *Emotions and Peace of Mind: From Stoic Agitation to Christian Temptation* (Oxford: Oxford University Press, 2000); Malcolm Schofield, "Stoic Ethics," in Inwood, *Cambridge Companion to the Stoics*, 233–56; Guckes, *Zur Ethik der älteren Stoa*. The former model, which Philo also preferred, will be decisively adopted by many Christian authors, from Clement to Origen to the Cappadocians and beyond, all strongly influenced by Platonism and also by Stoicism. See the full documentation in my philosophical essay in *Gregorio di Nissa*. The divine represents the highest ethical ideal, because, as we have seen in the commentary on the previous fragment, it constitutes the moral paradigm for human beings.

6. Plato had already distinguished between the punitive aspect and the educative or therapeutic aspect of the punishments inflicted upon human beings by God: the former looks to the past and is a punishment for evil that has been committed; the latter looks to the future and has as its goal that the person who has been punished not incur such guilt again, but rather that one reform and improve. Clearly, at least in the second perspective, the punishment is destined to end at a certain moment. Only in the case of those sinners who are so hardened as to be irredeemable does Plato hold that their torments must continue eternally in Tartarus and serve only as punishment for them, without any therapeutic function or amelioration; even in this case, however, their punishment is not wholly lacking in benefit, since it is at least useful to others, as a deterrent (see *Phaed.* 113E; *Gorgias* 525C; *Resp.* 10.615C–616A). For the topic of punishment in Plato and in Socratic thought, see Richard F. Stalley, "Punishment and the Physiology of the *Timaeus*," *CQ* 46 (1996): 357–70; Thomas C. Brickhouse and Nicholas D. Smith, "The Problem of Punishment in Socratic Philosophy," *Apeiron* 30 (1997): 95–107; Hope E. May, "Socratic Ignorance and the Therapeutic Aim of the Elenchos," *Apeiron* 30 (1997): 37–50. In Neoplatonism, however, some thinkers, such as Macrobius, asserted against the evidence that Plato held that every soul will conclude its period of purification and return to its original bliss: *necesse est omnem animam ad originis suae sedem reverti*. This is not Plato's view, but rather Macrobius's own; see my "Macrobio allegorista neoplatonico e il tardo platonismo latino," in *Macrobio: Commento al Sogno di Scipione* (ed. Moreno Neri; Bompiani il pensiero occidentale; Milan: Bompiani, 2007), 5–163.

7. This is a concept on which Hierocles much insists (see the notes to the preceding fragment) and which is clearly at the core of the problem of human liberty and its compatibility with determinism and fate in Stoic philosophy from the beginning; see, among many studies, R. W. Sharples,

"Necessity in the Stoic Doctrine of Fate," *Symbolae Osloenses* 56 (1981): 81–97; idem, "Soft Determinism and Freedom in Early Stoicism," *Phronesis* 31 (1986): 266–79; Heinrch Otto Schröder, "Marionetten: Ein Beitrag zur Polemik des Karneades," *RhM* 126 (1983): 1–24; Jaap Mansfeld, "The Idea of Will in Chrysippus, Posidonius, and Galen," *Boston Area Colloquium in Ancient Philosophy* 7 (1991): 107–45; David N. Sedley, "Chrysippus on Psychophysical Causality," in *Passions and Perceptions: Studies in Hellenistic Philosophy of Mind: Proceedings of the Fifth Symposium Hellenisticum* (ed. Jacques Brunschwig and Martha Nussbaum; Cambridge: Cambridge University Press, 1993), 313–31; Susanne Bobzien, "The Inadvertent Conception and Late Birth of the Free-Will Problem," *Phronesis* 43 (1998): 133–75; idem, *Determinism and Freedom in Stoic Philosophy* (Oxford: Clarendon, 1998), with the review by Tad Brennan, "Fate and Free Will in Stoicism," *OSAP* 21 (2001) 259–86; and Dorothea Frede, "Stoic Determinism," in Inwood, *Cambridge Companion to the Stoics*, 179–205. See also André-Jean Voelke, *L'idée de volonté dans le Stoïcisme* (Paris: PUF, 1973); Albrecht Dihle, *The Theory of Will in Classical Antiquity* (Berkeley and Los Angeles: University of California Press, 1982); Christopher Gill, "Did Chrysippus Understand Medea?" *Phronesis* 28 (1983): 136–49; Charles H. Kahn, "Discovering the Will: From Aristotle to Augustine," in *The Question of Eclecticism* (ed. John M. Dillon and Anthony A. Long; Berkeley and Los Angeles: University of California Press, 1988), 234–59. Further references on the relationship between freedom, fate, and human responsibility, specifically in Chrysipus, who is the major exponent of this question in Stoicism, are provided in the notes to §5b of the introductory essay. Related to this issue are also the reflections of Saint Paul (on whom see Abraham J. Malherbe, "Determinism and Free Will in Paul: The Argument of 1 Corinthians 8 and 9," in *Paul in His Hellenistic Context* [ed. Troels Engberg-Pedersen; Minneapolis: Fortress, 1994], 231–55). In Roman Stoicism the concept of will is developed and is especially important in Seneca; see, at a minimum, Brad Inwood, "The Will in Seneca the Younger," *CP* 95 (2000): 44–60, who recognizes the importance of Seneca in the formation of the concept of "will," although he does not deem it sufficient simply to adduce the repeated use of the terms *voluntas* and *velle* in support of the idea that Seneca invented the concept: rather, Inwood analyzes specific passages in which the idea of the will emerges from the sense of the argument (34.3; 37.5; 71.36; 80.4; 81.13), and he notes some notions in Seneca that will contribute to the subsequent development of the concept of will, such as the attention to self-control and the vocabulary of self-mastery, as well as the isolation of a moment of deci-

sion or active judgment in the process of reacting to certain stimuli; see also Rainer Zöller, *Die Vorstellung vom Willen in der Morallehre Senecas* (Munich: Saur, 2003). On the development of the idea of free choice in the late phase of Roman Stoicism and especially in Epictetus, see Robert F. Dobbin, "Προαίρεσις in Epictetus," *AncPhil* 11 (1991): 111–35; Elizabeth Asmis, "Choice in Epictetus' Philosophy," in Collins and Mitchell, *Antiquity and Humanity*, 387–412. Stoicism, and in particular Neo-Stoicism, seem to have been well known also to Bardaisan of Edessa, a contemporary of Clement of Alexandria who, like Clement and Origen, was strongly committed to the defense of human free will, especially as against gnostic and astrological determinism. Bardaisan, however, who seems closer to Middle Platonism (as is apparent above all from the fragments of his *De India* preserved by Porphyry), inclines toward ethical intellectualism, just as Origen and other early supporters of the doctrine of apocatastasis did. See my "Bardesane e la sua scuola tra la cultura occidentale e quella orientale: Il lessico della libertà nel *Liber Legum Regionum* (testo siriaco e versione greca)," in *Pensiero e istituzioni del mondo classico nelle culture del Vicino Oriente, Atti del Seminario Nazionale di Studio, Brescia, 14–16 ottobre 1999* (ed. Rosa Bianca Finazzi and Alfredo Valvo; Alessandria: Edizioni dell'Orso, 2001), 237–55; idem, "Origen, Bardaisan, and the Origin of Universal Salvation." *HTR* 102 (2009): 135–68); idem, *Bardesane Κατὰ Εἱμαρμένης* (Bologna: Edizioni Studio Domenicano, 2009).

8. *Od.* 1.32; the citations immediately preceding correspond to 1.33–34, which immediately follow in the Homeric passage. Here Homer is cited positively for having expressed an important concept. See the notes to the preceding fragment for Hierocles' complex attitude toward Homer, whom he sometimes cites approvingly and in support of his own arguments but at other times critically, adducing him as a negative example.

9. *Resp.* 1.335D. In the background there is also Plato's myth of Er, with the above-quoted denial of divine responsibility for human evils, since the divine, which is good, cannot be the cause of any evil, but only of goods (see the notes to the preceding fragment). Here Hierocles does not confine himself to repeating that guilt for human evils may not be ascribed to God but further explains what the cause of such evils is: wickedness, vice, and the choice of evil on the part of humans themselves.

10. That the only evil is vice or things that derive directly from it and the sole good is virtue and its effects is a basic doctrine of Stoic ethics, just like divine providence in respect to humankind and the category of indifferents (ἀδιάφορα), that is, what falls neither among true goods (= the virtues and their consequences) nor true evils (= the vices and their

consequences), and which are discussed by Hierocles in what follows. See also the introductory essay above, §5 and n. 71; Chiesa, "Le problème du mal"; and Giuseppina Allegri, "La ricchezza e le cause di male," *Paideia* 52 (1997): 5–23.

11. Lacuna. This second point concerning the negativity of matter, listed right alongside vice among the causes of evil, since it is not endowed with rational nature, seems to reveal influences foreign to orthodox Stoicism, perhaps deriving from a current of thought closer to Platonism. For in "pure" Stoicism, as we have noted, all that exists is corporeal and material, and at the same time it is also wholly rational, since the seeds of *logos*, which are also divine, are inherent in matter itself. One cannot say, then, in strict Stoic circles, that the sublunary world is qualitatively different from the celestial, given that both are composed of the same corporeal substance, although in the ether this is more rarefied and refined, inasmuch as ether, in Stoic allegorizing, is the physical equivalent of the supreme divinity, Zeus, and is the ruling faculty or *hêgemonikon* of the cosmos: to the degree that it is igneous, it is identified with the fiery *pneuma* itself, which is God (see Ramelli, *Allegoria*, ch. 2; Cornutus, *Theol.* 1, 3, 19, 20 and *passim*). So too Isnardi notes that, "despite the insistence in the Stoa, from Zeno onwards, on the idea of ether as a privileged element, this theory, expressed in these terms, is odd for a Stoic, and leads one to imagine some eclecticising contamination" ("Ierocle," 2207). See also the introductory essay above. In fact, in Roman Stoicism it seems possible to identify some Platonic, and especially Middle Platonic, influences as well; see Reale, *Scetticismo, eclettismo, neoaristotelismo e neostoicismo*, 52–55. It is not implausible, perhaps, to see also an Aristotelian touch in the division between the sublunary and celestials worlds, although the idea of matter as the principle of evil, which is as foreign to Aristotelianism as it is to Stoicism, would seem to point mainly to Middle Platonic developments, which were adopted also, in another context but not far removed in time, in gnostic and hermetic circles, for instance. On matter in Plato and the Platonic tradition, understood as the principle of becoming and disorder, and ultimately as the cause of evil, see Giovanni Reale, *Per una nuova interpretazione di Platone* (11th ed.; Milan: Vita e pensiero, 1993), 598–631; Jean-Marc Narbonne, "Le réceptacle platonicien: nature, fonction, contenu," *Dialogue* 36 (1997): 253–79, who analyzes the representation of matter as a receptacle and principle of necessity in the *Timaeus*, where there is a notion of sensible substance not very far removed from Aristotle's idea of matter; John Simons, "Matter and Time in Plotinus," *Dionysius* 9 (1985): 53–74, on the representation of matter in

Plotinus as the cause of becoming and of evil. Two patristic philosophers who were influenced by Middle Platonism and by Plato's *Timaeus*, Origen and Bardaisan, regarded the celestial bodies as superior to the sublunar elements (but not to human beings, or at least their noetic and spiritual component); they considered them to be creatures, not divine entities, but rational creatures serving God's providence and endowed with extraordinary beauty and purity and even with a minimum of free will.

12. The primary parent in Stoicism from the very beginning of the Old Stoa is in truth the highest god, Zeus, whose paternity in respect to humanity is thereafter strongly emphasized in Neo-Stoic circles, and particularly by Musonius; see, e.g., my "La concezione di Giove," 292–320; idem, "Dio come padre nello Stoicismo romano al tempo della predicazione cristiana e nell'*Epistola Anne*," in *Scripta antiqua in honorem Ángel Montenegro Duque et José María Blázquez Martínez* (ed. Santos Crespo Ortiz de Zárate and Ángel Montenegro Duque; Valladolid: Universidad de Valladolid, 2002), 343–51; idem, "L'interpretazione allegorica filosofica di Zeus come padre nello Stoicismo," in *Visiones mítico-religiosas del padre en la antigüedad clásica* (ed. Marcos Ruiz Sánchez; Monografías y Estudios de Antigüedad Griega y Romana 12; Madrid: Signifer Libros, 2004), 155–80.

13. Note the recourse to etymology in the argument, which is typical of the Stoics, who often use it in combination with allegory in their philosophical treatises: see my *Allegoria*, chs. 2, 6–7, and 9.

14. Note Hierocles' insistence on giving priority to the whole rather than to the individual part and at the same time on the tight unity between part and whole, a theme on which the Old Stoa had already concentrated (see Nicholas P. White, *Individual and Conflict in Greek Ehics* [Oxford: Clarendon, 2002]); for Cleanthes in particular, see Patrice Cambronne, "L'universel et le singulier: L'Hymne à Zeus de Cléanthe: Notes de lecture," *REA* 100 (1998): 89–114. The dialectic between whole and individual component in the Old Stoics is examined by Michael Gass, "Eudaimonism and Theology in Stoic Accounts of Virtue," *JHI* 61 (2000): 19–37, who observes, on the basis above all of Epictetus, *Diss.* 2.8–10, that among the Roman Stoics, and probably too already in the Old Stoa, the ideal of integrating the part in the whole was prominent; thus the cosmic perspective ends up being an expression of the thought and will of the part, which in turn is adapted, in the *sapiens*, to the will of God and to universal law. I myself, in this regard, think especially of Cleanthes' poem as translated by Seneca: *duc o parens celsique dominator poli ... ducunt volentem fata, nolentem trahunt* ["Lead, O Father, ruler of the high heaven.... The fates lead the willing, drag the unwilling"] (*SVF* 1.527; see Joachim Dalfen,

"Das Gebet des Kleanthes an Zeus und das Schicksal," *Hermes* 99 [1971]: 174–83; Hellfried Dahlmann, "Nochmals 'Ducunt volentem fata, nolentem trahunt,'" *Hermes* 105 [1977]: 342–51; Aldo Setaioli, "Due messe a punto senecane," *Prometheus* 17 [1991]: 137–54; Gisela Striker, "Following Nature: A Study in Stoic Ethics," *OSAP* 9 [1991]: 1–73, repr. in idem, *Essays on Hellenistic Epistemology and Ethics* [Cambridge: Cambridge University Press, 1996], 221–80; Frede, "Stoic Determinism," 179–205; Ramelli, *Allegoria*, ch. 2.3.2 on Zeus as fate and universal law in Cleanthes, à propos the fragment under discussion). In fact, in the immanentist view of the Stoics, everything is God, and every single part is a fragment of God, that unique and highest divinity of whom the various minor deities represent determinate aspects and partial manifestations. See Mansfeld, "Theology," 452–78; Martin L. West, "Towards Monotheism," in Athanassiadi and Frede, *Pagan Monotheism in Late Antiquity*, 21–41; Algra, "Stoic Theology," 153–78; Rainer Hirsch-Luipold, ed., *Gott und die Götter bei Plutarch: Götterbilder–Gottesbilder–Weltbilder* (Religionsgeschichtliche Versuche und Vorarbeiten 54; Berlin: de Gruyter, 2005), esp. the following essays in this volume: Franco Ferrari, "Der Gott Plutarchs und der Gott Platons" (13–25); Frederick E. Brenk, "Plutarch and His Middle-Platonic God: About to Enter (or Remake) the Academy" (27–49); and Rainer Hirsch-Luipold, "Der eine Gott bei Philon von Alexandrien und Plutarch" (141–68). See also the introductory essay above, §5b.

15. Note the assimilation of the emotions (πάθη) to diseases, which as such are to be completely eliminated for the health of the soul (ἀπάθεια). The medical metaphor is part and parcel of the idea of philosophy as *animi medicina*, which is found in Seneca, for example, and has a long tradition behind it. See, e.g., the introduction by Antonella Borgo in *Lessico morale di Seneca* (Studi Latini 33; Naples: Loffredo, 1998), with my review of Borgo's volume in *Aevum* 74 (2000): 372–74, and Garro, "La concezione dei πάθη," 183–95; also Martha Nussbaum, *The Therapy of Desire: Theory and Practice in Hellenistic Ethics* (Princeton: Princeton University Press, 1994); Pier Luigi Donini, "*Pathos* nello stoicismo romano," *Elenchos* 16 (1995): 193–216; Roberto Gazich, "La *Fedra* di Seneca tra pathos ed elegia," *Humanitas (Brescia)* NS 52 (1997): 348–75; Paola Migliorini, *Scienza e terminologia medica nella letteratura latina di età neroniana* (Frankfurt am Main: Lang, 1997); Giovanni Reale, *La filosofia di Seneca: Come terapia dei mali dell'anima* (Milan: Bompiani, 2003); Margaret Graver, *Stoicism and Emotion* (Chicago: University of Chicago Press, 2007), who stresses that the Stoic ideal of *apatheia* did not entail the absence of all emotions, but only of the negative ones, the *pathê*, whereas the *eupatheiai*

were not only admitted but also encouraged and regarded positively. The Stoic theory of the *pathê* is also treated by Christopher Gill in the second part of his *The Structured Self in Hellenistic and Roman Thought* (Oxford: Oxford University Press, 2006), reviewed by Gretchen Reydams-Schils in *CP* 103 (2008): 189–95 and Brad Inwood in *Philosophical Quarterly* 57, 228 (2007): 479–83. In particular, in ch. 4 Gill shows how, in the Hellenistic-Roman philosophical landscape, a tension developed between the Platonic-Aristotelian conception of *pathos*, based on a nonholistic model of the self, and the Stoic one, which conceived of the human person as a holistic psycho-physical unit. The development of the Stoic conception of *pathê* is analyzed by Richard Sorabji, "What Is New on Emotion in Stoicism after 100 BC?" in *Greek and Roman Philosophy 100 BC–200 AD* (ed. Richard Sorabji and Robert W. Sharples; London: Institute for Classical Studies, 2007), 163–74.

From the point of view of philosophy as a cure for the illnesses of the soul, suicide itself, seen by the Stoics as an extreme remedy, can be regarded as a form of therapy, albeit rather a drastic one; see Jason Xenakis, "Stoic Suicide Therapy," *Sophia* 40 (1972): 88–99; also, on Stoic suicide and the motives for it, Miriam Griffin, "Philosophy, Cato, and Roman Suicide," *GR* 33 (1986): 64–77, 192–202; Mariella Menchelli, "La morte del filosofo o il filosofo di fronte alla morte," *SIFC* 15 (1997): 65–80; Timothy Hill, *Ambitiosa Mors: Suicide and Self in Roman Thought and Literature* (New York: Routledge, 2004), esp. ch. 7 on Seneca, whom the author regards as "obsessed by suicide" and "suicidocentric" (146), ch. 8 on suicide among the Roman nobility under Nero and Domitian, where it is remarked that these senators were often sympathetic to Stoicism, and ch. 9 on suicide in Lucan.

16. Zaleucus was the lawgiver of Locri in the seventh century B.C. The sources seem to indicate that his law code was inspired by the principle of retaliation. See Max Mühl, *Die Gesetze des Zaleukos und Charondas* (Leipzig: Dieterich, 1929; repr., Aalen: Scientia-Verl, 1964); Kurt von Fritz, "Zaleukos," PW 9.A2:2298; Andrew Szegedy-Maszak, "Legends of the Greek Lawgivers," *GRBS* 19 (1978): 199–209; René van Compernolle, "La législation aristocratique de Locres Épizéphyrienne, dite législation de Zaleukos," *L'Antiquité Classique* 50 (1981): 759–69; Giorgio Camassa, "Il pastorato di Zaleuco," *Athenaeum* 64 (1986): 139–45, who assimilates the figure of Zaleucus to those of the kings and herdsman-lawgivers of Crete and the Near East, but also to later Greek lawgivers; Maddalena Luisa Zunino, "Scrivere la legge orale, interpretare la legge scritta: I *Nomoi* di Zaleuco," *QS* 24 (1998): 151–59, with an analysis of Aristotle, frag.

548 in Valentin Rose, *Aristotelis qui ferebantur librorum fragmenta* (3rd ed.; Leipzig: Teubner, 1886; repr., Stuttgart: Teubner, 1967), 342 = frag. 555 in Olof Gigon, *Librorum deperditorum fragmenta* (vol. 3 of *Aristotelis opera*; Berlin: de Gruyter, 1987), 678–79; Anne Fitzpatrick-McKinley, "Ezra, Nehemiah and Some Early Greek Lawgivers," in *Rabbinic Law in Its Roman and Near Eastern Context* (ed. Catherine Hezser; TSAJ 97; Tübingen: Mohr Siebeck, 2003), 17–48, who finds parallels between the tradition on Ezra and Nehemiah and the Hellenistic tradition concerning Lycurgus, Zaleucus, and Charondas; Stefan Link, "Die Gesetzgebung des Zaleukos im epizephyrischen Lokroi," *Klio* 74 (1992): 11–24.

For the importance of laws in the Stoic tradition and the harmony between natural law and positive laws, see my *Il basileus come nomos empsychos tra diritto naturale e diritto divino: spunti platonici dell'idea stoica e sviluppi di età imperiale* (Naples: Bibliopolis, 2007); for the idea of natural law in Stoicism, see at a minimum Gerard Watson, "The Natural Law and Stoicism," in Long, *Problems in Stoicism*, 216–38, who argues that the concept of natural law is typical of the Stoics and attains a clear expression among them for the first time, later to be adopted by Cicero and the church fathers; Joseph DeFilippo and Phillip T. Mitsis, "Socrates and Stoic Natural Law," in Vander Waerdt, *The Socratic Movement*, 252–71; Brad Inwood, "Natural Law in Seneca," *StudPhiloAnn* 15 (2003): 81–99; John M. Cooper, "Eudaimonism, the Appeal to Nature, and 'Moral Duty' in Stoicism," in *Aristotle, the Stoics, and Kant: Rethinking Happiness and Duty:* (ed. Stephen P. Engstrom and Jennifer Whiting; Cambridge: Cambridge University Press, 1996), 261–84; idem, *Knowledge, Nature, and the Good: Essays on Ancient Philosophy* (Princeton: Princeton University Press, 2004); Christopher Gill, "Stoic Writers of the Imperial Era," in *The Cambridge History of Greek and Roman Political Thought* (ed. Christopher Rowe and Malcolm Schofield; Cambridge: Cambridge University Press, 2000), 597–615, esp. 606–7. See also James E. G. Zetzel, "Natural Law and Poetic Justice: A Carneadean Debate in Cicero and Vergil," *CP* 86 (1991): 297–319.

With this motif is connected that of veneration for the ancient legislators or νομοθέται, the founders of laws and customs (νόμος has both senses in Greek, and Hierocles has both in mind, as he makes explicit), who are placed on a par with the ancient theological poets and with the creators of myths and rites; the idea begins with Chrysippus's speculations in *SVF* 2.1009; see my *Allegoria*, chs. 2, 6–7, and 9. Annaeus Cornutus shows great respect for this veneration of the ancients, to whom he attributes the ability to philosophize and whose wisdom was expressed in symbols

and riddles in their myths, rituals, and representations of the gods, all to be interpreted allegorically (*Theol.* 35; see Ramelli, *Cornuto*, "Saggio integrativo"). On the ancient Greek νομοθέται, see Karl-Joachim Hölkeskamp, *Schiedsrichter, Gesetzgeber und Gesetzgebung im archaischen Griechenland* (Stuttgart: Steiner, 1999). The application of Stoic theological allegoresis not only to literary traditions but also to iconography and cult is rightly emphasized by Glenn W. Most, "Cornutus and Stoic Allegoresis: A Preliminary Report," *ANRW* 36.3:2014–65.

From this point onward, von Arnim based his edition of the Stobaean excerpts of Hierocles on Meineke rather than on the edition by Wachsmuth and Hense, because the fourth volume of the latter had not yet been published (it appeared three years later). As the critical apparatus of von Arnim indicates, he did not simply reproduce Meineke's text but edited it, making a number of improvements. For the fragments based on Meineke, I have carefully checked the corresponding texts in volume 4 of Wachsmuth and Hense, *Ioannis Stobaei anthologium* and verified that there are very few significant departures from von Arnim's edition.

17. It is worth comparing Hierocles' treatise on marriage with the surviving diatribes on the subject by Musonius Rufus, the Roman Stoic of the time of Nero, on whom see Ramelli, *Musonio Rufo*, 7 and 17–23; idem, "La tematica *de matrimonio*," 145–62; idem, "Musonio Rufo," 8:7696–97. On Musonius and his literary and philosophical context, see also Tim Whitmarsh, *Greek Literature and the Roman Empire*, 141–55; Mark Morford, *The Roman Philosophers*, 189–201. Specifically on Musonius's attitude toward marriage, the family, and women, see Charles Favez, "Un féministe romain: Musonius Rufus," *Bulletin de la Société des Études de Lettres, Lausanne* 20 (1933): 1–8; Emiel Eyben, "De latere stoa over het huwelijk," *Hermeneus* 50 (1978): 15–32, 71–94, 337–58 (with introductions, texts, and translations of Antipater, Musonius, Hierocles, and Epictetus on marriage, along with commentary); Mario Adinolfi, "Le diatribe di Musonio Rufo sulla donna e il matrimonio alla luce delle lettere paoline," in *Studia Hierosolymitana 3: Nell'ottavo centenario francescano (1182–1982)* (ed. Giovanni Claudio Bottini; Studium Biblicum Franciscanum 30; Jerusalem: Franciscan Printing Press, 1982), 121–35; Roy B. Ward, "Musonius and Paul on Marriage," *NTS* 36 (1990): 281–89; Engel, "The Gender Egalitarianism of Musonius Rufus," 377–91; Nussbaum, "Incomplete Feminism of Musonius Rufus," 283–326; Wöhrle, "Wenn Frauen Platons Staat lesen," 135–43; Gaca, *The Making of Fornication*, 60, 82–86, 90–93, 113–15; Laurand, "Souci de soi et mariage," 85–116; Reydams-Schils, *The Roman Stoics*, esp. chs. 4–5, with my review in *RFN* 98

(2006): 605–10; Ramelli, *Stoici romani minori*, essay on Musonius Rufus; idem, "Neo-Stoicism and Household."

One may also mention, by way of comparison, the parallel treatment of marriage by Seneca, reported by Jerome in *Against Jovinianus* and translated by me in Giovanni Reale, ed., *Seneca: Tutte le opere* (Milan: Bompiani, 2000); on this treatise, see above all Chiara Torre, *Il matrimonio del* sapiens: *Ricerche sul* De matrimonio *di Seneca* (Genoa: Università di Genova, Facoltà di lettere, Dipartimento di archeologia, filologia classica e loro tradizioni, 2000). See also Ramelli, "La tematica de matrimonio"; idem, "Il matrimonio cristiano in Clemente: Un confronto con la legislazione romana e gli Stoici romani," in *Il matrimonio cristiano: XXXVII Incontro di studiosi dell'Antichità cristiana, Roma, Augustinianum, 6–8 Maggio 2008* (Studia Ephemeridis Augustinianum 114; Rome: Institutum patristicum Augustinianum, 2009), 351–72; and, for a collection of ancient sources on this topic, Konrad Gaiser, *Für und wider die Ehe: Antike Stimmen zu einer offenen Frage* (Dialog mit der Antike 1; Munich: Heimeran, 1974).

As Isnardi observes ("Ierocle", 2202), many themes in Hierocles' reflections on marriage, as they appear in the Stobaean extracts, have significant parallels not only in neo-Stoics such as Seneca and still more in Musonius, but already in Antipater of Tarsus, who was a disciple of Chrysippus and of Diogenes of Babylon and was head of the school after the latter, as well as being the teacher of Posidonius; an edition of the fragments with interpretive essay may be found in Hermann Cohn, *Antipater von Tarsos: Ein Beitrag zu Geschichte der Stoa* (Berlin: Fromholz, 1905), to which add the new edition of Papyrus Berolinensis inv. 16545, dating to the second century A.D., which contains a text of Antipater's on representations: Thamer Backhouse, "Antipater of Tarsus on False *Phantasiai*," in *Papiri filosofici: Miscellanea di studi 3* (Studi e testi per il CPF 10; Firenze: Olschki, 2000), 7–31, which replaces the edition by Mikołaj Szymanski, "P. Berol. Inv. 16545: A Text on Stoic Epistemology with a Fragment of Antipater of Tarsus," *Journal of Juristic Papyrology* 20 (1990): 139–41; critical study and bibliography in Steinmetz, "Die Stoa," 4.2:637–42 and 644–45; for further and more recent refrences, see the introductory essay above, n. 60. Indeed, in fragments 62–63 (*SVF* 3.62–63:254–57), both quoted by Stobaeus alongside excerpts from Hierocles, we find pronounced affinities with various ideas on wedlock developed also by Hierocles. The first fragment, in *Anth.* 4.22d.103 (4:539,5–540,6 Wachsmuth and Hense), is drawn from Antipater's work *On Living Together with a Wife* (Περὶ γυναικὸς συμβιώσεως) and argues that one

must not choose a wife because of her wealth, noble status, or beauty but rather on the basis of her parents' behavior and her own. The second extract, quoted by Stobaeus at 4.22a.25 (4:507,6–512,7 Wachsmuth and Hense), derives from Antipater's *On Marriage* (Περὶ γάμου) and argues in favor of marrying: a family or house (οἰκία) is not complete without a wife and children; man has a social nature and the obligation to increase and perpetuate his *polis*, and in addition must make sure that there will always be someone to render thanks to the gods. The love between spouses, and their union, which is entirely in accord with nature, is not a simple juxtaposition but a total fusion of birthrights, children, bodies, and souls; this last idea of the spiritual communion between spouses will be dear also to Musonius and Hierocles. The presence of a wife in the house is a great relief to a husband, especially in times of adversity and sickness, and it also has a moral value, since it helps one avoid immoderate behavior. A wife is certainly not an encumbrance, or if so a very light one, but is rather a helper, like an additional hand. Whoever loves study can, by taking a wife, assign the handling of the patrimony and of the household to her, and so have more freedom for his own activities. The convergence of all these ideas of Antipater's with those of Hierocles in the extract under consideration, as well as with the diatribes of Musonius on the same topic, is evident. Eyben ("De latere stoa over het huwelijk," 15–32, 71–94, 337–58) lines up the texts of Antipater on marriage with the much later texts by Musonius, Hierocles, and Epictetus and highlights the deep affinities between them. Will Deming, *Paul on Marriage and Celibacy: The Hellenistic Background of 1 Corinthians 7* (2nd ed.; Grand Rapids: Eerdmans, 2004), 47–104, includes a Greek text and translation of the fragments of *De matrimonio* by Antipater of Tarsus and shows how the question of marriage was fully treated only in Stoic and Cynic circles: the Stoics, apart from Zeno in his *Republic*, approved of marriage as a duty of the *sapiens*. Zeno, in his *Republic*, did not admit of marriage at all, since he favored communalism, which Chrysippus did not reject in principle (*SVF* 3.743–746:185–86 and 728:183), although he did not accept adultery in established states (*SVF* 3.729:183), whereas later Stoics did reject adultery outright, as Philodemus attests (*Stoic.* XIV.4). It is in Middle Stoicism and even more in Neo-Stoicism that the marriage theme receives close attention. See Roberto Radice, *Oikeiôsis*, 63–75 for the tendency to mitigate Zeno's (and Chrysippus's) view. The Cynics, instead, tended to regard marriage as a burden; so too the Peripatetic Theophrastus, along with Epicurus and his followers, were inclined to see marriage as incompatible with the commitments of a sage.

The theme of "whether one should marry" is also treated in the rhetorical tradition. Libanius offers it as an exercise in thesis in his *Progymnasmata*: Εἰ γαμητέον, now translated into English by Craig A. Gibson, *Libanius's* Progymnasmata*: Model Exercises in Greek Prose Composition and Rhetoric* (SBLWGRW 27; Atlanta: Society of Biblical Literature, 2008). Libanius's argument is based on the fact that the gods and demigods themselves marry and beget children and that the behavior of animals also shows that marriage is according to nature (as opposed to Socrates and some Stoics, Libanius does not seem to make any distinction here between marriage and animal mating). Moreover, Libanius contends that, if one refuses to marry, one damages his own city and that marriage brings financial advantage and the sharing of delights and pains, the presence of a housekeeper and co-worker, a relief in time of illness, a new family to be joined with one's own, a better reputation, and children who will work and tend their father in his old age; the father will also be able to share in their fame (it may be noted that the argument is entirely from the husband's perspective). Gibson (511 n. 1) lists the other relevant places where this theme is found in rhetorical materials: Aelius Theon, *Prog.* 120, 121, 128; Pseudo-Hermogenes, *Prog.* 24–26; Aphthonius, *Prog.* 41–46; and Nicolaus, *Prog.* 71–75. I am extremely grateful to John Fitzgerald and the author for providing me with the relevant section of the book before its publication.

18. This is one of the many arguments common to Hierocles and Musonius, with roots in the Stoic tradition *de matrimonio*: Musonius also argues dialectically, in *Diss.* 14, that if matrimony were eliminated, families, cities, and the entire human race would be eliminated as well (see Ramelli, *Musonio Rufo*, 184–85). For this reason he considers marrying to be a duty both civic and religious, since it is in conformity with the law of nature and, at the same time, the law of Zeus, given the Stoic view of the coextension of God and nature and of the total immanence of the highest deity in nature (see Ramelli, *Musonio Rufo*, 21–22).

19. Just as for Musonius (as Reydams-Schils, *Roman Stoics*, 143–59, has made especially clear), so too for Hierocles, the end of marriage is not only procreation but also the ideal of leading a life in common both harmoniously and in the pursuit of virtue. Indeed, Musonius makes the bond between souls—their ὁμόνοια and φιλία—the ultimate end of marriage, beyond that of procreation itself, which remains central, to be sure, but in itself can very well be achieved in other kinds of relationship. As we read in *Diss.* 13, a married couple must join together in such a way as "to share their lives with one another and produce children.... For the generation

of the human race, which this bond achieves, is a great thing. But this is not sufficient for the man who marries, since it can occur outside of matrimony if people join in other ways, in the way that animals join with each other. But in marriage there must always be sharing of lives [συμβίωσις] and the caring [κηδεμονία] of husband and wife for one another, when they are healthy and when they are ill and in every circumstance" (these same ideas are taken up by Clement of Alexandria in the second book of his *Stromata*; see Ramelli, *Musonio Rufo*, 174–75). Musonius continues:

> It is in pursuit of this caring, as well as of the procreation of children, that they enter upon marriage. Where this caring is complete, and the couple living together grant it completely to one another, each competing to outdo the other, this marriage is as it should be and is worthy of being emulated, for such a communion [κοινωνία] is beautiful [καλή, sc. morally]. Where, however, each looks only to his own interest without concern for the other, or even, by Zeus, only one of the two is like this, and though he dwells in the same house, in his mind [τῇ γνώμῃ] he gazes outside it and he does not wish to strive together and coalesce with [συντείνειν τε καὶ συμπνεῖν] his mate, it is inevitable that in this case the communion be destroyed.

Again, in *Diss.* 13B Musonius speaks of κοινωνία and ὁμόνοια as the most important thing in wedlock (see Ramelli, *Musonio Rufo*, 176–77; idem, "Transformations of the Household and Marriage Theory between Neo-Stoicism, Middle-Platonism, and Early Christianity," *RFN* 100 [2008]: 369–96). In this way, as Reydam-Schils, *Roman Stoics*, ch. 5, has made clear, philosophers such as Musonius and, after him, Hierocles elevate the marriage bond to the same level of dignity as that of friendship, traditionally understood as a tie between virtuous men, and so extend the basic instantiation of virtue also to the relation between spouses. Both relationships, indeed, arise from the affective bond of φιλία. See also the introductory essay above and references in n. 36.

20. For this doctrine of οἰκείωσις, see the more developed version of it by Hierocles himself in the *Elements of Ethics*, with the commentary above; also Radice, *Oikeiôsis*, with up-to-date references, the most important of which are indicated in n. 7 of the introductory essay above.

21. "In the way one ought" means "according to the duties of each": marriage is among the duties or καθήκοντα, which were treated more in more depth in the time of Panaetius and Middle Stoicism within the theory of preferable indifferents but were nevertheless already present in the Old Stoa. See Nebel, "Der Begriff ΚΑΘΗΚΟΝ," 439–60; Engberg-

Pedersen, "Discovering the Good," 145–83; D. Sedley, "Stoic-Platonist Debate," 128–52; Sorabji, *Emotions and Peace of Mind*, 29–77, 93–132. Reason serves to enable us to make just choices in conformity with our duties, Hierocles says—this is the *logos* that is grafted onto each of us insofar as we are human beings; here Hierocles returns to the Stoic tripartition that was already noted in the *Elements of Ethics*: plants have only nature (φύσις); animals also a soul (ψυχή); and in human beings there is added reason (λόγος). In respect to nature, nevertheless, reason is not something different or contrary: as a faculty present in human beings, it agrees with nature when making the best choices, drawing inspiration from nature itself, as Hierocles asserts. But if *logos* too, in a human being, looks to nature for its criterion of action, what is the difference between the action of a human being and that of a plant, given that both have nature as their guide? In a plant, every action or state is unconscious; in a human being, choices are conscious and voluntary.

22. Musonius Rufus made an effort above all to demonstrate that marriage is in conformity with divine will, even going so far as to find support in etymological considerations relating to the epithets of Zeus, Hera, and Aphrodite:

> That marriage is a great thing and worthy of serious effort is clear from the following—for great gods are in charge of it, according to what is believed among human beings: first Hera, and for this reason we address her as "protrectress of marriage" [ζυγία]; then Eros, and next Aphrodite: for we suppose that all these perform the function of bringing husband and wife together for the procreation of children. For where would Eros more justly be present than in the lawful association of husband and wife? Where Hera? Where Aphrodite? When could one more opportunely pray to these gods than when entering upon marriage? What might we more properly call "the work of Aphrodite" [ἔργον ἀφροδίσιον] than the union of a married woman with him who married her? Why, then, would one say that such great gods superintend and are in charge of marriage and procreation but that these things were not suitable for a human being? (*Diss.* 14; see Ramelli, *Musonio Rufo*, 188–89)

> How can we not offend against our ancestral gods and against Zeus protector of the family [ὁμόγνιος] if we behave in this way? For just as someone who is unjust toward guests offends against Zeus protector of guests [ξένιος] or toward friends against Zeus protector of friends [φίλιος], so too whoever is unjust toward his own ancestors offends against the ancestral gods [πάτριοι] and against Zeus protector of the

> family [ὁμόγνιον], who is the overseer of sins concerning the family: but he who sins against the gods is impious. (*Diss.* 15A; cf. Ramelli, *Musonio Rufo*, 143–145).

A claim similar to that of Musonius invited a polemical response on the part of Seneca, nominally directed against Chrysippus but implicitly, it is likely, also against more recent followers of Chrysippus. See my *Musonio Rufo*, 22–23, and, especially for the etymologies and the polemic with Seneca, my *Allegoria*, ch. 6.4. In *De matrimonio* (*SVF* 3.727:183), Seneca writes: "Chrysippus instructs the sage to take a wife so as not to offend Jupiter *Gamelius* and *Genethlius*," a precept that, however, Seneca ridicules. Chrysippus *ridicule praecipit*, he says, since, "on this account among the Latins one will not have to take a wife, since they do not have a Jupiter *Nuptialis*!" According to Seneca, moral precepts cannot be derived from the epithets of the gods; this is absurd and leads to absurdities. However, this is precisely what the Stoic allegorists did, from the Old Stoa down to the contemporaries of Seneca such as Cornutus and Musonius: in the names of the deities, and also in the details of their myths, they believed that the truth lay hidden, both physical or cosmological and ethical truths. Seneca, in launching such an attack, not only distances himself from the Old Stoic Chrysippus, whom he openly ridicules, and from the neo-Stoic Cornutus, who was an admirer of the Chrysippean exegesis of myth and probably knew his work directly (as I attempt to demonstrate in *Allegoria*, ch. 6.3.4a), but also from his contemporary Musonius, who, as we have seen, based his conjugal precepts precisely on a reference to Zeus, placing marriage under the protection of Zeus, Hera, and the greatest deities and who invokes Ζεὺς ὁμόγνιος and Hera ζυγία as custodians of the family and its offspring. Analogously, the respect for guests and friends is grounded by him in Zeus's epithets ξένιος and φίλιος; in addition, the adjective ἀφροδίσιος is brought back to its basic meaning, "of Aphrodite," so conjugal sex is placed under the jurisdiction of the goddess, in line with the etymologizing and allegorizing practice systematically applied by Cornutus to divine epithets. Seneca, on the contrary, criticizes the idea that love is a god; in his *Phaedra*, in response to the affirmation by the protagonist that it is useless to fight against the passion of love, since it is a god (184–194), i.e., the winged Eros, who makes even the most powerful gods succumb, the nurse replies that it was simply *furor*, the *turpis libido vitio favens*, that made a divinity of erotic passion (195–203). In any case, apart from the connection with mythological gods and allegorical interpretations, that marriage conforms to divine

will is primarily demonstrated by the Stoics on the basis of its conformity to nature.

In the present section, Hierocles, after having argued that marriage is a duty, seeks to demonstrate as well that it is useful, that is, advantageous to those who enter into it, and he illustrates above all the advantages that accrue to the father of a family from his wife and children.

23. Here Hierocles touches on the most important point: marriage is not only a duty, and is not only useful, but it is also a "beautiful" thing, which is to be understood as morally fine, in accord with a common sense of *καλόν*, since it is oriented toward the pursuit of virtue. This idea of sharing the path to virtue is no longer the privilege only of philosophers who are friends with one another but also of wives and husbands, in a communion that, for Hierocles as well as for Musonius, is not just one of bodies with a view to procreation but still more one of souls, carrying with it a moral commitment: marriage becomes a spiritual bond in the pursuit of virtue, which is the goal of the philosophical life itself, according to the Stoics. Musonius, in *Diss.* 13B, entitled "What Is the Most Important Thing in a Marriage," observes, as does Hierocles, that this is not one of the seeming goods but rather true concord and a spiritual bond between spouses:

> Therefore those who marry should not look to lineage and whether it is from nobility, nor to money and whether they possess much of it, nor to bodies and whether they have beautiful ones. For neither wealth nor beauty nor birth are such as to increase communion [κοινωνία] or concord [ὁμόνοια] more, nor again do these things make the procreation of children firmer. Rather, they should look for bodies that are sufficiently healthy for marriage, middling in appearance and strong enough for work, which will also be less subject to attack by wanton people, will work harder at bodily chores, and will amply produce children. One must consider those souls best adapted [for marriage] that are by nature most disposed to temperance, justice, and in general to virtue. For what marriage is beautiful, without concord? Or what communality good? And how can human beings who are wicked be in accord with one another? Or how could a good person be in accord with a wicked one? (see Ramelli, *Musonio Rufo*, 176–79)

In addition, Musonius too, like Hierocles, declares that the communion characteristic of marriage is *καλή* in *Diss.* 13A (Ramelli, *Musonio Rufo*, 174–75). This is why Musonius also insists on a philosophical education for women: for the pursuit of virtue is common to both sexes in

equal measure. To this thesis *Diss.* 2, 3, and 4 are dedicated, the last of these especially lengthy (Ramelli, *Musonio Rufo*, 50–77). *Discourse* 2 provides the theoretical foundation for Musonius's argument, demonstrating that in all human beings virtue is innate: "All of us are so disposed by nature as to live faultlessly and nobly, and not one of us yes, another no.... It is clear, then, that there is no other cause of this than that a human being is born for virtue.... There is in the soul of a human being a natural capacity for honorable conduct, and a seed of virtue resides in each one of us." *Discourse* 3 draws the logical conclusion from these premises: women too should practice philosophy, as the title itself proclaims, since "women have received from the gods the same reasoning as men," have the same sense, the same limbs, and "a desire for and natural orientation toward virtue occurs not only in men but also in women." There follow examples of the various virtues that it is good for a woman to possess in the same degree as a man. *Discourse* 4, entitled, "Whether Sons and Daughters Should Be Given an Education," replies in the affirmative with lengthy arguments (which makes it clear that this was not the usual practice in the classical world), rehearsing again the claims in the preceding diatribes and demonstrating that women should achieve the same virtues as the other sex and by means of the same education, especially in ethics: "just as no man can be rightly educated without philosophy, so too no woman can." See Reydams-Schils, *Roman Stoics*, ch. 5, with my review in *RFN* 8 (2006): 605–10; also Ramelli, *Musonio Rufo*, 17–20.

24. *Od.* 6.182–183. This is evidently a sign of admiration for Homer, although Hierocles does not hesitate to criticize him openly, as at the end of the first of the Stobaean extracts. Here, however, as in other passages, Hierocles uses Homer in support of his own argument, as Chrysippus had done (see my *Allegoria*, ch. 2.4) and as was common practice among not a few Stoic and Stoicizing writers. For the importance of Homer in the Stoic tradition, which subjected him to allegorizing interpretation in the conviction that his verses contained philosophical truths, see the notes to the first two extracts from Stobaeus above.

25. Foolishness, which is one with vice, since it instantly yields to it, is what is truly evil and leads to evil; this is a cardinal principle of Stoic ethics, on which the Neo-Stoics also insisted. Cleanthes, in the *Hymn to Zeus* (see the introductory essay above, §5b with related notes), had already prayed to the highest deity to drive grim foolishness out of his soul (ἀπειροσύνης ἀπὸ λύγρης, ἣν σύ, πάτερ, σκέδασον ψυχῆς ἄπο), since it is the cause of all its evils (see Johan C. Thom, "Kleantes se Himne aan Zeus," *Akroterion* 41 [1996]: 44–57; idem, "The Problem of Evil in Cleanthes'

Hymn to Zeus," *AClass* 41 [1998]: 45–57; idem, *Cleanthes' Hymn to Zeus*). Zeus, who is called upon to liberate him from foolishness, is thus far from being the cause of it (see Helmut Quack, "Der Zeushymnus des Kleanthes als Paralleltext zum Vaterunser," *AU* 39 [1996]: 86–97). Persius, a Stoic poet in the time of Nero, a friend of the Stoic Thrasea Paetus, who was part of the opposition to Nero, and a pupil of Annaeus Cornutus, takes up this theme in *Sat.* 5, which is dedicated to his teacher Cornutus: here he treats the central Stoic topic of true freedom as the moral freedom of the person who lives rightly (5.104–109) and knows how to control the passions (5.109–112). Persius presents his master as a follower of the purest strain of Stoicism, in particular that of Cleanthes ("for you, as an educator of youths, plant in their purified ears the harvest of Cleanthes," 5.63–64), who is not by accident the only source whom Cornutus cites in his *Theologiae Graecae compendium*. What is more, the teachings of Cornutus are represented as inspired by Socrates, just as in the case of his contemporary Musonius ("you receive their tender years [those of his pupils] in your Socratic bosom"). Persius owned approximately seven hundred books by Chrysippus, which at his death he bequeathed to Cornutus (Valerius Probus, *Vita Persii* 7), whose admiration for and emulation of Chrysippus is attested also by Dio Cassius, *Hist. Rom.* 62.29.3: "Chrysippus, whom you [sc. Cornutus] praise and imitate [ἐπαινεῖς καὶ ζηλοῖς]," and by the many ideas of Chrysippean origin that I have pointed out in his *Theologiae Graecae compendium* (*Allegoria*, ch. 6). For Cornutus and Persius, then, foolishness is the incapacity to make good use of the faculty that is characteristic of a human being, namely, reason; from this derive continual faults in behavior: the *publica lex hominum naturaque* contain the divinely sanctioned rule (*fas*) that he who does not have wisdom cannot live properly or be truly free (*Sat.* 5.96–99). For God himself is identified with reason-Logos and does not allow foolishness to be mixed with rectitude: where the former exists, which is the greatest evil, the latter cannot, and neither, therefore, can there be true freedom, that is, moral freedom from the passions, which are the masters of the ignorant and constitute the true sicknesses of the soul, in accord with characteristically Stoic notions. Persius writes, in verses that represent a synthesis of the ethical teachings of his master: "Reason has granted you [sc. the fool] nothing; raise but a finger, and you commit an error.... No incense you offer will make even a little half-ounce of rectitude [*recti*] stick to fools [*stultis*].... It is unlawful to mix these things.... 'I am free' [*liber ego*]. Whence do you derive this idea, you who are a slave to so many things [*tot subdite rebus*]...? Within you, in your sick liver, your masters are born [*intus in iecore aegro/nascun-*

tur domini]" (*Sat.* 5.119–30). See my "La concezione di Giove," 292–320, and *Allegoria*, ch. 6.4.4–5, with an analysis of the key philosophical concepts in *Sat.* 5 and further references; also J. C. Zietsman, "A Commentary on Persius Satire 5: Themes and Structure" (Ph.D. diss., University of Pretoria, 1988); idem, "Persius, Saturn and Jupiter," *Akroterion* 36 (1991): 94–103; Giuseppe La Bua, "La *laus Cornuti* nella V satira di Persio e Lucrezio III 1–30," *Bollettino di Studi Latini* 27 (1997): 82–101; Morford, *The Roman Philosophers*, 194–95; Franco Bellandi, "Anneo Cornuto nelle *Saturae* e nella *Vita Persi*," in *Gli Annei: Una famiglia nella storia e nella cultura di Roma imperiale, Atti del Convegno Internazionale, Milano-Pavia, 2–6 maggio 2000* (ed. Isabella Gualandri and Giancarlo Mazzoli; Como: New Press, 2003), 185–210, esp. 187ff., who recognizes the importance of *Sat.* 5 for documenting Cornutus's ethical concerns.

26. The recommendations of Musonius are analogous, and they are based on the same premises: one should not choose a wife (or a husband: Musonius, in contrast to the more traditionalist Hierocles, contemplates both cases, in conformity with his more egalitarian conception of the two genders) on the basis of false criteria, which are based on external goods, but ought rather to consider the true goods and ends of marriage, that is, the concord and community of the two partners in respect to virtue and procreation. One's spouse, then, need not be rich, beautiful, noble, and so forth, but rather physically and still more morally healthy, which is to say, predisposed to virtue. See Musonius, *Diss.* 13B, quoted above; Reydams-Schils, *The Roman Stoics*, 67–68 and 143–59.

27. Most likely Homer, *Od.* 20.135: "Do not blame her, my son, for she is blameless." Again, Hierocles exhorts everyone to assume responsibility for themselves, without blaming others (the divine, earlier; here, one's neighbor), and to be conscious that it is we ourselves who provoke evils, in our ignorance, which brings with it erroneous choices. Immediately following this, the term I render as "ignorance" is ἄγνοιαν, a conjecture due to Praechter and followed by Wachsmuth and Hense; Meineke conjectured rather ἀπειρίαν. The reading ἀσθένειαν, however, may also make sense: "our own inability regarding, precisely, their usefulness."

28. There is a close analogy here with Musonius Rufus, *Diss.* 15A and B of (see my *Musonio Rufo*, which keeps the text of Hense but supplements it with a discovered-subsequently papyrus that allows us to unify both parts of *Diss.* 15: Ramelli, *Musonio Rufo*, 192–203): according to Musonius, too, all children who are born are to be raised and not to be destroyed in order to secure greater wealth for those that remain, which is considered impious and contrary to divine law. In *Diss.* 15A, indeed, he notes first of all

that the legislators or νομοθέται revered by the Stoics (see my *Allegoria*, chs. 2.4.1 and 9) and called by Musonius himself "divine men dear to the gods" seek to encourage πολυπαιδία among citizens, which is also protected by Zeus ὁμόγνιος and, as such, conforms to divine will. Besides this, Musonius seeks to show that it is also advantageous on the practical plane, since it confers power and prestige and is morally a fine thing (καλόν); it is also a beautiful sight to see a father surrounded by numerous offspring. In the papyrus fragment Rendel Harris I, which joins the two halves of the diatribe (ed. Cora E. Lutz, "Musonius Rufus, the Roman Socrates," *YCS* 10 [1947]: 3–147, here 98, vv. 18–27; see also 6 n. 12; Ramelli, *Musonio Rufo*, 198–99), in response to one who objects that he does not have sufficient money to raise all the children born to him, Musonius replies by adducing the example of birds who nourish all their chicks, though they are poorer and less gifted than human beings (this bears an obvious affinity to the saying of Jesus in Matt 6:26; see Pieter W. van der Horst, "Musonius Rufus and the New Testament," *NovT* 16 [1974]: 306–15, with many other parallels), and in *Diss.* 15B he attacks those who, although they are quite rich, rid themselves of their last-born in order to keep the patrimony undivided for their earlier children, "contriving wealth for their children by way of impiety…, little knowing how much better it is to have many siblings than much money." For this reason, too, Musonius was a writer especially praised by Christians, so much so that Clement of Alexandria considered him a martyr of the Logos for having been sent into exile by Nero and drew frequently and extensively on Musonius's *Discourses* in his *Pedagogue* and in the *Stromata*; Origen (*Cels.* 3.66) considered Musonius a παράδειγμα τοῦ ἀρίστου βίου: documentation in my *Musonio Rufo*, 25–30, with many additional parallels with the Gospels. For the echoes in Clement, see José M. Blázquez, "El uso del pensamiento de la filosofía griega en el *Pedagogo* de Clemente de Alejandria," *Anuario de Historia de la Iglesia* 3 (1994): 59–62; for Musonius's thinking concerning children, Reydams-Schils, *The Roman Stoics*, 115–42. In his insistence on not destroying one's own children, Hierocles too expresses a similar view. See my "Il matrimonio cristiano in Clemente," with documentation on infant exposure in Rome, the (very late) legislation against it, and the opposition to it on the part of philosophers, Jews, and Christians. The term πολυτεκνία is first attested in Aristotle, who deems it to be among the things needed if one is to be self-sufficient in the highest degree (αὐταρκέστατος, *Rhet.* 1360b19–1361a6).

29. The need affirmed here to provide more citizens for one's country, along with the support and pleasure that derive from children that

Hierocles emphasized shortly before, are motives that Musonius also fully endorsed in order to prove that marrying and procreating constitute a good. In *Diss.* 14, indeed, where he shows that marriage is not an obstacle to the exercise of philosophy, Musonius argues:

> Is it not appropriate for each person to consider the interests of his neighbor, both so that there be other families in his city and the city not be deserted, and so that the commonwealth will prosper…? Human nature most resembles that of the bee, which cannot live alone.… If love for one's fellow human being is considered a virtue, along with goodness, justice, and a beneficent and considerate attitude toward one's neighbor, then each person must take thought also for his city and furnish his city with a household. (see Ramelli, *Musonio Rufo*, 182–84)

See also Antipater of Tarsus, *SVF* 3.63:254–55: "For cities cannot be preserved unless the citizens who are best in their natures, the children of the nobles … marry early," and, a little later in time, Panaetius, whose writings Musonius and Hierocles probably knew well, cited in Cicero, *Off.* 1.17.54: "The primary society is in marriage itself, the next in children; then there is a househod, with all in common. This is the beginning of the city and the seed, so to speak, of the republic." That wedlock is also fine and pleasurable is affirmed by Musonius again in *Diss.* 14: "One cannot find another union more necessary or pleasing than that between husbands and wives. For what companion is so kind to his companion as a wife is mindful of the man who married her? What brother to his brother? What son to his parents? Who, when he is away, is so missed as a husband by his wife and a wife by her husband? Whose presence can better alleviate pain or increase joy or set right a misfortune?" (see Ramelli, *Musonio Rufo*, 186–87).

30. The filial bond that unites human beings with the gods, discussed in the first part of the treatise, is analogous to that which unites us with our parents, yet the latter is even stronger in that our parents are closer to us and are like us. A bit further on, the parallel is strengthened in the definition of parents as "domestic gods" and again in the following argument that assimilates the care bestowed on parents in the home to the worship of the gods in a temple. In this way the Roman ideas of *pietas erga deos* and *pietas erga parentes*, which were undoubtedly assimilated by Neo-Stoics along with other elements of the *mos maiorum*, gain a foothold. See the documentation on the Roman Stoic conception of divine parentage adduced in the commentary on the fourth Stobaean fragment.

31. Hierocles is here addressing the issue of the physical care that children should provide to their aging parents out of gratitude, before

turning to care of the soul. These attentions are but one way of thanking one's parents for the care that they have continually bestowed on us, especially when we were very young and they had not only to satisfy our needs but even to go so far as to guess what they were, given that we were not yet able to express ourselves. This identical idea, in the same context of the requirement that one be grateful to parents, is ascribed to Socrates by Xenophon in a conversation with his elder son, Lamprocles, who had been lamenting the harshness of his mother Xanthippe. In this case, too, the loving attentions of the mother for her newborn son, who was still incapable of indicating his own needs, are regarded as a wholly adequate motive for feeling gratitude toward her, for she first carries the child,

> weighed down, risking her life, and sharing the nourishment by which she herself is nourished; and after she has borne it with much effort and has given birth, she nourishes and cares for it, without her having experienced any prior good or the infant realizing by whose graces it is flourishing or even being able to indicate what it needs, but she, guessing what is good and pleasant for it, tries to fulfill them. And she nourishes it for a long time, enduring the drudgery day and night, not knowing whether she will ever receive any compensation for it.... How many troubles, with your voice and your actions, do you imagine you caused her from the time when you were a child, giving her aggravation day and night—how many pains, when you were sick? (Xenophon, *Mem.* 2.2.5 and 8; see the entire passage 1–14)

It is not surprising to find such close connections with the Socrates of Xenophon, for not only was the Stoa a Socratic movement, but the Roman Stoics often imitated Socrates closely; it is enough to mention Musonius Rufus, who is dubbed by Cora E. Lutz "The Roman Socrates." See also Klaus Döring, *Exemplum Socratis: Studien zur Sokratesnachwirkung in der kynisch-stoischen Popularphilosophie der frühen Kaiserzeit und im frühen Christentum* (Wiesbaden: Steiner, 1979); Aldo Brancacci, "Le Socrate de Dion Chrysostome," *PhilosAnt* 1 (2001): 166–82. Most recently, Reydams-Schils (*The Roman Stoics*, 92 and *passim*) has insisted on the fact that the Roman Stoics recalled aspects of Socrates quite different from those emphasized by Plato: Socrates' behavior rather than Plato's more theoretical constructs—qualities (which Reydams-Schils finds principally in Hierocles, Seneca, Musonius, Epictetus, and Marcus Aurelius, along with some Ciceronian passages; for the constitution of this group, see, however, my review in *RFN*; also the review by Brad Inwood, *CP* 101 [2006]: 88–93) inspired directly by a Socrates of whom these thinkers had their own view,

distinct from that of the Platonists, whom Reydams-Schils considers to be the major antagonists of the Roman Stoics. For the Socratic heritage among the Roman Stoics, with special reference to Epictetus, see Klaus Döring, "Sokrates bei Epiktet," in *Studia Platonica: Festschrift für Hermann Gundert zu seinem 65. Geburtstag am 30.4.1974* (ed. Klaus Döring and Wolfgang Kullman; Amsterdam: Grüner, 1974), 195–226; idem, *Exemplum Socratis*; Francesca Alesse, *La Stoa e la tradizione socratica* (Naples: Bibliopolis, 2000); Jean-Baptiste Gourinat, "Le Socrate d'Epictète," *PhilosAnt* 1 (2001): 137–65; Anthony A. Long, "Socrates in Hellenistic Philosophy," *CQ* 38 (1988) 150–71, repr. in idem, *Stoic Studies* (Cambridge: Cambridge University Press, 1996), 1–34; idem, "Epictetus as Socratic Mentor," *PCPhS* 46 (2000): 79–98; idem, *Epictetus: A Stoic and Socratic Guide to Life* (Oxford: Clarendon, 2002); idem, "The Socratic Imprint of Epictetus' Philosophy," in *Stoicism: Traditions and Transformations* (ed. Steven K. Strange and Jack Zupko; Cambridge: Cambridge University Press, 2004), 10–31.

32. Hierocles here gives evidence of a certain psychological delicacy and refinement, developed in connection with the idea of "types," in this case that of the elderly parent, who is treated not in respect to his body and physical needs but rather in regard to his psyche, in a way that is strictly speaking psychological. For the psychological understanding of old age and the attitude toward the elderly in Roman Stoicism, see Gretchen Reydams-Schils, "La vieillesse et les rapports humains dans le Stoïcisme Romain," in *L'ancienneté chez les Anciens* (ed. Béatrice Bakhouce; 2 vols.; Montpellier: Université Paul-Valéry Montpellier, 2003), 2:481–89. The analysis of character types was pursued, as is well known, in Peripatetic circles and is associated above all with the name of Theophrastus, who followed the moral phenomenology underlying Aristotle's *Nicomachean Ethics*; it is properly part of the study of ethics and of the faculties of the soul, explaining their function at the level of behavior, as well as of the virtues and vices that the various human types exemplify. For the characters of Theophrastus and their psychology, see, e.g., Markus Stein, *Definition und Schilderung in Theophrasts Charakteren* (Stuttgart: Teubner, 1992); Luigi Torraca, *Teofrasto Caratteri. Introduzione, traduzione, e note* (Milan: Garzanti, 1994); Han Baltussen, *Theophrastus against the Presocratics and Plato* (PhAnt 86; Leiden: Brill, 2000); William W. Fortenbaugh, *Theophrastean Studies* (Philosophie der Antike 17; Stuttgart: Steiner, 2003); James Diggle, *Theophrastus: Characters* (CCTC 43; Cambridge: Cambridge University Press, 2004). For the study of psychology in connection with ethics in Stoicism, see Tad Brennan, "Stoic Moral Psychology," in Inwood, *Cambridge Companion to the Stoics*, 257–94; Graver, *Stoicism and Emo-*

tion, 133–71; for the impulses and their philosophical explanation, John A. Stevens, "Preliminary Impulse in Stoic Psychology," *AncPhil* 20 (2000): 139–68.

33. This is also the principle enunciated in the Gospels that one should not do to others what we would not wish done to us and, vice versa, to do to them what we would wish done to us. This putting of oneself "in the shoes of the other" is what is meant by συμπάθεια, and it is also an application of complete sociable *oikeiôsis* on the part of a person who thinks of and takes an interest in what concerns another as though it were his or her own, up to the point of being as concerned for the other as one is for oneself. This "other" is not only someone near and dear, as Hierocles specifies; the principle is valid in respect to all people. For parallels between the New Testament and Hierocles and Hellenistic moral philosophy generally, taking account also of popular morality and the diatribe tradition, see van der Horst, "Hierocles the Stoic," 156–60; Abraham J. Malherbe, *Paul and the Popular Philosophers* (Philadelphia: Fortress, 1988); idem, "Hellenistic Moralists and the New Testament," *ANRW* 26.2:267–333; also Marcia L. Colish, "Stoicism and the New Testament: An Essay in Historiography," *ANRW* 26.2:334–379; Troels Engberg-Pedersen, *Paul and the Stoics* (Louisville: Westminster John Knox, 2000); Bruce W. Winter, *Philo and Paul among the Sophists* (Cambridge: Cambridge University Press, 1997); idem, *After Paul Left Corinth: The Influence of Secular Ethics and Social Change* (Grand Rapids: Eerdmans, 2001); Jonathan Barnes, "Ancient Philosophers," in *Philosophy and Power in the Graeco-Roman World: Essays in Honour of Miriam Griffin* (ed. Gillian Clark and Tessa Rajak; Oxford: Oxford University Press, 2002), 293–306, on the "wide" notion of philosophy in antiquity; see also the research promoted by the groups Hellenistic Moral Philosophy and Early Christianity and Corpus Hellenisticum Novi Testamenti in the Society of Biblical Literature; good surveys of studies devoted to the connections between Hellenistic philosophy and the New Testament may be found in John T. Fitzgerald, Thomas H. Olbricht, and L. Michael White, eds., *Early Christianity and Classical Culture: Comparative Studies in Honor of Abraham J. Malherbe* (NovTSup 110; Leiden: Brill, 2003; repr., Atlanta: Society of Biblical Literature, 2005), which contains among other things a bibliography of the works of Abraham Malherbe oriented precisely to the study of these relationships; also Ilaria Ramelli, "Philosophen und Prediger: Pagane und christliche weise Männer: Der Apostel Paulus," in *Dion von Prusa: Der Philosoph und sein Bild* (ed. Eugenio Amato and Sotera Fornaro; SAPERE 13; Tübingen: Mohr Siebeck, forthcoming), ch. 4. For συμπάθεια and its connection with φιλία

and pity see David Konstan, *The Emotions of the Ancient Greeks: Studies in Aristotle and Greek Literature* (Toronto: University of Toronto Press, 2006), chs. 8 and 10. For the transcending of Stoic altruistic *oikeiôsis* in the New Testament, see Troels Engberg-Pedersen, "Radical Altruism in Philippians 2:4," in Fitzgerald, Olbricht, and White, *Early Christianity and Classical Culture*, 197–214. On the conception of friendship in Paul's letters, where God is the first friend, see John T. Fitzgerald, "Paul and Friendship," in *Paul in the Greco-Roman World: A Handbook* (ed. J. Paul Sampley; Harrisburg, Pa.: Trinity Press International, 2003), 319–43; idem, "Christian Friendship: John, Paul, and the Philippians," *Int* (2007): 284–96, with further documentation.

34. The principle is that of opposing evil and vice not with another evil and another vice but rather with a good and with virtue and of repaying evil with good, a principle that Hierocles explicitly ascribes to Socrates and that is such as to remove the ground from every kind of vendetta and to require freedom from anger. See Janine Fillion-Lahille, *Le* De ira *de Sénèque et la philosophie stoïcienne des passions* (Paris: Klincksieck, 1984); Konstan, *The Emotions of the Ancient Greeks*, ch. 2; also my "Il tema del perdono" and Griswold, *Forgiveness*, esp. 1–19.

35. In the case of brothers, thanks to their consanguinity, οἰκείωσις is particularly evident: they are directly part of our own body and, still more, of our self. In addition, the equal relationship that binds one to a brother makes "appropriation" easier; in the case of other ties that are less equal and not so much between like partners, such as those cited by Hierocles in this passage, between parents and children or masters and slaves, the reciprocal exchange of identities is not so immediate. In *Diss.* 15B Musonius too had extolled the bond of brotherhood, noting its beauty and usefulness: "What can one compare for beauty with the goodwill of a brother in regard to our safety? What more pleasing partner of one's goods could one have than an upright brother…? I believe that the most enviable man is he who lives among many likeminded brothers, and I consider that man most dear to God who derives his goods from his own home" (see Ramelli, *Musonio Rufo*, 202–3).

36. Hierocles contrasts both with the condition that is not ἐφ' ἡμῖν and with κακία, which depends on us and for which each person is responsible in his own case even if he cannot control it in others, the opposite of κακία, that is, virtue or goodness, the only true good according to the Stoics. Virtue is opposed to all that does not depend on the choosing subject, that is, the fortune or malice of others. Virtue belongs to that "interior citadel" of Stoic ethics, discussed in detail in the Roman Stoic context by Marcus

Aurelius, which is protected from everything that is not ἐφ' ἡμῖν; see Pierre Hadot, *La citadelle intérieure: Introduction aux* Pensées *de Marc Aurèle* (Paris: Fayard, 1992). Hierocles, at all events, does not leave the individual moral subject locked up in his own private citadel (which, for Reydams-Schils, *Roman Stoics*, 98, is never in any case a mere "ivory tower") but rather allies with each person in this ethical endeavor his dearest companions in virtue: brothers and relatives here, one's marriage partner earlier, and friends, with whom the tie is grounded not in blood but exclusively in *logos*, as Hierocles states, though he associates with this bond, as we have seen, the marital relation as well, as does Musonius. On the conception of friendship in ancient philosophy and particularly in Stoicism, see Glenn Lesses, "Austere Friends: The Stoics and Friendship," *Apeiron* 26 (1993): 57–75; Luigi Franco Pizzolato, *L'idea di amicizia nel mondo antico classico e cristiano* (Torino: Einaudi, 1993); John T. Fitzgerald, ed., *Greco-Roman Perspectives on Friendship* (SBLRBS 34; Atlanta: Scholars Press, 1997); Anne Banateanu, *La théorie stoïcienne de l'amitié* (Fribourg: Editions Universitaires, 2001); David Konstan, *Friendship in the Classical World* (Cambridge: Cambridge University Press, 1997); idem, "Reciprocity and Friendship," in *Reciprocity in Ancient Greece* (ed. Christopher Gill and Norman Postlethwaite; Oxford: Oxford University Press, 1998), 279–301; idem, *The Emotions of the Ancient Greeks*, ch. 8 on φιλία. The institutional, utilitarian, and economic aspects of the bond of friendship (on which see, e.g., Koenraad Verboven, *The Economy of Friends: Economic Aspects of Amicitia and Patronage in the Late Republic* [Brussels: Latomus, 2002]) tend to give way before affective and ethical qualities in the ideal of friendship theorized and developed by philosophers from Aristotle onward.

37. See Homer, *Od.* 19.163; *Il.* 22.126; Plato, *Resp.* 544; *Apol.* 34.

38. Hierocles expands the circle of intimates ever more widely, following the progression of ever larger concentric circles, which is explained in the following sentence; it is probably the most famous passage of Hierocles.

39. For this image of circles that share the same center but expand progressively outward as an effective symbol of sociable *oikeiôsis*, see the introductory essay above. Richard Sorabji ("What Is New on the Self in Stoicism after 100 BC?" in Sorabji and Sharples, *Greek and Roman Philosophy*, 141–62) includes Hierocles' vision of the concentric circles among the "expansive theories of self," given his extension of the self to include society (155).

40. Thus, Stoic sociable *oikeiôsis* (on which see also Reydams-Schils, "Human Bonding and *Oikeiôsis*," 221–51), as Hierocles' image shows quite

well, extends all the way up to a concern for all humanity, in perfect accord with the ideal of the Stoic cosmopolite, on whose role in Roman Stoicism and connection with the theory of *oikeiôsis* see Greg R. Stanton, "The Cosmopolitan Ideas of Epictetus and Marcus Aurelius," *Phronesis* 13 (1968): 183–95; Malcolm Schofield, *The Stoic Idea of City* (Cambridge: Cambridge University Press, 1991); Dirk Obbink, "The Stoic Sage in the Cosmic City," in *Topics in Stoic Philosophy* (ed. Katerina Ierodiakonou; Oxford: Clarendon, 1999), 178–95; my "La 'Città di Zeus' di Musonio Rufo nelle sue ascendenze vetero-stoiche e nell'eredità neostoica," *Stylos* 11 (2002): 151–58; Radice, *Oikeiôsis*, 222–34. Nevertheless, the bond that this implies, as it widens in extension, inevitably tends to lose something in intensity, as noted by Martha C. Nussbaum ("The Worth of Human Dignity: Two Tensions in Stoic Cosmopolitanism," in Clark and Rajak, *Philosophy and Power*, 31–50), who examines Cynic cosmopolitanism, defined in terms of characteristics grounded in *logos* and in human moral capacities and which are shared by all human beings, including women, barbarians, and slaves, and the Stoic conception, in which the idea of benevolence toward humanity cannot be more than generic: each person can manifest true benevolence only toward a limited circle of people. Benevolence and concern for others, according to Nussbaum, are in contradiction with the doctrine of *apatheia* and with that of indifferents. However, we have already had occasion to mention that, beginning with the Middle Stoa, *apatheia* was mitigated and, among indifferents, the value of preferables was emphasized along with the *kathêkonta*, which are the ground of social relations, and was linked directly to the discussion of *oikeiôsis*. These developments were retained by the Neo-Stoics such as Musonius in the first century A.D. (see Ramelli, *Musonio Rufo*, 5–17) and Hierocles himself shortly afterwards, in the first half of the second century A.D.

41. For each circle there is attached a series of *kathêkonta*; in the previous note I observed how the theory of sociable *oikeiôsis*, as fully expounded by Hierocles, developed quite naturally on the soil of Middle Stoic ethics, which was characterized precisely by the theorization of the *kathêkonta*. This integrated doctrine is found again in the present extract from Hierocles. For the order of the several groups of people in this passage and that of the sequence of Hierocles' treatises πῶς χρηστέον in the Stobaean fragments, see the introductory essay, §5b. Like Inwood ("Hierocles," 181) and Malherbe (*Moral Exhortation*, 96–97), Long and Sedley, *The Hellenistic Philosophers*, 2:348 (§57G), take κατὰ τὸν ἐντεταμένον (61,24 von Arnim) as referring to a person (similarly for κατὰ τὸν φιλοίκειον at 61,26), whereas I take it to refer to the "most stretched out"

circle (similarly, I render *κατὰ τὸν φιλοίκειον* "in respect to love of one's family," taking *φιλοίκειον*, which can mean "pertaining to one's family," as referring to *κύκλον*: "as for the circle pertaining to one's family/embracing one's family…"). Of course, both renderings are grammatically possible. In the first case, I also propose to understand "according to the extension of each circle," all the more in that there is a textual problem: where Meineke and Hense write *κατὰ τὸν ἐντεταμένον*, MSS AB of Stobaeus read *κατὰ τὸ ἐντεταγμένον*, "according to the category of persons who are listed under each circle." Hierocles is referring to a passage from circle to circle, according to the extension and the characteristics of each single circle, composed of persons. A lacuna also makes it difficult to assess the precise meaning of κατὰ τὸν φιλοίκειον, but a reference to the circle of one's family seems most appropriate.

42. Hierocles was clearly aware of the problem highlighted in the penultimate note and brought out by Nussbaum ("The Worth of Human Dignity," 31–50), relative to the impossibility of maintaining the same intensity of benevolence as one proceeds gradually to relations with ever-wider circles of individuals. Thus, he seeks to offer a realistic answer, but of a sort that does not violate the spirit of his conception: while progressively extending the range of *oikeiôsis*, it is true that benevolence will decrease, since this is inevitable, but the important thing is that one nevertheless maintain a sense of affinity with all people: "we must make an effort about assimilating them," that is, all human beings. This affinity is grounded by Hierocles in another Stoic argument that we have already had occasion to underline and to document in the notes to the fourth excerpt: the common origin or descent of all human beings from the supreme deity, who is also the father of all.

43. Hierocles is attentive also to the use of names that, in Stoicism, have an important value. To address people by the terms used for closer relatives helps people to feel closer. This foreshortening of distances in interhuman relations is indicated by Hierocles by way of the metaphorical image of a "contraction of circles." In the ancient world, moreover, there was a nice example of this in common practice: the use of "brother" in the wide sense, understood to designate also cousins and other degrees of kinship even though they were less close than brotherhood strictly speaking, not to speak of the adoption of this term in a religious context, where it might refer even to people who had no blood relation between them at all. See, e.g., the documentation in my "Una delle più antiche lettere cristiane extra-canoniche?" *Aegyptus* 80 (2000): 169–88; and, with further references, Philip A. Harland, "Familial Dimensions of Group

Identity: 'Brothers' (ΑΔΕΛΦΟΙ) in Associations of the Greek East," *JBL* 124 (2005): 491–551, who studies the terminology of fictive relations, in particular those of brotherhood, in Greek associations in the East, both religious and profane. For the significance of names in Stoicism and the consequent importance of etymology, see my *Allegoria*, ch. 9, with further documentation and bibliography. Particularly illuminating as parallels with Hierocles are, I think, the ideas of Plutarch, very likely a contemporary of his, in *De fraterno amore* (*On Brotherly Love*; on which see Reidar Aasgaard, *My Beloved Brothers and Sisters: Christian Siblingship in Paul* [JSNTSup 265; London: T&T Clark, 2004], ch. 6). In particular, Plutarch represents relations of friendship as a reflection of these closer bonds of kinship (479C–D): "For most friendships are really shadows, imitations, and images of that first φιλία that is implanted in children toward their parents and in brothers toward brothers." For the basis of the kinship relation is held by Plutarch to be εὔνοια ("benevolence" or "goodwill," 481C), and brothers are united in both their emotions and their actions (480B).

44. The father is a figure for Zeus, as I noted in commenting on the fourth Stobaean fragment; the mother evidently has less authority, in conformity with the norms of the ancient family. Probably this is why, in the ninth Stobaean fragment (*Anth.* 4.67.23 [3:8,19–24 Meineke]; cf. *Anth.* 4.22a.23 = 4:503,11–16 Wachsmuth and Hense), Hierocles assimilates the family to a relationship between one who rules, clearly the father, and one who is ruled, presumably the wife or children or both: "a household without marriage is incomplete, since neither can what governs be conceived without that which is governed, nor what is governed without that which governs." If the fragment is understood in this way, it certainly yields a conception that is thoroughly traditional and indeed banal. Nevertheless, in the present fragment Hierocles attributes to the mother the primary affective role, and thus we face not so much a hierarchy as a differentiation: to the mother, who incidentally is mentioned first, is awarded more love, to the father more honor. On the basis of this difference, Hierocles can derive the *kathêkonta* for other relations as well, on the analogy respectively with the father or the mother. It is always a question of establishing the greatest possible continuity between the wider circles of sociable *oikeiôsis* and the narrower ones, so as to be able to produce the above-mentioned contraction or constriction of the circles and to feel that other people are as closely bound to us as possible, in benevolence or at least in affinity, the key bonds in Hierocles' theory of *oikeiôsis*.

45. For this section, derived from Hierocles' *Oeconomicus* or *Household Management*, with its various ideas on the traditional division of

labor in the family, one can adduce interesting parallels, among others especially with Xenophon and Musonius. In Xenophon's *Oec.* 3 and 7–10, Socrates speaks of the importance of education for virtue even for women and of the equal importance of husband and wife, in their respective roles, in the management of the household (3.15: "I believe that a woman, if she is a good partner in the household, has exactly the same weight as the man in respect to their good; for assets, for the most part, enter the home through the activities of the husband, but they are mainly spent through dispensations by the wife"), roles that remain, however, well-defined, with the wife's domain being in the house and the husband's outside, without overlapping areas. For attitudes toward household management in the Hellenistic period, see Carlo Natali, "Oikonomia in Hellenistic Political Thought," in *Justice and Generosity: Studies in Hellenistic Social and Political Philosophy: Proceedings of the Sixth Symposium Hellenisticum* (ed. André Laks and Malcolm Schofield; Cambridge: Cambridge University Press, 1995), 95–128.

For comparison with Musonius, we may adduce the diatribes concerning the family and the activities of both spouses. Like Hierocles, so too Musonius had already allowed for interchanges of activities between spouses and above all insisted that the activities that lead to virtue be assigned in the same measure and manner to both spouses. Thus, in *Diss.* 4 we read:

> to each nature [that of man and of woman] there should be assigned the most suitable tasks, and the heavier should be given to those who are stronger, the lighter to those who are weaker. Thus, weaving is more appropriate for women than for men, as is too care of the house; gymnastics, on the other hand, is more appropriate for men than for women, as too is the outdoors. Sometimes, however, certain men too might reasonably undertake also lighter tasks that seem feminine, and women might work at harsher ones that seem appropriate rather to men, when the qualities of their bodies suggest it or else some need or opportune occasion. For all human chores alike are instituted in common and are common to men and women, and none should be of necessity reserved for one or the other. Some, indeed, are more suitable to one nature, some to the other, which is why some are called "masculine," others "feminine"; but one may rightly say that all those that have it in them to lead to virtue are equally appropriate to either nature, if, at all events, we affirm that the virtues are not more appropriate to the one than to the other. (see Ramelli, *Musonio Rufo*, 72–73).

A more complete comparison between Musonius and Hierocles, in addition to the review of ancient works on household management provided in Chrēstos P. Baloglou, Ἡ οἰκονομικὴ σκῆψις τῶν ἀρχαίων Ἑλλήνων (Thessaloniki: Historikē kai Laographikē Hetaireia Chalkidikēs, 1995), is provided in idem, "Αἱ οἰκονομικαὶ ἀντιλήψεις τῶν Στωϊκῶν Ἱεροκλέους καὶ Μουσωνίου," *Platon* 44 (1992): 122–34, who notes, in addition to the obvious affinities, also a difference in perspective: Hierocles focuses attention above all on the division of tasks between husband and wife in the running of the household and the incidental interchanges and overlappings between their respective activities; Musonius organizes his exposition more specifically around the pursuit of virtue on the part of both spouses.

The Stoicizing orator and close contemporary of Hierocles, Dio Chrysostom, who was knowledgeable about Stoic allegoresis (Ramelli, "L'ideale del filosofo nelle orazioni dionee," with documentation), a disciple of Musonius, and the author of a well-known but lost work Πρὸς Μουσώνιον (on which see John L. Moles, "The Career and Conversion of Dio Chrysostom," *JHS* 98 [1978]: 79–100, esp. 82–83 and 85–88), also wrote a lost *Oeconomicus* attested to by Stobaeus; see Aldo Brancacci, *Rhêtorikê philosophousa: Dione Crisostomo nella cultura antica e bizantina* (Elenchos 11; Naples: Bibliopolis, 1985), 245–63; Hans-Josef Klauck, ed., *Dion von Prusa: Olympikos und Peri tês prôtês tou theou ennoias* (Darmstadt: Wissenschaftliche Buchgesellschaft, 2000), 18–20: it is likely that it presented points of contact with the analogous treatises by Musonius and Hierocles.

46. It is interesting to observe that Hierocles evinces a certain flexibility in allowing also for a moderate degree of interchange in the respective roles of the two spouses within the management of the household. Fundamental to this attitude is, it seems, the very goal of marriage as it is conceived by him, which is, as we have seen, not just legitimate procreation but also, and in equal degree, the spiritual growth of the couple, their common path to virtue in marital concord. For it is precisely on this basis that an interchange of tasks, to the extent possible, between the spouses can be seen as a positive opportunity for the further deepening of what they have in common, the spiritual bond between husband and wife. I have had occasion to emphasize that Hierocles states explicitly in the tenth extract that the nuptial bond does not concern merely the bodies of the couple but also and above all their souls: "the union of a husband and wife who share each other's destinies and are consecrated to the gods of marriage, generation, and the hearth, in concord with each other and setting everything in common up to their very bodies, or rather up to their

very own souls.... For what could be 'stronger and better ... than when a husband and wife, like-minded in their thoughts, maintain a home?'" Similarly, Musonius affirms in *Diss.* 14: "Of whom is it believed that they have all in common, bodies, souls, and riches, if not husband and wife?" (see Ramelli, *Musonio Rufo*, 186–87).

47. Hierocles, like other Stoics, and in contrast to a widespread attitude of contempt in the classical world (on which see Ronald F. Hock, *The Social Context of Paul's Ministry: Tentmaking and Apostleship* [Philadelphia: Fortress, 1980]), praises manual labor as well. For an interesting comparison between the view illustrated around the same time by the Stoicizing Dio Chrysostom in his *Euboicus* toward such occupations and that of the Greeks and Romans belonging to the privileged classes, see Brunt, "Aspects of the Social Thought," *PCPhS* 9–34, who supposes that Dio was influenced by his own life experiences during the time of his exile and by the views of the Stoics, particularly Cleanthes and Chrysippus; a further comparison is drawn with the position of Panaetius, as it is represented in Cicero, *Off.* 1.150–151. From the same perspective, there is a useful comparison between the *Euboicus* of Dio and a later inscription (*CIL* 8.11824) in Paolo Desideri, "L'iscrizione del mietitore (CIL vm. 11824): Un aspetto della cultura mactaritana del III secolo," in *L'Africa romana: Atti del IV convegno di studio, Sassari, 12–14.XII.1986* (ed. Attilio Mastino; Sassari: Gallizzi, 1987), 137–49; in the inscription (an epitaph), the life and work of a harvester is highly praised and indeed is offered as an *exemplum* for future imitation. This exceptionally positive assessment of a humble manual laborer does exhibit similarities with Dio's *Euboicus*, and Desideri compares it also with other evidence deriving from various literary genres, including Tacitus's *Agricola* and Petronius' novel *Satyrica*. On the Stoic orientation of Dio and his relationship to Musonius Rufus, who was his master, see "Musonio Rufo stoico romano-etruscoe e la prevalenza degli interessi etico-religiosi" in my *Stoicismo Romano Minore*.

In this connection, one may mention Philodemus's *On Household Management* (*De oeconomia*), which has been well discussed by Voula Tsouna, "Epicurean Attitudes to Management and Finance," in *Epicureismo Greco e romano* (ed. Gabriele Giannantoni and Marcello Gigante; 3 vols.; Naples: Bibliopolis, 1996), 2:701–14; idem, *The Ethics of Philodemus* (Oxford: Oxford University Press, 2007); and Elizabeth Asmis, "Epicurean Economics," in *Philodemus and the New Testament World* (ed. John T. Fitzgerald, Dirk Obbink, and Glenn S. Holland; NovTSup 111; Leiden: Brill, 2004), 133–76. See also David L. Balch, "Philodemus, 'On Wealth' and 'On Household Management': Naturally Wealthy Epicureans against

Poor Cynics," in Fitzgerald, Obbink, and Holland, *Philodemus and the New Testament World*, 177–96.

Hierocles first points to agriculture as a manual activity that can be directly assigned to the husband; Musonius also, in conformity with his ideal of excercise and πόνος and as an ascetic with Cynic leanings (see Marie-Odile Goulet-Cazé, "Le cynisme à l'époque impériale," *ANRW* 36.4:2720–2833 and, with particular reference to the emphasis on πόνος in Musonius and Dio, 2759–63; Richard Valantasis, "Musonius Rufus and Roman Ascetical Theory," *GRBS* 40 [1999]: 201–31; Ramelli, *Musonio Rufo*, 12–13), recommends the healthy and toilsome life of the farmer, which acquires positive characteristics at the ethical level. According to Musonius, indeed, work in the fields is the ideal activity for a philosopher, since it requires exercise and effort, tempers the body and the soul by means of a simple life in conformity with nature, and allows those who practice it to be self-sufficient, thus realizing the ideal of *autarkeia*. Musonius affirms in *Diss.* 11, devoted to establishing the source of income most suitable for a philosopher, that the best is

> that which comes from the earth.... For no one who is not a gossip or effeminate can say that any of the agricultural activities is shameful or not suitable to a good man.... Of all agricultural activities, it is that of the herdsman that is most pleasing to me, since it provides the soul with more free time to think and investigate.... But if, indeed, one philosophizes and farms simultaneously, I would not compare any other life to this one.... For how could it not be more in accord with nature to make a living from the earth, which is our nurse and mother, than from any other source...? How could it not be more healthful to live out of doors than to grow up in the shade...? Not to depend on another for our own needs is clearly far more dignified than to depend. So fine is it, then, and happy and dear to God to live off agriculture.... It would really be a terrible thing if working the earth impeded philosophizing or helping guide others to philosophy.... But what prevents a disciple from listening, even as he works, to his teacher speak of temperance or justice or endurance...? Among the true lovers of philosophy, there is no one who would not wish to live in the country with a good man.... If, especially, the disciple is most of the time together with the teacher and the teacher has the disciple at hand: if this is the case, then a livelihood from agriculture is seen to be most suitable of all for a philosopher.

See further Reydams-Schils, *The Roman Stoics*, 108–10; Ramelli, *Musonio Rufo*, 152–65 and 331 s.v. *Agricoltura*. The excellence of agriculture among the various profitable activities is similarly proclaimed by two authors

who both draw upon Stoic sources: Varro, *Rust.* 2.1–3; and Cicero, *Off.* 1.42.151.

48. A man who is free of prejudices and comfortably aware of his own worth has no problem even in turning to activities conventionally regarded as feminine and unsuitable for a man, such as domestic chores. Hierocles, as a philosopher, gives proof of his own freedom from such prejudices, just as Musonius did in condemning double standards whether in the education of boys and girls, which in his view should be the same (*Diss.* 4, cited above: see Emiel Eyben and Alfons Wouters, "Musonius Rufus, Εἰ *παραπλησίως παιδευτέον τὰς θυγατέρας τοῖς υἱοῖς*," *Lampas* 8 [1975]: 185–213; Emiel Eyben, "Musonius Rufus: Ook vrouwen moeten filosofie studeren," *Hermeneus* 48 [1976]: 90–107), or in comportment in marriage, where he affirms that, if some husbands do not find it blameworthy to have sexual relations with their female slaves, they should find it equally legitimate for their wives to have them with their male slaves. Indeed, in *Diss.* 12, Περὶ ἀφροδισίων (*On Sex*), Musonius offers a clear and well-reasoned exposition of his principles, beginning with the affirmation that ἀφροδίσια, in and of themselves, are a manifestation of softness (τρυφή):

> Not the least part of softness resides in sex, too, since those who live a soft life need a variety of beloveds, not just lawful ones but also illegitimate, and not just female but also male … in their pursuit of shameful couplings: all these things constitute grave charges against a person. One must maintain that … the only sex that is just is that in marriage and undertaken for the production of children and that this is also the only lawful sex. That which pursues bare pleasure [ψιλὴ ἡδονή] is unjust and illegitimate [*ἄδικα καὶ παράνομα*], even if it occurs within marriage.

There is a similar idea in the *Sententiae* (*Sentences*) of Sextus (*Sent.* 231–232; Anton Elter, *Sexti Pythagorei Sententiae* [Bonn: George, 1891–92]): "Every dissolute person [*ἀκόλαστος*] is an adulterer with his own wife. Do nothing for the sake of bare pleasure [ψιλῇ ἡδονῇ]." Later, Clement of Alexandria, in the *Paedagogus* (2.10.92), closely reproduces the passage of Musonius: "For bare pleasure [ψιλὴ ἡδονή], even when it is obtained within marriage, is illegitimate, unjust [*παράνομος, ἄδικος*], and irrational"; lust is similarly condemned by Dio Chrysostom (Elisabetta Berardi, "Avidità, lussuria, ambizione: Tre demoni in Dione di Prusa, *Sulla regalità* IV 5–139," *Prometheus* 24 [1998]: 37–56). Musonius continues:

> All sexual relations with women that are not adulterous are stripped of legitimacy and are shameful, if they are performed out of dissoluteness [δι' ἀκολασίαν]. Just as a person cannot manage to have sex temperately, indeed, with a courtesan, so too he cannot do so with a free woman outside of marriage, nor even, by Zeus, with his own slave girl.... "By Zeus," one will say, "not like a person who wrongs a husband by corrupting his wife, it is not like this—a man who has sex with a courtesan who has no husband wrongs no one, by Zeus...." I rather insist on saying that whoever commits a fault [ἁμαρτάνει] simultaneously commits a wrong [ἀδικεῖ], and if it is not against his neighbor, it is against himself.... Every master believes that he has full power to do whatever he wishes to his own slave. Against this, my argument is simple: if someone believes that it is not shameful or absurd for a master to have sex with his own slave..., let him think how it would seem to him if a mistress had sex with a slave: for would he not think it intolerable, not only if a woman who had a legitimate husband should approach a slave, but even if an unmarried woman should do this?

Another Roman Stoic, Seneca in *Ep.* 94.26, advances a not dissimilar idea: "You know that a man who demands modesty of his own wife but is himself a seducer of others' wives is dishonorable; you know that, just as she ought to have nothing to do with an adulterer, so too you should have nothing to do with a concubine." Musonius concludes his reasoning with a critique of the claim on the part of men to govern women, at least if they prove incapable of being also morally superior: "It is proper that men be much stronger [sc. and much more able to control themselves], if they think they should be in charge of women; but if they show themselves to be [weaker and] more dissolute, they will also be worse. That it is a matter of dissoluteness and nothing else for a master to have sex with his slave, what need is there to say? For it is well known." See Ramelli, *Musonio Rufo*, 164–73; Engel, "Gender Egalitarianism," 377–91; Martha C. Nussbaum, "Musonius Rufus—Enemy of Double Standards for Men and Women?" in *Double Standards in the Ancient World* (ed. Karla Pollmann; Göttingen: Duehrkohp & Radicke, 2000), 221–46; idem, "The Incomplete Feminism of Musonius Rufus," 283–326; Georg Wöhrle, "Wenn Frauen Platons Staat lesen," 135–43. David M. Engel, "Women's Role in the Home and the State: Stoic Theory Reconsidered," *HSCP* 101 (2003): 267–88, rightly challenges the view that the Stoics, including Middle and Late Stoics such as Antipater, Musonius, and Hierocles, were protofeminists and points out that, "although the Stoics throughout their history asserted that women possessed the same capacity for virtue as men, they never inferred from

that or any other premise that women deserved treatment equal to that of men in any sphere except perhaps education" (268). He correctly points out that Antipater speaks only from the point of view of the husband's advantage and that Musonius's interest is in providing good wives and housekeepers (I take the same view in my "Transformations of the Household"). Engel also discusses the fragment of Hierocles under discussion in this note and observes that Hierocles certainly did not mean that women should share in men's political activities. Engel is right that the Stoics were not at all social revolutionaries. He does, however, allow that the Stoics did not think of women as morally inferior by nature, as Aristotle did. He also accepts the view—disputed by some scholars, e.g., Teun Tieleman—that Stoicism underwent changes during its history, and thus a periodization into Ancient, Middle, and Late Stoicism is appropriate (273). More on this in my "Ierocle Neostoico in Stobeo."

49. I insert a question mark that is missing in the edition of von Arnim, *Ethische Elementarlehre*, 63, for it is clear from what follows that this sentence is not a negation but rather a rhetorical question that invites a positive reply: among the labors within the house there are some that are especially tiring and that are better adapted to a man than to a woman; therefore, the husband might well perform them, and if it is the wife who usually does so, this means that she is able also to perform those tasks that are traditionally assigned to men.

Fragments of Hierocles in the *Suda*

[1] Suid. s. v. ἐμποδών·

ἐχρήσατο δὲ τῇ λέξει Ἱεροκλῆς τε καὶ ἄλλοι ἀντὶ τοῦ ἐμποδίου. φησὶν ἐν β′ Φιλοσοφουμένων περὶ τῶν φιλοσόφων·Τίς γὰρ αὐτῶν οὐχὶ καὶ ἔγημε καὶ παῖδας ἀνείλατο καὶ οὐσίας ἐπεμελήθη μηδενὸς ἐμποδὼν ὄντος.

[2] Suid. s. v. λέσχη·

πολλὴ ὁμιλία, φλυαρία. τὸ δὲ παλαιὸν αἱ καθέδραι καὶ οἱ τόποι, ἐν οἷς εἰώθεσαν ἀθροιζόμενοι φιλοσοφεῖν, λέσχαι ἐκαλοῦντο. Οὕτω φησὶ καὶ Ἱεροκλῆς ἐν α′ Φιλοσοφουμένων.

[3] Suid. s. v. διαλέγοιντο γυναιξίν·

ὁμιλοῖεν ἢ συνουσιάζοιεν. οὕτως Ἱεροκλῆς.

[4] Suid. s. v. διότι.

ἔσθ’ ὅτε καὶ ἀντὶ τοῦ «ὅτι» λαμβάνεται. οὕτω γὰρ ἄλλοι τε πολλοὶ καὶ Ἱεροκλῆς.

[5] Suid. s. v. τέμνουσι φάρμακον.

τιμῶσιν, ἡγοῦνται. οὕτως ἄλλοι τε καὶ Ἱεροκλῆς.

1. *Suda*, s.v. ἐμποδών ["obstacle," properly adverb]:

Hierocles and others used this word instead of ἐμπόδιον, "impediment." In book 2 of the *Philosophizings* [Φιλοσοφούμενα], he says concerning philosophers: "For which of them did not marry and raise children and take care of his property, if there was no obstacle?"[1]

2. *Suda*, s.v. λέσχη ["portico, meeting-place"]:

A great crowd, chatter. In ancient times, the seats and places in which people used to gather to discuss philosophy were called λέσχαι. So says Hierocles too in book 1 of Philosophizings.

3. *Suda*, s.v. διαλέγοιντο with women:

They would converse or associate with them. Thus Hierocles.

4. *Suda*, s.v. διότι ["because"]:

It is sometimes used instead of ὅτι ["that, because"]. So many others, and also Hierocles.

5. *Suda*, s.v. τέμνουσι ["cut"] a drug:

Esteem, believe. So others, and also Hierocles.

1. I insert a question mark that is missing in the edition of von Arnim, *Ethische Elementarlehre*, 64.

Bibliography

Aasgaard, Reidar. *My Beloved Brothers and Sisters: Christian Siblingship in Paul.* JSNTSup 265. London: T&T Clark, 2004.

Acosta Méndez, Eduardo. "Diogenes Babylonius, fr. 104 *SVF* III, p. 238 von Arnim." *Lexis* 9–10 (1992): 155–61.

Adinolfi, Mario. "Le diatribe di Musonio Rufo sulla donna e il matrimonio alla luce delle lettere paoline." Pages 121–35 in *Studia Hierosolymitana 3: Nell'ottavo centenario francescano (1182–1982).* Edited by Giovanni Claudio Bottini. Studium Biblicum Franciscanum 30. Jerusalem: Franciscan Printing Press, 1982.

Alesse, Francesca. *Panezio di Rodi, Testimonianze.* Naples: Bibliopolis, 1997.

———. *Panezio di Rodi e la tradizione stoica.* Naples: Bibliopolis, 1994.

———. "La *Repubblica* di Zenone di Cizio e la letteratura socratica." *SIFC* 16 (1998): 17–38.

———. "Socrate dans la littérature de l'ancien et du moyen stoïcisme." *PhilosAnt* 1 (2001): 119–35.

———. *La Stoa e la tradizione socratica.* Naples: Bibliopolis, 2000.

———. "Lo stoico Boeto di Sidone." *Elenchos* 18 (1997): 359–83.

Algra, Keimpe. "Stoic Theology." Pages 163–78 in *The Cambridge Companion to the Stoics.* Edited by Brad Inwood. Cambridge: Cambridge University Press, 2003.

Allegri, Giuseppina. "La ricchezza e le cause di male." *Paideia* 52 (1997): 5–23.

Alpers-Gölz, Roswitha. *Der Begriff Skopos in der Stoa und seine Vorgeschichte.* Spoudasmata 8. Hildesheim: Olms, 1976.

André, Jacques. *De Physiognomonia liber.* Paris: Belles Lettres, 1981.

Annas, Julia. *La morale della felicità in Aristotele e nei filosofi dell'età ellenistica.* Temi metafisici e problemi del pensiero antico: Studi e testi 64. Milan: Vita e Pensiero, 1998.

———. *The Morality of Happiness.* Cambridge: Cambridge University Press, 1993.

———. "My Station and Its Duties: Ideals and the Social Embeddedness of Virtue." *Proceedings of the Aristotelian Society* 102 (2002): 109–23.

Appel, Wlodzimierz. "Zur Interpretation des vierten Verses von Kleanthes' Hymnus auf Zeus." *Eranos* 82 (1984): 179–83.

Armato, Giorgio. "Possibilità, necessità e verità nella teoria deterministica di Crisippo." *PP* 53 (1998): 241–54.

Arnim, Hans Friedrich August von. "Eudromos," PW 6.1:950.

———. "Hierokles." PW 8.2:1479.

———, ed., in collaboration with Wilhelm Schubart, *Ethische Elementarlehre (Papyrus 9780): Nebst den bei Stobaios erhaltenen ethischen Exzerpten aus Hierokles*. Berliner Klassikertexte 4. Berlin: Weidmann, 1906.

Asmis, Elizabeth. "Choice in Epictetus' Philosophy." Pages 387–412 in *Antiquity and Humanity: Essays on Ancient Religion and Philosophy Presented to Hans Dieter Betz on His 70th Birthday.* Edited by Adela Yarbro Collins and Margaret M. Mitchell. Tübingen: Mohr Siebeck, 2001.

———. "Epicurean Economics." Pages 133–76 in *Philodemus and the New Testament World.* Edited by John T. Fitzgerald, Dirk Obbink, and Glenn S. Holland. NovTSup 111. Leiden: Brill, 2004.

Aujoulat, Noël. "De la phantasia et du pneuma stoïciens, d'après Sextus Empiricus, au corps lumineux néo-platonicien (Synésios de Cyrène et Hiéroclès d'Alexandrie)." *Pallas* 34 (1988): 123–46.

———. "Hiéroclès d'Alexandrie d'après Damaskios et la Souda." *Pallas* 44 (1996): 65–77.

———. *Le néo-platonisme alexandrin: Hiéroclès d'Alexandrie.* PhAnt 45; Leiden: Brill, 1986.

Aymard, Jacques. "La querelle du cobra et de la mangouste dans l'antiquité." *Mélanges de l'École Française de Rome* 71 (1959) : 227–62.

Backhouse, Thamer. "Antipater of Tarsus on False *phantasiai*." Pages 7–31 in *Papiri filosofici: Miscellanea di studi 3.* Studi e testi per il CPF 10. Firenze: Olschki, 2000.

Badalamenti, Guido. "Ierocle stoico e il concetto di *synaisthesis*." *Annali del Dipartimento di Filosofia dell'Università di Firenze* 3 (1987): 53–97.

Balch, David L. "Philodemus, 'On Wealth' and 'On Household Management': Naturally Wealthy Epicureans against Poor Cynics." Pages 177–96 in *Philodemus and the New Testament World.* Edited by John T. Fitzgerald, Dirk Obbink, and Glenn S. Holland. NovTSup 111. Leiden: Brill, 2004.

Baloglou, Chrēstos P. "Αἱ οἰκονομικαὶ ἀντιλήψεις τῶν Στωϊκῶν Ἱεροκλέους καὶ Μουσωνίου," *Platon* 44 (1992): 122–34.

———. *Ἡ οἰκονομικὴ σκῆψις τῶν ἀρχαίων Ἑλλήνων*. Thessaloniki: Historikē kai Laographikē Hetaireia Chalkidikēs, 1995.

Balch, David L. "The Areopagus Speech." Pages 52–79 in *Greeks, Romans and Christians: Essays in Honor of Abraham J. Malherbe*. Edited by David L. Balch, Everett Ferguson, and Wayne A. Meeks. Minneapolis: Fortress, 1990.

Baltussen, Han. *Theophrastus against the Presocratics and Plato*. PhAnt 86. Leiden: Brill, 2000.

Banateanu, Anne. *La théorie stoïcienne de l'amitié*. Fribourg: Editions Universitaires, 2001.

Barker, Andrew D. "Diogenes of Babylon and Hellenistic Musical Theory." Pages 353–70 in *Cicéron et Philodème: La polémique en philosophie*. Edited by Clara Auvray-Assayas and Daniel Delattre. Études de Littérature Ancienne 12. Paris: Rue d'Ulm, 2001.

Barnes, Jonathan. "Ancient Philosophers." Pages 293–306 in *Philosophy and Power in the Graeco-Roman World: Essays in Honour of Miriam Griffin*. Edited by Gillian Clark and Tessa Rajak. Oxford: Oxford University Press, 2002.

———. "Antiochus of Ascalon." Pages 51–96 in *Essays on Philosophy and Roman Society*. Vol. 1 of *Philosophia Togata*. Edited by Jonathan Barnes and Miriam T. Griffin. Oxford: Clarendon, 1989.

———. *Logic and the Imperial Stoa*. PhAnt 75; Leiden: Brill, 1997.

———. "Monotheists All?" *Phoenix* 55 (2001): 142–62.

Barton, Tamsyn. *Power and Knowledge: Astrology, Physiognomics and Medicine under the Roman Empire*. Ann Arbor: University of Michigan Press, 2003.

Bastianini, Guido, and Anthony A. Long. "Ierocle: Elementi di Etica." Pages 296–362 in vol. 1.1.2 of *Corpus dei papiri filosofici greci e latini: Testi e lessico nei papiri di cultura greca e latina*. Florence: Olschki, 1992.

Bees, Robert. *Die Oikeiosislehre der Stoa I: Rekonstruktion ihres Inhaltes*. Würzburg: Königshausen & Neumann, 2004.

Bellandi, Franco. "Anneo Cornuto nelle *Saturae* e nella *Vita Persi*." Pages 185–210 in *Gli Annei: Una famiglia nella storia e nella cultura di Roma imperiale, Atti del Convegno Internazionale, Milano-Pavia, 2–6 maggio 2000*. Edited by Isabella Gualandri and Giancarlo Mazzoli. Como: New Press, 2003.

Bellincioni, Maria Scarpat. "Clementia liberum arbitrium habet." *Paideia* 39 (1984): 173–83. Repr. as pages 113–25 in idem, ed., *Studi senecani e altri scritti*. Brescia: Paideia, 1986.

———. *Potere ed etica in Seneca*: Clementia *e* voluntas *amica*. Brescia: Paideia, 1984.

Bénatouïl, Thomas. *Faire usage: La pratique du stoïcisme*. Paris: Vrin, 2006.

Bennet, Julian. *Trajan: Optimus Princeps*. London: Routledge, 1997.

Berardi, Elisabetta. "Avidità, lussuria, ambizione: Tre demoni in Dione di Prusa, *Sulla regalità* IV 5–139." *Prometheus* 24 (1998): 37–56.

Berry, Edmund. "Dio Chrysostom the Moral Philosopher." *GR* NS 30 (1983) 70–80.

Birley, Anthony R. *Hadrian: The Restless Emperor*. London: Routledge, 1997.

Blank, David L. "Diogenes of Babylon and the *kritikoi* in Philodemus." *CErc* 24 (1994): 55–62.

Blázquez, José M. "El uso del pensamiento de la filosofía griega en el *Pedagogo* de Clemente de Alejandría." *Anuario de Historia de la Iglesia* 3 (1994): 59–62.

Blundell, Mary Whitlock. "Parental Nature and Stoic οἰκείωσις." *AncPhil* 10 (1990): 221–42.

Bobzien, Susanne. *Determinism and Freedom in Stoic Philosophy*. Oxford: Clarendon, 1998.

———. "The Inadvertent Conception and Late Birth of the Free-Will Problem." *Phronesis* 43 (1998): 133–75.

Bonhoeffer, A. "Hierokles." *Deutsche Literaturzeitung* 2 (1907): 86–89.

Borgo, Antonella. *Lessico morale di Seneca*. Studi Latini 33. Naples: Loffredo, 1998.

Bost-Pouderon, Cécile. "Dion de Pruse et la physiognomonie dans le Discours XXXIII." *REA* 105 (2003): 157–74.

Boys-Stones, George R. "Eros in Government: Zeno and the Virtuous City." *CQ* NS 48 (1998): 168–74.

———. *Post-Hellenistic Philosophy: A Study of Its Development from the Stoics to Origen*. Oxford: Oxford University Press, 2001.

———. "The Stoics' Two Types of Allegory." Pages 189–216 in *Metaphor, Allegory, and the Classical Tradition: Ancient Thought and Modern Revisions*. Edited by George R. Boys-Stones. Oxford: Oxford University Press, 2003.

Brancacci, Aldo. "Dio, Socrates, and Cynicism." Pages 240–60 in *Dio Chrysostom: Politics, Letters, and Philosophy*. Edited by Simon Swain. Oxford: Oxford University Press, 2000.

———. "Le Socrate de Dion Chrysostome." *PhilosAnt* 1 (2001): 166–82.

———. *Rhêtorikê philosophousa: Dione Crisostomo nella cultura antica e bizantina*. Elenchos 11. Naples: Bibliopolis, 1985.

Brehier, Émile. *Chrysippe et l'ancien stoïcisme.* 3rd ed. Paris: Presses Universitaires de France, 1971.

Bremmer, Jan N. "Aetius, Arius Didymus and the Transmission of Doxography." *Mnemosyne* 51 (1998): 154–60.

Brenk, Frederick E. "Dio on the Simple and Self-Sufficient Life." Pages 261–78 in *Dio Chrysostom: Politics, Letters, and Philosophy.* Edited by Simon Swain. Oxford: Oxford University Press, 2000.

———. "Plutarch and His Middle-Platonic God: About to Enter (or Remake) the Academy." Pages 27–49 in *Gott und die Götter bei Plutarch: Götterbilder–Gottesbilder–Weltbilder.* Edited by Rainer Hirsch-Luipold. Religionsgeschichtliche Versuche und Vorarbeiten 54. Berlin: de Gruyter, 2005.

Brennan, Tad. "Fate and Free Will in Stoicism." *OSAP* 21 (2001): 259–86.

———. *The Stoic Life: Emotions, Duties, and Fate.* Oxford: Clarendon, 2005.

———. "Stoic Moral Psychology." Pages 257–94 in *The Cambridge Companion to the Stoics.* Edited by Brad Inwood. Cambridge: Cambridge University Press, 2003.

Brickhouse, Thomas C., and Nicholas D. Smith. "The Problem of Punishment in Socratic Philosophy." *Apeiron* 30 (1997): 95–107.

Brink, Charles O. "*Oikeiôsis* and *oikeiotês*: Theophrastus and Zeno on Nature in Moral Theory." *Phronesis* 1–2 (1955–57): 123–45.

Brunschwig, Jacques. "The Cradle Argument in Epicureanism and Stoicism." Pages 113–45 in *The Norms of Nature: Studies in Hellenistic Ethics.* Edited by Malcolm Schofield and Gisela Striker. Cambridge: Cambridge University Press, 1986.

———. "Stoic Metaphysics." Pages 206–32 in *The Cambridge Companion to the Stoics.* Edited by Brad Inwood. Cambridge: Cambridge University Press, 2003.

Brunschwig, Jacques, and David N. Sedley. "Hellenistic Philosophy." Pages 151–83 in *The Cambridge Companion to Greek and Roman Philosophy.* Edited by David N. Sedley. Cambridge: Cambridge University Press, 2003.

Brunt, Peter A. "Aspects of the Social Thought of Dio Chrysostom and of the Stoics." *PCPhS* 19 (1973): 9–34.

Burnyeat, Myles F. "Antipater and Self-Refutation: Elusive Arguments in Cicero's *Academica*." Pages 277–310 in *Assent and Argument: Studies in Cicero's Academic Books: Proceedings of the 7th Symposium Hellenisticum (Utrecht, August 21–25, 1995).* Edited by Brad Inwood and Jaap Mansfeld. PhAnt 76. Leiden: Brill, 1997.

Camassa, Giorgio. "Il pastorato di Zaleuco." *Athenaeum* 64 (1986): 139–45.

Cambronne, Patrice. "L'universel et le singulier: L'Hymne à Zeus de Cléanthe: Notes de lecture." *REA* 100 (1998): 89–114.

Campanella, Lorenza, and Barbara Wilkens. "Una mangusta egiziana ('Herpestes ichneumon') dall'abitato fenicio di Sant'Antioco." *Rivista di Studi Fenici* 32 (2004): 25–48.

Cavallini, Eleonora. "L'Elegia alle Muse di Solone e l'Inno a Zeus di Cleante." *RFIC* 117 (1989): 424–29.

Chiesa, Curzio. "Le problème du langage intérieur chez les Stoïciens." *RIPh* 45 (1991): 301–21.

———. "Le problème du mal concomitant chez les Stoïciens." *StudPhil* 52 (1993): 45–65.

Clay, Diskin. *Lucretius and Epicurus.* Ithaca: Cornell University Press, 1983.

Cohn, Hermann. *Antipater von Tarsos: Ein Beitrag zur Geschichte der Stoa.* Berlin: Fromholz, 1905.

Colish, Marcia L. "Stoicism and the New Testament: An Essay in Historiography." *ANRW* 26.2:334–379.

———. *The Stoic Tradition from Antiquity to the Early Middle Ages.* 2 vols. Studies in the History of Christian Thought 34–35. Leiden: Brill, 1985; corr. repr., 1995.

Colombo, Anna Maria. "Un nuovo frammento di Crisippo." *PP* 9 (1954): 376–81.

Compernolle, René van. "La législation aristocratique de Locres Épizéphyrienne, dite législation de Zaleukos." *L'Antiquité Classique* 50 (1981): 759–69.

Cooper, John M. "Eudaimonism, the Appeal to Nature, and 'Moral Duty' in Stoicism." Pages 261–84 in *Aristotle, the Stoics, and Kant: Rethinking Happiness and Duty.* Edited by Stephen P. Engstrom and Jennifer Whiting. Cambridge: Cambridge University Press, 1996.

———. *Knowledge, Nature, and the Good: Essays on Ancient Philosophy.* Princeton: Princeton University Press, 2004.

Dahlmann, Hellfried. "Nochmals 'Ducunt volentem fata, nolentem trahunt.'" *Hermes* 105 (1977): 342–51.

Dalfen, Joachim. "Das Gebet des Kleanthes an Zeus und das Schicksal." *Hermes* 99 (1971): 174–83.

Decleva Caizzi, Fernanda. "The Porch and the Garden: Early Hellenistic Images of the Philosophical Life." Pages 303–29 in *Images and Ideologies: Self-Definition in the Hellenistic World.* Edited by Anthony

Bulloch et al. Berkeley and Los Angeles: University of California Press, 1994.

Delattre, Daniel. "Une 'citation' stoïcienne des Lois (II, 669 B–E) de Platon dans les Commentaires sur la musique de Philodème?" *RHT* 21 (1991): 1–17.

———. "Speusippe, Diogène de Babylone et Philodème." *CErc* 23 (1993): 67–86.

Delle Donne, Vittorio. "Per una nuova edizione dei Principi di etica di Ierocle Stoico (*P. Berol. 9780*)." *Annali dell'Istituto Italiano per gli Studi Storici* 10 (1987–88): 113–44.

———. "Sulla nuova edizione della 'Ηθικὴ στοιχείωσις di Ierocle stoico." *SIFC* 13 (1995): 29–99.

DeFilippo, Joseph, and Phillip T. Mitsis. "Socrates and Stoic Natural Law." Pages 252–71 in *The Socratic Movement*. Edited by Paul A. Vander Waerdt. Ithaca, N.Y.: Cornell University Press, 1994.

Deming, Will. *Paul on Marriage and Celibacy: The Hellenistic Background of 1 Corinthians 7*. 2nd ed. Grand Rapids: Eerdmans, 2004.

Des Places, Édouard. "Des temples faits de main d'homme (Actes des Apôtres XVII, 24)." *Bib* 42 (1961): 217–23.

Desideri, Paolo. *Dione di Prusa*. Messina: D'Anna, 1978.

———. "L'iscrizione *del mietitore* (CIL vm. 11824): *Un aspetto della* cultura mactaritana del III secolo." Pages 137–49 in *L'Africa romana: Atti del IV convegno di studio, Sassari, 12–14.XII.1986*. Edited by Attilio Mastino. Sassari: Gallizzi, 1987.

———. "Religione e politica nell'*Olimpico* di Dione." *QS* 15 (1980): 141–61.

Di Stefano, Eva. "Antioco di Ascalona tra Platonismo scettico e Medioplatonismo." Pages 37–52 in *Momenti e problemi di storia del platonismo*. Symbolon 1. Catania: Univerità di Catania, 1984.

Diels, Hermann. *Elementum: Eine Vorarbeit zum griechischen und lateinischen Thesaurus*. Leipzig: Teubner, 1899.

Diels, Hermann, and Wilhelm Schubart, eds. *Anonymer kommentar zu Platons Theaetet (papyrus 9782): Nebst drei bruchstücken philosophischen inhalts (pap. n. 8; p. 9766. 9569)*. Berliner Klassikertexte 2. Berlin: Weidmann, 1905.

Diggle, James. *Theophrastus: Characters*. CCTC 43. Cambridge: Cambridge University Press, 2004.

Dihle, Albrecht. *The Theory of Will in Classical Antiquity*. Berkeley and Los Angeles: University of California Press, 1982.

Dirkzwager, Arie. "Ein Abbild der Gottheit haben und Weiteres zum Kleanthes-Hymnus." *RhM* 123 (1980): 359–60.

Dirlmeier, Franz. *Die Oikeiôsis-Lehre Theophrasts*. Philologus Supplementband 30.1. Leipzig: Dieterich, 1937.

Dobbin, Robert F. "Προαίρεσις in Epictetus." *AncPhil* 11 (1991): 111–35.

Donini, Pier Luigi. "Fato e volontà umana in Crisippo." *Atti dell'Accademia di Torino* 109 (1975): 187–230.

———. "*Pathos* nello stoicismo romano." *Elenchos* 16 (1995): 193–216.

———. "Testi e commenti, manuali e insegnamento: la forma sistematica e i metodi della filosofia in età post-ellenistica." *ANRW* 36.7:5027–5100.

Dorandi, Tiziano. "Contributo epigrafico alla cronologia di Panezio." *ZPE* 79 (1989): 87–92.

———. "Filodemo: Gli Stoici (PHerc 155 e 3339)." *CErc* 12 (1982): 91–133.

Döring, Klaus. *Exemplum Socratis: Studien zur Sokratesnachwirkung in der kynisch-stoischen Popularphilosophie der frühen Kaiserzeit und im frühen Christentum*. Wiesbaden: Steiner, 1979.

———. "Sokrates bei Epiktet." Pages 195–226 in *Studia Platonica: Festschrift für Hermann Gundert zu seinem 65. Geburtstag am 30.4.1974*. Edited by Klaus Döring and Wolfgang Kullman. Amsterdam: Grüner, 1974.

Doull, James A. "A Commentary on Plato's *Theaetetus*." *Dionysius* 1 (1977): 5–47.

Dragona-Monachou, Myrto. "Providence and Fate in Stoicism and Prae-Neoplatonism: Calcidius as an Authority on Cleanthes' Theodicy." *Philosophia* 3 (1973): 262–306.

———. "'Ο ὕμνος στὸ Δία ... Ἡ ποιητικὴ θεολογία τοῦ Κλεάνθη καὶ ἡ ὀρφικο-πυθαγορικὴ παραδόση." *Philosophia* 1 (1971): 339–78.

Dumont, Jean-Paul. "Le citoyen-roi dans la *République* de Zénon." *CPhPJ* 4 (1983): 35–48 .

———. "Diogène de Babylone et la déesse Raison: La Métis des Stoïciens." *Bulletin de l'Association G. Budé* (1984): 260–78.

———. "Diogène de Babylone et la preuve ontologique." *RPFE* (1982): 389–95.

Dyck, Andrew R. "The Plan of Panaetius' *Peri tou Kahêkontos*." *AJP* 100 (1979): 408–16.

Edelstein, Ludwig, and I. G. Kidd, eds. *Fragments 150–293*. Vol. 2.2 of *Posidonius*. Cambridge: Cambridge University Press, 1988.

Edwards, Mark J. "Quoting Aratus." *ZNW* 83 (1992): 266–69.

Engberg-Pedersen, Troels. "Discovering the Good: Οἰκείωσις and καθήκοντα in Stoic Ethics." Pages 145–83 in *The Norms of Nature:*

Studies in Hellenistic Ethics. Edited by Malcolm Schofield and Gisela Striker. Cambridge: Cambridge University Press, 1986.

———. *Paul and the Stoics*. Louisville: Westminster John Knox, 2000.

———. "Radical Altruism in Philippians 2:4." Pages 197–214 in *Early Christianity and Classical Culture: Comparative Studies in Honor of Abraham J. Malherbe*. Edited by John T. Fitzgerald, Thomas H. Olbricht, and L. Michael White. NovTSup 110. Leiden: Brill, 2003. Repr., Atlanta: Society of Biblical Literature, 2005.

———. *The Stoic Theory of Οἰκείωσις: Moral Development and Social Interaction in Early Stoic Philosophy*. Studies in Hellenistic Civilization 2. Aarhus: Aarhus University Press, 1990.

Engel, David M. "The Gender Egalitarianism of Musonius Rufus." *AncPhil* 20 (2000): 377–91.

———. "Women's Role in the Home and the State: Stoic Theory Reconsidered." *HSCP* 101 (2003): 267–88.

Erler, Michael. "Stoic *Oikeiosis* and Xenophon's Socrates." Pages 239–58 in *The Philosophy of Zeno*. Edited by Theodore Scaltsas and Andrew S. Mason. Larnaka, Cyprus: Municipality of Larnaca, 2002.

Erskine, Andrew. "Zeno and the Beginning of Stoicism." *Classics Ireland* 7 (2000): 51–60.

Evans, Elizabeth C. "The Study of Physiognomics in the I Century A.D." *TAPA* 72 (1941): 96–108.

Eyben, Emiel. "De latere stoa over het huwelijk." *Hermeneus* 50 (1978): 15–32, 71–94, 337–58.

———. "Musonius Rufus: Ook vrouwen moeten filosofie studeren." *Hermeneus* 48 (1976): 90–107.

Eyben Emiel, and Alfons Wouters. "Musonius Rufus, Εἰ παραπλησίως παιδευτέον τὰς θυγατέρας τοῖς υἱοῖς." *Lampas* 8 (1975): 185–213.

Favez, Charles. "Un féministe romain: Musonius Rufus." *Bulletin de la Société des Études de Lettres, Lausanne* 20 (1933): 1–8.

Ferrante, Domenico. *La Semantica di logos in Dione Crisostomo alla luce del contrasto tra retorica e filosofia*. Naples: Loffredo, 1981.

Ferrari, Franco. "Der Gott Plutarchs und der Gott Platons." Pages 13–25 in *Gott und die Götter bei Plutarch: Götterbilder–Gottesbilder–Weltbilder*. Edited by Rainer Hirsch-Luipold. Religionsgeschichtliche Versuche und Vorarbeiten 54. Berlin: de Gruyter, 2005.

Fillion-Lahille, Janine. *Le* De ira *de Sénèque et la philosophie stoïcienne des passions*. Paris: Klincksieck, 1984.

Fitzgerald, John T. "Christian Friendship: John, Paul, and the Philippians." *Int* (2007): 284–96.

———. "The Passions and Moral Progress: An Introduction." Pages 1–25 in *Passions and Moral Progress in Greco-Roman Thought.* Edited by John T. Fitzgerald. London: Routledge, 2008.

———. "Paul and Friendship." Pages 319–43 in *Paul in the Greco-Roman World: A Handbook.* Edited by J. Paul Sampley. Harrisburg, Pa.: Trinity Press International, 2003.

———. "Paul and Paradigm Shifts: Reconciliation and Its Linkage Group." Pages 241–62 in *Paul beyond the Judaism/Hellenism Divide.* Edited by Troels Engberg-Pedersen. Louisville: Westminster John Knox, 2001.

———, ed. *Greco-Roman Perspectives on Friendship.* SBLRBS 34. Atlanta: Scholars Press, 1997.

Fitzgerald, John T., Thomas H. Olbricht, and L. Michael White, eds. *Early Christianity and Classical Culture: Comparative Studies in Honor of Abraham J. Malherbe.* NovTSup 110. Leiden: Brill, 2003. Repr., Atlanta: Society of Biblical Literature, 2005.

Fitzpatrick-McKinley, Anne. "Ezra, Nehemiah and Some Early Greek Lawgivers." Pages 17–48 in *Rabbinic Law in Its Roman and Near Eastern Context.* Edited by Catherine Hezser. TSAJ 97. Tübingen: Mohr Siebeck, 2003.

Fladerer, Ludwig. *Antiochos von Askalon.* Graz: Berger & Söhne, 1996.

Forschner, Maximilian. *Die stoische Ethik: Über den Zusammenhang von Natur-, Sprach- und Moralphilosophie im altstoischen System.* Stuttgart: Klett-Cotta, 1981.

Förster, Richard. *Scriptores physiognomonici graeci et latini.* 2 vols. Berlin: Teubner, 1893.

Fortenbaugh, William W. *Theophrastean Studies.* Philosophie der Antike 17. Stuttgart: Steiner, 2003.

Frede, Dorothea. "Stoic Determinism." Pages 179–205 in *The Cambridge Companion to the Stoics.* Edited by Brad Inwood. Cambridge: Cambridge University Press, 2003.

Frede, Michael. "Monotheism and Pagan Philosophy in Later Antiquity." Pages 41–68 in *Pagan Monotheism in Late Antiquity.* Edited by Polymnia Athanassiadi and Michael Frede. Oxford: Oxford University Press, 1999.

———. "On the Stoic Conception of the Good." Pages 71–94 in *Topics in Stoic Philosophy.* Edited by Katerina Ierodiakonou. Oxford: Clarendon, 1999.

———. *Die stoische Logik.* Göttingen: Vandenhoeck & Ruprecht, 1974.

Fredouille, Jean-Claude. "La théologie tripartite, modèle apologétique." Pages 220–35 in *Hommages à Henri Le Bonniec: Res sacrae.* Edited by

Danielle Porte and Jean-Pierre Néraudau. Brussels: Latomus, 1988.

Frings, Irene. "Struktur und Quellen des Prooemiums zum I. Buch Ciceros *De officiis*." *Prometheus* 19 (1993): 169–82.

Fritz, Kurt von. "Polemon." PW 21.2:2524–29.

———. "Zaleukos." PW 9.A2:2298.

Funghi, Maria Serena. "Un testo sul concetto stoico di progresso morale (PMilVogliano Inv. 1241)." Pages 85–124 in *Aristoxenica, Menandrea, fragmenta philosophica*. Edited by Aldo Brancacci et al. Florence: Olschki, 1988.

Furley, David. "Cosmology, III: The Early Stoics." Pages 432–51 in *The Cambridge History of Hellenistic Philosophy*. Edited by Keimpe A. Algra et al. Cambridge: Cambridge University Press, 1999.

Gaca, Kathy L. *The Making of Fornication: Eros, Ethics, and Political Reform in Greek Philosophy and Early Christianity*. Berkeley and Los Angeles: University of California Press, 2003.

Gaiser, Konrad. *Für und wider die Ehe: Antike Stimmen zu einer offenen Frage*. Dialog mit der Antike 1. Munich: Heimeran, 1974.

García de Sola, María del Carmen. "La representación en el estoicismo antiguo." *Estudios de Filosofía Griega* 2 (1986): 247–52.

Garro, Paolo. "La concezione dei πάθη da Zenone e Crisippo a Panezio." *SMSR* 13 (1989): 183–95.

Gärtner, Hans Armin. *Cicero und Panaitios: Beobachtungen zu Ciceros Schrift* De officiis. Heidelberg: Winter, 1974.

Gass, Michael. "Eudaimonism and Theology in Stoic Accounts of Virtue." *JHI* 61 (2000): 19–37.

Gazich, Roberto. "La *Fedra* di Seneca tra pathos ed elegia." *Humanitas (Brescia)* NS 52 (1997): 348–75.

Gibson, Craig A. *Libanius's* Progymnasmata*: Model Exercises in Greek Prose Composition and Rhetoric*. SBLWGRW 27. Atlanta: Society of Biblical Literature, 2008.

Gigante, Marcello. "Dossografia stoica." Pages 123–26 in *Varia papyrologica*. Edited by Fernanda Decleva Caizzi et al. STCPF 5. Florence: Olschki, 1991.

Giangrande, Giuseppe. "Cleanthes' *Hymn to Zeus*, line 4." *Corolla Londiniensis* 2 (1982): 95–97.

Gill, Christopher. "Did Chrysippus Understand Medea?" *Phronesis* 28 (1983): 136–49.

———. "The School in the Roman Imperial Period." Pages 33–58 in *The Cambridge Companion to the Stoics*. Edited by Brad Inwood. Cambridge: Cambridge University Press, 2003.

———. "Stoic Writers of the Imperial Era." Pages 597–615 in *The Cambridge History of Greek and Roman Political Thought*. Edited by Christopher Rowe and Malcolm Schofield. Cambridge: Cambridge University Press, 2000.

———. *The Structured Self in Hellenistic and Roman Thought*. Oxford: Oxford University Press, 2006.

Giordano-Zecharya, Manuela. "As Socrates Shows, the Athenians Did Not Believe in Gods." *Numen* 52 (2005): 325–55.

Giusta, Michelangelo. "Antioco di Ascalona e Carneade nel libro V del *De finibus bonorum et malorum* di Cicerone." *Elenchos* 11 (1990): 29–49.

Glucker, John. *Antiochus and the Late Academy*. Göttingen: Vandenhoeck & Ruprecht, 1978.

Gomoll, Heinz, ed. *Der stoische Philosoph Hekaton, seine Begriffswelt und Nachwirkung unter Beigabe seiner Fragmente*. Bonn: Cohen, 1933.

Göransson, Tryggve. *Albinus, Alcinous, Arius Didymus*. Göteborg: Acta Universitatis Gothoburgensis, 1995.

Görler, Woldemar. "Älterer Pyrrhonismus—Jüngere Akademie: Antiochos von Askalon." Pages 717–989 in vol. 4.2 of *Grundriss der Geschichte der Philosophie*. Edited by Friedrich Ueberweg and Hellmut Flashar. Basel: Schwabe, 1994.

Gould, Josiah B. *The Philosophy of Chrysippus*. Leiden: Brill, 1970.

Goulet-Cazé, Marie-Odile. "Le cynisme à l'époque impériale." *ANRW* 36.4:2720–2833.

———. *Les Kynika du stoïcisme*. Wiesbaden: Steiner, 2003.

Gourinat, Jean-Baptiste. "L'embryon végétatif et la formation de l'âme selon les stoïciens." Pages 59–77 in *L'embryon dans l'Antiquité et au Moyen-Âge*. Edited by Luc Brisson and Marie-Helène Congourdeau. Paris: Vrin, 2008.

———. "Le Socrate d'Epictète." *PhilosAnt* 1 (2001): 137–65.

Graeser, Andreas. *Zenon von Kition: Positionen und Probleme*. Berlin: de Gruyter, 1975.

Graver, Margaret. *Stoicism and Emotion*. Chicago: University of Chicago Press, 2007.

Griffin, Miriam. "Nerva to Hadrian." Pages 84–131 in *The High Empire, A.D. 70–192*. Vol. 11 of *The Cambridge Ancient History*. Edited by Alan K. Bowman, John B. Bury, and Averil Cameron. 2nd ed. Cambridge: Cambridge University Press, 2000.

———. "Philosophy, Cato, and Roman Suicide." *GR* 33 (1986): 64–77, 192–202.

Grilli, Alberto. *Il problema della vita contemplativa nel mondo greco-romano.* Milan: Fratelli Bocca, 1953.

———. "Studi paneziani." *SIFC* 29 (1957): 31–97.

Griswold, Charles L. *Forgiveness: A Philosophical Exploration.* Cambridge: Cambridge University Press, 2007.

Guckes, Barbara. *Zur Ethik der älteren Stoa.* Göttingen: Vandenhoeck & Ruprecht, 2004.

Guthrie, Kenneth Sylvan. *Pythagoras: Source Book and Library.* 2 vols. Yonkers: Platonist, 1920.

———, comp. and trans. *The Pythagorean Sourcebook and Library.* Edited by David R. Fiedler. 2nd ed. Grand Rapids: Phanes, 1987.

Hadot, Ilsetraut. "Le démiurge comme principe dérivé dans le système ontologique d'Hiéroclès." *Revue des Études Grecques* 103 (1990): 241–62.

———. *Le problème du néoplatonisme alexandrin: Hiéroclès et Simplicius.* Paris: Études augustiniennes, 1978.

Hadot, Pierre. *La citadelle intérieure: Introduction aux* Pensées *de Marc Aurèle.* Paris: Fayard, 1992.

Hager, Paul. "Chrysippus' Theory of Pneuma." *Prudentia* 14 (1982): 97–108.

Hahm, David E. "The Ethical Doxography of Arius Didymus." *ANRW* 36.4:2935–3055, 3234–43.

———. "Zeno before and after Stoicism. Pages 29–56 in *The Philosophy of Zeno.* Edited by Theodore Scaltsas and Andrew S. Mason. Larnaka, Cyprus: Municipality of Larnaca, 2002

Hankinson, R. J. "Stoic Epistemology." Pages 59–84 in *The Cambridge Companion to the Stoics.* Edited by Brad Inwood. Cambridge: Cambridge University Press, 2003.

Harland, Philip A. "Familial Dimensions of Group Identity: 'Brothers' (ΑΔΕΛΦΟΙ) in Associations of the Greek East." *JBL* 124 (2005): 491–551.

Häsler, Berthold. *Favorin über die Verbannung.* Berlin: Postberg, 1935.

Hill, Timothy. *Ambitiosa Mors: Suicide and Self in Roman Thought and Literature.* New York: Routledge, 2004.

Hillgruber, Michael. "Dion Chrysostomos 36 (53), 4–5 und die Homerauslegung Zenons." *MH* 46 (1989): 15–24.

Hirsch-Luipold, Rainer. "Der eine Gott bei Philon von Alexandrien und Plutarch." Pages 141–68 in *Gott und die Götter bei Plutarch: Götterbilder–Gottesbilder–Weltbilder.* Edited by Rainer Hirsch-Luipold. Religionsgeschichtliche Versuche und Vorarbeiten 54. Berlin: de Gruyter, 2005.

———, ed. *Gott und die Götter bei Plutarch: Götterbilder–Gottesbilder–Weltbilder.* Religionsgeschichtliche Versuche und Vorarbeiten 54. Berlin: de Gruyter, 2005.

Hock, Ronald F. *The Social Context of Paul's Ministry: Tentmaking and Apostleship.* Philadelphia: Fortress, 1980.

Hölkeskamp, Karl-Joachim. *Schiedsrichter, Gesetzgeber und Gesetzgebung im archaischen Griechenland.* Stuttgart: Steiner, 1999.

Holladay, Carl R. *Aristobulus.* Vol. 3 of *Fragments from Hellenistic Jewish Authors.* SBLTT 39. Atlanta: Scholars Press, 1995.

Holwerda, Douwe. *Sprünge in die tiefen Heraklits.* Groningen: Bouma, 1978.

Horst, Pieter W. van der. "Hierocles the Stoic and the New Testament: A Contribution to the Corpus Hellenisticum." *NovT* 17 (1975): 156–60.

———. "Musonius Rufus and the New Testament." *NovT* 16 (1974): 306–15.

Houser, J. Samuel. "Eros and Aphrodisia in Dio Chrysostom." Pages 327–53 in *The Sleep of Reason: Erotic Experience and Sexual Ethics in Ancient Greece and Rome.* Edited by Martha Nussbaum and Juha Sihvola. Chicago: University of Chicago Press, 2002.

Invernizzi, Giuseppe. "Un commento medioplatonico al *Teeteto* e il suo significato filosofico." *RFN* 68 (1976): 215–33.

Inwood, Brad. "Comments on Professor Görgemanns' Paper: The Two Forms of Oikeiôsis in Arius and the Stoa." Pages 190–201 in *On Stoic and Peripatetic Ethics: The Work of Arius Didymus.* Edited by William W. Fortenbaugh. New Brunswick, N.J.: Transaction, 1983.

———. *Ethics and Human Action in Early Stoicism.* Oxford: Clarendon, 1985.

———. "Goal and Target in Stoicism." *JPh* 10 (1986): 547–56.

———. "Hierocles: Theory and Argument in the 2nd Century A.D." *OSAP* 2 (1984): 151–84.

———. "Kanones kai syllogistiki sti stoiki Ithiki." *Deukalion* 15 (1997): 107–43.

———. "Natural Law in Seneca." *StudPhiloAnn* 15 (2003): 81–99.

———. "L'οἰκείωσις sociale chez Épictète." Pages 243–64 in *Polyhistor: Studies in the History and Historiography of Ancient Philosophy.* Edited by Keimpe A. Algra, Pieter W. van der Horst, and David T. Runia. PhAnt 72. Leiden: Brill, 1996.

———. Review of Christopher Gill. *The Structured Self in Hellenistic and Roman Thought. Philosophical Quarterly* 57, 228 (2007): 479–83.

———. Review of Gretchen Reydams-Schils, *The Roman Stoics: Self, Responsibility, and Affection. CP* 101 (2006): 88–93.

———. "Seneca in His Philosophical Milieu." *HSCP* 97 (1995): 63–76.

———. "The Will in Seneca the Younger," *CP* 95 (2000): 44–60.

———, ed. *The Cambridge Companion to the Stoics*. Cambridge: Cambridge University Press, 2003.

Inwood, Brad, and Pier Luigi Donini. "Stoic Ethics." Pages 675–738 in *The Cambridge History of Hellenistic Philosophy*. Edited by Keimpe A. Algra et al. Cambridge: Cambridge University Press, 1999.

Ioppolo, Anna Maria. *Aristone di Chio e lo Stoicismo antico*. Naples: Bibliopolis, 1980.

———. *Opinione e scienza: Il dibattito tra stoici e accademici nel III e nel II secolo a.C.* Naples: Bibliopolis, 1986.

Irwin, Terrence H. "Stoic Inhumanity." Pages 219–41 in *The Emotions in Hellenistic Philosophy*. Edited by Juha Sihvola and Troels Engberg-Pedersen. Dordrecht: Kluwer Academic, 1998.

Isnardi Parente, Margherita. "Ierocle stoico: Oikeiôsis e doveri sociali." *ANRW* 36.3:2201–26.

Janda, Jan. "Einige ethisch-soziale Probleme in der Philosophie des Zenon von Kition: Zur *Politeia* des Zenon." Pages 99–116 in *Soziale Probleme im Hellenismus und im römischen Reich: Akten der Konferenz (Liblice 10. bis 13. Oktober 1972)*. Edited by Pavel Olivia and Jan Burian. Prague: CSAV, 1973.

Janko, Richard. "A First Join between P. Herc. 411 + 1583 (Philodemus, *On Music* IV): Diogenes of Babylon on Natural Affinity and Music." *CErc* 22 (1992): 123–29.

Kahn, Charles H. "Discovering the Will: From Aristotle to Augustine." Pages 234–59 in *The Question of Eclecticism*. Edited by John M. Dillon and Anthony A. Long. Berkeley and Los Angeles: University of California Press, 1988.

Kerferd, George B. "The Search for Personal Identity in Stoic Thought." *BJRL* 55 (1972): 177–96.

Kidd, Douglas, ed. *Aratus: Phaenomena*. Cambridge: Cambridge University Press, 1997.

Klauck, Hans-Josef. "Pantheisten, Polytheisten, Monotheisten—Eine Reflexion zur griechisch-römischen und biblischen Theologie." Pages 3–56 in idem, *Religion und Gesellschaft im frühen Christentum: Neutestamentliche Studien*. WUNT 152. Tübingen: Mohr Siebeck, 2003.

———. *The Religious Context of Early Christianity: A Guide to Graeco-Roman Religions*. Minneapolis: Fortress, 2003.

———, ed. *Dion von Prusa: Olympikos und Peri tês prôtês tou theou ennoias*. Darmstadt: Wissenschaftliche Buchgesellschaft, 2000.

Kleywegt, Adrianus Jan. "Fate, Free Will, and the Text of Cicero." *Mnemosyne* 26 (1973): 342–49.

Kobusch, Theo. *Studien zur Philosophie des Hierokles von Alexandria.* Munich: Berchmans, 1976.

Köhler, Friedrich Wilhelm. *Hieroclis in aureum Pythagoreorum carmen commentarius.* BSGRT. Leipzig: Tuebner, 1974.

———. *Kommentar zum Pythagoreischen goldenen Gedicht.* Griechische und lateinische Schriftsteller. Stuttgart: Teubner, 1983.

Kohnke, F. W. "Γαστὴρ ἐργαστήριον φύσεως: Ein Chrysippzitat." *Hermes* 93 (1965): 383–84.

Konstan, David. *The Emotions of the Ancient Greeks: Studies in Aristotle and Greek Literature.* Toronto: University of Toronto Press, 2006.

———. *Friendship in the Classical World.* Cambridge: Cambridge University Press, 1997.

———. "Reciprocity and Friendship." Pages 279–301 in *Reciprocity in Ancient Greece.* Edited by Christopher Gill and Norman Postlethwaite. Oxford: Oxford University Press, 1998.

Kühn, Karl Gottlob. *Claudii Galeni opera omnia.* 20 vols. Leipzig: Knobloch, 1821–33.

La Bua, Giuseppe. "La *laus Cornuti* nella V satira di Persio e Lucrezio III 1–30." *Bollettino di Studi Latini* 27 (1997): 82–101.

Lanzi, Silvia. *Theos Anaitios: Storia della teodicea da Omero ad Agostino.* Rome: Il calamo, 2000.

Laurand, Valéry. "Souci de soi et mariage chez Musonius Rufus: Perspectives politiques de la κρᾶσις stoïcienne." Pages 85–116 in *Foucault et la philosophie antique.* Edited by Frédéric Gros and Carlos Lévy. Paris: Editions Kimé, 2003.

Lee, Chang-Uh. *Οἰκείωσις: Stoische Ethik in naturphilosophischer Perspektive.* Freiburg: München Alber, 2002.

Lefèvre, Eckard. *Panaitios' und Ciceros Pflichtenlehre.* Stuttgart: Steiner, 2001.

Lehmann, Yves. *Varron théologien et philosophe romain.* Brussels: Latomus, 1997.

Lesky, Albin. *Geschichte der griechischen Literatur.* Munich: Taschenbuch, 1993.

Lesses, Glenn. "Austere Friends: The Stoics and Friendship," *Apeiron* 26 (1993): 57–75.

Levick, Barbara. "Women, Power, and Philosophy at Rome and Beyond." Pages 134–55 in *Philosophy and Power in the Graeco-Roman World.* Edited by Gillian Clark and Tessa Rajak. Oxford: Oxford University

Press, 2002.
Lieberg, Godo. "Die *theologia tripertita* in Forschung und Bezeugung." *ANRW* 1.4:63–115.
Lilla, Salvatore. *Introduzione al Medio-platonismo.* Rome: Istituto patristico Augustinianum, 1992.
Link, Stefan. "Die Gesetzgebung des Zaleukos im epizephyrischen Lokroi." *Klio* 74 (1992): 11–24.
Long, Anthony A. "Arius Didymus and the Exposition of Stoic Ethics." Pages 41–65 in *On Stoic and Peripatetic Ethics: The Work of Arius Didymus.* Edited by William W. Fortenbaugh. New Brunswick, N.J.: Transaction, 1983.
———. "Carneades and the Stoic *Telos*." *Phronesis* 12 (1967): 59–90.
———. *Epictetus: A Stoic and Socratic Guide to Life.* Oxford: Clarendon, 2002.
———. "Epictetus as Socratic Mentor." *PCPhS* 46 (2000): 79–98.
———. *Hellenistic Philosophy: Stoics, Epicureans, Sceptics.* London: Duckworth, 1974.
———. "Representation and the Stoic Self." Pages 102–20 in *Psychology.* Edited by Stephen Everson. Vol. 2 of *Companions to Ancient Thought.* Cambridge: Cambridge University Press, 1991.
———. "Roman Philosophy." Pages 184–210 in *The Cambridge Companion to Greek and Roman Philosophy.* Edited by David N. Sedley. Cambridge: Cambridge University Press, 2003.
———. "Socrates in Hellenistic Philosophy." *CQ* 38 (1988) 150–71. Repr. as pages 1–34 in idem, *Stoic Studies.* Cambridge: Cambridge University Press, 1996.
———. "The Socratic Imprint of Epictetus' Philosophy." Pages 10–31 in *Stoicism: Traditions and Transformations.* Edited by Steven K. Strange and Jack Zupko. Cambridge: Cambridge University Press, 2004.
———. "Soul and Body in Stoicism." *Phronesis* 27 (1982): 34–57.
———. "The Stoics on World-Conflagration and Everlasting Recurrence." Pages 13–58 in *Recovering the Stoics.* Edited by Ronald H. Epp. Supplement to the Southern Journal of Philosophy. Memphis: Dept. of Philosophy, Memphis State University, 1985.
Long, Anthony A., and David N. Sedley. *The Hellenistic Philosophers.* 2 vols. Cambridge: Cambridge University Press, 1987.
Lutz, Cora E. "Musonius Rufus, the Roman Socrates." *YCS* 10 (1947): 3–147.
Luzzatto, Maria Tanja. "Dio Prusaensis." *CPF* 1.1.2:34–85.
Magnaldi, Giuseppina. *L'οἰκείωσις peripatetica in Ario Didimo e nel De*

finibus di Cicerone. Firenze: Casa Editrice Le Lettere, 1991.

Malherbe, Abraham J. "Determinism and Free Will in Paul: The Argument of 1 Corinthians 8 and 9." Pages 231–55 in *Paul in His Hellenistic Context.* Edited by Troels Engberg-Pedersen. Minneapolis: Fortress, 1994.

———. "Hellenistic Moralists and the New Testament." *ANRW* 26.2:267–333.

———. *Moral Exhortation: A Greco-Roman Sourcebook.* LEC 4. Philadelphia: Westminster, 1986.

———. *Paul and the Popular Philosophers.* Philadelphia: Fortress, 1988.

Mansfeld, Jaap. "Chrysippus' Definition of Cause in Arius Didymus." *Elenchos* 22 (2001): 99–109.

———. "Doxography and Dialectic: The Sitz im Leben of the 'Placita.'" *ANRW* 36.4:3186–90.

———. "The Idea of Will in Chrysippus, Posidonius, and Galen." *Boston Area Colloquium in Ancient Philosophy* 7 (1991): 107–45.

———. "Notes on Some Passages in Plato's *Theaetetus* and in the Anonymous Commentary." Pages 108–14 in *Zetesis: Album amicorum aangeboden aan E. de Strycker.* Antwerp: Nederlandsche boekh, 1973.

———. "Providence and the Destruction of the Universe in Early Stoic Thought." Pages 129–88 in *Studies in Hellenistic Religions.* Edited by Maarten J. Vermaseren. ÉPRO 78. Leiden: Brill, 1979.

———. "Some Stoics on the Soul (*SVF* I 136)." *Mnemosyne* 37 (1984): 443–45.

———. "Theology." Pages 452–78 in *The Cambridge History of Hellenistic Philosophy.* Edited by Keimpe A. Algra et al. Cambridge: Cambridge University Press, 1999.

———. "Zeno and Aristotle on Mixture." *Mnemosyne* 36 (1983): 306–10.

Marrone, Livia. "La logica degli epicurei e degli stoici." *CErc* 30 (2000): 111–18.

Martin, Jean, ed. *Aratos: Phénomènes.* 2 vols. Paris: Belles lettres, 1998.

Martínková, D. "Neomon." *Zpravy Jednoty Klassickych Filologuring* 9 (1967): 1–4.

Mattioli, Augusta. "Ricerche sul problema della libertà in Crisippo." *RIL* 73 (1939–41): 161–201.

May, Hope E. "Socratic Ignorance and the Therapeutic Aim of the Elenchos." *Apeiron* 30 (1997): 37–50.

Mazzarelli, Claudio. "Bibliografia medioplatonica, I: Gaio, Albino e Anonimo commentatore del *Teeteto.*" *RFN* 72 (1980): 108–44.

Meineke, August. *Iōannou Stobaiou Anthologion.* 4 vols. Leipzig: Teubner: 1855–57.

——. *Stephani Byzantii ethnicorum quae supersunt.* Berlin: Reimer, 1849.

Menchelli, Mariella. "La morte del filosofo o il filosofo di fronte alla morte." *SIFC* 15 (1997): 65–80.

Merz, Annette, and Teun L. Tieleman. "The Letter of Mara Bar Sarapion: Some Comments on Its Philosophical and Historical Context." Pages 107–33 in *Empsychoi Logoi—Religious Innovations in Antiquity: Studies in Honour of Pieter Willem van der Horst.* Edited by Alberdina Houtman, Albert de Jong, and Magda Misset-van de Weg. Ancient Judaism and Early Christianity 73. Leiden: Brill, 2008.

Michel, Alain. "Rhétorique et philosophie au second siècle ap. J.-C." *ANRW* 34.1:5–74.

Migliorini, Paola. *Scienza e terminologia medica nella letteratura latina di età neroniana.* Frankfurt am Main: Lang, 1997.

Moles, John L. "The Career and Conversion of Dio Chrysostom." *JHS* 98 (1978): 79–100.

——. "Dio und Trajan." Pages 165–85 in *Philosophie und Lebenswelt in der Antike.* Edited by Karen Piepenbrink. Darmstadt: Wissenschaftliche Buchgesellschaft, 2003.

Moreschini, Claudio. *Apuleio e il platonismo.* Firenze: Olschki, 1978.

——. "Aspetti della cultura filosofica negli ambienti della Seconda Sofistica." *ANRW* 36.7:5101–33.

——. *Storia della filosofia patristica.* Brescia: Morcelliana, 2004.

Morford, Mark P. O. *The Roman Philosophers: From the Time of Cato the Censor to the Death of Marcus Aurelius.* London: Routledge, 2002.

Moricca, U. "Un trattato di etica stoica poco conosciuto." *Bilychnis* 34 (1930): 77–100.

Most, Glenn W. "Cornutus and Stoic Allegoresis: A Preliminary Report." *ANRW* 36.3:2014–65.

——. "Philosophy and Religion." Pages 300–22 in *The Cambridge Companion to Greek and Roman Philosophy.* Edited by David N. Sedley. Cambridge: Cambridge University Press, 2003.

Mühl, Max. *Die Gesetze des Zaleukos und Charondas.* Leipzig: Dieterich, 1929. Repr., Aalen: Scientia-Verl, 1964.

Mussies, Gerard. *Dio Chrysostom and the New Testament.* SCHNT 2. Leiden: Brill, 1972.

Nachov, I. M. "Le cynisme de Dion Chrysostome" [Russian]. *Voprosy Klassiceskoj Filologii* 6 (1976): 46–104.

Narbonne, Jean-Marc. "Le réceptacle platonicien: nature, fonction, contenu." *Dialogue* 36 (1997): 253–79.

Natali, Carlo. "Oikonomia in Hellenistic Political Thought." Pages 95–128 in *Justice and Generosity: Studies in Hellenistic Social and Political Philosophy: Proceedings of the Sixth Symposium Hellenisticum*. Edited by André Laks and Malcolm Schofield. Cambridge: Cambridge University Press, 1995.

Nebel, Gerhard. "Der Begriff ΚΑΘΗΚΟΝ in der alten Stoa." *Hermes* 70 (1935): 439–60.

Nesselrath, Heinz-Günther, Balbina Bäbler, Maximilian Forschner, and Albert De Jong, eds. *Dion von Prusa: Menschliche Gemeinschaft und göttliche Ordnung: Die Borysthenes-Rede*. Darmstadt: Wissenschaftliche Buchgesellschaft, 2003.

Nussbaum, Martha C. "The Incomplete Feminism of Musonius Rufus, Platonist, Stoic, and Roman." Pages 283–326 in *The Sleep of Reason: Erotic Experience and Sexual Ethics in Ancient Greece and Rome*. Edited by Martha Nussbaum and Juha Sihvola. Chicago: University of Chicago Press, 2002.

———. "Musonius Rufus—Enemy of Double Standards for Men and Women?" Pages 221–46 in *Double Standards in the Ancient World*. Edited by Karla Pollmann. Göttingen: Duehrkohp & Radicke, 2000.

———. "Philosophy and Literature." Pages 211–41 in *The Cambridge Companion to Greek and Roman Philosophy*. Edited by David N. Sedley. Cambridge: Cambridge University Press, 2003.

———. *The Therapy of Desire: Theory and Practice in Hellenistic Ethics*. Princeton: Princeton University Press, 1994.

———. "The Worth of Human Dignity: Two Tensions in Stoic Cosmopolitanism." Pages 31–50 in *Philosophy and Power in the Graeco-Roman World: Essays in Honour of Miriam Griffin*. Edited by Gillian Clark and Tessa Rajak. Oxford: Oxford University Press, 2002.

Obbink, Dirk. "The Stoic Sage in the Cosmic City." Pages 178–95 in *Topics in Stoic Philosophy*. Edited by Katerina Ierodiakonou. Oxford: Clarendon, 1999.

Obbink, Dirk, and Paul A. Vander Waerdt. "Diogenes of Babylon: The Stoic Sage in the City of Fools." *GRBS* 32 (1991): 355–96.

Opsomer, Jan. *In Search of the Truth: Academic Tendencies in Middle Platonism*. Brussels: Paleis der Academiën, 1998.

Parsons, Mikeal C. *Body and Character in Luke and Acts: The Subversion of Physiognomy in Early Christianity*. Grand Rapids: Baker, 2006.

Peck, Arthur L. *Aristotle: Historia Animalium IV–VI*. LCL. Cambridge: Harvard University Press, 1970.

Pembroke, S. G. "Oikeiôsis." Pages 114–49 in *Problems in Stoicism*. Edited by Anthony A. Long. London: Athlone, 1971.

Pépin, Jean. *Mythe et allégorie*. 2nd ed. Paris: Études augustiniennes, 1976.

———. "La théologie tripartite de Varron." *REAug* 2 (1956): 265–94.

Philippson, Robert. "Hierokles der Stoiker." *RhM* 82 (1933): 97–114.

Pizzolato, Luigi Franco. *L'idea di amicizia nel mondo antico classico e cristiano*. Torino: Einaudi, 1993.

Pohlenz, Max. *Grundfragen der stoischen Philosophie*. Göttingen: Vandenhoeck & Ruprecht, 1940.

———. *Die Stoa*. Göttingen: Vandenhoeck & Ruprecht, 1949.

———. *La Stoa: Storia di un movimento spirituale*. Translated by Ottone De Gregorio and Beniamino Proto. 2 vols. Florence: La nuova Italia, 1967.

———. Review of Hans Friedrich August von Arnim, *Ethische Elementarlehre (Papyrus 9780): Nebst den bei Stobaios erhaltenen ethischen Exzerpten aus Hierokles*. *Göttingische Gelehrte Anzeigen* 11 (1906): 914–20.

Pomeroy, Arthur J., trans. *Arius Didymus, Epitome of Stoic Ethics*. SBLTT 44. Atlanta: Society of Biblical Literature, 1999.

Pounder, Robert L. "The Origin of θεοί as Inscription-Heading." Pages 243–50 in *Studies Presented to Sterling Dow on His Eightieth Birthday*. Edited by Alan L. Boegehold. Durham, N.C.: Duke University, 1984.

Praechter, Karl. *Hierokles der Stoiker*. Leipzig: Dieterich, 1901. Repr. as pages 311–474 in idem, *Kleine Schriften*. Edited by Heinrich Dörrie. Hildesheim: Olms, 1973.

Prost, François. "L'éthique d'Antiochus d'Ascalon." *Philologus* 145 (2001): 244–68.

———. "La psychologie de Panétius." *Revue des Études Latines* 79 (2001): 37–53.

Puglia, Enzo. "Le biografie di Filone e di Antioco nella Storia dell'Academia di Filodemo." *ZPE* 130 (2000): 17–28.

Puhle, Annekatrin. *Persona: Zur Ethik des Panaitios*. Frankfurt: Lang, 1987.

Quack, Helmut. "Der Zeushymnus des Kleanthes als Paralleltext zum Vaterunser." *AU* 39 (1996): 86–97.

Radice, Roberto. *La filosofia di Aristobulo e i suoi nessi con il "De mundo" attribuito ad Aristotele*. Milan: Vita e pensiero, 1995.

———. *Oikeiôsis: Ricerche sul fondamento del pensiero stoico e sulla sua genesi*. Introduction by Giovanni Reale. Temi metafisici e problemi

del pensiero antico: Studi e testi 77. Milan: Vita e Pensiero, 2000.

———. *Stoici antichi: Tutti i frammenti secondo la raccolta di H. von Arnim.* Milan: Rusconi, 1998.

Ramelli, Ilaria. "Alcune osservazioni su *credere*." *Maia* NS 51 (2000): 67–83.

———. *Anneo Cornuto: Compendio di teologia greca.* Milan: Bompiani, 2003.

———. "Anneo Cornuto e gli Stoici Romani." *Gerión* 21 (2003): 283–303.

———. "Aspetti degli sviluppi del rapporto fra Stoicismo e Cristianesimo in età imperiale." *Stylos* 12 (2003): 103–35.

———. "Bardesane e la sua scuola tra la cultura occidentale e quella orientale: Il lessico della libertà nel *Liber Legum Regionum* (testo siriaco e versione greca)." Pages 237–55 in *Pensiero e istituzioni del mondo classico nelle culture del Vicino Oriente, Atti del Seminario Nazionale di Studio, Brescia, 14–16 ottobre 1999.* Edited by Rosa Bianca Finazzi and Alfredo Valvo. Alessandria: Edizioni dell'Orso, 2001.

———. *Bardesane* Κατὰ Εἱμαρμένης. Bologna: Edizioni Studio Domenicano, 2009.

———. "La 'Città di Zeus' di Musonio Rufo nelle sue ascendenze vetero-stoiche e nell'eredità neostoica." *Stylos* 11 (2002): 151–58.

———. "La coerenza della soteriologia origeniana: Dalla polemica contro il determinismo gnostico all'universale restaurazione escatologica." Pages 661–88 in *Pagani e cristiani alla ricerca della salvezza: Atti del XXXIV Incontro di Studiosi dell'Antichità Cristiana, Roma, Augustinianum, 5–7.V.2005.* Studia ephemeridis Augustinianum 96. Rome: Institutum patristicum Augustinianum, 2006.

———. "La colpa antecedente come ermeneutica del male in sede storico-religiosa e nei testi biblici." Pages 11–64 in *Origine e fenomenologia del male: Le vie della catarsi vetero-testamentaria: XIV Convegno di Studî vetero-testamentarî dell'Associazione Biblica Italiana, Roma-Ciampino, Il Carmelo, 5–7.IX.2005.* Edited by Innocenzo Cardellini. Bologna: Dehoniane, 2007 = *Ricerche Storico-Bibliche* 19 (2007).

———. "La concezione di Giove negli stoici romani di età neroniana." *Rendiconti dell'Istituto lombardo accademia di scienze e lettere* 131 (1997): 292–320.

———. *Corpus Hermeticum.* Milan: Bompiani, 2005.

———. "Una delle più antiche lettere cristiane extra-canoniche?" *Aegyptus* 80 (2000): 169–88.

———. "Dio come padre nello Stoicismo romano al tempo della predicazione cristiana e nell'*Epistola Anne*." Pages 343–51 in *Scripta antiqua*

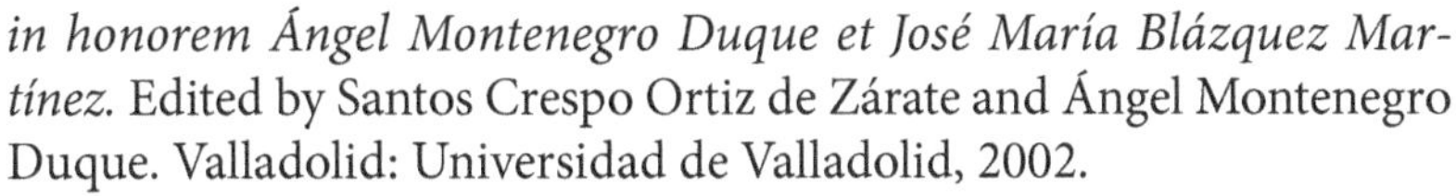

in honorem Ángel Montenegro Duque et José María Blázquez Martínez. Edited by Santos Crespo Ortiz de Zárate and Ángel Montenegro Duque. Valladolid: Universidad de Valladolid, 2002.

———. "Diogene Laerzio storico del pensiero antico tra biografia e dossografia, 'successioni di filosofi' e scuole filosofiche." Pages xxxiii–cxxxvi in Giovanni Reale, *Diogene Laerzio: Vite e dottrine dei più celebri filosofi*. Milan: Bompiani, 2005.

———. *L'età classica*. Vol. 1 of *Allegoria*. Milan: Vita e Pensiero, 2004.

———. "Gesù tra i sapienti greci perseguitati ingiustamente in un antico documento filosofico pagano di lingua siriaca." *RFN* 97 (2005): 545–70.

———. *Gregorio di Nissa: Sull'anima e la resurrezione*. Milan: Bompiani, 2007.

———. "L'ideale del filosofo nelle orazioni dionee." In *Dione Crisostomo: Tutti i discorsi*. Edited by Eugenio Amato. Milan, forthcoming.

———. "Ierocle Neostoico in Stobeo: I *Kathêkonta* e l'evoluzione dell'etica stoica." In *Deciding Culture: Stobaeus' Collection of Excerpts of Ancient Greek Authors*. Edited by Gretchen Reydams-Schils. Turnhout: Brepols, 2009.

———. *Il basileus come nomos empsychos tra diritto naturale e diritto divino: spunti platonici del concetto e sviluppi di età imperiale*. Naples: Bibliopolis, 2007.

———. "Il matrimonio cristiano in Clemente: Un confronto con la legislazione romana e gli Stoici romani." Pages 351–72 in *Il matrimonio cristiano: XXXVII Incontro di studiosi dell'Antichità cristiana, Roma, Augustinianum, 6–8 Maggio 2008*. Studia Ephemeridis Augustinianum 114. Rome: Institutum patristicum Augustinianum, 2009.

———. "Il tema del perdono in Seneca e in Musonio Rufo." Pages 191–207 in *Responsabilità, perdono e vendetta nel mondo antico*. Edited by Marta Sordi. CISA 24. Milan: Vita e pensiero, 1998.

———. "L'interpretazione allegorica filosofica di Zeus come padre nello Stoicismo." Pages 155–80 in *Visiones mítico-religiosas del padre en la antigüedad clásica*. Edited by Marcos Ruiz Sánchez. Monografías y Estudios de Antigüedad Griega y Romana 12. Madrid: Signifer Libros, 2004.

———. "La lettera di Mara Bar Serapion." *Stylos* 13 (2004): 77–104.

———. "Macrobio allegorista neoplatonico e il tardo platonismo latino." Pages 5–163 in *Macrobio: Commento al Sogno di Scipione*. Edited by Moreno Neri. Bompiani il pensiero occidentale. Milan: Bompiani, 2007.

———. "Monoteismo." Pages 3350–58 in vol. 2 of *Nuovo Dizionario Patristico e di Antichità Cristiane.* Edited by Angelo Di Berardino. 3 vols. Genoa: Marietti, 2007.

———. "Musonio Rufo." Pages 7696–97 in vol. 8 of *Enciclopedia Filosofica.* Edited by Virgilio Melchiorre. 2nd ed. Milan: Bompiani, 2006.

———. *Musonio Rufo: Diatribe, frammenti, testimonianze.* With introductory essay, Greek text, translation, notes, apparatuses, and bibliography. Milan: Bompiani, 2001.

———. "Μυστήριον negli *Stromateis* di Clemente Alessandrino: Aspetti di continuità con la tradizione allegorica greca." Pages 83–120 in *Il volto del mistero.* Edited by Angela Maria Mazzanti. Castel Bolognese: Itaca, 2006.

———. *Opere e frammenti: Allegoristi dell'età classica.* Il Pensiero occidentale. Milan: Bompiani, 2007.

———. "Origen, Bardaisan, and the Origin of Universal Salvation." *HTR* 102 (2009): 135–68.

———. "Le origini della filosofia: greche o barbare? L'enigmatico mito del Boristenitico di Dione." *RFN* 99 (2007): 185–214.

———. "Philosophen und Prediger: Pagane und christliche weise Männer: Der Apostel Paulus." In *Dion von Prusa: Der Philosoph und sein Bild.* Edited by Eugenio Amato and Sotera Fornaro. SAPERE 13. Tübingen: Mohr Siebeck, forthcoming.

———. Review of Antonella Borgo, *Lessico morale di Seneca. Aevum* 74 (2000): 372–74.

———. Review of Brad Inwood, ed., *The Cambridge Companion to the Stoics. RFN* 97 (2005): 152–58.

———. Review of George R. Boys-Stones, *Post-Hellenistic Philosophy: A Study of Its Development from the Stoics to Origen. Aevum* 78 (2004): 196–200.

———. Review of Gretchen Reydams-Schils, *The Roman Stoics: Self, Responsibility, and Affection. RFN* 8 (2006): 605–10.

———. "Stoicismo e Cristianesimo in area siriaca nella seconda metà del I secolo d.C." *Sileno* 25 (1999): 197–212.

———. *Stoici romani minori.* Milan: Bompiani, 2008.

———. "La tematica *de matrimonio* nello Stoicismo romano: alcune osservazioni." *'Ilu* 5 (2000): 145–62.

———. "Transformations of The Household and Marriage Theory between Neo-Stoicism, Middle-Platonism, and Early Christianity." *RFN* 100 (2008): 369–96.

———. "'*Tristitia*': Indagine storica, filosofica e semantica su un'accusa

antistoica e anticristiana del I secolo." *Invigilata Lucernis* 23 (2001): 187–206.

———. "Varrone." Pages 12018–19 in vol. 12 of *Enciclopedia Filosofica*. Edited by Virgilio Melchiorre. 2nd ed. Milan: Bompiani, 2006.

Reale, Giovanni. *Cinismo, epicureismo e stoicismo*. Vol. 5 of *Storia della filosofia greca e romana*. Milan: Bompiani, 2004.

———. *Diogene Laerzio: Vite e dottrine dei più celebri filosofi*. In collaboration with Ilaria Ramelli and Giuseppe Girgenti, with introductory essay, edition, commentary, and bibliography by Ilaria Ramelli, translation by Giovanni Reale, and indexes by Giuseppe Girgenti. Milan: Bompiani, 2005.

———. *La filosofia di Seneca: Come terapia dei mali dell'anima*. Milan: Bompiani, 2003.

———. *Per una nuova interpretazione di Platone*. 11th ed. Milan: Vita e pensiero, 1993.

———. *Scetticismo, Eclettismo, Neoaristotelismo e Neostoicismo*. Vol. 6 of *Storia della filosofia greca e romana*. Milan: Bompiani, 2004.

———, ed. *Seneca: Tutte le opere*. Milan: Bompiani, 2000.

Reesor, Margaret E. *The Nature of Man in Early Stoic Philosophy*. London: Duckworth, 1985.

Reinhardt, Karl. "Poseidonios von Apameia." PW 22.1:558–826.

Renehan, Robert F. "Acts 17.28." *GRBS* 20 (1979): 347–53.

Rensberger, David. "Reconsidering the Letter of Mara Bar Serapion." In *Aramaic Studies in Judaism and Early Christianity*. Edited by Paul V. M. Flesher and Eric M. Meyers. Duke Judaic Studies Monograph Series 3. Winona Lake, Ind.: Eisenbrauns, forthcoming.

Reydams-Schils, Gretchen. "Human Bonding and οἰκείωσις in Roman Stoicism." *OSAP* 2 (2002): 221–51.

———. Review of Christopher Gill. *The Structured Self in Hellenistic and Roman Thought*. *CP* 103 (2008): 189–95.

———. *The Roman Stoics: Self, Responsibility, and Affection*. Chicago: University of Chicago Press, 2005.

———. "La vieillesse et les rapports humains dans le Stoïcisme Romain." Pages 481–89 in vol. 2 of *L'ancienneté chez les Anciens*. Edited by Béatrice Bakhouce. 2 vols. Montpellier: Université Paul-Valéry Montpellier, 2003.

Rist, John M. *Stoic Philosophy*. Cambridge: Cambridge University Press, 1980.

———. "Zeno and Stoic Consistency." *Phronesis* 22 (1977): 161–74.

Roskam, Geert. *On the Path to Virtue: The Stoic Doctrine of Moral Progress*

and Its Reception in (Middle-)Platonism. Ancient and Medieval Philosophy 33. Leuven: Leuven University Press, 2005.

Russell, Donald A., and David Konstan, *Heraclitus*: Homeric Problems. SBLWGRW 14. Atlanta: Society of Biblical Literature, 2005.

Sacks, Oliver W. *The Man Who Mistook His Wife for a Hat.* London: Duckworth, 1985.

Salmeri, Giovanni. *La politica e il potere: Saggio su Dione di Prusa.* Catania: Facoltà di Lettere e Filosofia, Università di Catania, 1982.

Sandbach, Francis H. *The Stoics.* London: Chatto & Windus, 1975.

Schäfer, Maximilian. "Diogenes der Mittelstoiker." *Philologus* 91 (1936): 174–96.

Schibli, Hermann S. *Hierocles of Alexandria.* Oxford: Oxford University Press, 2002.

Schofield, Malcolm. "Stoic Ethics." Pages 233–56 in *The Cambridge Companion to the Stoics.* Edited by Brad Inwood. Cambridge: Cambridge University Press, 2003.

———. *The Stoic Idea of City.* Cambridge: Cambridge University Press, 1991.

———. "The Syllogisms of Zeno of Citium." *Phronesis* 28 (1983): 31–58.

———. "Two Stoic Approaches to Justice." Pages 191–212 in *Justice and Generosity: Studies in Hellenistic Social and Political Philosophy, Proceedings of the Sixth Symposium Hellenisticum.* Edited by André Laks and Malcolm Schofield. Cambridge: Cambridge University Press, 1995.

Schönrich, Gerhard. "*Oikeiôsis*: Zur Aktualität eines stoischen Grundbegriffs." *PhJ* 96 (1989): 34–51.

Schröder, Heinrch Otto. "Marionetten: Ein Beitrag zur Polemik des Karneades." *RhM* 126 (1983): 1–24.

Sedley, David N. "Chrysippus on Psychophysical Causality." Pages 313–31 in *Passions and Perceptions: Studies in Hellenistic Philosophy of Mind: Proceedings of the Fifth Symposium Hellenisticum.* Edited by Jacques Brunschwig and Martha Nussbaum. Cambridge: Cambridge University Press, 1993.

———. "The Stoic-Platonist Debate on *kathêkonta*." Pages 128–52 in *Topics in Stoic Philosophy.* Edited by Katerina Ierodiakonou. Oxford: Clarendon, 1999.

———. "Three Platonist Interpretations of the *Theaetetus*." Pages 79–103 in *Form and Argument in Late Plato.* Edited by Christopher Gill and Mary Margaret McCabe. Oxford: Oxford University Press. 1996.

———, ed. *The Cambridge Companion to Greek and Roman Philosophy.*

Cambridge: Cambridge University Press, 2003.

Setaioli, Aldo. "Due messe a punto senecane." *Prometheus* 17 (1991): 137–54.

Sharples, R. W. "Necessity in the Stoic Doctrine of Fate." *Symbolae Osloenses* 56 (1981): 81–97.

———. "Soft Determinism and Freedom in Early Stoicism." *Phronesis* 31 (1986): 266–79.

Sharples, R. W., and M. Vegetti. "Fato, valutazione e imputabilità: un argomento stoico in Alessandro, *De fato* 35." *Elenchos* 12 (1991): 257–70.

Sherrington, Charles S. *The Integrative Action of the Nervous System.* New York: Scribner, 1906.

Simons, John. "Matter and Time in Plotinus." *Dionysius* 9 (1985): 53–74.

Sohlberg, David. "Aelius Aristides und Diogenes von Babylon: Zur Geschichte des rednerischen Ideals." *MH* 29 (1972): 177–200, 256–77.

Solmsen, Friedrich. "Greek Philosophy and the Discovery of the Nerves." *MH* 18 (1961): 150–97.

Sorabji, Richard. *Emotions and Peace of Mind: From Stoic Agitation to Christian Temptation.* Oxford: Oxford University Press, 2000.

———. "Soul and Self in Ancient Philosophy." Pages 8–32 in *From Soul to Self.* Edited by M. James C. Crabbe. London: Routledge, 1999.

———. "What Is New on Emotion in Stoicism after 100 BC?" Pages 163–74 in *Greek and Roman Philosophy 100 BC–200 AD.* Edited by Richard Sorabji and Robert W. Sharples. London: Institute for Classical Studies, 2007.

———. "What Is New on the Self in Stoicism after 100 BC?" Pages 141–62 in *Greek and Roman Philosophy 100 BC–200 AD.* Edited by Richard Sorabji and Robert W. Sharples. London: Institute for Classical Studies, 2007.

Soreth, Marion. "Die zweite Telosformel des Antipater von Tarsos." *AGPh* 50 (1968): 48–72.

Speller, Elizabeth. *Following Hadrian: A Second-Century Journey through the Roman Empire.* Oxford: Oxford University Press, 2003.

Stadter, Philip A., and Luc Van der Stockt, eds. *Sage and Emperor: Plutarch, Greek Intellectuals and Roman Power in the Time of Trajan (98–117 A.D.).* Leuven: Leuven University Press, 2002.

Stalley, Richard F. "Punishment and the Physiology of the *Timaeus.*" *CQ* 46 (1996): 357–70.

Stanton, Greg R. "The Cosmopolitan Ideas of Epictetus and Marcus Aurelius." *Phronesis* 13 (1968): 183–95.

Stein, Markus. *Definition und Schilderung in Theophrasts Charakteren.*

Stuttgart: Teubner, 1992.

Steinmetz, Peter. "Die Stoa." Pages 635–36 in vol. 4.2 of *Grundriss der Geschichte der Philosophie*. Edited by Friedrich Ueberweg and Hellmut Flashar. Basel: Schwabe, 1994.

Stevens, John A. "Preliminary Impulse in Stoic Psychology." *AncPhil* 20 (2000): 139–68.

Straaten, Modestus van. *Panaetii Rhodii Fragmenta*. 3rd ed. PhAnt 5. Leiden: Brill, 1962.

Striker, Gisela. "Antipater or the Art of Living." Pages 185–204 in *The Norms of Nature: Studies in Hellenistic Ethics*. Edited by Malcolm Schofield and Gisela Striker. Cambridge: Cambridge University Press, 1986.

———. "Following Nature: A Study in Stoic Ethics." *OSAP* 9 (1991): 1–73. Repr. as pages 221–80 in idem, *Essays on Hellenistic Epistemology and Ethics*. Cambridge: Cambridge University Press, 1996.

———. "The Role of οἰκείωσις in Stoic Ethics." *OSAP* 1 (1983): 145–67.

Swain, Simon, ed. *Dio Chrysostom: Politics, Letters, and Philosophy*. Oxford: Oxford University Press, 2000.

———. *Seeing the Face, Seeing the Soul: Polemon's Physiognomy from Classical Antiquity to Medieval Islam*. Oxford: Oxford University Press, 2007.

Szegedy-Maszak, Andrew. "Legends of the Greek Lawgivers." *GRBS* 19 (1978): 199–209.

Szymanski, Mikołaj. "P. Berol. Inv. 16545: A Text on Stoic Epistemology with a Fragment of Antipater of Tarsus." *Journal of Juristic Papyrology* 20 (1990): 139–41.

Tarrant, Harold. "The Date of Anonymous *In Theaetetum*." *CQ* 33 (1983): 161–87 .

———. "Peripatetic and Stoic Epistemology in Antiochus and Boethus." *Apeiron* 20 (1987): 17–37.

———. *Scepticism or Platonism? The Philosophy of the Fourth Academy*. Cambridge: Cambridge University Press, 1985.

Tatum, Jeffrey W. "Plutarch on Antiochus of Ascalon." *Hermes* 129 (2001): 139–42.

Taylor, Thomas. *Political Fragments of Archytas, Charondas, Zaleucus, and Other Ancient Pythagoreans Preserved by Stobaeus, and Also, Ethical Fragments of Hierocles, the Celebrated Commentator on the Golden Pythagorean Verses, Preserved by the Same Author*. Chiswick: Whittingham, 1822.

Theiler, Willy, ed. *Poseidonios: Die Fragmente*. Berlin: de Gruyter, 1982.

Thom, Johan C. *Cleanthes' Hymn to Zeus: Text, Translation, and Commentary*. STAC 33. Tübingen: Mohr Siebeck, 2005.

———. "Cleanthes' Hymn to Zeus and Early Christian Literature." Pages 477–99 in *Antiquity and Humanity: Essays on Ancient Religion and Philosophy Presented to Hans Dieter Betz on His 70th Birthday*. Edited by Adela Yarbro Collins and Margaret M. Mitchell. Tübingen: Mohr Siebeck, 2001.

———. "Kleantes se Himne aan Zeus." *Akroterion* 41 (1996): 44–57.

———. "The Problem of Evil in Cleanthes' Hymn to Zeus." *AClass* 41 (1998): 45–57.

Tieleman, Teun L. "Diogenes of Babylon and Stoic Embryology: Ps. Plutarch, *Plac.* V 15. 4 Reconsidered." *Mnemosyne* 44 (1991): 106–25.

———. *Galen and Chrysippus on the Soul: Argument and Refutation in the* De placitis, *Books II–III*. PhAnt 68. Leiden: Brill, 1996.

———. "Panaetius' Place in the History of Stoicism, with Special Reference to His Moral Psychology." Pages 107–42 in *Pyrrhonists, Patricians, Platonizers: Hellenistic Philosophy in the Period 155–86 BC. Tenth Symposium Hellenisticum*. Edited by Anna Maria Ioppolo and David N. Sedley. Naples: Bibliopolis, 2007.

Torraca, Luigi. *Teofrasto Caratteri. Introduzione, traduzione, e note*. Milan: Garzanti, 1994.

Torre, Chiara. *Il matrimonio del* sapiens: *Ricerche sul* De matrimonio *di Seneca*. Genoa: Università di Genova, Facoltà di lettere, Dipartimento di archeologia, filologia classica e loro tradizioni, 2000.

Tortorelli, Marisa Ghidini. "Morfologia cleantea di Zeus." *Atti dell'Accademia Pontaniana* 22 (1973): 327–42.

Trapp, Michael B. *Maximus of Tyre: The Philosophical Orations*. Oxford: Oxford University Press, 1997.

———. "Plato in Dio." Pages 213–39 in *Dio Chrysostom: Politics, Letters, and Philosophy*. Edited by Simon Swain. Oxford: Oxford University Press, 2000.

Traversa, Augusto, ed. *Index Stoicorum Herculanensis*. Genoa: Istituto di filologia classica, 1952.

Tsekourakis, Damianos. *Studies in the Terminology of Early Stoic Ethics*. Wiesbaden: Steiner, 1974.

Tsouna, Voula. "Epicurean Attitudes to Management and Finance." Pages 701–14 in vol. 2 of *Epicureismo Greco e romano*. Edited by Gabriele Giannantoni and Marcello Gigante. 3 vols. Naples: Bibliopolis, 1996.

———. *The Ethics of Philodemus*. Oxford: Oxford University Press, 2007.

Valantasis, Richard. "Musonius Rufus and Roman Ascetical Theory."

GRBS 40 (1999): 201–31.

Vander Waerdt, Paul A. "Zeno's Republic and the Origins of Natural Law." Pages 272–308 in *The Socratic Movement.* Edited by Paul A. Vander Waerdt. Ithaca, N.Y.: Cornell University Press, 1994.

Verboven, Koenraad. *The Economy of Friends: Economic Aspects of Amicitia and Patronage in the Late Republic.* Brussels: Latomus, 2002.

Vimercati, Emmanuele. *Panezio: Testimonianze e frammenti.* Milan: Bompiani, 2002.

Voelke, André-Jean. *L'idée de volonté dans le Stoïcisme.* Paris: PUF, 1973.

Wachsmuth, Curt, and Otto Hense, eds. *Ioannis Stobaei anthologium.* 5 vols. in 4. Berlin: Weidmann, 1884–1923.

Ward, Roy B. "Musonius and Paul on Marriage." *NTS* 36 (1990): 281–89.

Watson, Gerard. "The Natural Law and Stoicism." Pages 216–38 in *Problems in Stoicism.* Edited by Anthony A. Long. London: Athlone, 1971.

West, Martin L. "Towards Monotheism." Pages 21–41 in *Pagan Monotheism in Late Antiquity.* Edited by Polymnia Athanassiadi and Michael Frede. Oxford: Oxford University Press, 1999

Westerink, Leendert G. "Hierokles II (Neuplatoniker)." *RAC* 15:109–17.

White, Michael J. "Stoic Natural Philosophy (Physics and Cosmology)." Pages 124–52 in *The Cambridge Companion to the Stoics.* Edited by Brad Inwood. Cambridge: Cambridge University Press, 2003.

White, Nicholas P. "The Basis of Stoic Ethics." *HSCP* 83 (1979): 143–78.

———. *Individual and Conflict in Greek Ehics.* Oxford: Clarendon, 2002.

Whitmarsh, Tim. *Greek Literature and the Roman Empire.* Oxford: Oxford University Press, 2001.

Winter, Bruce W. *After Paul Left Corinth: The Influence of Secular Ethics and Social Change.* Grand Rapids: Eerdmans, 2001.

———. *Philo and Paul among the Sophists.* Cambridge: Cambridge University Press, 1997.

Wöhrle, Georg. "Wenn Frauen Platons Staat lesen, oder: Epiktet und Musonius konstruieren Geschlechtenrollen." *Würzburger Jahrbücher für die Altertumswissenschaft* 26 (2002): 135–43.

Xenakis, Jason. "Stoic Suicide Therapy." *Sophia* 40 (1972): 88–99.

Yousif, Ephrem-Isa. *La floraison des philosophes syriaques.* Paris: L'Harmattan, 2003.

Zagdoun, Mary-Anne. "Problèmes concernant l'*oikeiôsis* stoïcienne." Pages 319–34 in *Les Stoïciens.* Edited by Gilbert Romeyer-Dherbey and Jean-Baptiste Gourinat. Paris: Presses universitaires de France, 2005.

Zeller, Eduard. *Die Philosophie der Griechen.* 4th ed. 3 vols. in 6. Leipzig: Reisland, 1922, repr. 1963.

Zetzel, James E. G. "Natural Law and Poetic Justice: A Carneadean Debate in Cicero and Vergil." *CP* 86 (1991): 297–319.

Zietsman, J. C. "A Commentary on Persius Satire 5: Themes and Structure." Ph.D. diss., University of Pretoria, 1988).

———. "Persius, Saturn and Jupiter." *Akroterion* 36 (1991): 94–103.

Zöller, Rainer. *Die Vorstellung vom Willen in der Morallehre Senecas.* Munich: Saur, 2003.

Zunino, Maddalena Luisa. "Scrivere la legge orale, interpretare la legge scritta: I *Nomoi* di Zaleuco." *QS* 24 (1998): 151–59.

Zuntz, Günther. "Vers 4 des Kleanthes-Hymnus." *RhM* 122 (1979): 97–98.

Index

Note: the index is intended to identify the major topics discussed in Hierocles' texts as well as in the introduction and commentary. It does not aim to provide a complete word list or to include every name and source mentioned—to do so would make the the index more cumbersome than useful. References to Hierocles' text are keyed to the page number of the English translation.

CPSIA information can be obtained
at www.ICGtesting.com
Printed in the USA
BVHW042030070622
639061BV00008B/31

9 781589 834187